The Payroll Process

A Basic Guide to U.S. Payroll Procedures and Requirements

The Payroll Process

A Basic Guide to U.S. Payroll Procedures and Requirements

Gregory Mostyn
Mission College

Worthy & James Publishing

Before you buy or use this book you should understand . . .

Names: Mostyn, Gregory R., author.
Title: The payroll process 2022: a basic guide to payroll procedures and requirements / Gregory R. Mostyn.
Description: Milpitas, CA: Worthy and James Publishing, 2022. |Previous edition in 2020| Includes index.
Identifiers: LCCN 2018901226 (print) | ISBN 978-0-9914231-8-7 (paperback)
Subjects: LCSH: Payrolls. | Payroll tax—United States. | Accounting. | Wages. | Employee fringe benefits—United States. | Labor laws and legislation—United States. | BISAC: BUSINESS & ECONOMICS / Accounting / General. | BUSINESS & ECONOMICS / Taxation / General.
Classification: LCC HF5681.W3 M67 2022 (print) | DDC 657/.742—dc23.

Worthy and James Publishing
P.O. Box 362015
Milpitas, CA. 95036, USA
www.worthyjames.com

For All Students,
As Employees or Employers
Past, Present, and Future

Contents

About the Author

Greg Mostyn is an accounting instructor at Mission College, Santa Clara, California. He is a member of the American Accounting Association and American Institute of Certified Public Accountants. He has worked as a practicing CPA, consultant, and educator. He also has extensive experience in accounting curriculum design and course development. He has authored several books and published articles in the areas of learning theory and its application to accounting instruction, textbook design and use, and accounting education research.

Acknowledgements

Sincere gratitude and appreciation are extended to the following professionals and academics. They have provided creative ideas, corrected mistakes, shared their experiences, and immeasurably improved the quality of this work.

Karina Godoy, Esq.
JML Law; Southwestern Law School

Francis J. Mootz III, AM, JD
McGeorge School of Law University of Pacific

Janel Greiman, CPA, M.T.
Monfort College of Business, University of Northern Colorado

Howard Randall, CPA, (Retired), MBA
Mission College

Morris Jennings, FLSA Consultant
Principal, Wage and Hour Consulting Service, former DOL Investigator

Richard Schickel, Tax Consultant
Principal, RMS Tax Consulting, former IRS Revenue Officer

Myra McGill, CPA, MAcc
Allan Hancock College

Also by the author:

Basic Accounting Concepts, Principles, and Procedures, Vol. 1, 2nd edition *(Worthy and James Publishing)*

Basic Accounting Concepts, Principles, and Procedures, Vol. 2, 2nd edition *(Worthy and James Publishing)*

Getting Started:
What You Should Know

Read Me First

This reference book is designed to be used in three ways:

- The book will explain the steps needed to complete a proper payroll process.
- The book can be used as an efficient first-source reference to help understand compliance requirements and to help resolve payroll questions.
- The book also functions as a reference to more detailed information and advanced resources if more information is needed or more complex issues arise.

The table below is a suggested guide for your initial steps:

Step	Procedure
1	Refer to the illustration on page 4. This is an overview of the process. Each section in the book explains the details of each of the five elements.
2	Because there are many filing deadlines, **you will need a tax calendar**. An IRS calendar is available online as **Publication 509**. It is a comprehensive federal resource; it contains three calendars: a general calendar, an employer calendar, and an excise tax calendar. Be sure to contact your state/local tax authorities for similar information.
3	Read the "Overview" of payroll at the beginning of this book. This provides a guideline for accessing additional resouces. It is important to know that especially the IRS provides many detailed resouces that are accessible on the Internet—for forms, use the form numbers from our discussion and search for form instructions. For more in-depth information, as you read by topic you often will see publication number references. These are IRS and/or Department of Labor publications, which are **available online**. Again, check state and local references; many are also available online by topic search.
4	**Older edition use:** If you are using an older edition of this book, probably the only difference is that rates, dollar limits, or table amounts may have changed, and these can be easily obtained online for a particular item. Procedures infrequently change. These are a foundation that you should understand first and always keep as a point of reference.

Why Be Informed About Payroll: Payroll Errors Are Frequent and Can Be Costly

As a business, governmental, non-profit, or charity manager, and espe-cially as a payroll employee, it is vital to understand the key elements of the entire payroll process and to maintain a working knowledge that permits informed access to payroll references. Failure in any part of the process can lead to expensive errors and penalties. From a positive per-spective, knowledge can improve efficiency, cost savings, and profitability that improve a competitive position. Here are some of the data:

For example, in 2017 the American Payroll Association reported that 54%[1] of employees had paycheck errors. The IRS alone reported in FY 2020 that it assessed approximately 4.3 million payroll tax-related penalties (over about 8 months due to COVID-19) with total assessments of about $6 billion.[2] This does not include state and local payroll tax assessments.

The Department of Labor Wage and Hour Division reported that in FY 2020 its actions recovered approximately $258 million in back wages for an average of approximately $1,120 per employee. More than half of this came from failure to pay correct overtime.[3] The above statistics typically result from the following:

Common and Important Payroll Errors

- Hiring errors: employment eligibility, worker rights, and employee information
- Misclassification between employee and independent contractor
- Misclassification between exempt and non-exempt
- Errors in overtime calculation
- Underpayment of minimum wage
- During employment: Violation of fair employment and worker rights laws
- Missed/delinquent payroll tax deposits and and/or form filing
- Bad checks used for payroll deposits
- Errors in form preparation
- Improper payroll records maintenance
- Incorrect exclusion of payments from wages
- Inadequate workers' compensation coverage

[1]American Payroll Associate Trendline Survey.
[2]IRS Data Book 2020.
[3]U.S. Department of Labor Wage and Hour Division, https://www.dol.gov/agencies/whd/data/charts/all-acts 8/9/21.

Overview of the Payroll Process

Overview of "Payroll"

Overview

The term "payroll" encompasses many activities that are critical to the successful operation of a business or other organization with employees, or even businesses or organizations that may require the services of others who are not employees. As well, practically all payroll activitities are subject to numerous legal compliance requirements of federal, state, and local agencies, all of which will impose various penalties if requirements are violated. An organization has no control over these requirements. Therefore, "payroll" actually involves two broad areas of knowledge: 1) An understanding of the process within which payroll activities take place. These activities also include human resources, management, accounting, and reporting functions. 2) An understanding of the legal rules imposed on all the activities, to which a business must comply in order to prevent losses due to penalties or financial damages. This book provides a basic reference, primarily for federal rules, to the essential elements of both of these knowledge domains.

Finding Resources for Compliance Procedures and Questions

Although this book serves as a useful guide through many payroll topics, more than one source should be utilized; it is always wise to seek as much help as possible when dealing with compliance procedures and questions. Here are some suggestions for additional resources:

- **IRS Publications:** IRS publications are generally available online. Many of these relevant payroll publications are referenced in this book (also see index). The basic IRS employer publication is called Publication 15, also known as Circular E. Many Department of Labor publications and guidelines are also available online.
- **DOL Publications:** www.dol.gov/whd/, use resources menu.
- **State and Local Information:** Despite many similiarites to federal requirements, state and local rules vary. Therefore, this book focuses primarily on federal requirements. However, state and local information is often available online; for example, for state requirements you can: 1) Do an Internet search for "state (name of state) payroll taxes" 2) As of this writing some useful websites are www.taxnews.ey.com and the American Payroll Association site. 3) Reference departments in local or school libraries may also provide help.
- **Professional Help:** If you are in business or going into business, it is prudent to obtain expert professional help, because requirements can change and at times can be complex to apply. Obtain client references and check with state licensing boards to find a competent CPA or attorney who has clients in the same type of business that you are in, and who is familiar with your type of business and payroll issues.

Overview of "Payroll", *continued*

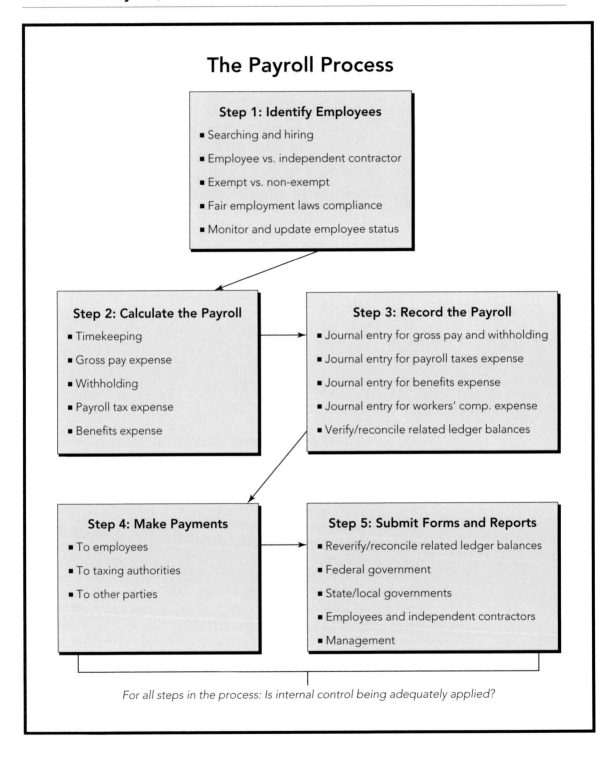

The Payroll Process

Step 1: Identify Employees

- Searching and hiring
- Employee vs. independent contractor
- Exempt vs. non-exempt
- Fair employment laws compliance
- Monitor and update employee status

Step 2: Calculate the Payroll

- Timekeeping
- Gross pay expense
- Withholding
- Payroll tax expense
- Benefits expense

Step 3: Record the Payroll

- Journal entry for gross pay and withholding
- Journal entry for payroll taxes expense
- Journal entry for benefits expense
- Journal entry for workers' comp. expense
- Verify/reconcile related ledger balances

Step 4: Make Payments

- To employees
- To taxing authorities
- To other parties

Step 5: Submit Forms and Reports

- Reverify/reconcile related ledger balances
- Federal government
- State/local governments
- Employees and independent contractors
- Management

For all steps in the process: Is internal control being adequately applied?

Section 1 Identify Employees

Introduction

As illustrated on page 4, the payroll process begins with searching for, evaluating, and hiring employees, and the relationship continues until the employee leaves. For a new business, also see Appendix IV for additional information. The key elements of searching and hiring are summarized below in the ordinary sequence of occurance.

Searching and Hiring

Procedure

New Employee Approval

A request and justification for a new employee should be formalized in a written requisition form in which specific duties are identified. Cost/benefit analysis should be included as part of the decision process, including pre-employment costs. Supervisory approval should be required at different levels, coordinated by the Human Resoures department. If an applicant is hired this requistion form should be placed in the employee's file.

Job Description

Every position should have a detailed and dated job description that identifies duties and responsbilities, specific skill sets, required experience and certifications, job title, number of employees supervised, compensation including benefits, and verification of independent contractor vs. employee status, (If unsure, submit form SS-8 to the Internal Revenue Service and check with Department of Labor Wage and Hour Division district office and/or employment counsel), and also verification of exempt vs. nonexempt status. (If unsure, check with the Department of Labor Wage and Hour Division, and/or counsel.) The necessity for an employee contract should be considered if specific noncompete requirements and nondisclosure and term of employment issues are important. The job description should demonstrate no discrimination or preferences in its development and the planning for search, hiring, and employment based on race, color, religion, sex (including gender identity, sexual orientation, and pregnancy), national origin, age, disability, or any genetic information. If an applicant is hired the job description goes to the employee 's file.

Advertising

A job-advertising budget is used and the job description is placed in the desired media. These generally consist of print and Internet media and the use of recruitment firms. An employer must be cautious about advertising that inadvertently creates discrimination-related liability. First, as many sources as possible should be utilized not only for the practical purpose of attracting more qualified candidates but also to demonstrate greater access and therefore greater potential diversity. Secondly,

continued ▶

Procedure, *continued*

Advertising, Continued	certain adjectives as well as some common-use nouns/pronouns should be thoughtfully vetted to avoid any type of implied discrimination. Examples: "Dominant", "Ninja", "He/She", "Secretary" (gender identity) or "Recent", "New", "Energetic", "Beginning", "Older" (age identity). Finally, edit for cliché, trite, exaggerated, and vague language. This usually does nothing to attract qualified people.
Application Form	Applicants will complete a formal written application and submit a resumé. Questions on the form should relate strictly to factors related to performance of job duties; however, an employer should also ask if the applicant has any restrictive agreements such as confidentiality or non-compete covenants from a previous employer. Questions concerning age, birthdate, gender, arrests, physical traits (including photographs), drug use, smoking, citizenship and immigration status (see Form I-9), credit history, marital status, and education level, if advanced education is not relevant to job performance, should not be used. Do not note or use volunteered information that is unrelated to performance of duties. The application form can require an applicant to sign a certification that all information supplied by the applicant is accurate and truthful. Selected candidates receive an interview invitation and others receive a courteous rejection.
Interviews	Interviews are conducted that include standardized questions in a consistent, structured, process. Multi-level inteviews with experienced staff allow for greater interaction and improve communication for all parties. A written guideline should be used, standarized as much as possible, to guide the employees conducting the interviews. Interview questions should be clearly job-related and concerned only with determining the applicant's ability to perform job duties. No applicant should be singled out for special or unique questioning, unless the interviewer is following up on an applicant's experience or knowledge. If an applicant volunteers information not related to the job requirements, such as family or other personal information, it should be noted that this was not relevant to the decision process.

If an applicant for an at-will (see page 15) position falsifies or misrepresents information and is later hired, that person can be fired immediately upon discovering the falsification. Employees with contracts who have provided falsified information may be discharged if the information is material (significant) and the employer relied on that information when offering the job. It is good practice to have the employment contract terminable upon discovery of false information. Clearly trivial discrepencies such as typographical errors are not grounds for dismissal. Unfortunately, these circumstances can be so subjective that only a court decision or settlement can provide a resolution.

Procedure, *continued*

Background Checks	After one or a few candidates are selected as finalists, it is appropriate to begin background checks prior to an offer of employment. Background checks include contacting (often calling) references and prior employers, obtaining a copy of the applicant's driving record (where relevant), and drug testing if the employer is prepared to fully comply with state statutes governing such testing. In some cases criminal convictions can be checked if relevant to the job duties. Generally, arrest records are not relevant unless a case is still pending. Background checks should conform to information on the application and on the resumé. Note: many states have laws that regulate how and what information can be disclosed by a former employer. The federal Employee Polygraph Protection Act of 1988 prohibits the use or suggestion of lie detector tests by private employers unless engaged in the security business or the manufacture of controlled substances, or in certain conditions.

Some states have limitations on disclosure of employee files by prior employers, as well as other limitations.

The federal Fair Credit Reporting Act (FCRA), enforced by the federal Consumer Financial Protection Bureau (CFPB), places limits on background checks by third parties, including "consumer reporting agencies". When using this type of background check:

1) An employer must request the described report from the candidate in writing as a separately identifiable document.
2) Written approval must be obtained from the interview candidate for credit, education, medical, and military service information as a separately identifiable document. This information must be job-related and not used in a discriminatory manner.
3) The applicant is entitled to receive results of the resulting report by written request.
4) If the employer makes an adverse employement decision using any information in the report, the employer must first notify the applicant, provide a copy of the report, the name and address of the third party supplying the report, and a statement explaining the applicant's rights related to the decision based on the report (also on the CFPB website). The CFPB website has a complaint process available at www. consumerfinance.gov (Tel. 855-411- 2372).
5) The EEOC as an administrative agency enforces anti-discrimination provisions in the use of background checks.

The application of the FCRA rules applies when using third-party consumer reporting agency background checks. If an employer conducts its own background check by using tools such as an Internet search for information, the employer is not fully subject to these rules. However, a prudent employer would always request the applicant or employee for written permission for any type of background check. Finally, as usual, be sure to check state laws, which vary widely in respect to background checks.

Procedure, *continued*

Testing	Testing by employers is permitted, and is particularly useful for technical positions. However, there are legal limits on how testing can be applied which target the use of testing as a means of discrimination. Group or individualized adjustment of scores or use of different cutoff scores or generally altering the results of tests is very likely to be considered discriminatory.
Adverse Impact Analysis	Major federal government agencies concerned with fair employment use "adverse impact analysis" to identify potential "disparate impact" discrimination.
	The first test element is called the "four-fifths test" or "80% test". If a selection process results in a selection rate that is less than 80% for a race, ethnic, or gender group of the selection rate of an identifiable group with the highest selection rate, the results will be considered as evidence of an "adverse impact" which is regarded as discriminatory. Because this test is not statisically valid (i.e. adverse impact results could happen by chance rather than indicate an underlying condition), a second element is then required. An employer should then conduct statistical tests to validate the selection process. The EEOC provides guidelines for these tests.
Offer of Employment	When an applicant is selected a written offer of employment should be preprepared. It should include the details of the job description and date of beginning employment. As well, it should require a signature and date of acceptance by the applicant, and be returned to the employer. The offer should expire if not accepted within a reasonable time.
Medical Exam	A medical exam can be required only after an offer of employment and after all other conditions of the employment are satisfied. The employment may be conditioned upon the outcome of the exam if:

1) All offers in the job category are subject to medical exams.
2) Medical exams are not used as a means of discrimination (See Americans With Disability Act, Family Medical Leave Act, and the obligation to provide reasonable accomodations.)
3) The exam is clearly job-related and necessary for job performance.
4) The medical information must be treated as confidential.

Final Tasks	After the applicant has accepted the offer, the following documentation is required to formalize the relationship:

1) Complete employee information data using an employee self-identification form for employee file. (e.g. name, address, email, telephone, emegency contacts, etc.)
2) Obtain evidence of eligibility to work (See Form I-9 and E-verify below)

continued ▶

Procedure, *continued*

Final Tasks,
Continued

3) Required information (such as employee number, salary/wage, pay period, W-4 form, direct deposit, etc.) must be sent to the payroll department. Note: If there is no completed W-4, withholding is based on status of single, no allowances.

4) Contact state employment department per guidelines (W-4 info. /employee info.)

5) Suggest that the employee enroll in direct deposit. Supply the form and process the application.

6) Human resources department completes the PRWORA notice (see below).

7) Check if EEO-1 report is required (generally companies with 100 or more employees and some federal contractors) to categorize by race/ethnicity, gender, and job category; if so, collect information and file report. Report is confidential.

8) Employee receives a policy and procedures manual (employee handbook) and job description, and employer receives a signed receipt from employee for each. Employee also receives location and parking information, keys, access codes, and badge. Employee is introduced to key employees with whom new employee will interact.

TIP

As a result of COVID-19, more potential employees might want a position that allows at least partial work from home, or alternatively, flexible working hours. A company can consider developing a plan for new employees, such as an initial on-site period, so that it could be discussed during interviews.

Initial Documentation

Required
Employment
Documentation

When a candidate accepts employment the following documentation must be completed. Copies of all items are retained in the employee file in the human resources department.

continued

Initial Documentation, *continued*

1) **Job description, application, and acceptance forms**
2) **Testing, social security card, credit report, and medical results:** As applicable
3) **Agreements:** As applicable: non-disclosure, non-compete, arbitration agreements, and employment contract
4) **Signed permission from applicant:** Background check, medical test
5) **Signed receipt from employee:** For employee handbook and job description
6) **Form I-9:** *Employment Eligibility Verification:* This is required by the Department of Homeland Security (DHS). Complete within three business days of date employee begins work. The signed form (employee/employer) is retained in secure employer files according to requirements, not sent to DHS. Employer can retain copies of documentation.
7) **PRWORA notice:** *Personal Responsibility and Work Opportunity Act:* Follow state reporting requirements to report new employees. Report new hire information to State Directory of New Hires in the state(s) in which the employee works. Employers may register online or by paper form. For further information go to www.acf.hhs.gov /css/employers.
8) **W-4 and state equivalent:** Prior to a first paycheck, an employee needs to provide a completed federal W-4 form and equivalent state (and sometimes local) form to the employer; otherwise, withholding is at single status rate. These are used to determine federal and state income tax withholding. (Note: Form W-9 is required for independent contractors. Some states, such as California, may require new independent contactor reporting.)
9) **Benefit enrollment forms:** If benefits such as health, insurance, and savings plans are available, provide benefits summary. Employee should provide choices and personal data to employer prior to first paycheck.
10) **Updates for workers' compensation insurance:** Contact provider.
11) **Frequently used non-resident alien forms as needed:** I-129 (Petition for a Non-Immigrant Worker to temporarily work in U.S.); ETA 9089 (Part of the process for a U.S. employer to hire a foreign worker who wishes to obtain a "green card"—permanent residence based on employment.); I-140 (Immigrant Petition for Alien Worker to permanently work and reside in U.S.).

TIP

Form I-9 is very important. It is illegal to knowingly hire or employ a person not eligible for work in the United States. By law, (Immigration and Control Reform Act of 1986) every employer must have a completed Form I-9 for every compensated worker and must retain and safeguard the form in a separate file (three separate files are best: for non-reverify, for reverify due to work authorization expiration date, and for separated) for at least three years after date of hire or one year after termination, whichever is later. Also, an employer must complete a key verification section **within three days** after an applicant is hired. See next page for Form I-9 (date extended by DHS).

Penalties for compliance failure vary depending on the number of employees affected and other factors. For example, technical/form errors range from $230 to about $2,300 and knowing/continued violations range from about $600 to about $24,000 with even criminal penalties. Details are at ice.gov/factsheets/i9-inspection.

Initial Documentation, *continued*

Illustration 1.1: Form I-9

Employment Eligibility Verification **Department of Homeland Security** U.S. Citizenship and Immigration Services		**USCIS** **Form I-9** OMB No. 1615-0047 Expires 10/31/2022

▶ **START HERE:** Read instructions carefully before completing this form. The instructions must be available, either in paper or electronically, during completion of this form. Employers are liable for errors in the completion of this form.

ANTI-DISCRIMINATION NOTICE: It is illegal to discriminate against work-authorized individuals. Employers **CANNOT** specify which document(s) an employee may present to establish employment authorization and identity. The refusal to hire or continue to employ an individual because the documentation presented has a future expiration date may also constitute illegal discrimination.

Section 1. Employee Information and Attestation *(Employees must complete and sign Section 1 of Form I-9 no later than the* **first day of employment,** *but not before accepting a job offer.)*

Last Name *(Family Name)*	First Name *(Given Name)*	Middle Initial	Other Last Names Used *(if any)*
Address *(Street Number and Name)*	Apt. Number	City or Town	State	ZIP Code

Date of Birth *(mm/dd/yyyy)*	U.S. Social Security Number	Employee's E-mail Address	Employee's Telephone Number

I am aware that federal law provides for imprisonment and/or fines for false statements or use of false documents in connection with the completion of this form.

I attest, under penalty of perjury, that I am (check one of the following boxes):

☐ 1. A citizen of the United States

☐ 2. A noncitizen national of the United States *(See instructions)*

☐ 3. A lawful permanent resident   (Alien Registration Number/USCIS Number): _____

☐ 4. An alien authorized to work   until (expiration date, if applicable, mm/dd/yyyy): _____
    Some aliens may write "N/A" in the expiration date field. *(See instructions)*

Aliens authorized to work must provide only one of the following document numbers to complete Form I-9:
An Alien Registration Number/USCIS Number OR Form I-94 Admission Number OR Foreign Passport Number.

1. Alien Registration Number/USCIS Number: _____

OR

2. Form I-94 Admission Number: _____

OR

3. Foreign Passport Number: _____

Country of Issuance: _____

QR Code - Section 1
Do Not Write In This Space

Signature of Employee	Today's Date *(mm/dd/yyyy)*

Preparer and/or Translator Certification (check one):

☐ I did not use a preparer or translator.   ☐ A preparer(s) and/or translator(s) assisted the employee in completing Section 1.
(Fields below must be completed and signed when preparers and/or translators assist an employee in completing Section 1.)

I attest, under penalty of perjury, that I have assisted in the completion of Section 1 of this form and that to the best of my knowledge the information is true and correct.

Signature of Preparer or Translator	Today's Date *(mm/dd/yyyy)*
Last Name *(Family Name)*	First Name *(Given Name)*	
Address *(Street Number and Name)*	City or Town	State	ZIP Code

🛑 *Employer Completes Next Page* 🛑

Form I-9 10/21/2019 | Page 1 of 3

Initial Documentation, *continued*

Illustration 1.1: Form I-9 *continued*

	Employment Eligibility Verification **Department of Homeland Security** U.S. Citizenship and Immigration Services	**USCIS** **Form I-9** OMB No. 1615-0047 Expires 10/31/2022

Section 2. Employer or Authorized Representative Review and Verification
(Employers or their authorized representative must complete and sign Section 2 within 3 business days of the employee's first day of employment. You must physically examine one document from List A OR a combination of one document from List B and one document from List C as listed on the "Lists of Acceptable Documents.")

Employee Info from Section 1	Last Name *(Family Name)*	First Name *(Given Name)*	M.I.	Citizenship/Immigration Status

List A **Identity and Employment Authorization**	OR	**List B** **Identity**	AND	**List C** **Employment Authorization**

List A	List B	List C
Document Title	Document Title	Document Title
Issuing Authority	Issuing Authority	Issuing Authority
Document Number	Document Number	Document Number
Expiration Date *(if any) (mm/dd/yyyy)*	Expiration Date *(if any) (mm/dd/yyyy)*	Expiration Date *(if any) (mm/dd/yyyy)*
Document Title		
Issuing Authority	Additional Information	QR Code - Sections 2 & 3 Do Not Write In This Space
Document Number		
Expiration Date *(if any) (mm/dd/yyyy)*		
Document Title		
Issuing Authority		
Document Number		
Expiration Date *(if any) (mm/dd/yyyy)*		

Certification: I attest, under penalty of perjury, that (1) I have examined the document(s) presented by the above-named employee, (2) the above-listed document(s) appear to be genuine and to relate to the employee named, and (3) to the best of my knowledge the employee is authorized to work in the United States.

The employee's first day of employment *(mm/dd/yyyy)*: _____   *(See instructions for exemptions)*

Signature of Employer or Authorized Representative	Today's Date *(mm/dd/yyyy)*	Title of Employer or Authorized Representative
Last Name of Employer or Authorized Representative	First Name of Employer or Authorized Representative	Employer's Business or Organization Name

Employer's Business or Organization Address *(Street Number and Name)*	City or Town	State	ZIP Code

Section 3. Reverification and Rehires *(To be completed and signed by employer or authorized representative.)*

A. New Name *(if applicable)*			**B. Date of Rehire** *(if applicable)*
Last Name *(Family Name)*	First Name *(Given Name)*	Middle Initial	Date *(mm/dd/yyyy)*

C. If the employee's previous grant of employment authorization has expired, provide the information for the document or receipt that establishes continuing employment authorization in the space provided below.

Document Title	Document Number	Expiration Date *(if any) (mm/dd/yyyy)*

I attest, under penalty of perjury, that to the best of my knowledge, this employee is authorized to work in the United States, and if the employee presented document(s), the document(s) I have examined appear to be genuine and to relate to the individual.

Signature of Employer or Authorized Representative	Today's Date *(mm/dd/yyyy)*	Name of Employer or Authorized Representative

continued   ▶

Initial Documentation, *continued*

Illustration 1.1: Form I-9 *continued*

LISTS OF ACCEPTABLE DOCUMENTS
All documents must be UNEXPIRED

Employees may present one selection from List A
or a combination of one selection from List B and one selection from List C.

LIST A Documents that Establish Both Identity and Employment Authorization		LIST B Documents that Establish Identity	LIST C Documents that Establish Employment Authorization
	OR		**AND**
1. U.S. Passport or U.S. Passport Card		1. Driver's license or ID card issued by a State or outlying possession of the United States provided it contains a photograph or information such as name, date of birth, gender, height, eye color, and address	1. A Social Security Account Number card, unless the card includes one of the following restrictions: (1) NOT VALID FOR EMPLOYMENT (2) VALID FOR WORK ONLY WITH INS AUTHORIZATION (3) VALID FOR WORK ONLY WITH DHS AUTHORIZATION
2. Permanent Resident Card or Alien Registration Receipt Card (Form I-551)			
3. Foreign passport that contains a temporary I-551 stamp or temporary I-551 printed notation on a machine-readable immigrant visa		2. ID card issued by federal, state or local government agencies or entities, provided it contains a photograph or information such as name, date of birth, gender, height, eye color, and address	
4. Employment Authorization Document that contains a photograph (Form I-766)			2. Certification of report of birth issued by the Department of State (Forms DS-1350, FS-545, FS-240)
		3. School ID card with a photograph	
5. For a nonimmigrant alien authorized to work for a specific employer because of his or her status:		4. Voter's registration card	3. Original or certified copy of birth certificate issued by a State, county, municipal authority, or territory of the United States bearing an official seal
		5. U.S. Military card or draft record	
a. Foreign passport; and		6. Military dependent's ID card	
b. Form I-94 or Form I-94A that has the following:		7. U.S. Coast Guard Merchant Mariner Card	4. Native American tribal document
(1) The same name as the passport; and		8. Native American tribal document	5. U.S. Citizen ID Card (Form I-197)
(2) An endorsement of the alien's nonimmigrant status as long as that period of endorsement has not yet expired and the proposed employment is not in conflict with any restrictions or limitations identified on the form.		9. Driver's license issued by a Canadian government authority	6. Identification Card for Use of Resident Citizen in the United States (Form I-179)
		For persons under age 18 who are unable to present a document listed above:	7. Employment authorization document issued by the Department of Homeland Security
6. Passport from the Federated States of Micronesia (FSM) or the Republic of the Marshall Islands (RMI) with Form I-94 or Form I-94A indicating nonimmigrant admission under the Compact of Free Association Between the United States and the FSM or RMI		10. School record or report card	
		11. Clinic, doctor, or hospital record	
		12. Day-care or nursery school record	

Examples of many of these documents appear in the Handbook for Employers (M-274).

Refer to the instructions for more information about acceptable receipts.

Employment Eligibility Verification

An employer is required to review the information entered on Form I-9 by an employee. It is also the employer's responsibility to examine the employee's employment eligibility documents and identification documents and to decide if they reasonably appear to be genuine, and if they relate to the employee, and to the Form I-9 being completed. A list of acceptable documents is on the last page of Form I-9.

E-Verify

One comprehensive and potentially time-saving method to comply with verification requirements is *E-Verify*. E-Verify is a free Internet-based system that is operated by the federal Department of Homeland Security (DHS) and the Social Security Administration (SSA).

An authorized employer obtains permission to access the system by registering with the DHS. Go to www.dhs.gov/E-Verify. "Click on appropriate block." (Instructions are also available on the Internet from the U.S. Citizenship and Immigration Services (uscis.gov; click on "Forms", "All Forms" and search for "I-9"), which also publishes *Handbook For Employers*, Publication M-274.)

An employer uses the system by inputting information obtained from Form I-9. This creates a "case". The system then compares information on Form I-9 with information contained in the Social Security Administration database, the Department of Homeland Security database, and the Department of State database. The system then provides a "case result" to determine an applicant's work eligibility.

The case result can be initial, interim, or final. Initial case results can be: 1) Employment authorized 2) SSA or DHA tentative non-confirmation or DHS verification in process. 3) Final non-confirmation. Tentative non-confirmation or a verification in process case results require further action. The employee must be immediately notified and has the right to appeal the results within 10 days of notice. E-Verify provides a further action notice that explains how to contact the SSA and DHS for what to do next. Interim case results require further information and final case results provide a final determination.

An employer cannot take adverse action while a case is still pending or being appealed. Violations can be reported on an E-Verify hotline: 888-897-7781 and TTY hearing impaired 877-875-6028. E-Verify information is available at www.e-verify.gov.

The E-Verify system requires that an employer create a case within three days after a new employee has started work. E-Verify does not perform reverification.

Generally, use of E-Verify is voluntary. Exceptions are:

- Federal contracts that require the use of E-Verify
- States that require the use of E-Verify.

Employer Misrepresentation and Negligence in Hiring

Misrepresentation What if an employer misrepresents an offer of employment, the applicant relies on the offer, and the offer is later withdrawn, or some employer statements were untrue and the terms of the employment are less than promised? The employer misrepresentation could be intentional misrepresentation (fraudulent-intent to deceive, or reckless) or could simply be negligent, for which reasonable care and judgment is not exercised.

The answer to this question depends on several factors and really requires the services of employment legal counsel. One element is at-will employment (See page 15/16). If the offer is for at-will employment, there may not be a remedy for the applicant because the employment can be ended at any time with or without reason. Some courts have used promissory estoppel (the legal principal that requires a person who makes a promise that induces another to rely on the promise to pay damages that result from the reliance) or misrepresentation to provide the applicant with relief for damages such as relocation expenses or loss of income. Only negligence is unlikely to result in a remedy but is possible in some jurisdictions Any given outcome as described above often depends on the law and courts of a particular state. A final issue is the degree of difficulty in proving the existence of misrepresentation.

If the employment is not at-will and involves an employment contract, an applicant will have a stronger case if the agreement is secured by promises or misrepresentations.

TIP
An employer may want to consider **employment practices liability insurance (EPLI)**. This provides employer coverage for claims based on various kinds of discrimination, harassment, and wrongful discharge. It can also provide coverage for wage and hour claims such as based on Fair Labor Standards Act requirements. (See next section.)

At-Will Employment

Overview Most employee-employer relationships are "at-will" (except Montana). It is the default rule. "At-will" employment means that both the employee and employer are free to terminate the relationship at any time, for any reason, or no reason at all. Of course the employer may not terminate for illegal reasons such as discrimination and the exceptions described below. If an employer terminates an employee and an exception applies, the employee can sue the employer with the possbile results of money damages and employment reinstatement. Application of at-will exceptions varies by jurisdication.

At-Will Employment, *continued*

Employment Contracts: Explicit and Implied

An employment contract is an agreement between an employee and employer that the employment will be for a definite period and/or the employee can be discharged only for good cause or specified reasons. Furthermore, a contract will contain various specific elements that include items such as job description, required duties, compensation, benefits, vacation, legal jurisdication, possibly confidentiality, non-competition, arbitration, and other possible provisisons. With some exceptions, employment contracts require good faith and fair dealing — honesty and open communication between the parties—to avoid possible violation. In all cases, a contract should be written and reviewed by employment legal counsel.

In some cases an employment contract may be implied, such as language in an offer of employment that refers to the length or term of employment, or language in an employee handbook discussing firing for only good cause. Although more difficult to prove, even oral communication such as references to job security or length of employment can create an implied contract if there is sufficient corroboration.

Public Policy

A second common exception to at-will employment is if an employer violates the public policy of federal or state jurisdication with the termination. For example, a jurisdication may have established a public policy that protects whistle blowers (employees who reveal illegal business activity), those who refuse to break the law or not perform a duty required by law, those who file worker compensation claims, or that protects employees from on-the-job harassment (a form of discrimination under various federal and state laws). "Public policy" is usually found in constitutions, statutes and regulations. In some jurisdications, public policy can be found in court decisions and well-established administrative history. Public policy varies by jurisdiction and competent local employment law counsel should be consulted if issues arise.

Collective Bargaining Agreements

Labor law that concerns union activities and collective bargaining is a complex and extensive topic, and employers would be well advised to utilize the services of labor law counsel. The govening federal law is the National Labor Relations Act (NLRA) primarily enforced by the National Labor Relations Board (NLRB). Union employees under collective bargaining agreements and the NLRA have various rights and are not at-will employees. As well, it is important to understand that the NLRA does not just apply to unionized workplaces. Under Section 7, an employer may not threaten or interfere with organizing activity by employees, *even if there is no union or even a formal effort to establish one.*

Employee vs. Independent Contractor

Employees

Overview

Not all people who perform services for a business are employees. It is very important to accurately identify which workers qualify as employees because laws impose different requirements for workers who are employees and for those who are not. Not only is it necessary to comply with various laws, but correct identification also permits an employer to have a flexible workforce and reduces fraud and waste.

"Employee" Defined

Under the traditional, "common law" (law that results from court decisions) test, any person who performs services for another (the "employer"—see below) is an employee if the employer has the right to control:

- what will be done, and
- how it will be done,

whether or not the employer actually exercises this control.

This definition must be applied to each individual. It makes no difference what job title or name is used, frequency or means of payment, or whether the work is full time or part time. Generally, courts broadly interpret the term "employee" for the purpose of protecting workers. (Also see "ABC test" later.)

> *Note:* Form SS-8 can be submitted to the Internal Revenue Service to determine employee status. This form can be filed either by a business or a worker and can also be submitted online. It is highly recommended that an employer seek the assistance of employment law counsel before seeking an IRS determination. Contact state employment offices for state rules.

Example of an Employee

Jane performs secretarial services for Smith Company and is given word-processing tasks that include preparing management reports. Jane is expected to be at the business location during certain hours and to allow her manager to review and make changes to her work at any time. She must use the business office and equipment and software used by the business. She also receives a regular paycheck from Smith Company. Jane is an employee primarily because Smith Company supervises and controls not only what is done but also *how the work is done*.

Not an Employee

Mary also performs the same type of services for Smith Company. Mary is given a management report to complete, and she completes the job from her own office during her own work schedule. Mary uses her own equipment and software , and she completes the work during her own hours without review from Smith Company managers. Mary submits a

continued ▶

Employees, *continued*

Not an Employee, Continued	bill to Smith Company for the work completed. Mary is not an employee primarily because Mary controls how the work is done. Mary would be regarded as an independent contractor.
Temporary Workers	"Temp" workers, whether full or part time, are employees. They are entitled to minimum wage and overtime hours and meal and rest breaks just as other employees, even if they are paid by an employment agency and their payroll is processed by an agency.
Business Owners	▪ Proprietorship: A sole proprietor is not an employee of the business. ▪ Partnership: A partner performing duties as a partner is not an employee of a partnership. ▪ Corporation: Owners (shareholders) of a corporation who work in the business are employees of the corporation if they otherwise qualify under the common law "control" test.
"Employer" Defined	The word "employer" is a general term. An employer is one who employs the services of another. In other words, under common law an employer is the party who employs the services of another and controls what work is done and how it is done. A legalistic and broader definition is found in the Fair Labor Standards Act (FLSA), that provides that an employer is one who suffers or permits another to work. Most statutory law (law enacted by a legislature), such as the FLSA, identify an employee and then define an employer as the one who provides compensation and "suffers (allows) the employee to work"; in other words, first determine whether or not a worker is an employee before trying to identify the employer.

⚑ Independent Contractors ⚑

Overview	It is important to identify independent contractors, because an independent contractor is not an employee, even though an independent contractor may do the same kind of work or similar work as an employee. Documentation and compliance rules that a business must follow are very different than for employees, so the distinction is significant. Only employees are considered to be part of a business "payroll." This is important because it means that for an independent contractor, a business does not withhold income tax, withhold or pay social security taxes, employment taxes, provide workers compensation insurance, or follow fair labor laws.
Definition	An "independent contractor" is the party who is in control of the manner in which services are performed. Therefore, independent contractors are not employees (and don't receive employee protection such as minimum wage).

Independent Contractors, *continued*

Examples
- People who are in work for themselves such as doctors, lawyers, and construction contractors, are independent contractors.
- If an employer has someone from the maintenance department fix a leaky sink in the restroom, the work is performed by an employee. If an employer calls a plumber to come to the premises to fix the sink, the plumber is an independent contractor.
- In the example on the previous page, Mary in an independent contractor.

TIP

Independent contractors are not employees. Temporary workers and seasonal workers who are not independent contractors are employees, even if an agency processes their payroll.

Guidelines
In some circumstances following the above definition in order to determine exactly who is an independent contractor and who is an employee can be complicated, and an employer may need to seek professional help. The IRS, the Department of Labor, and individual states have their own guidelines in this matter. Here are some key (but not all) indicators of an independent contractor for various situations:

- The person doing the work determines how the work is to be done.
- The person doing the work also offers services to the public.
- The person doing the work operates as a business that makes a profit or loss.
- There is a contract for the services to be performed.
- Payment is not by paycheck, but rather when invoices for work are submitted.
- The person doing the work sets his/her own working hours and schedule.

IRS and DOL Guidelines to Determine Worker Status

IRS Guidelines
The Internal Revenue Service (IRS) uses the following guidelines in the determination of worker status:

- **Behavioral Control:** Behavioral control refers to an employer's right to control how work is done (without necessarily needing to exercise that right). Behavioral control factors fall into these categories:
  - Type of instruction: 1) When and where work is to be done 2) Tools or equipment that are to be used. 3) The workers that are to be hired or that will help with the work 4) Where supplies or services are to be purchased 5) Specific individual assignments 6) Order or sequence of work activity

continued ▶

IRS and DOL Guidelines to Determine Worker Status, *continued*

IRS Guidelines,
Continued

- Degree of instruction: The greater the detail of instruction, the stronger the indication that the worker is an employee.
- Evaluation: If an evaluation procedure or system is in place, then the greater the focus on details of how the work was done, the stronger the indication that the worker is an employee. Evaluation of only end results indicates an independent an contractor.
- Training: If the worker receives training by or on behalf of the employer on how to do a job, this is a good indication that the worker is an employee. Regular or ongoing training strenghthens this presumption.

■ **Financial Control:** The type of employer financial commitment or influence related to a worker is an indicator of status.

- Investment in equipment used: The greater an employer's investment in equipment used by a worker, the stronger the presumption of employee status.
- Expense reimbursement: Worker expense reimbursement by employer is an indicator of employee status.
- Profit or loss: The absence of an opportunity for an individual profit or loss is an indicator of employee status.
- Availability of services: A worker is not offering his or her services to the general public, which indicated employee status.
- Payment method: Wage payment (e.g. hourly or by other period of time or by commission), rather than being billed or invoiced for completed projects is an indicator of employee status.

■ **Relationship:** The manner in which the parties perceive their relationship to each other is an indicator of a worker's status.

- Contract: A contract referencing the above factors can be an indicator. However, a statement of employee or independent contractor status in the contract is itself not determinative. The issue is a factual question.
- Benefits: Items that are usually considered to be in the nature of fringe benefits (e.g. unemployment insurance, workers' compensation, health plan, retirement plan, vacation pay) indicate employee status.
- Permanency: An expectation that the work relationship is indefinite rather than for a specific task or tasks is an indication of employee status.

Employment Tax
Questions

800-829-4933 or 800-829-4059 for hearing/speech impaired.

continued ▶

IRS and DOL Guidelines to Determine Worker Status, *continued*

TIP

How expensive can worker misclassification be? Sometimes pretty expensive. In a famous Microsoft case, workers who were classified as independent contractors were determined to be employees by the IRS. This required Microsoft to pay substantial back payroll taxes, penalties, and interest. Microsoft was then required to pay the workers overtime for the misclassification period as required by the Department of Labor. Upon the reclassification, employees then sued Microsoft for full benefits including 401(k) and stock purchase plan rights, for the period of misclassification. The appeals court decided in favor of the employees. In another case, FedEx paid almost $230 million to settle a case in which delivery drivers had been classified as independent contractors. The moral of these stories? Correct worker classification is incredibly important.

DOL Guidelines

The Department of Labor (DOL) uses its own guidelines for the purpose of determining employee or independent contractor status under the Fair Labor Standards Act (page 40.) There is no single determinative factor in this regard; rather, according to the Supreme Court the entirety or totality of the relationship must be considered when making a decision. Accordingly, the Department of Labor applies what it calls an "economic realities test" that rejects the focus on "control" of the work in favor of the following factors relating to the economic reality of the worker's position with regard to the employer.

- **Extent to which a worker's services are integral to employer:** This generally means the importance of a worker's services in completing an employer's product or service. The idea is that work that is a key part of the process means that the worker is likely to be financially dependent on the employer as an employee and less likely to be in business as an independent contractor.
- **A worker's managerial or entrepeneurial skills:** The greater these skills, the greater a worker's opportunity for profit or loss as an independent contractor.
- **Relative investments in facilities and equipment:** Has a worker has made a significant investment in tools and equipment necessary for completion of work? If a worker's investment is sufficient to bear a risk of loss with the employer, that is an indication of independent contractor status. However, a worker may also own tools in a capacity as an employee.
- **Worker skill and initiative:** Greater skills and judgment are considered to be associated with independent contractor status.

continued ▶

IRS and DOL Guidelines to Determine Worker Status, *continued*

DOL Guidelines,
Continued

- If a worker demonstrates skills sufficient to indicate independent business judgment, that may indicate independent contractor status.
- If a worker offers services to the general public and is competing in an open market, that is an indicator of independent contractor status.

■ **Permanency of relationship with employer:** Indefinite relationship with an employer is an indictor of employee status; however, lack of an indefinite relationship does not necessarily suggest independent contractor status.

■ **Nature and degree of control of employer:** The greater the degree of employer control, the greater the likelihood of employee status. Examples of analysis of this element includes, but is not limited to, the following:

- Who determines pay and working hours?
- Who determines how the work is performed?
- Is the worker free to hire others?

The following factors generally are immaterial to determining whether an employee or independent contractor relationship exists: 1) The wording in a signed agreement stating the status of the relationship, 2) Whether the worker is incorporated or licensed, 3) Financial method or timing of pay. The Department of Labor provides the following contacts for further information: www.wage/hour.dol.gov or toll-free 1-866-487-9243.

The ABC Test

Many States Use
the ABC Test

Many states use some version of what is known as the "ABC test" for certain employment law statutes. This test places the burden of proof on an employer to show that a worker is *not* an employee. This requires meeting three requirements, hence the term "ABC." For example, in California a hiring entity must establish that:

A) The worker is free from the control and direction of the hiring entity for the performance of work, both in contract for performance and in fact.
B) The worker performs work that is outside the usual course of the hiring entity's business.
C) The worker is customarily engaged in an independently established trade, occupation, or business of the same nature as the work performed.

Employment law varies, sometimes conflicts, and is evolving in this area in different jurisdictions. In California for example, although the Supreme Court only applied the ABC test to wage and hour claims, the

continued ▶

The ABC Test, *continued*

Many States Use the ABC Test, Continued	legislature has expanded the scope of coverage to other employment settings and employment laws. This indicates that knowledgeable employment counsel should be consulted on all identification issues in a local jurisdiction.

Other Agencies

Also Check Other Agencies

Other agencies are empowered to audit businesses and enforce the laws and requirements that they administer. In addition to the IRS and DOL discussed above, examples of other agencies are the Equal Employment Opportunity Commission (EEOC), the Occupational Safety and Health Administration (OSHA), individual state wage and hour departments, state unemployment insurance departments, and workers' compensation administrators. All the agencies and departments have their own individual guidelines for evaluating employee and independent contractor status; however, a common tendency is to more rigorously question independent contractor status. This is because the agencies are aware that employers frequently wish to avoid the additional costs (payroll taxes, workmen's compensation insurance, benefits, human resources and payroll administration costs, etc.) and responsibilities (fair hiring and employment laws) associated with employee classification, and it is precisely the role of the agencies to enforce these laws.

TIP

If an employer is concerned that existing contractor classifications may be incorrect, for IRS purposes a voluntary program can provide relief. It is called the Voluntary Classification Settlement Program ("VCSP"). Also available is Section 530 safe harbor relief. See pages 266, 268.

Fair Employment: Employee Rights Compliance

Overview

Federal and State/Local Law

Employment is an extremely important part of society and most people's lives, and is a major factor affecting quality of life. Federal and state, and sometimes even local governments place a high priority on protection of employee rights and working conditions and have enacted numerous laws related to this goal. These are often referred to as "fair employment laws" that

continued ▶

Overview, *continued*

Federal and State/Local Law, Continued	protect the welfare of employees, job seekers and retirees. Two primary administrative authorities at the federal level are the U.S. Department of Labor (DOL), which administers various federal wage and hour laws and the Equal Employment Opportunity Commission (EEOC) administering equality in employment. Other agencies are also listed in Table 1.1. They have authority to investigate businesses, assess penalities, and undertake civil and criminal prosecution on behalf of both employees and government. Table 1.1 below provides a summary of some key federal laws and compliance requirements that employers must follow. Further information from the DOL and EEOC can be obtained directly from the DOL (www.dol.gov, or toll-free 1-866-487-2365) and EEOC (www.eeoc.gov or toll-free 1-800-669-4000).

States have also enacted fair employment laws that protect worker rights. Table 1.2 lists important categories of these laws. However, both employer and employee should review state law in greater detail to determine specifically what rules apply in their own state. Employers generally must comply with highest federal or state requirements. Individual states each have a state department of labor that can answer questions and provide further guidance. As well, professional legal advice is available in this area of specialization.

Important Federal Fair Employment Laws

Table 1.1: Important Federal Fair Employment Laws

Key Employer Compliance Requirements	Name of Law
Large employers must offer affordable health insurance. (See page 163).	Affordable Care Act (ACA)
Requires that there is no age discrimination in hiring practices or employment, according to guidelines.	Age Discrimination in Employment Act (ADEA)
Agricultural employers must disclose employment terms at time of recruitment and comply with those terms. Farm labor contractors that recruit, supervise, and transport farmworkers must register and be licensed with the DOL. Providers of housing and transportation must meet minimum safety standards. Provides whistleblower protection and prohibits retaliation.	Agricultural Worker Protection Act (AWPA) Full name: Migrant and Seasonal Agricultural Worker Protection Act. (Does not apply to family farms and certain other exemptions.) Enforced by DOL.
Employer must ensure that there is no disability-related discrimination in hiring practices or employment, and maintain reasonable accommodations for disabled employees, according to guidelines. "Disability" is determined medically on a case-by-case basis as impairment of major life functions, according to guidelines. Applies to employers with 15 or more employees.	Americans with Disabilities Act (ADA). Enforced primarily by the Equal Employment Opportunity Commission (EEOC) and the DOL.

continued ▶

Important Federal Fair Employment Laws, *continued*

Table 1.1: Important Federal Fair Employment Laws, *continued*

Key Employer Compliance Requirements	Name of Law
Employers (except churches and church-related organizations) with group health plans and 20 or more employees (counting part-time as fractional) on more than 50% of normal business days in the prior year must allow workers and dependents to elect to pay 100% for continuing coverage for at least 18 (possibly 36) months if coverage is lost due to "qualifying events", including quitting, being fired, loss of work, divorce or separation, and death.	Consolidated Omnibus Budget Reconciliation Act of 1985 (COBRA)
For employers with federal government contracts (minimum contract size in parentheses) the listed laws apply. (Many other provisions apply. Contact help desk at ofccphelpdesk.dol.gov or call 800-397-6251.)	Davis-Bacon Act ($2,000), McNamara-O'Hara Service Contract Act ($2,500) also now called Service Contract Labor Standards (SCLS), Vocational Rehabilitation Act ($2,500), Vietnam Era Veterans Readjustment Act ($10,000), Walsh-Healy Act ($15,000), Federal Contractor Compliance Program ($10,000)
In all aspects of hiring and employment, employers cannot engage in the various specified types of discrimination, according to guidelines, particularly discrimination based on race, sex, color, national origin, or religion. Contact the local EEOC field office for requirements and details. Note: discrimination prevention training is considered essential.	Title VII of the Civil Rights Act, also called "Equal Employment Opportunity" (EEO) and enforced by the Equal Employment Opportunity Commission (EEOC).
Ensure that there are no compensation disparities based on gender, according to guidelines.	Equal Pay Act (amendment to FLSA)
When outsourced, an investigative ("background check") or credit report about a job applicant or employee, employer must first notify that person in writing and receive written permission. Employer must provide advance notice that the report will be used, provide a copy of the report, and explanation of the person's rights. If adverse action is taken, the employer must notify the person that he/she was not hired in whole or in part as a result of information in the report.	Fair Credit Reporting Act (FCRA). Act is enforced the Consumer Financial Protection Bureau and the Federal Trade Commission.

continued ▶

Important Federal Fair Employment Laws, *continued*

Table 1.1: Important Federal Fair Employment Laws, *continued*

Key Employer Compliance Requirements	Name of Law
Regulates working conditions including minimum wage, overtime, child labor, and recordkeeping according to guidelines. (See page 40)	Fair Labor Standards Act (FLSA) Administered and enforced by the Department of Labor (DOL)
Private sector employers with 50 or more employees within a 75-mile radius of the worksite and public agency and elementary and secondary school employers regardless of number of employees must grant qualified employees unpaid, job-protected leave (or can be paid) for family or medical emergencies, according to guidelines. Eligible employees are also eligible for: 1) Continuation of group medical coverage with same terms as if employee had not taken leave or changed terms while on leave that apply to all employees, 2) Twelve workweeks (they do not have to be continuous) of leave in a single 12-month period for designated medical issues including childbirth and newborn care, child adoption or foster care placement and care, care for spouse, child, or parent with a serious medical condition, a serious health condition of employee, and an emergency arising out of military active duty. Twenty-six weeks in a single 12-month period is allowed for military caregiver leave for a family member. See https://www.dol.gov/whd/fmla.	Family and Medical Leave Act (FMLA) Administered and enforced by the Department of Labor (DOL) Note: check state law for more favorable employee terms.
Workers must be able to access their own full personnel files up to two years after termination.	Lilly Ledbetter Fair Pay Act
OSHA provides employer training and guidance rules for safety in the workplace, and also conducts audits and enforces results. Complaints of violations and/or employer retaliation can be made at 800-321-6742 or regional or local office within 30 days of retaliation.	Occupational Safety and Health Act (OSHA) Administered and enforced by the Occupational Safety and Health Administration. Free onsite consultation/exemption. See OSHA Consultation Directory.
It is unlawful for an employer discriminate on the basis of pregnancy, childbirth, or related medical conditions, for both employees and job applicants. **NOTE:** Private employers of more than 100 employees and federal contracts of more than 50 must submit **Form EEO-1** annually.	Pregnancy Discrimination Act (Amendment to Title VII of Civil Rights Act) Administered and enforced by the Equal Employment Opportunity Commission (EEOC).
Employer must allow a leave of absence and reemploy with accrued seniority those employees required to perform active military service.	Uniformed Service and Reemployment Rights Act (USERRA) Administered and enforced by the Department of Labor (DOL)

continued ▶

Important Federal Fair Employment Laws, *continued*

Table 1.1: Important Federal Fair Employment Laws, *continued*

Key Employer Compliance Requirements	Name of Law
Protects employees from retaliation for reporting violations under various laws. See www.whistleblowers .gov/ and www.whistleblowers.org/know-your-rights/. (Also check state laws, which can be broader.)	Whistleblower Protection Act of 1989 and other whistleblower protection laws. Administered and enforced by the relevant agencies.

State Fair Employment Law Categories

Overview   States and some local governments have enacted their own fair employment laws. Because these are numerous and vary by state and locality, only the common general categories are listed here. However, each individual state will have a department of labor that can be contacted for details on their own fair employment laws. Additionally, the following link can be used to access further information on state employment laws: https://www.dol.gov/whd/state/state.htm.

Table 1.2: Important State Fair Employment Law Categories

Key Employer Compliance Requirements	Category
Many states have enacted their own minimum wage rates; additionally, local jurisdictions may enact their own minimum wage, often called "living wage" (minimum wage at or above local poverty level, particularly where cost of living is high) laws. One living wage calculator is available at livingwage.mit.edu/. Some states also have living wage calculators available online. Employer must pay the greater of FLSA, state, local, or living wage pay requirement.	Minimum Wage and "Living Wage" laws.
Currently there are no federal requirements for paid sick leave. However there are some state/local laws at various levels. The states are Arizona, California, Colorado, Connecticut, Maine, Maryland, Massachusetts, Michigan, Nevada, New Jersey, New Mexico, New York, Oregon, Rhode Island, Vermont, Washington, and District of Columbia.	Mandatory paid sick leave
Some states have enacted laws that require a mandatory employee-paid insurance plan to provide disability benefits for disabilities that are not work-related. The payments are made via employer withholding for each payroll period. At this time the states are: California, Hawaii, New Jersey, New York, and Rhode Island, and the territory of Puerto Rico.	State Disability Insurance (SDI)

continued ▶

State Fair Employment Law Categories, *continued*

Most states have "Pay Day" laws that require a minimum frequency of paying employees, most often in the range of about every two to four weeks, sometimes depending on occupation.	State "Pay Day" Laws
Employer must enroll in insurance coverage for medical expenses and wage replacement for employees for work-related injury, disability, or death. (See page 171.)	Workers' Compensation

Monitor and Update Employee Status

Employment and Termination Overview

Overview After an employee is hired and status has been determined, a continuing relationship exists that requires regular monitoring of the employee status and related payroll procedures. This relationship ends when an employee leaves; the termination of the relationship has its own requirements. Table 1.3 below identifies key procedures for current employees.

Current Employees

Monitor and Review Status Table 1.3 below identifies key procedures for current employees.

Table 1.3: Monitoring Employee Status

Current Employees
▪ Update personnel file with all employee status changes such as address, pay, withholding, reviews, job title, job description.
▪ Update payroll department with individual changes in status, job title, pay rate, withholding amounts and payment method.
▪ Review for any changes in minimums and limits requirements such as for minimum wage rates, living wage rates, overtime status (exempt vs. non-exempt), and individual withholding items. Review workers' compensation insurance coverage.
▪ Communicate and document (to employee file) regular feedback, performance reviews, training, and mentoring. With a secure system, also communicate the data digitally to employees so they have access. Develop, monitor, and document a performance improvement plan if applicable. Maintain related data such as vacation and sick leave time.
▪ Maintain and document compliance with federal, state, and local fair employment laws. (Review applicable items in tables 1.1 and 1.2, and a self-audit plan.)
▪ Update and distribute employee handbook as needed, and obtain signed receipts from employees.

Separation Procedures

Overview

Unfortunately, employment separation in some cases can be an unpleasant experience which in turn can create a range of feelings including disappointment, anger, fear, resentment, and so on. In the case of involuntary separation, for ethical and practical reasons, including avoidance of a variety of liability claims, it is clearly in the best interests of an employer to act in a manner that ensures full legal compliance, follows good business practice, and also supports the best interests of an employee. The following discussion addresses these procedures and potential issues.

Is It Necessary?

As previously discussed, in most cases the employer-employee relationship is "at-will". However, regardless of the employer's right to fire an employee at any time, with or without cause, it may be sub-optimal for an employer to do so. It can be expensive to search for, hire, and train a new employee and involuntary terminations for no good reason will adversely affect morale.

When feasible, a useful alternative is to work with an employee who is not performing satisfactorily to develop a written ***performance improvement plan***. The plan should identify deficiences, performance goals and deadlines, and the specific means of training or mentoring. This can have several valuable benefits:

1) When an employee receives collaborative training and mentoring and addresses deficencies, performance improves, and business productivity improves. 2) Employer-employee relations and morale improve. 3) If the employer ultimately determines that it must terminate the employee, there is documented evidence that the employer made a good-faith effort to retain the employee, which will help protect against a variety of wrongful termination claims.

Pre-Termination Checklist

1) If involuntary separation, is authority to fire clearly defined?
2) If involuntary separation, are there regular performance reviews that clearly document the specifically-identified deficiencies?
3) Were the performance reviews discussed with the employee? What was noted as the main elements of the discussions? What were employee responses?
4) Has the employee made complaints? How were these addressed —have there been reasonable and good-faith efforts by the employer and are these documented? Can the complaints plausibly relate to fair employment law violations? Was employment legal counsel consulted and were recommendations followed?
5) Was a peformance improvement plan implemented?
6) Is the employee at-will or is there an employee or collective bargaining contract with requirements that must be followed? Is there risk of implied contract?

continued ▶

Separation Procedures, *continued*

Pre-Termination Checklist, Continued

7) Are there state/local requirements for written notice? (Not required by the FLSA, but suggested for best practices.).
8) Is the employee on leave? Some require job protection while on leave.
9) Review employee handbook so that no protocol is overlooked.
10) Should a security person be available?
11) Calculate separation costs including possible increase in state unemployment insurance. In applicable situations consider severance payments including a waiver of employee claims.
12) Calculate final paycheck and any accrued amounts to be included such as vacation pay. Verify state/local requirement for final paycheck date.
13) Contact benefits advisors to inform them of plan participant changes and to determine benefits changes in order to advise the employee.

Termination Procedures

1) A private face-to-face meeting in an exit interview is advantageous for an employer because it facilitates communication and usually is more respectful to the employee than using media. (A third-party mangement person should be present to listen.) Specific documented reasons should be reviewed to preclude innacurate suspicions by the employee. Carefully listen and document employee comments. This is especially important if the employee is voluntarily quitting his or her job. However, unless there is a contractual requirement, an employee is never required to attend an exit interview. From an employee perspective, it may in some cases be disadvantageous if the wrong things are said.
2) Inform human resources department of details and date of termination.
3) Inform payroll department of date of termination.
4) Advise the employee of all rights and benefits following termination, such as unemployment benefits, workers' compensation, severance, and COBRA if applicable. Complete employee notices required by state/local law (typically rights and benefits).
5) Contact benefits advisors and workers' compensation insurance to confirm employee departure. Check with benefit advisors to calculate amounts due from employee in the final period that are paycheck withholding amounts.
6) Final paycheck: Must be timely per federal and state laws. Inform employee of final paycheck amount and date and explain calculations. Verify contact information.
7) Advise the employee of the time period for departure and to remove all personal items by the end of that period.
8) Advise employee of the duty to maintain confidentiality and non-competition according to any agreements.

continued ▶

Separation Procedures, *continued*

Termination Procedures, Continued	9) Collect all company property such as laptops, credit cards, badges, timecards, passcards, and keys, etc. from employee by the end of the time period. 10) Passwords and systems access should be changed at appropriate time. Cancel any signatory authority. 11) Notify directly affected (not most) employees and security of departure without giving reasons (See "Defamation" below.). 12) Garnishment: For employees with garnishment orders, termination will require notice to each issuing agency. Some states have online forms. 13) Review and comply with requirements for notice to state/local authorities of separated employees. 14) If employee requests a W-2, provide within 30 days of earlier of request or final wage payment. If no request, file according to normal deadlines. 15) Approval authority: If employee has approval authority (such as signing checks, payroll processing approvals, or reports approval) remove name and reassign.

Other Separation Liability Issues

Discrimination	As previously indicated discrimination can take numerous forms, including retaliation through harassment, demotion, threats, intolerable conditions, and termination to discourage or prevent employees from exercising their employment rights. Also refer to fair employment laws in Tables 1.1 and 1.2 and the discussion of modifications to at-will employment on page 15. The DOL and EEOC and state agencies investigate these employee claims.
Underpaid Compensation	A liability exists for a separated employee who has not received full compensation. The DOL and state agencies investigate these claims.
Defamation	"Defamation" means intentionally damaging someone's reputation by making a false claim that is presented as a fact to another party, either verbal (slander) or written (libel). Defamation in termination situations can occur if the employer states a defamatory reason for termination. Defamation also occurs in the context of employer references when a prior employer defames a prospective employee to another employer. (This does not mean that a very positive reference prevents liability claims; in fact, a previous employer may be liable for damages suffered by a subsequent employer because of a misleading positive reference.) *Note:* Treating a current employee in an extremely demeaning manner may also constitute defamation if those actions amount to factual assertions.

Other Separation Liability Issues, *continued*

Public Policy: Wrongful Discharge	As indicated earlier in the discussion about at-will employment, termination may violate public policy. This is usually called "wrongful discharge in violation of public policy". A wrongful discharge/wrongful termination definition can be subjective and varies by jurisdiction.
Severance Agreements	Severance agreements are sometimes used. An employee receives payment and continued benefits during a specified period after departure to recognize prior good services and to create goodwill. As part of a severance agreement an employer can require that an employee agree to waive ("release") some or all of the potential claims that the employee may have against the employer.
	However, a severance agreement is not a blanket insurance policy. First, such an agreement is not enforceable if the employee has received nothing additional in return, beyond what they are already entitled to receive. Second, an employee cannot relinquish certain rights, such as filing a whistleblower claim. Third, a release is not enforceable as to future harms such as later defamation. Finally, a release of some claims must allow an employee time to change his or her mind before and after signing: specifically, age discrimination under the Age Discrimination in Employment Act (ADEA) which requires a 21-day period to think before signing, and a 7-day period after to revoke the agreement.

Human Resource Information Systems (HRIS)

Overview	As probably evident from the prior discussion, human resource management (HRM) functions encompass numerous responsiblities that concern legal compliance and data management. One method of streamling human resource duties is the use of a human resource information system.
What It Does	A HRIS is software (often modular, with each module specializing in a type of functionality) that is designed to assist with human resource duties. Various vendors provide a variety of software that can include the following functionality:

- Application and interview documentation
- Appraisal and performance assessment data
- Benefits choices and management (such as enrollment periods)
- Employee access permissions
- Employee exempt/non-exempt status for various requirements
- Employment contracts
- Employee handbook development and updates
- Hiring and recruitment requirements documentation
- Pay rate and withholding data
- Personal data
- PTO (paid time off) and absence tracking

continued ▶

Human Resource Information Systems (HRIS), *continued*

What It Does, Continued

- Status changes
- Title and job description
- Termination/job change data
- Tools for both employers and employees (timekeeping, time management, document management)
- Training data

Some of these systems are also designed to access a database that can provide customized reports. The greatest ongoing time and cost saving is an HR system that is integrated with the payroll processing system so that data entry is minimized; in other words, data can be updated from human resources and accessed in payroll processing. As well, payroll data can be accumulated for the use of human resource management reports.

Internal Control

Overview

Internal control means the policies, procedures, and organizational structure that safeguard assets from theft and from loss due to mismanagement. Internal control applies to all the steps in the payroll process that are illustrated on page 4.

For the first step, "Identify Employees" that we have been discussing, internal control is primarily a matter of fair employment laws compliance to prevent FLSA and other fededal and state statute violations. Violations result in penalties and interest, and in the worst case, lawsuits. Prevention is accomplished by an undertanding of and conformance to legal requirements, using checklists, regular monitoring of relevant activities, clearly communicating policies, consultation with legal or human resource professionals when necessary, and an overall fair treatment of employees. Internal control is discussed further in Section 7.

Disciplinary Actions

Summary

First and foremost employee discplinary procedures should be written— clearly explained in a current policy and procedures manual (or union agreement) for all employees. Regarding reductions in pay, the manual should clearly state the following: what deductions are permitted, an employee complaint process for pay deductions, and a reimbursements process for improper deductions; additionally, the company policy is compliant with FLSA requirements.

- Non-exempt employees and exempt outside sales employees: The FLSA does not prohibit an employer from docking (making a reduction in) an employee's pay or suspending an employee from work, for

continued ▶

Disciplinary Actions, *continued*

Summary,
Continued

a variety of disciplinary reasons, provided that the pay does not fall below minimum wage. State and local jurisdiction wage and hour laws should be checked.

■ Other exempt employces: These employees are generally paid on a salary basis and must be paid full salary for any week in which they perform some work. However, the following exceptions permit deductions made on a per full-day basis: 1) pay decreases are allowed if the employee is absent for one or more full days for personal reasons other than illness or disability if there is no provsion for personal time off, 2) for absence for one or more full days from illness or disability and there is a bona fide plan in place that provides compensation for illness or disability, 3) for serious violations such as safety, sexual misconduct, violence, or excessive absences as defined in regulations; however, work performance quality is excluded. 4) For any week in which the employee performs no work at all. Monetary penalties are permitted for violation of safety rules.

TIP

If an employer makes improper deductions from an exempt employee's compensation, the employer risks losing the exemption such that the employee will be considered as non-exempt during the period in which improper deductions were made. Furthermore, the same change will apply to all employees in the same job category/classification who work for the same supervisors or managers. This very expensive outcome can be mitigated or avoided by a genuine good-faith effort to follow the guidelines in the first paragraph of the above summary.

Joint Employers

Definition

A joint employer is an organization that employs a worker while that same worker is simultaneously employed by another organization, and each organization benefits from the arrangement; at the same time, each organization exercises some significant degree of control over the worker and the worker is economically dependent upon each organization. Common examples of this arrangement are the use of staffing agencies (the direct employer) that provides temporary workers to a client of the agency (the secondary employer) for which the worker performs daily duties. Other common examples are farm labor contractors and construction subcontractors that provide workers. The reason that this arrangement is important is that a joint employer may be jointly liable for ensuring and paying minimum wage and overtime under the FLSA.

In March of 2020 the DOL enacted a "final ruling" that identified the arrangement as either "horizontal" or "vertical" and set specific guidelines to identify a joint employment relationship. Specifically, a "horizontal" arrangement

continued ▶

Joint Employers, *continued*

Definition,
Continued

occurs when a worker works for two or more related organizations during the same week such as different companies owned by the same entity. A "vertical" arrangement is when a worker is hired by one firm for worker services to be provided to another, such as staffing agency that hires a "temp" worker and often handles the payroll.

Prior to the DOL final ruling, the most important factor in the judgement of the DOL and most courts was the degree of economic control that each organization could exercise over a worker. Although this was not the only factor, it was often a decisive one. As stated above, the 2020 DOL ruling was an attempt to clarify this by setting forth specific factors that defined a joint employment relationship. However, on August 31 of 2021 the DOL withdrew the final ruling.

Why It Matters

The August 2021 DOL action for now returns employers to prior status as before, i.e. DOL auditors and courts will likely primarily use a worker's economic dependence upon each organization, although this is not the sole factor (see guideline below). Currently it would be highly prudent to consult a labor law counsel that works in this area before entering what might be a joint employer relationship. Secondarily, especially for vertical arrangements, employers should be aware of contractual safeguards such as indemnification and up-to-date liability insurance. Finally, in the meantime this area of employment will remain in flux, as the DOL considers its options.

Possibly Not
Determinative

The following factors may not by themselves influence joint employer analysis:

- The existence a franchisor business model
- Providing sample employee handbooks to a franchisee
- Allowing an employer to operate a facility on company property
- Jointly participating with an employer in an apprenticeship program
- Offering an association health or retirement plan to an employer or participating in such a plan with an employer.
- Requiring a business partner to establish minimum health and safety, sexual harassment prevention, and other workplace standards.

Using a Staffing Agency

Overview

Using a staffing agency (sometimes called a "temp agency") to provide a temporary employment solution is a common occurrence. A temporary worker can be a valuable resource when the right employee cannot be found or the time is not right for a permanent employee. Aside from the importance of finding the right worker for a job (skills test, resume´, background check, interview, etc.), other issues generic to the procedure also should be considered. Some of them are listed below. If the list raises

continued ▶

Using a Staffing Agency, *continued*

Overview,
Continued

doubts or creates uncertainty, it may be best to consult employment law counsel to help before finalizing a decision.

- **Review the contract**. Obtain proposals and contracts from several agencies, and read and compare. 1) What are the agency and client respective duties? 2) Will the agency hold the client harmless and indemnify the client for agency acts or omissions that create losses, penalties, and worker claims against the client? This is especially important if federal or state law deems that the arrangement is one of joint employment and therefore joint liability. 3) Does the agency warrant that it will comply with laws and regulations? 4) What is the payment structure; are rates likely to change? 5) Will information remain confidential? 6) Is there a minimum hour requirement before a temporary worker could be hired as regular employee?
- **Obtain proof of insurance and check financial resources**. 1) Does the staffing firm have the financial resources and/or insurance to indemnify clients (employment practices insurance with client as additional named insured) ? 2) Is the workers' compensation insurance up to date? 3) What is the credit rating of the agency? 4) Does the firm have any industry or professional certifications or awards?
- **Check prior performance of staffing agency**. 1) Can a prospective client contact prior and current clients for their evaluation? 2) A litigation search can provide a history of litigation.

Indian Tribal
Governments

For a discussion of Indian tribal government special rules and tax guidance, see Publications 4268 and 5343. Also search online for "Employment Taxes for Tribes" by the IRS. Also go to https://secure.ssa.gov/poms.nsf/lnx/0301901700 for additional details by the Social Security Administration. If certain types of gaming profit distributions are made to tribal members in excess of $12,950/yr., withholding is required. See Publication 15-T for a quick summary and tables.

The Payroll Process

Step 1: Identify Employees

- Searching and hiring
- Employee vs. independent contractor
- Exempt vs. non-exempt
- Fair employment laws compliance
- Monitor and update employee status

Step 2: Calculate the Payroll

- Timekeeping
- Gross pay expense
- Withholding
- Payroll tax expense
- Benefits expense

Step 3: Record the Payroll

- Journal entry for gross pay and withholding
- Journal entry for payroll taxes expense
- Journal entry for benefits expense
- Journal entry for workers' comp. expense
- Verify/reconcile related ledger balances

Step 4: Make Payments

- To employees
- To taxing authorities
- To other parties

Step 5: Submit Forms and Reports

- Reverify/reconcile related ledger balances
- Federal government
- State/local governments
- Employees and independent contractors
- Management

For all steps in the process: Is internal control being adequately applied?

Section 2 Calculate the Payroll

Introduction

A calculation of a payroll is at the heart of the payroll process. Depending on a number of factors, the calculation can be relatively straightforward or complex. Issues can involve both Department of Labor and tax authorities compliance. This section is subdivided into each of the key areas that play essential roles in the calculation procedure.

Before proceeding with gross pay calculations, it should be understood that the amounts used in the various gross pay calculations, particularly for wages, depend on an accurate *timekeeping* function. Hours worked are usually needed before dollar costs can be determined. Timekeeping also provides data for some benefit calculations and allocations of payroll costs between jobs. Timekeeping is discussed in greater detail in Appendix II. Finally, the constant application of *internal control* procedures is essential to reduce the chances of fraud and error. See Section 7 for a procedures checklist.

Gross Pay

Gross Pay Overview

Overview and Examples

Gross pay is the total, called "gross" compensation earned by an employee. This usually is an amount shown on a paycheck before any deductions, but can also include other items such as various property and services. Typical examples of gross pay include:

- **Salary:** The term "salary" generally refers to a fixed amount per period that is not determined by hours worked. Salaries are usually earned by managers, administratiors, supervisors, and other professional staff.
- **Wage:** The term "wage" may be used generally to refer to compensation, but usually "wage" means an amount that is determined by hours worked or units of product completed. Typically wages are earned by skilled and unskilled workers in manufacturing, manual labor, retail positions, and customer service positions.
- **Commission:** Commissions are usually earned based on a percentage of sales.
- **Bonus:** Bonus earnings are extra amounts usually given as a reward for some kind of achievement or meeting performance goals.
- **Tip:** A tip is an extra amount, also called a "gratuity", paid at the discretion of a customer as a reward for good service.
- **In-kind:** Payment in some form of property or services (rather than money) is called "in-kind".

The Fair Labor Standards Act (FLSA) and Gross Pay

Importance

The FLSA significantly affects the amount and method of determining gross pay for employees. Employers must be aware of the numerous FLSA compliance requirements to avoid related penalties, back wages, and liquidated damages. Likewise, employees should be aware of the FLSA in order to understand their employment rights and to verify the accuracy of their paychecks. The following pages discuss major elements of this topic.

FLSA Overview

The *Fair Labor Standards Act (FLSA)* is a federal law that sets working condition requirements related to minimum wage, overtime, child labor, and record-keeping. The FLSA, as a result of both statute and broad case law interpretation, for practical purposes applies to virtually all employers and employees. Employee immigration status or citizenship does not affect FLSA coverage.

The Department of Labor's Wage and Hour Division (WHD) enforces the FLSA. Additionally, employees have a private right to sue. For questions and more information, the Department of Labor WHD call center is 1-866-487-2365. FLSA-related guidance, including fact sheets and regulations, may be accessed at the WHD website, www.dol.gov/whd/. Remember to also check state and local laws for wage and hour and working condition requirements.

Key FLSA provisions are:

- Employment relationship: The FLSA applies to "employees." There are very broad statutory definitions of "employ," "employer," and "employee." The mere designation of a worker as an "independent contractor" or "contract labor" does not invalidate an employment relationship. See DOL Fact Sheet #13, "Employment Relationship."
- Minimum wage: At this writing, the federal minimum wage is $7.25 per hour, except federal workers and contractors at $15. (Caution: Some states and localities have higher minimum wage rates.)
- Workweek: The FLSA applies on a workweek basis. An employee's workweek is a fixed and regularly recurring period of 168 hours—seven consecutive 24-hour periods. It is not necessary that the workweek coincide with the calendar week; it may begin on any day and at any hour of the day. See Fact Sheet #23, "Overtime Pay Requirements."
- Working hours: The FLSA requires that employees be paid for all time worked. See Fact Sheet #22 ("Hours Worked") and the "Hours Worked" regulations.

continued ▶

The Fair Labor Standards Act (FLSA) and Gross Pay, *continued*

FLSA Overview, Continued

- Fractional hours calculation: It is preferred that employees are paid to the full minute of work. However, the "Hours Worked" regulations permit rounding if the arrangement is used consistently and results in employees being compensated for all hours of work. Three methods are cited in the DOL Interpretive Bulletin: Rounding starting and stopping time to the nearest five minutes, nearest tenth of an hour or quarter hour.
- Overtime: All hours worked in excess of 40 hours per workweek must be paid at a rate 1.5 times the "regular pay rate" for non-exempt employees. Overtime compensation must be paid to non-exempt employees (see below), irrespective of the compensation arrangement (e.g., hourly, salary, commission, piece rate, job rate, day rate, or a combination of various methods). Applicable overtime requirements cannot be waived or avoided by any employee/employer agreement. (Caution: check state and local law for higher overtime rates. See Appendix I for states with daily overtime requirements.)
- Anti-discrimination and anti-retaliation rules, and child labor law are part of FLSA.
- Coverage and Exemptions: FLSA coverage will be discussed below, and some of the common exemptions will be discussed in the following pages. Coverage is broadly construed, while most exemptions are applied narrowly. There are minimum wage and overtime exemptions, but most of the exemptions apply only to the overtime standards.
- With the exception of the Equal Pay Act (part of the FLSA), the FLSA does not prohibit pay discrimination based on gender, color, race, religion, age, disability, national origin, or sexual identity, which are addressed by other laws. The Equal Pay Act and most other federal employment discrimination laws are enforced by the Equal Employment Opportunity Commission (EEOC). Most states also have laws that prohibit employment discrimination on the basis of the above factors. The DOL's Office of Federal Contract Compliance Programs (OFCCP) enforces certain employment discrimination provisions that apply to the performance of federal contracts.

Application of the FLSA to Employees

An employee who is engaged in interstate or foreign commerce, or in the production of goods (or whose work is closely related and directly essential to such production) for interstate or foreign commerce, is a covered employee under the FLSA. This is commonly called "traditional coverage." (Caution: "interstate commerce" is very broadly interpreted, such as any of the following examples: using mail or telephone on an interstate basis, shipping or receiving products moving interstate, preparing credit card transactions, or utilizing email, the Internet, a GPS system, or, in most cases, text messaging). Generally, most employees are involved in interstate commerce directly or indirectly. If an enterprise has at least two such employees, it is covered.

continued ▶

The Fair Labor Standards Act (FLSA) and Gross Pay, *continued*

Application of the FLSA to Employees, Continued	Employees of an enterprise whose annual gross volume of sales made or business done is not less than $500,000, and employees of certain "named" enterprises, (hospitals, nursing homes, schools) are also covered by the FLSA. Because traditional (interstate) coverage is so broadly construed, and enterprise coverage is so common, there are very few employees who are not covered by the FLSA.

An employee is not subject to certain FLSA provisions if:

- The employee is not covered on a traditional or enterprise basis, or
- The employee qualifies for an exemption.

What the FLSA Does Not Address	Some employment issues are not addressed by the FLSA. Following are some key items:

- Total hours worked per day or per week for persons 16 years of age or older
- Overtime pay based on weekend or holiday work
- Requirement to give holidays off
- Requirement to give vacation time
- Requirement to grant sick leave
- Meals or rest periods
- Pay raises or fringe benefits

Statute of Limitations	The FLSA has a two-year statute of limitations for violations (three years if the employer willfully violates FLSA requirements). What this means is that a claim for wages for work performed more than two (three) years before a federal lawsuit is filed by the DOL or individually filed is not collectible. Complaints to the DOL are confidential and there are no charges or fees. Contact is: (1-866-487-9243) TTY: 1-877-889-5627 and www.dol.gov. The statutes of limitations under state laws vary. For discrimination issues, the Equal Employment Opportunity Commission (EEOC) requires a complaint to be filed within 180 calendar days of the time the discrimination occurred, extended to 300 calendar days if the enforced law of the state or locality prohibits similar discrimination, except age discrimination is extended based only on state law. Federal employees generally have 45 days. EEOC can be contacted at 1-800-669-4000 and by online search for "EEOC field office". For health and safety violations, employees contact OSHA at 1-800-321-OSHA (6742).

Employee Wage Claims	Under the FLSA (and state laws) employees may initiate legal action against an employer for employment law violations, if within the statute of limitations, and (under many state laws) after an unsuccessful good-faith effort to resolve the issue with the employer. For wage and hour violations, an employee has several options:

- File a federal wage claim with the DOL. If investigation indicates violations, the DOL on behalf of the employee, may 1) take administrative

continued   ▶

The Fair Labor Standards Act (FLSA) and Gross Pay, *continued*

*Employee
Wage Claims,
Continued*

action against the employer for back pay/additional damages, 2) File a lawsuit against the employer for back pay/additional damages/costs, 3) Refer the matter to the U. S. Department of Justice for criminal action.

- File a wage claim with a state agency (the employee might have greater rights and greater claims under state law).
- An employee can obtain his/her own attorney and file a lawsuit. State statute of limitations for an individual lawsuit will apply if the action is filed under state law.

More on Minimum Wage

Overview

As indicated above, an important objective of the FLSA is to ensure that workers receive a minimum wage. The FLSA requires that a $7.25 hourly minimum wage rate be paid to all employees for all full or fractional hours worked. This includes work taken home and off-business site premises work. Minimum wage is required unless employees are exempted by the FLSA, as described below.

If you review the diagram on page 38, you will see that one important part of the first step in the payroll process is identifying workers as exempt or non-exempt. These terms apply to both minimum wage and overtime. Both federal and state rules apply in this process, with whatever rule resulting in the highest compensation as the rule that applies.

*Employees
Exempt from
Minimum Wage
Requirements
Under FLSA*

Certain employees are exempt from minimum wage under the FLSA:

- Employed on a small farm—small farm: The employer did not, during any calendar quarter during the preceding calendar year, use more than five hundred man-days of agricultural labor. 'Man day': any day during which an employee performs agricultural work for at least one hour Also immediate family. (Fact sheet #12 online).
- Worker principally engaged on the range in the production of livestock
- Local hand harvest laborers who commute daily from their permanent residence, are paid on a piece rate basis in traditionally piece-rated occupations, and are engaged in agriculture less than thirteen weeks during the preceding calendar year
- Non-local minors, 16 years of age or under, who are hand harvesters, paid on a piece rate basis in traditionally piece-rated occupations, employed on the same farm as their parent, and paid the same piece rate as those over 16.
- Babysitters on a casual basis and companions to the elderly or infirm (See Fact Sheet #79A).
- Employees in certain seasonal, amusement, and recreational businesses that meet a set of very specific requirements. (See Fact Sheet #18.)

continued ▶

More on Minimum Wage, *continued*

Employees Exempt from Minimum Wage Requirements Under FLSA, Continued

- Fishermen, marine farm workers, and at-sea processing workers incident to fishing or marine harvesting operations (see regulations, 29 CFR Part 784).
- Newspaper delivery persons (delivery of newspapers to the consumer)
- Seamen on non-American ships
- Small circulation (< 4,000) newspaper employees. (See 29 CFR Part 786)
- Homeworkers engaged in the making of evergreen wreaths
- "White collar" jobs exemption (as defined by DOL regulations): executive, administrative, professional, outside sales, and certain computer-related employees (See below).

Executive Exemption

To qualify for the executive employee exemption, all of the following tests must be met:

- The employee must be compensated on a salary basis at a rate not less than $684 per week for a calendar 52-week period. A catch-up for a shortage is allowed for a 52-week period if fully paid by the start of the next pay period. Up to 10% of pay can be incentive pay such as bonuses or commissions;
- The employee's primary duty must be managing a business, or managing a customarily recognized department or subdivision of the business;
- The employee must customarily and regularly direct the work of at least two or more other full-time employees or their equivalent; and
- The employee must have the authority to hire or fire other employees, or the employee's suggestions and recommendations as to the hiring, firing, advancement, promotion or any other change of status of other employees must be given significant weight.

Note: The DOL uses a number of specific factors to evaluate whether a business has correctly applied this category. These factors relate to the nature and degree of authority, judgment, independence, and responsibilities.

Administrative Exemption

To qualify for the administrative employee exemption, all of the following tests must be met:

- The employee must be compensated on a salary basis at a rate not less than $684 per week;
- The employee's primary duty must be the performance of office or non-manual work directly related to the management or general business operations of the employer or the employer's customers;
- The employee's primary duty includes the exercise of discretion and independent judgment with respect to matters of significance.

Note: The DOL uses a number of specific factors to evaluate whether a business has correctly applied this category. These factors relate to the nature and degree of authority, judgment, independence, and responsibilities.

More on Minimum Wage, *continued*

Professional Exemption: Learned Professional	To qualify for the learned professional exemption, all of the following tests must be met:

- The employee must be compensated on a salary or fee basis at a rate not less than $684 per week (not applicable to teachers or employees practicing law or medicine);
- The employee's primary duty must be the performance of work requiring advanced knowledge, defined as work that is predominantly intellectual in character and that includes work requiring the consistent exercise of discretion and judgment;
- The advanced knowledge must be in a field of science or learning;
- The advanced knowledge must be customarily acquired by a prolonged course of specialized intellectual instruction.

Professional Exemption: Creative Professional	To qualify for the creative professional exemption, all of the following tests must be met:

- The employee must be compensated on a salary basis at a rate not less than $684 per week;
- The employee's primary duty must be the performance of work requiring invention, imagination, originality or talent in a recognized field of artistic or creative endeavor.

Computer Employee Exemption	To qualify for the computer employee exemption, all of the following tests must be met:

- The employee must be compensated on a salary or fee basis at a rate not less than $684 per week, or if by hourly rate, not less than $27.63 per hour;
- The employee must be employed as a computer systems analyst, computer programmer, software engineer or other similarly skilled worker in the computer field performing the duties described below;
- The employee's primary duty must consist of any of the following:

1) The application of systems analysis techniques and procedures, including consulting with users to determine hardware, software or system functional specifications;
2) The design, development, documentation, analysis, creation, testing or modification of computer systems or programs, including prototypes, based on and related to user or system design specifications;
3) The design, documentation, testing, creation or modification of computer programs related to machine operating systems; or
4) A combination of the aforementioned duties, the performance of which requires the same level of skills. Note: It should be remembered that workers could be entitled to overtime even though they are paid a salary, depending on work and salary level.

More on Minimum Wage, *continued*

Outside Sales Exemption	To qualify for the outside sales employee exemption, all of the following tests must be met:

- The employee's primary duty must be making sales (as defined by DOL regulations), or obtaining orders or contracts for services or for the use of facilities for which a consideration will be paid by the client or customer; and
- The employee must be customarily and regularly engaged away from the employer's place or places of business

Highly Compensated Employee Exemption	To qualify as a "highly compensated employee", the following tests must be met:

- The employee must be compensated total annual compensation of at least $107,432 per year and receive a weekly salary or fee of at least $684;
- The employee customarily and regularly performs at least one of the duties of exempt executive, administrative, or professional described above.

Fee Basis	Administrative, professional, and computer employees may be paid on a fees basis instead of a salary basis. "Fee basis" means that an employee is paid a single agreed amount for each individual job. The total of weekly fee compensation must equal at least $684. To determine this, divide the job fee total received by the hours required and multiply by 40 (for the 40 hour weekly wage standard).
"Make-up" Time	Under the FLSA employers can require exempt employees to make up time off work of less than a day, hour-for-hour. However, an employer may not dock an employee's salary for failing to make up the time, but may discipline the employee in other ways.
Exemptions Do Not Apply To...	The "White collar" exemptions do not apply to police officers, firefighters, paramedics, and emergency medical technicians. As well, manual laborers are not exempt, regardless of pay rate or duties description.
Higher Minimum Wage Rates	In some cases a higher hourly minimum wage than $7.25 is required for non-exempt employees. This situation occurs with:

- State and local minimum wage requirements exceeding FLSA requirements.
- Employees of federal contracting companies. (At least $11.25 per hour through January 30, 2022; entered into or extended after that date $15.)

Reduced Minimum Wage Rates (Subminimum Wage)	Infrequently, a lower hourly minimum wage rate than $7.25 is allowed. Certificates from the Department of Labor are required for this kind of employment. The rule is shown at the lowest amount.

- Initial 90 days for new employees under 20 years old ($4.25/hr.)

continued ▶

More on Minimum Wage, *continued*

Reduced Minimum Wage Rates (Subminimum Wage), Continued	▪ Student trainees in an a bona fide vocational training program employed part-time and enrolled at an accredited school ($5.44/hr.) ▪ Full-time students doing retail, service, or farm work (Limited hours at $6.17/hr.) ▪ Full-time college and university students working at the school at which they are enrolled (Limited hours at $6.17/hr.) ▪ Workers with disabilities (employers with DOL certification)
Involuntary Deductions Overview	Under the FLSA, an employer can make deductions to exempt employee pay only under specific conditions as listed below (In all cases review state law.). Improper unreimbursed deductions that are material or recurring will generally result in loss of employee exempt status.
Permitted Involuntary Deductions: Exempt Employees	Legally required deductions such as FICA taxes, tax assessments, judgments, garnishments, child and spousal support are allowed. ▪ It is not required that the salary be paid if the exempt employee performs no work at all during a full workweek. ▪ Accrued leave can be reduced for days or portions of days not worked provided that full salary continues to be paid. ▪ Employee is absent from work one or more full days for personal reasons other than sickness or disability. (Deduction is per full day, not partial.) ▪ Employee is absent from work one or more full days for sickness or disability and a bona fide plan is in place and employee has used all paid days allowed. (Deduction is per full day, not partial.) ▪ As an offset to amounts received for jury or witness fees ▪ As an offset to amounts received for military pay ▪ For violations of major significance of safety policy imposed in good faith ▪ As disciplinary suspensions for violations of work conduct rules imposed in good faith according to stated policy. ▪ Periods in which employee takes leave under the Family and Medical Leave Act. It is also permissible to convert employee to an hourly basis during this period for intermittent work. ▪ Partial work week during initial and final week of employment: Salary may be prorated. Physicians, lawyers, outside salespersons, and teachers in bona fide educational institutions are not subject to salary FLSA requirements. Deductions from the pay of such employees for partial days work will not result in loss of the exemption.
Voluntary Deductions	An employer can make a deduction from employee pay (if not in conflict with the regulations) when an employee makes written voluntary deduction requests. Examples are income tax withholding (Form W-4. Paying taxes, however, is not voluntary.), savings plans, insurance, and dues.

continued ▶

More on Minimum Wage, *continued*

Interns and Volunteers (No Employment Relationship)

An internship is an arrangement in which a worker (the "intern") performs services in exchange for training and job experience. Under certain conditions the DOL does not classify interns working for "for-profit" employers as employees; therefore, the interns would not require compensation. The DOL provides a seven-factor test called a "primary beneficiary" test to analyze the economic reality of an internship arrangement. If an employer is deemed to be the primary beneficiary, an employee status exists and DOL wage and hour rules apply. No single factor is controlling and the test is to be applied for each unique set of circumstances. Because of the potentially subjective nature of the test, legal counsel may be advisable. As usual, state rules may vary. The factors are:

1. The extent to which the intern and the employer clearly understand that there is no expectation of compensation; any promise of compensation, express or implied, suggests that the intern is an employee–and vice versa.
2. The extent to which the internship provides training that would be similar to that which would be given in an educational environment, including the clinical and other hands-on training provided by educational institutions,
3. The extent to which the internship is tied to the intern's formal education program by integrated coursework or the receipt of academic credit,
4. The extent to which the internship accommodates the intern's academic commitments by corresponding to the academic calendar,
5. The extent to which the internship's duration is limited to the period in which the internship provides the intern with beneficial learning,
6. The extent to which the intern's work complements, rather than displaces, the work of paid employees while providing significant educational benefits to the intern,
7. The extent to which the intern and the employer understand that the internship is conducted without entitlement to a paid job at the conclusion of the internship.

The same test also applies to "non-profit" employers; however, an exception provides that even if the employer is the primary beneficiary, if an intern volunteers without an expectation of compensation for religious, charitable, civic, or humanitarian purposes to a charitable organization, the intern is not an employee.

An FLSA exemption provides that people who volunteer to perform services for a state or local government agency are not employees. However, if an *employee's* volunteer activities are to be excluded, the volunteer services must not be the same type of services that the individual is employed to perform for the public agency. Another exemption provides that the term "employee" does not include individuals who volunteer their services solely for humanitarian purposes to private non-profit food banks and who receive groceries from the food banks.

Overtime Principles and Common Examples

Overview of Overtime

"Overtime" as defined by the FLSA is a pay rate not less than 1½ (1.5) times the regular hourly pay rate. The general rule is that all hours worked in excess of 40 hours per week (7 consecutive 24-hour recurring periods) must be paid at the overtime rate.

Three basic issues arise when applying these requirements: 1) What is the pay per workweek? In some cases it becomes necessary to convert the pay for the actual pay period into its equivalent for a 7-day weekly pay period. 2) What are the regular hours and what are the overtime hours for a workweek? 3) How do we calculate the "regular rate" of pay? Various forms of compensation (salary, bonus, commission, tips, etc.) must be included in the regular rate (never less than minimum wage). We address these topics with examples in the next section.

Overtime Exempt Employees

Overtime requirements do not apply to all employees. The same exempt categories (including executive, administrative, professional, computer employees, outside sales, and highly-compensated) that you see for minimum wage on pages 43–46 also apply to overtime. In addition to this, a number of other specific job categories have also been exempted from overtime. These can be found by contacting the Department of Labor (and state employment departments).

Commonly applied overtime exemptions are:

- Drivers, driver's helpers, loaders, or mechanics whose duties affect the safety of operation of motor vehicles in transportation on public highways in interstate or foreign commerce (the small vehicle exception often invalidates this exemption, however). See DOL Fact Sheet #19 (online), "The Motor Carrier Exemption."
- Agricultural employees. See Fact Sheet #12, "Agricultural Employers."
- Certain commissioned employees of retail or service establishments. See Fact Sheet #20, "Employees Paid Commissions By Retail Establishments." (See page 66 for retail employees paid on a commission basis.)
- Automobile, truck, and farm implement dealer mechanics and sales and parts employees who are primarily engaged in selling or servicing the vehicles or implements. See Fact Sheet #11, Automobile Dealers."
- Small public agency (fewer than 5 law enforcement or fire protection employees); the fire protection and law enforcement activities are considered separately. See 29 CFR Part 553.
- Small forestry or lumbering operations. (See 29 CFR Part 788.)

continued ▶

Overtime Principles and Common Examples, *continued*

Overtime Exempt Employees, Continued

Additional examples include:

- Taxi drivers
- Various airline employees
- Movie theater employees

- Live-in domestic employees
- Some rail carrier employees

What the Overtime Rate Means

The FLSA overtime premium rate is one-half of the "regular" rate of pay. The regular rate is paid for all hours of work, and the half-time overtime premium rate is computed for all overtime hours. Referring to the overtime rate as 1½ times the regular rate is simply a useful "shortcut" calculation that combines the regular hourly rate plus the *overtime premium* of 50% of the regular hourly rate. For example, if the regular rate is $18 per hour, 50% of that is a $9 overtime premium that results in a combined total of $27 that is both regular rate plus the premium. This makes it easy to calculate both regular pay plus overtime premium. However, this shortcut is not practical if there are pay supplements or multiple wage rates. In such instances, the total regular wages must first be calculated, the regular rate determined, and then the overtime premium pay is computed. This method and the records that will correlate with it conform to the FLSA overtime compensation and record keeping rules.

> *Note:* FLSA record-keeping regulations require that payroll records should show both regular wages and overtime wages.

TIP

Posters: Did you know...? Employers are required by law to display posters that inform employees of their rights under various labor laws. These may be federal, state, or local laws. The U.S. Department of Labor has a website that an employer can check for federal poster requirements. There is a federal poster advisor at the Department of Labor 'elaws' Internet website.

What the "Regular Hourly Rate" Means

The hourly "regular rate" as defined by the FLSA is total straight time pay divided by the hours that the pay is intended for (which is hours worked unless an agreement exists for fixed lower hours) within a weekly work period. The regular rate as defined above by the FLSA is a common point of reference for all overtime calculations because overtime is calculated as a multiple of the regular rate. In the clearest situation, a base hourly rate is given and this is the regular rate. Example: Bill earns $20 per hour and worked 46 hours for the week. His regular hourly rate is $20 and his required compensation is ($20 × 46) + ($10 × 6) = $980 or alternatively, using the shortcut method: ($20 × 40 hrs.) + ($20 × 1.5 × 6 hrs. overtime) = $980.

However, there are other circumstances in which the regular rate must be determined. The table below summarizes regular hourly rate determination in various circumstances (however, never less than minimum wage). The hours are on a weekly basis as defined by the Department of Labor.

continued ▶

Overtime Principles and Common Examples, *continued*

Table 2.1: Overtime Calculations Summary, Non-exempt Employees

	If...	**Then the Regular Hourly Rate Is...**
1.	Base (hourly) rate is given, and there is no other form of compensation (Example above)	The base rate that is given.
2.	Base (hourly) rate is given, and there is other compensation, such as a fixed bonus or commission. (Example 1, Page 52)	Base rate + (Other compensation/Total hours worked); OR: [(Base rate × Total hours) + Other compensation]/Total hours worked
3.	Compensation is a fixed amount (salary) for a fixed number of hours. (Examples 2, 5, 6,)	Total compensation/Fixed hours
4.	Compensation is a fixed amount (salary) for a variable number of hours. (Examples 3, 4, 7)	Total compensation/Total hours worked (and rarely other methods)
5.	Total compensation is variable, such as a commissions or tips. (See commissions and tips.)	Total compensation/Total hours worked

Table items 3 and 4 refer to salary compensation. Although most non-exempt employees are hourly or otherwise have variable compensation, there are also salaried non-exempt employees. Non-exempt salaries can create a variety of total compensation outcomes depending on how many weekly hours worked the employee and employer agree that the salary covers:

1. If a salary is for 40 hours of work: the regular rate is multiplied by over-time hours and added to the salary as additional regular wages for hours in excess of 40; then the half-time premium rate is applied as overtime wages for the excess hours (over 40).

2. If a salary is intended to cover an amount over 40 hours–such as 50 hours–a half-time overtime premium on the regular rate is added to the salary for all hours above 40 up to 50 hours (here, regular hours to 50 are in the salary); then for the additional hours above 50, first the regular rate would be multiplied by the additional hours and added to other regular wages; then last, the half-time premium rate would be multiplied by the same additional hours and added as overtime pay.*

3. If a salary is for less than 40 hours: Pay, in addition to the salary, the regular rate multiplied by all hours in excess of the agreed number of hours worked up to 40. For all hours in excess of 40, multiply one-half of the regular rate by the overtime hours as the overtime premium compensation.

4. For a salary that covers all hours worked: Pay, in addition to the salary, the .5 overtime premium above 40 hours. (Regular wages for hours worked are included in the salary). However, in some cases there may be certain variations here.

---

*If fewer than the designated number of hours is worked the salary may be reduced accordingly; if not, the effect is an increase in the regular rate. This would not be the case, however, if failure to work the designated hours is the result of holiday, PTO, or other authorized leave. If the fixed number of hours is greater than 40, and the salary is not reduced proportionately when fewer than the designated hours have been worked, the regular rate is total compensation / hours actually worked.

Principles and Common Examples, *continued*

Example #1:
Hourly Rate
Plus Other
Compensation;
Pay Conversion
from Biweekly
Pay Period

Example: Haru, an hourly non-exempt employee, earns $35 per hour and is paid biweekly. As well, the employer pays a $180 biweekly fixed bonus ("non-discretionary" bonus) for 100% non-absence for the period, which Haru earned. Haru worked 95 hours in the biweekly period: 45 hours in the first week and 50 hours in the second week. What is her biweekly pay?

Step	Procedure
1	Determine weekly total, regular, and overtime hours.
2	Determine regular hourly pay rate
3	Calculate regular pay.
4	Determine overtime premium rate (regular rate × .5).
5	Calculate overtime pay.
6	Calculate total pay: regular plus overtime.

Step	Calculation
1	Information is given: 45 hours in week 1 and 50 hours in week 2. Therefore 5 hours overtime and 10 hours overtime.
2	Week 1: $35/hr. + [($180/2)/45] = $37.00/hr. Week 2: $35/hr. + [($180/2)/50] = $36.80/hr.
3	Week 1: $37.00 × 45 = $1665.00 Week 2: $36.80 × 50 = $1840.00
4	Week 1: $37.00 × .5 = $18.50 OT premium Week 2: $36.80 × .5 = $18.40 OT premium
5	Week 1: $18.50 × 5 = $92.50 Week 2: $18.40 × 10 = $184.00
6	Week 1: $1665.00 + $92.50 = $1,757.50 Week 2: $1840.00 + $184.00 = $2,024.00 Biweekly pay: $3,781.50

TIP

Weekly equivalent: Although the regular rate is determined on a weekly basis, employees' wages can be paid in other periods such as biweekly, semi-monthly, or monthly. Because the FLSA requires that minimum wage and overtime be determined weekly, compensation using other time periods must be converted to a weekly basis, as illustrated by some of these examples, such as you see happening above for the biweekly bonus in Step 2. Other compensation types such as bonuses, commissions, tips, etc. are included as part of weekly pay.

Overtime Principles and Common Examples, *continued*

Example #2: Salary for Hours Fixed at 40; Pay Conversion from a Biweekly Pay Period

Example: Maxie Donig, an hourly non-exempt employee, worked 90 hours during the biweekly period, with 4 hours of overtime in the first week and 6 hours in the second week. Maxie earns a $3,000 salary every two weeks **for working 40-hour weeks**. What is the total pay for the biweekly period?

Step	Procedure
1	Determine weekly total, regular, and overtime hours.
2	Calculate regular pay covered by the salary.
3	Determine regular hourly pay rate.
4	Determine overtime pay rate premium.
5	Calculate overtime pay.
6	Calculate total pay: regular plus overtime.

Step	Calculation
1	Information is given: 44 hours in week 1 and 46 hours in week 2. Therefore 4 hours overtime and 6 hours overtime.
2	$3,000/2 = $1,500 per week (or $3,000 × 26/52)
3	Week 1: ($1,500)/40 hrs. = $37.50/hr. Week 2: ($1,500)/40 hrs. = $37.50/hr.
4	Week 1: $37.50 × .5 = $18.75 OT premium Week 2: $37.50 × .5 = $18.75 OT premium
5	Week 1: $18.75 × 4 = $75.00 Week 2: $18.75 × 6 = $112.50
6	Week 1: $1,500.00 + $150.00 + $75.00 = $1,725.00 Week 2: $1,500.00 + $225.00 + $112.50 = $1,837.50 Biweekly pay: $3,562.50
Note: There are 26 biweekly periods per year.	

In this example, biweekly gross pay is converted to weekly by dividing the $3,000 by 2, for each weekly pay period (alternatively $3,000 × 26/52). Note that the specific 40-hour agreement means that hours in excess of 40 are calculated with a .5 overtime premium and added to all hours at the regular rate (or alternatively, overtime hours at a 1.5 rate) because the salary does not apply to more than 40 hours.

TIP

In practice the end of the payroll period precedes the pay date by several days, but that doesn't concern us here.

Overtime Principles and Common Examples, *continued*

TIP

Payroll periods: Biweekly is the most popular payroll period, except for businesses with less than 10 employees, for which weekly is slightly more popular. As well, service and technical businesses use biweekly more often while manufacturing, construction, and transportation use weekly more often. According to the Bureau of Labor Statistics, about 43% of U.S. businesses use a biweekly payroll period. Next in frequency are weekly pay period periods at about 33%, with semi-monthly and monthly at about 19% and 5%.

(Source: U.S. Bureau of Labor Statistics report, Current Employment Statistics Survey, February 2020.)

Overview: Conversion from a Semi-Monthly Pay Period

A semi-monthly pay period means that pay is earned over two periods per month, and that employees are paid twice per month, such as on the 15th and last day of a month. However, the FLSA requires that: 1) A company must use a fixed 7- consecutive day workweek; 2) Overtime is calculated at the end of a workweek for hours in excess of 40 hours for that workweek.

Semi-monthly periods add complexity to overtime calculations (non-exempt employees) because usually there are not an exact number of full workweeks that begin and end within a semi-monthly period. The result is that a workweek may begin during the last days of one semi-monthly period and end during the first days of the next semi-monthly period. The overtime resulting from the part of a workweek that begins in the last days of one semi-monthly period and ends early in the next semi-monthly period will be totaled and paid for in the next semi-monthly period. Therefore, when a workweek begins near the end of a semi-monthly period and ends in the next period, no overtime wages (half-time premium pay) for that workweek are computed until the next pay period.

Also it is important to note that employees always receive their regular pay for hours worked even if overtime pay premium is delayed because of the above overlapping effect. Therefore, when those regular hours are used as part of total hours in a workweek ending in a later pay period to calculate overtime hours, only the overtime premium is paid in the later period.

Example #3: Salary for All Hours; Pay Conversion from a Semi-Monthly Pay Period

John Evans, a non-exempt employee, earns a $2,600 salary semi-monthly as his base pay **for all hours worked**. He is paid on the 15th and last day of a month. The workweek is Sunday-Saturday. The illustration below shows John's hours worked for March 28 to April 17. What is John's gross pay for his April 15th paycheck?

continued ▶

Overtime Principles and Common Examples, *continued*

Sunday	Monday	Tuesday	Wednesday	Thursday	Friday	Saturday
MARCH				APRIL		
3/28	3/29	3/30	3/31	4/1	4/2	4/3
0	8	9	8	10	8	2
4/4	4/5	4/6	4/7	4/8	4/9	4/10
0	9	8	8	8	7	0
4/11	4/12	4/13	4/14	4/15	4/16	4/17
0	11	8	8	8	8	3

Example #3: Salary for All Hours; Pay Conversion From a Semi-Monthly Pay Period, Continued

Step	Procedure
1	Both workweeks ending in the current period: ■ Determine total hours worked in each week. ■ Calculate overtime hours in a week.
2	Calculate regular pay.
3	Determine regular hourly rate.
4	Determine overtime pay rate.
5	Calculate overtime pay.
6	Calculate total pay: regular plus overtime.

Step	Calculation
1	First week ending in current period: (8 + 9 + 8 + 10 + 8 + 2) = 45 hours Second week ending in current period: (9 + 8 + 8 + 8 + 7) = 40 hours Overtime is 5 and 0 hours respectively.
2	$2,600 × 24/52 = $1,200 per week
3	First week: $1,200/45 = $26.67/hr. (rounded) Second week: $1,200/40 = $30.00/hr. (Hours are not fixed, so divide by total hours worked.) Third week: This week does not end in the current pay period ending April 15, so overtime is not calculated or paid until the next period.
4	First week: $26.67 × .5 = $13.335 OT premium Second week: $0 (No overtime hours)
5	First week: $13.335 × 5 = $66.68 (rounded)
6	$2,600.00 + $66.68 = $2,666.68 April 15th gross pay
Note: There are 24 semi-monthly periods per year.	

continued ▶

Overtime Principles and Common Examples, *continued*

To determine overtime, semi-monthly gross pay is converted to weekly by annualizing ($2,600 × 24) and dividing by 52 (or multiply by coefficient .4615). The regular rate is: $1,200 salary/all hours worked; in other words, salary is the total regular pay for all hours, so only the .5 overtime premium is needed for the overtime hours.

In the example above, the salary is for all weekly hours worked. What would be the result if the salary were based on an agreement for only 40 hours? The regular rate would be $1,200/40 = $30 per hour every week. Above 40 hours, hourly rate adds $15/hr. overtime.

If John were an hourly employee, payment at the regular rate plus overtime in the current period is still required, including hours in the third week *within the current pay period* (here, semi-monthly ending on April 15). 35 hours at the regular rate would be paid for the third week (and 20 hours for the first week). The last 11 hours at the regular rate for April 16 and 17 are part of the April 30 pay. The 6 hours of overtime in week 3 would not be paid until next payday on April 30. Assuming $30/hr., ($600 + $1,200 + $1,050 + $75 OT) = $2,925 April 15 pay.

Conversion From a Monthly Pay Period

Although most monthly pay periods probably apply to exempt salaried employees, there could be cases in which monthly pay periods apply to non-exempt salaried employees or hourly employees. Therefore, overtime calculations may be needed. This is illustrated below for a salary.

A monthly pay period means that pay is earned over a full month, and payment is made once per month. However, the FLSA requires that: 1) A company must use a fixed 7- consecutive day workweek; 2) For an employee who is entitled to overtime, the overtime is calculated at the end of a workweek for hours in excess of 40 hours for that workweek.

Example #4: Salary for All Hours; Pay Conversion From a Monthly Pay Period

Melanie Jones, a non-exempt employee, earns a $5,700 monthly salary for all hours worked. She is paid on the last day of the month, and there is a Sunday-Saturday workweek. The illustration below shows Melanie's hours worked from March 28 to May 1. What is her April pay?

Sunday	Monday	Tuesday	Wednesday	Thursday	Friday	Saturday
MARCH				APRIL		
3/28	3/29	3/30	3/31	4/1	4/2	4/3
4	8	8	8	11	8	4
4/4	4/5	4/6	4/7	4/8	4/9	4/10
0	8	8	8	8	8	4

continued ▶

Overtime Principles and Common Examples, *continued*

4/11	4/12	4/13	4/14	4/15	4/16	4/17
0	8	8	10	8	8	3

48

4/18	4/19	4/20	4/21	4/22	4/23	4/24
0	8	8	8	8	8	0

40

						MAY
4/25	4/26	4/27	4/28	4/29	4/30	5/1
4	8	8	10	8	8	4

46

└D GOES TOWARDS NEXT PAYCHECK OVERTIME

Example #4: Salary for All Hours; Pay Conversion From a Monthly Pay Period, Continued

Step	Procedure
1	Workweeks ending in the current period: ■ Determine total hours worked in the week. ■ Calculate overtime hours in the week.
2	Calculate regular pay.
3	Determine regular hourly rate.
4	Determine overtime pay rate.
5	Calculate overtime pay.
6	Calculate total pay: regular plus overtime.

Step	Calculation
1	First week ending in current period: (4 + 8 + 8 + 8 + 11 + 8 + 4) = 51 hours Second week ending in current period: (8 + 8 + 8 + 8 + 8 + 4) = 44 hours Third week ending in current period: (8 + 8 + 10 + 8 + 8 + 3) = 45 hours Fourth week ending in current period: (8 + 8 + 8 + 8 + 8) = 40 hours Fifth week: 50 hours worked; however, as this week does not end in the current pay period, the daily recorded hours are not totaled to determine overtime until the next month. Current month weekly overtime is 11, 4, 5, and 0 hours respectively.
2	$5,700 × 12/52 = $1,315.39 per week
3	First week: $1,315.39/51 = $25.79/hr. (rounded) Second week: $1,315.39/44 = $29.90/hr. (rounded) Third week: $1,315.39/45 = $29.23/hr. (rounded) Fourth week: $1,315.39/40 = $32.88/hr. (rounded) (Hours are not fixed, so divide by total hours worked.)

continued ▶

rinciples and Common Examples, *continued*

Example #4: Salary for All Hours; Pay Conversion From a Monthly Pay Period, Continued

4	First week: $25.79 × .5 = $12.895 OT premium Second week: $29.90 × .5 = $14.95 OT premium Third week: $29.23 × .5 = $14.615 OT premium Fourth week: $0 (No overtime hours)
5	First week: $12.895 × 11 = $141.85 (rounded) Second week: $14.95 × 4 = $59.80 Third week: 14.615 × 5 = $73.08 (rounded)
6	$5,700 + $141.85 + 59.80 + $73.08 = $5,974.73 April gross pay

In this example, monthly gross pay is converted to weekly by annualizing ($5,700 × 12) and dividing by 52 (or multiply by coefficient .2308). Note that the regular rate is based on the total $5,700 salary, which is total pay for all hours, and the .5 overtime premium rate is used for the overtime hours.

Fifth week: If Melanie were an hourly employee, payment for 46 regular hours in the fifth week in the current period (monthly) is still required, while the remaining 4 regular hours are paid next month. The 10 overtime hours are paid next month. Assuming $30/hr., April 30th pay: ($690 + $1,320 + $1,350 + $1,200 + $1,380 + $300.00 OT) = $6,240.00

Example #5: Salary for Fixed Hours Greater Than 40; Weekly Pay Period

Leslie and her employer have agreed on a weekly salary of $1,800 for 50 hours of work. Leslie worked 55 hours this week. What is her gross pay?

Step	Procedure
1	Determine weekly total, regular, and overtime hours.
2	Calculate regular pay.
3	Determine regular hourly pay rate.
4	Determine overtime pay rate ("shortcut" method shown).
5	Calculate overtime pay.
6	Calculate total pay: regular plus overtime.

Step	Calculation
1	Information is given: 55 hours. Overtime: 55 – 40 = 15 hours.
2	Given as $1,800 per week
3	$1,800/50 = $36.00 regular hourly rate
4	$36.00 × 1.5 = $54.00 "time and a half" overtime
5	(10 hrs. × $18) + (5 hrs. × $54, alternate method) = $450
6	$1,800 + $450 = $2,250

continued ▶

Overtime Principles and Common Examples, *continued*

This example reflects the common method of computing wages in this scenario. The 10 hours between 40 and 50 are paid at the overtime premium rate because the salary covers all regular hours up to 50. Hours above 50 are calculated using the popular "time and half" method.

However, as seen previously careful adherence to the preferred FLSA calculation method is what would conform to regulations, as follows:

- $1,800 + (5 hrs. × $36) = $1,980 total regular pay for all hours
- 15 hrs. × $18 = $270 total overtime pay for OT hours
- Total pay: $1,980 + $270 = $2,250

TIP

State daily overtime requirements: Some states require overtime to be calculated on a daily basis. The following states and territories require overtime to be paid for hours worked in excess of 8 per day: Alaska, California, Nevada, Puerto Rico, and Virgin Islands. Colorado requires overtime for hours in excess of 12 per day. Also check local requirements in your location. **In all cases the highest overtime (FLSA vs. state vs. local) is what must be paid.**

See Appendix I for discussion of the above state daily overtime requirements.

Example #6: Salary for Fixed Hours Less Than 40; Pay Conversion from a Biweekly Pay Period

Walter Smith, a non-exempt employee, agrees to receive a biweekly salary of $2,300 and to work 38 hours per week. This week was unusual and Walter worked 47 hours. What is Walter's total gross pay this week?

Step	Procedure
1	Determine weekly total, regular, and overtime hours.
2	Calculate regular pay.
3	Determine regular hourly pay rate.
4	Determine overtime pay rate ("shortcut" method shown).
5	Calculate overtime pay.
6	Calculate total pay: regular plus overtime.

Step	Calculation
1	Information is given: 47 hours. Overtime: 47 − 40 = 7 hours.
2	$2,300/2 = $1,150 per week
3	$1,150/38 = $30.26 (rounded) regular hourly rate
4	$30.26 × 1.5 = $45.39
5	$45.39 × 7 = $317.73 "time and a half" overtime
6	$1,150 + [(40 − 38) × $30.26] + $317.73 = $1,528.25

continued ▶

Overtime Principles and Common Examples, *continued*

Example #6: Salary for Fixed Hours Less Than 40; Pay Conversion from a Biweekly Pay Period, Continued

The two hours below 40 weekly hours are paid at the regular rate*. Beyond 40, overtime is earned. (This example shows the common method of computing wages at a 1.5 rate. As in the previous example, the FLSA method that identifies both regular and overtime pay is: 1) $1,150 + (9 × $30.26) = $1,422.34 total regular pay; 2) 7 × $15.13 overtime premium = $105.91 total overtime pay; 3) Total pay: $1,422.34 + $105.91 = $1,528.25)

*When overtime is worked, all hours must be compensated. In *non-overtime* workweeks or in workweeks in which the overtime provisions do not apply, a non-exempt employee (with certain exceptions, such as the "fluctuating workweek" arrangement) is considered to be paid in compliance if the overall earnings for the workweek equal or exceed the amount due at the applicable minimum wage. For example, if there is an agreement for less than 40 hours, the difference between the lower agreed hours and 40 hours, called "gap time," do not have to be compensated when up to 40 weekly hours are worked, provided the minimum wage requirement is not violated. It should be noted that this rule ("Klinghoffer Rule") ordinarily has no application under state laws, as they typically require payment for all hours of work, even in non-overtime workweeks.

More on Variable Hours

When a non-exempt employee is paid a salary (fixed payment) for variable weekly hours of work, the regular hourly rate is calculated each week by dividing the fixed salary amount by the number of hours worked. This will result in a changing regular rate and therefore a changing overtime rate from one week to the next. We saw this applied in examples 3 and 4. This is called the ***fluctuating workweek method***. The FLSA requires an advance clear and mutual understanding between employee and employer that the fixed salary is compensation for all hours worked. Hours must fluctuate from week to week (including weeks below 40) and the regular rate cannot be below minimum wage. Caution is recommended prior to adopting this pay plan, as violations result in significant back pay liabilities. (See 29 CFR Part 778, §§778.114 and 778.306(b)). Some states prohibit or constrain use of this method (e.g. Alaska, California, New Mexico, Pennsylvania).

Example #7: Salary for All Hours; Pay Conversion from a Biweekly Pay Period

Assume that in Example 6 Walter's salary is for whatever hours are worked, as needed. What is Walter's total gross pay this week?

Step	Procedure
1	Determine weekly total, regular, and overtime hours.
2	Calculate regular pay.
3	Determine regular hourly pay rate.
4	Determine overtime pay rate
5	Calculate overtime pay.
6	Calculate total pay: regular plus overtime.

continued ▶

Overtime Principles and Common Examples, *continued*

Example #7:
Salary for All
Hours; Pay
Conversion from
a Biweekly Pay
Period, Continued

Step	Calculation
1	Information is given: 47 hours. Overtime: 47 − 40 = 7 hours.
2	$2,300/2 = $1,150 per week (or $2,300 × 26/52)
3	$1,150/47 = $24.47 (rounded) regular hourly rate
4	$24.47 × .5 = $12.235 OT premium
5	$12.235 × 7 = $85.65 (rounded)
6	$1,150 + $85.65 = $1,235.65

Note that because the hours worked beyond 40 are already compensated by the salary, which is straight time, the overtime for these hours is calculated by using only the overtime .5 premium. Be sure to double-check with DOL before using.

Alternate Method
for Fluctuating
Workweek

If the employer, to avoid weekly computations, chooses to pay extra half-time based on the salary divided by 40 hours, such a method is permissible. This results in a higher .5 overtime premium rate, but the rate obtained through this method does not become the actual regular rate. The method chosen must be consistently applied. Example: $1,150/40 = $28.75 based on 40 hours. $28.75 × .5 = $14.375 overtime premium. $1,150 + ($14.375 × 7) = $1,250.63 total gross pay.

The Belo Plan

A "Belo plan" derives from the Supreme Court case *Walling v. A.H. Belo Corporation*. (Statutory authorization to utilize this pay plan is found in §7(f) of the FLSA.) A Belo contract is a special case that allows an employer to pay a fixed amount (a "guaranty") that includes a predetermined amount of overtime regardless of the hours worked. The guaranty is calculated as: (40 hours × regular rate) + (overtime at a 1.5 rate for overtime hours agreed).

Example: Under a Belo plan, a non-exempt employee and employer agree that the employee will receive a guaranty based on $25 per hour for 40 hours per week plus 12 hours of overtime, for a total of 52 guaranteed hours. Regardless of how many hours are worked below 40 or up to 52 in any week, the weekly guaranty is fixed at:

$25 × 40 hours = $1,000
$25 × 1.5 × 12 hours = $ 450
Weekly guaranty $1,450

If the employee worked 54 hours (2 hours beyond the agreed limit), the total compensation would be: $1,450 + (2 hours × $25 × 1.5) = $1,525.

A Belo contract has numerous specific legal requirements. Among them are:

- There should be a written agreement between employee and employer.
- There must be significant weekly fluctuations above and below 40 hours, as well as above the guaranteed weekly hours.

continued ▶

Overtime Principles and Common Examples, *continued*

The Belo Plan,
Continued

- The nature of the job itself (job duties, not personal reasons) requires fluctuating hours not controllable by the employer.
- The regular rate cannot include any other forms of compensation and cannot be below minimum wage.
- Maximum weekly guaranteed hours for the calculation cannot exceed 60.
- The full guaranty is paid for a week in which any work is done.

Caution: Employers should not attempt to utilize the Belo overtime pay plan without professional guidance. This is one of the most complex areas of the FLSA, and flawed efforts to use this plan result in substantial back wage liabilities.

TIP

As this book was being written, an experienced Department of Labor auditor remarked the following: "During my thirty-eight year enforcement career, involving thousands of enforcement actions, I saw attempts to apply the Belo plan fewer than ten times, and I can recall only one or two investigations in which the employer had actually utilized a Belo plan correctly and, consequently, did not owe back wages. I discovered attempts to use an illegal hourly guaranty plan, similar to Belo, by investigated employers perhaps fifty times, resulting in back wages in each case."

Other Types of Regular Pay and Overtime Calculations

Pay Types
Included in
Regular Rate

The purpose of calculating a regular rate is to use it to correctly calculate overtime. In addition to hourly wages and salaries, "regular rate" also includes other compensation. In general, any form of compensation is included unless specifically excluded. Common examples are:

- Commissions
- Retail sales employees earnings
- Tips (Up to limit of employer's tip credit. See page 66)
- Piecework
- Alternative work period pay
- Non-discretionary bonus
- Longevity pay
- Pay by the job
- "Off the clock" work
- Training time
- Travel time
- Meal and rest periods in some circumstances
- Retroactive pay

continued ▶

Other Types of Regular Pay and Overtime Calculations, *continued*

Pay Types Included in Regular Rate, Continued	■ Shift differential ■ Multiple rates ■ Deferred compensation

These are discussed in the following pages.

Excluded from the Regular Rate	The "regular rate" does not include all compensation. In general, fringe benefits are excluded from the definition of "regular rate". Examples of items excluded:

- Gifts unrelated to work or output, such as holiday gifts
- Payments made for periods when no work is performed (vacation, holiday, illness, insufficient work)
- Awards for service or performance if they are either: 1. Discretionary, 2. Made according to a bona fide profit sharing or thrift plan, 3. Paid as talent fees
- Employee expense reimbursements according to a bona fide plan
- Discretionary bonuses (See page 76)
- Contributions irrevocably made by employer to a bona fide retirement, accident, insurance, or health plan on behalf of employee The DOL has also excluded other fringe benefits. See "Final Rule: Regular Rate under the Fair Labor Standards Act" available online.
- Stock rights and grants in a qualified incentive stock option and stock purchase plans as defined by the FLSA. (Note that there is disagreement in some state courts such as California.)
- True premium payments for working overtime on weekends or holidays

Commission Employees

Commission Employees: Examples	Commissions are earnings that are typically calculated as a percentage of sales revenue. Also, commissions can be calculated in various ways– examples:

- As only a percentage commission: Arthur is a non-exempt inside salesman for a manufacturing company and earns a 10% commission on all sales from his customers, which for the 40-hour week are $22,000. Arthur's gross pay is: $22,000 × .10 = $2,200.
- As a combination of hourly wages plus commission: Jane is a non-exempt employee real estate appraiser assistant and worked 40 hours during the week at $18 per hour, plus she receives a 10% commission on total appraisal billings. For the current week these billings are $12,000. Jane's gross pay is: $720 of hourly earnings + ($12,000 × .10) = $1,920.

continued ▶

Commission Employees, *continued*

Commission Employees: Examples, Continued	▪ As a combination of salary plus commission: Susan is a non-exempt employee and earns a weekly salary of $1,500 plus 5% commission on all sales in a specific territory, for which she is responsible. For the week these sales are $28,000. Jane's gross pay is: $1,500 + ($28,000 × .05) = $2,900.
	▪ Other examples: certain products with higher or lower commission rates, multiple percentages, a percentage of company profits, commissions paid on sales resulting from development of innovative products.
Minimum Wage	In general, for non-exempt employees FLSA minimum wage and over-time requirements apply to compensation by commission.
	A non-exempt commission employee must receive minimum wage for all hours worked whether the amount comes from commissions, commissions plus wage or salary, or some other combination.
Example #1	A full-time non-exempt commission sales person makes no sales during a week. That person must receive minimum wage for all hours worked.
Example #2	A non-exempt commission sales person earns $500 of commissions during a week in which 45 hours were worked. Therefore the regular hourly compensation for that week is $500/45 = $11.11, which exceeds the FLSA minimum wage of $7.25. In this example overtime is $11.11 × .5 × (45 – 40) = $27.78. (Remember to check state minimum wage and overtime requirements.)
Example #3	The same commission sales person earns $200 of commissions during the next week in which 40 hours were worked. The regular hourly compensation for that week is $200/40 = $5.00, which does not meet the hourly FLSA minimum wage of $7.25 per hour. The employer pays an additional ($7.25 – $5.00) × 40 = $90.
Example #4	A non-exempt sales person worked 45 hours in a week. He earned $150 base weekly salary plus $120 commissions. Therefore, the regular rate of pay is ($150 + $120)/45 = $6.00. The employer must increase regular pay to minimum wage plus pay overtime based on the minimum wage rate. The total wages would be: $270 + [($7.25 – $6.00) × 45] + ($7.25 × .5 × 5) = $344.38.
Overtime	As we know, the FLSA requires overtime pay for hours worked in excess of 40 hours per week for non-exempt employees. Commission compensation must be included in the regular rate. This is commission compensation plus other compensation divided by weekly hours worked. Overtime is still calculated for hours in excess of 40 hours per week.

Commission Employees, *continued*

Example #1	Commission with overtime (no fixed hours): Arthur is a non-exempt inside salesman for a manufacturing company and earns a 10% commission on all sales from his customers, which for the week are $22,000. Assume that Arthur worked 45 hours during the week. Therefore Arthur's regular rate becomes $2,200/45 = $48.89. Overtime *premium* (Arthur already received $2,200 straight pay for his 45 hours): $48.89 × .5 = $24.45. Gross pay: $2,200 + 5 hours overtime × $24.45 = $2,322.25
Example #2	Commission plus hourly wages with overtime (no fixed hours): Jane is a non-exempt employee real estate appraiser assistant and worked 50 hours during the week at $18 per hour, plus she receives a 10% commission on total appraisal billings which for the week are $12,000. Jane now earns $18 × 50 = $900 + $1,200 = $2,100. Regular rate: $2,100/50 = $42. Overtime *premium*: $42 × .5 = $21. Gross pay: $2,100 + (10 hours overtime × $21) = $2,310.
Example #3	Salary for fixed hours plus commission with overtime, salary is intended to cover **up to 40 hours** per week: Susan is a non-exempt employee and earns a weekly salary of $1,500 plus 5% commission on all sales in a specific territory, for which she is responsible. For the week these sales are $28,000. Assume that Susan worked 55 hours in the current week. Susan is owed her equivalent hourly rate for hours in excess of 40; $1,500/40 = $ 37.50. Fifteen hours × $37.50 = $562.50 additional wages owed. Susan's regular wages are: $1500.00 + $562.50 + $1,400 commissions = $3,462.50. Her regular rate is $3,462.50/55 = $62.95 (a commission regular rate uses all earnings for all hours in a week). Susan's overtime premium rate is $31.48. Gross pay is $3,462.50 regular wages + ($31.48 × 15 = $472.20 overtime wages) = $3,934.70.
Example #4	Salary for fixed hours plus commission with overtime, salary is intended to cover **50 hours** per week: In the third example above, assume that Susan and her employer have agreed that her compensation is for 50 hours per week of work. Susan worked 55 hours. Susan's equivalent hourly rate is $1,500/50 = $30. Five hours × $30 = $150 to be added to the salary. Regular wages are $1,500 + $150 + $1400 commissions, = $3,050. Susan's regular rate is $3,050/55 = $55.45. Overtime wages are ($55.45 × .5) × 15 hours = $415.88. Gross wages total $3,465.88.
Deferred Commission Payments	Calculating a commission can be simple when it can be clearly identified at a point in time and paid in the same payroll period. However, there are circumstances in which the calculation and payment are delayed because the the commission is more complex and not calculated on a weekly basis and is paid at a later date. In this case the employer can temporarily disregard the commission in computing the weekly regular rate until the commission can be calculated. At that time the general

continued ▶

Commission Employees, *continued*

Deferred Commission Payments, Continued	rule is that the commission amount must be allocated back over the weeks in which it was earned, and any applicable overtime calculated for those weeks. The commission and overtime are then paid in the later payroll period as soon as the commission can be calculated. If it is not possible to relate the commission to specific periods, it may be allocated equally over the computational weeks. "Commissions" generally are in connection with sales but may also apply to services (e.g., automotive mechanics).

Retail Sales and Service Employees

Retail Sales/ Service Employees Overtime Exemption	In general, most employees receive overtime for hours worked in excess of 40 hours per week. However, under specific circumstances there is an exemption from overtime requirements for employees who are employed by a retail or service establishment. See Fact Sheet #20, "Employees Paid Commissions By Retail Establishments," for an explanation of this exemption. Also, retail employees sometimes receive commissions or other payments by manufacturers for promoting and selling their products (called "push money"). The requirements are:

- The employee is employed by a retail or service establishment. This is an establishment for which at least 75% of annual dollar sales of goods and/or services are not for resale and that is generally recognized as a retail or service establishment in its industry.
- The employee's regular rate must be greater than 1.5 times the minimum wage for every hour worked in a workweek in which overtime hours are worked. Rate of pay is total earnings divided by total hours worked in a workweek. Training and seminars for the job are part of total hours.
- More than half of the employee's total earnings in a representative period must consist of commissions. (The representative period may be as short as one month but not longer than one year.)

Tipped Employees

Minimum Wage Overview	A ***tipped employee*** is defined as an employee who customearily and regularly receives tips exceeding $30 per week. Non-exempt tipped employees must receive the same $7.25 per hour minimum wage that most other non-exempt employees receive. However, there is an additional element in calculating tipped employee minimum wage. For a tipped employee, an employer can elect a credit against the $7.25 requirement, called a ***tip credit***. The tip credit cannot exceed the difference between the minimum wage and $2.13, which means a maximum credit of $7.25 – $2.13 = $5.12 per hour; also, the credit cannot be more than the actual amount

continued ▶

Tipped Employees, *continued*

Minimum Wage Overview, Continued

amount of tips that an employee receives and reports, calculated on an hourly basis. If actual tips are less than $5.12, the credit is reduced to the amount of tips reported. If the reduced credit plus the cash wage do not equal at least $7.25 per hour, an employer must increase the cash wage until the total reaches $7.25. ***Cash wage*** includes hourly pay, salary, non-discretionary bonus, commission, and other employee compensation. In summary, the federal minimum cash wage paid to a non-exempt tipped employee using the full tip credit is $2.13 per hour (about 29% of the $7.25 requirement). Many states either reduce or do not allow tip credits. (The tip credit for federal contract employees is phased out by 1/1/2024.)

Electing the Tip Credit

In order to elect a tip credit (Section 3(m) of FLSA) for any employee, an employer must fulfill the following requirements:

1. Inform a tipped employee of the following –verbally or in writing however, it is prudent to obtain a written acknowledgement:

   - The amount of tip credit and the resulting minimum cash wage ($2.13 per hour is the federal minimum wage with a tip credit)
   - The tip credit cannot exceed the lesser of $5.12 per hour or the actual tips an employee receives (directly or indirectly) on an hourly basis.
   - Tips are always the property of the employee receiving the tip. It is unlawful for an employer to keep employee tips. (However, see tip pools, below.)
   - A tip credit cannot be applied to an employee who has not received this notice.

2. Be able to substantiate that employee compensation in fact is meeting all minimum wage requirements.
3. Increase the cash wage to make up for any shortfall between tip credit taken and actual tips received.
4. Wage deductions for walkouts, breakage, cash register shortages, and other employer deductions that reduce the actual hourly wage paid to below $7.25 are violations of the FLSA. Under very specific compliance rules an employer may reduce wages below $7.25 for the reasonable cost of providing "board, lodging, and other facilities".
5. Calculate overtime (see below) on the full regular rate, not the net cash wage. **The regular rate is not less than the minimum wage.**

Definition of "Tips"

- A tip is a gift, also sometimes called a "gratuity", that is cash or a cash equivalent, given to a worker by a customer for performing a service. Non-cash gifts are not tips. Tips are voluntarily made at the discretion of a customer and are not considered as part of cash wages.
- Mandatory service charges can be retained by a business; however, any amount of these charges paid to an employee is treated as wages, not tips.

continued ▶

Tipped Employees, *continued*

Minimum Wage Check	Use the procedure below to determine if the $7.25 hourly minimum wage requirement is being met.

Reported tips/ weekly hours worked:	$ _____	
Cash wage/ weekly hours worked:	$ _____	**Not < $2.13**
Total hourly rate:	$ _____	**Must be ≥ $7.25**

Example #1	A tipped employee worked 40 hours during a week and received $170 in wages and reported tips of $100. Is the employee receiving correct minimum wage? Does the employer need to increase the wage being paid?

Reported tips/ weekly hours worked:	$ 2.50	
Cash wage/ weekly hours worked:	$ 4.25	**Not < $2.13**
Total hourly rate:	$ 6.75	**Must be ≥ $7.25**

Even though the employee is receiving more than $2.13/hr. in wages, the employee is still not receiving correct minimum wage because the hourly total is less than $7.25. This is because actual tips are not enough at $2.50/hr. to reach $7.25/hr. when added to the cash wage. Only a $2.50 tip credit is allowed. Therefore, the employer must increase the hourly wage by $.50 to reach $7.25, and pay the employee an additional ($7.25 − $6.75) × 40 = $20. Check: $4.25 + $.50 + $2.50 = $7.25.

Example #2	Assume in the example above that the employee received $500 in tips during the week. Is the employee receiving correct minimum wage? Does the employer need to increase the wage being paid?

Reported tips/ weekly hours worked:	$ 12.50	
Cash wage/ weekly hours worked:	$ 4.25	**Not < $2.13**
Total hourly rate:	$ 16.75	**Must be ≥ $7.25**

The total hourly compensation is greater than $7.25, and the cash wage is greater than $2.13, so the employee is deemed to be receiving the correct minimum wage of $7.25. The employer's tip credit is $7.25 − $4.25 = $3.00/hr. The employer is paying an adequate wage to meet the $7.25 requirement. Check: $4.25 + $3.00 tip credit = $7.25, which is the regular rate, even though the actual hourly rate exceeds the minimum wage.

Example #3	A tipped employee worked 48 hours during the week and received $336 cash wages and $200 in tips. Is the employee receiving correct minimum wage? (overtime ignored)

Reported tips/ weekly hours worked:	$ 4.17	
Cash wages/ weekly hours worked:	$ 7.00	**Not < $2.13**
Total hourly rate:	$ 11.17	**Must be ≥ $7.25**

continued ▶

Tipped Employees, *continued*

Example #3, Continued	The total hourly rate is greater than $7.25, and the hourly cash wage is $7.00, greater than $2.13, so the employee is deemed to be receiving more than the minimum wage of $7.25. The tip credit is $.25 and total received exceeds minimum. Check: $7.00 + $4.17 = $11.17, greater than $7.25 minimum. It should be noted that the regular rate, for FLSA purposes, is $7.25, not $11.17. (Tips making cash wage plus total tips exceed $7.25 are gifts, not earnings, and are not used in overtime.)
Overtime Overview	Non-exempt tipped employees are entitled to overtime for hours in excess of 40 per week. **The regular rate for tipped employees** is the regular earnings (cash wages plus tip credit as allowed, times hours worked, plus other total compensation) divided by total hours. Using a regular rate below $7.25 per hour to calculate overtime, such as the wage rate of $2.13, is a violation the FLSA. Tips in excess of the tip credit (when cash wage is minimum) are not included in the regular rate because they are treated as discretionary customer gifts, not part of employer-paid compensation. I.e. when a tip credit is used, the employee is making minimum wage. A tip credit may be taken for overtime hours, but the half-time overtime premium compensation must be based on the full regular rate, not the cash wages paid.

Overtime and Earnings Calculations for a Tipped Employee

Use the procedure below to determine overtime and total earnings for a non-exempt, tipped employee:		
Step	**Action**	
1	Earnings without tip credit	$
2	Enter regular rate as defined above	$
3	Overtime premium Multiply (Step 2 by .5)	$
4	Overtime premium pay (Step 3 × overtime hours)	$
5	Total earnings: (Total hours × Step 2) + Step 4	$
6	Total cash received: (Total hours × cash wage rate) + Step 4 + other compensation	$

Alternate calculation for a non-exempt, variable hours tipped employee:		
Step	**Action**	
1	Enter regular rate as defined above.	$
2	Multiply Step 1 by 1.5	$
3	Pay for overtime hours: Step 2 × overtime hours	$
4	Straight-time pay: Step 1 × regular hours	$
5	Total earnings: add Steps 3 and 4	$
6	Total cash received: (cash wage rate × total hours) + Step 3 – (Step 1 × overtime hours) + other compensation	$

continued ▶

Tipped Employees, *continued*

Overtime and Earnings Calculation for a Tipped Employee, Continued

Advisory: It is best to use the alternative calculation as a means of verifying the calculations in the first table. The generally preferred FLSA method in most overtime calculations is to first determine total regular pay and then calculate the .5 rate premium as shown in the first table.

Step	Action	
1	Earnings without tip credit	$336.00
2	Enter regular rate as defined on page 69	$ 7.25*
3	Overtime premium Multiply (Step 2 by.5)	$ 3.625
4	Overtime premium pay (Step 3 × overtime hours)	$ 29.00
5	Total earnings: (Total hours × Step 2) + Step 4	$377.00
6	Total cash received: (Total hours × cash wage rate) + Step 4 + other compensation	$365.00**

*$336/48 = $7.00 cash rate, below minimum wage, so a $.25 tip credit is applied. Therefore $7.25 × 48 = $348 total regular earnings / 48 = $7.25.
**($7 × 48) + $29 = $365.

Example #4

In Example #3 above, A tipped employee worked 48 hours during the week and received $336 cash wages and $200 in tips. What are total earnings and cash wages?

Alternate earnings calculation:

Step	Action	
1	Enter regular rate as defined above.	$ 7.25
2	Multiply Step 1 by 1.5	$ 10.875
3	Pay for overtime hours: Step 2 × overtime hours	$ 87.00
4	Straight-time pay: Step 1 × regular hours	$ 290.00
5	Total earnings: add Steps 3 and 4	$ 377.00
6	Cash wages: (cash wage rate × total hours) + Step 3 – (Step 1 × overtime hours) + other compensation	$ 365.00*

*($7 × 48) + $87 – ($7.25 × 8) = $365.

It should be noted that the total earnings in row 5 are used for the purpose of verifying FLSA total minimum wage rate compliance. (The row has both OT premium plus regular hours using the tip credit since the employee is entitled to both.) Additionally, FLSA record keeping regulations and IRS rules require that tips received by an employee be a matter of record.

Tipped Employees, *continued*

Example #5

A non-exempt restaurant server is paid $3.00 per hour plus $4.25 tip credit. She sometimes works as a hostess (a separate job that is not tipped) and receives $10.00 per hour for these duties. This week, she worked 30 hours as a server and 20 hours as a hostess, for 50 total hours. The employee also received a $50 non-discretionary bonus. Her tips this week totaled $165.00 (in excess of the employer's claimed tip credit for the 30 tipped employment hours). (Draw the alternate table on your own.)

Step	Action	
1	Earnings without tip credit	$340.00
2	Enter regular rate as defined on page 69	$ 9.35*
3	Overtime premium Multiply (Step 2 by.5)	$ 4.675
4	Overtime premium pay (Step 3 × overtime hours)	$ 46.75
5	Total earnings: (Total hours × Step 2) + Step 4	$514.25
6	Total cash received: (Total hours × cash wage rate) + Step 4 + other compensation	$386.75**

* [($7.25 × 30) + ($10 × 20) + $50 = $467.50 total regular earnings] /50 = $9.35. It is useful to keep in mind that the regular rate is used only for the purpose of calculating an overtime rate. Exclude $50 if discretionary.
** [($3.00 × 30) + ($10 × 20) + $46.75 + $50] = $386.75. Also note that the total tip credit is (30 × $4.25) = $127.50.

Note that one part of the employee's work receives tips and is below minimum wage (MW), and therefore a tip credit is applied. The other type of work does not receive tips and also would not qualify for the tip credit because the rate is above MW. The $7.25 MW resulting from the tip credit is included in the regular earnings calculation to determine the regular rate.

Example #6

A restaurant senior service person received cash wages of $360 for 45 weekly hours and also received $400 in tips. What are total earnings and cash wages?

Step	Action	
1	Earnings without tip credit	$360.00
2	Enter regular rate as defined on page 69	$ 8.00*
3	Overtime premium Multiply (Step 2 by .5)	$ 4.00
4	Overtime premium pay (Step 3 × overtime hours)	$ 20.00
5	Total earnings: (Total hours × Step 2) + Step 4	$380.00
6	Total cash received: (Total hours × cash wage rate) + Step 4 + Other compensation	$380.00**

* $360/45 = $8.00 cash rate, above minimum wage, so no tip credit. Therefore $8.00 × 45 = $360 total regular earnings / 45 = $8.00.
** ($8 × 45) + $20 = $380.

In this example, the cash received is the same amount as total earnings since there is no tip credit.

continued ▶

Tipped Employees, *continued*

Example #7

A pizza delivery employee worked 50 hours, is paid cash wages of $3.13/hr. and received $250 in tips. **Personal vehicle expenses** are for 270 miles and reimbursed at the IRS rate of $.56/mile. For FLSA purposes, what are total earnings and cash wages? (Draw the alternate table on your own.)

Step	Action	
1	Earnings without tip credit	$156.50
2	Enter regular rate as defined on page 69	$ 7.25*
3	Overtime premium Multiply (Step 2 by.5)	$ 3.625
4	Overtime premium pay (Step 3 × overtime hours)	$ 36.25
5	Total earnings: (Total hours × Step 2) + Step 4	$398.75
6	Cash wages: (Total hours × cash wage rate) + Step 4 + other compensation	$192.75**
7	Reimbursements	$151.20

* Tip credit is ($7.25 – $3.13) = $4.12. Tips are $250/50 = $5.00, so tip credit does not exceed actual tip rate. When there is a tip credit and only tipped activities, the regular rate is $7.25. ($7.25 × 50 = $362.50)**(50 × $3.13) + $36.25 = $192.75

Use of the IRS rate is not required for vehicle expense reimbursement; it is accepted by the DOL as an alternative to the maintenance of actual and complete records.

Example #8

Same as example #7 except that employee tips are $190. Also, the employer has been advised by an associate that employee reimbursements are unnecessary.

Step	Action	
1	Earnings without tip credit (adjusted)	$172.50
2	Enter regular rate as defined on page 69	$ 7.25*
3	Overtime premium Multiply (Step 2 by.5)	$ 3.625
4	Overtime premium pay (Step 3 × overtime hours)	$ 36.25
5	Total earnings: (Total hours × Step 2) + Step 4	$398.75
6	Cash wages: (Total hours × cash wage rate) + Step 4 + other compensation	$208.75**
7	Reimbursements	$151.20

* This example is more complex because there are two points to emphasize: 1) The advice is wrong (and not used). MW employees (which happens with a tip credit) must be fully reimbursed. When less than full reimbursement is allowed: • An employee is not a tipped employee and the wage difference above MW (see pages 52–61) can absorb the cost. • An employer does not take the tip credit for a tipped employee and pays above MW (infrequent). Either way, only 40 hours is used to absorb expenses. (For overtime, the regular rate is always before expenses are subtracted.) Example: Cash wage of $10/hr.: ($10.00/hr. – $7.25 = $2.75 (above MW) × 40 = $110 max. may be unreimbursed.

** 2) A tip credit cannot exceed tips received. Here: $190/50 = $3.80; $4.12/hr. credit normally taken – $3.80 allowed = $.32 additional wage rate needed. ($.32/hr. + $3.13) × 50 + $36.25 = $208.75 cash wages. Check: $398.75 – $208.75 = $190. $190 = 50 × ($7.25/hr. – $3.45).

Tipped Employees, *continued*

Tips Paid by Credit Card	A tip may be given by credit card. In this case, the employer must pay the employee the tip amount by next payday, regardless of when the credit card bill is paid. A proportionate amount of credit card charges may be applied to reduce the tip payment. For example, if a credit card charge to the employer is 3%, then tips included in the credit card total can be reduced by 3% when paid to employees. Reductions cannot reduce employee compensation below minimum wage.
Tip Pooling	As indicated earlier, tips are always property of a tipped employee receiving the tip. It is unlawful for an employer, including managers and supervisors, to retain any employee tips for themselves. However, an employer may require tipped employees to participate in a tip sharing arrangement among themselves; this is a non-voluntary arrangement called *tip pooling.* When this is done and an employer uses a tip credit, tips can be shared only among employees receiving the tips; that is, only among those employees who customarily and regularly receive tips exceeding $30 per week.

However, when: 1) An employer does not elect to use the tip credit, and 2) The employer pays the full minimum wage (including state/local) to all employees, then the employer can require that the pooled tips be shared with other non-exempt support employees (excluding supervisors and managers) who do not receive tips, often called "back-of-the-house" employees, such as cooks and dishwashers. The method of allocation should reflect in some reasonable and proportionate way the employee interaction with customers.

Tip pooling does not change minimum wage and overtime requirements. On-line applications are available so that both employees and employers can automatically track a tip pool's amounts and allocations. There are state and local variations on tip pooling arrangements.

Dual Jobs	It is not unusual for an employee to perform different tasks that are related to the primary job. For example, a restaurant server might also be required at times to perform other related duties such as cleaning tables, folding napkins, setting tables, and so on. An issue can be created when other duties are not closely related to a primary job. For example, a server might be required to perform substantial time doing general cleaning. In effect an employee might then be working at two separate occupations. This is relevant for tipped employees when one activity meets the test as being performed by a tipped employee and the other does not. In this case, a tip credit could be applied only for the tipped employee. DOL policy is to focus on individual activity. An employee's work is tipped activity to which the tip credit can apply if either of the following is true: 1) The activity is tip-producing work, or 2) It is work that directly supports tip-producing work, if the support work is not done for a substantial

continued ▶

Tipped Employees, *continued*

Dual Jobs, Continued	amount of time. The DOL defines "substantial" as more than 1) 20% of a workweek's hours for which the employer takes a tip credit, or 2) 30 continuous minutes, after which full minimum wage is paid. Although the DOL identifies specific industries, the rules generally apply to all types of work activities; see Federal Register, 10/29/21, Vol. 86 No. 207, 60114-60158. Employers also can be guided by 29 CFR §531.56 (e) and (f), effective December 28, 2021.
	The best guidance for an employer is to use these sources and maintain a careful record of employee hours by task when there is a chance of dual jobs.
Employee Reporting Tips to the Employer	The Internal Revenue Service (IRS) requires an employee to report all net cash tips, received directly or indirectly, to the employer if the tips exceed $20 per month.
	Tip income (which is subject to both income tax and OASDI/Medicare withholding) must be reported to the employer no later than the 10th day of month following the month in which the tips were received. Employees use Form 4070 or equivalent for reporting. Form 4070A can be used for daily record keeping by employees. (See page 110 for tip reporting by employers.)

Piecework

Piecework Overview	Piecework is compensation paid to an employee based on the number of units the employee produces or completes.
Piecework and Minimum Wage	Piecework employees must be paid at least the required minimum wage for total hours worked. If an employee receives compensation by both piecework and hourly wage, each method must meet minimum wage requirements.
Piecework and Overtime	Overtime requirements apply to piecework employees. An employer must keep a detailed record of the number of units of output for each employee compensated by piecework. The regular hourly rate to calculate overtime is the total amount earned by piecework and all other sources such as bonuses, divided by hours worked, including wait time. If an employee who does piecework is guaranteed a minimum hourly rate, that rate is the regular rate if greater than as calculated above.
Piecework Payment Methods	There are two alternative payment methods that can be used:

- The employer must pay an overtime premium of one-half the regular hourly rate for hours worked in excess of 40 hours.
- Employees and employer agree–prior to doing the work–that the employees will be paid at 1½ times the regular piece rate for all piecework in overtime hours. (This method is based on a statutory exception, FLSA §7(g)(1), and must be used with caution in view of specific provisions. See also 29 CFR Part 778, §778.418.)

Piecework, *continued*

Example #1	A non-exempt employee earned $496 doing assembly piecework. The employee performed assembly for 45 hours and also spent another 3 hours waiting for parts to be delivered so that assembly could begin. The regular rate is $496/48 = $10.33 per hour. Overtime is: (8 hours × $5.17) = $41.36. Total pay is $496 + $41.36 = $537.36.
Example #2	If in the above example the employee was also guaranteed a minimum hourly rate of $11.00 per hour, that rate would be the regular rate because it exceeds $10.33. The overtime premium would then be $5.50.
Example #3	The employer and piecework employees have entered into an agreement pursuant to FLSA § 7(g)(1). Assume that in the example above, the piece rate is $8 per piece. Therefore, if the employees and employer agree that the employees will be paid at 1½ times the regular piece rate for all piecework in overtime hours, their overtime will be the piece rate of $12 per piece during overtime hours.

Alternative Method for Hospitals and Residential Care Establishments

Overview	Under FLSA provisions, employees of hospitals and other organizations primarily engaged in the care of the sick, aged, or mentally ill patients who reside on site can use an alternative overtime system called the "8 and 80 system" for hours worked at the site. The system requires a prior agreement between employer and employee. In this system, an employer pays overtime for the greater of all hours worked in excess of 8 hours per day (8-hour shifts) or 80 hours in a consecutive 14-day work period. The overtime rate is 1½ times the regular rate. The system can be applied on an individual employee basis, but it must be used continuously and not alternated with the workweek method for the purpose of reducing overtime pay. (See FLSA §7(j) and 29 CFR Part 778, § 778.601.)
Example #1	The example below shows the overtime hours worked in a consecutive 14-day period. A hospital employee in the 8/80 system is paid $18 per hour plus earned a $100 bonus during the pay period. Hours worked are shown below:

Day 1	Day 2	Day 3	Day 4	Day 5	Day 6	Day 7
-0-	12	10	8	8	8	-0-

Day 8	Day 9	Day 10	Day 11	Day 12	Day 13	Day 14
8	8	8	8	9	9	-0-

continued ▶

Alternative Method for Hospitals and Residential Care Establishments, *continued*

Example #1, | Total hours worked: 96; daily overtime hours: 8; biweekly overtime: 16
Continued |

Total hours worked: 96; daily overtime hours: 8; biweekly overtime: 16
Regular pay: (96 × $18) + $100 = $1,828
Regular rate: $1,828 / 96 hours = $19.04
Overtime premium rate: $19.04 × .5 = $9.52
Total pay: (96 hours × $18) +$100 bonus + (16 × $9.52) = $1,980.32

Example #2

The example below shows the overtime hours worked in a consecutive 14-day period. A hospital employee in the 8/80 system is paid $18 per hour plus earned a $100 bonus during the pay period. Hours worked are shown below:

Day 1	Day 2	Day 3	Day 4	Day 5	Day 6	Day 7
-0-	12	10	8	8	8	-0-

Day 8	Day 9	Day 10	Day 11	Day 12	Day 13	Day 14
-0-	-0-	4	8	8	8	-0-

Total hours worked: 74; daily overtime hours: 6; biweekly overtime: 0
Regular pay: (74 × $18) + $100 = $1,432
Regular rate: $1,432 / 74 hours = $19.35
Overtime premium rate: $19.35 × .5 = $9.68
Total pay: (74 hours × $18) + $100 bonus + (6 × $9.68) = $1,490.08

Related Overtime Matters

Bonus Pay

Non-discretionary bonus: A non-discretionary bonus is an amount that is in addition to regular compensation and that is paid according to a predetermined plan. In other words, the method for calculating the amount of the bonus has been fixed and disclosed in advance. (A discretionary bonus is not set in advance of payment.) Examples of a non-discretionary bonus are meeting productivity goals, attendance, hiring, and work quality, all based on a predetermined plan. Generally, if an employer gives up discretion with regard to any aspect of a bonus (e.g., employees are informed that there will be a bonus or how it will be computed if there is one), the bonus must be treated as non-discretionary. A non-discretionary bonus must be included as part of the regular rate unless the bonus qualifies for exclusion as a gift paid on a special occasion, such as a birthday or holiday gift.

Example

John is a non-exempt production employee who earns $30 per hour. For production employees who qualify, John's employer pays a $400 monthly efficiency bonus that is calculated following the end of the month. Because production is about equal each week, the employer allocates the bonus equally to each week as a "reasonable and equitable" method.

continued

Related Overtime Matters, *continued*

Example, *Continued*	John earned the bonus for June and worked the following hours in each workweek that ended in June: week 1: 40 hours; week 2: 46 hours; week 3: 44 hours; week 4: 42 hours.

John was already paid regular pay plus overtime premium based on regular pay. Now he is entitled to an additional overtime premium based on the bonus because it increases the earlier weekly regular rates, even though it is paid later. The additional overtime premium resulting from the bonus is: week 1: 0; week 2: ($92.31/46) × .5 = $1.00 × 6 hours = $6.00; for week 3: ($92.31/44) × .5 = $1.05 × 4 hours = $4.20; and week 4: ($92.31/42) × .5 = $1.10 × 2 hours = $2.20; total extra paid in the next pay period is $12.40 additional overtime premium plus the $400 bonus.

Key points: 1. A month averages 4.33 weeks, not 4 weeks; 2. A monthly supplement (bonus, commission, etc.) must be allocated into its weekly equivalent; 3. Each workweek that ends during the month is included in computing any additional overtime pay owed (even if 5 workweeks *ended* during a month), 4. The increase in the regular rate is multiplied by .5 in order to arrive at the additional overtime compensation owed.

TIP

One way to avoid overtime recalculations with bonuses for non-exempt employees is to make the bonus a percent of straight time pay plus overtime paid. The bonus will then result in the correct total amount, including any additional overtime premium required. However, this method involves some risk, so it is necessary to proceed with caution. Especially when workers are receiving relatively low wages, if the DOL perceives that proper overtime compensation is being evaded, back wages will be asserted. (See 29 CFR Part 778, § 778.210.)

Longevity Pay	Longevity pay is additional compensation or a wage adjustment received as a result of seniority. Just as all other forms of employee compensation that is not specifically excluded, longevity pay must be included in the regular rate. If longevity pay is paid on other than a weekly basis, the amount is simply adjusted to a weekly basis. For example, assume that a $5,000 lump sum of longevity pay is paid quarterly. ($5,000 × 4)/52 = $384.62 additional weekly amount to include in the regular rate.
Pay by Job	In general, when an employee is paid a flat or fixed either day rate or job rate, the regular rate is calculated by dividing the total compensation received by the number of hours worked. Overtime is then based on the regular rate. Payment for a single job is also called "fee basis" compensation by the DOL. (Also see determining exempt employee status, page 49).

continued ▶

Related Overtime Matters, *continued*

Example	John is paid $110 per day and worked 6 days for a total of 48 hours during the current week. The regular rate is: ($110 × 6) / 48 = $13.75 per hour. John's total compensation is: ($110 × 6) + [($13.75 × .5) × 8 overtime hours] = $715.

Other Activities

The following circumstances affect hours worked and are included in the tabulation of daily and weekly hours worked. These are often referred to as part of employee "principal activities":

- Waiting time: If an employee is on the job and idle, but ready to work and waiting for work or for equipment to become ready, this is regular hours worked. Note that this is different than being "on call" which allows personal activities and is often not part of hours worked.
- Setup time: Time required to set up equipment, software, tools, etc.
- Travel time: Travel time spent as part of employee duties qualifies as hours worked. Time spent commuting to and from work in most cases is not hours worked, but there are limited exceptions.
- Training time: Training directly related to an employee's work is part of principal activities.
- Medical assistance: Receiving or waiting for medical assistance at the place of work is part of principal activities.

Overview of "Comp Time": FLSA Rule for Compensatory Time in Lieu of Overtime

"Comp time" is an abbreviated expression for "compensatory time" off from work. This means that instead of receiving pay, an employee receives time off from work. Typically, employees will accumulate or "bank" time off to be used at a later date.

For non-exempt employees, the FLSA does not allow the use of compensatory time as a substitute for overtime pay, with this limited exception: State and local government agencies, with prior agreement with an employee, may allow employees to accumulate compensatory time off. Time off must be at the rate of 1½ hours for each overtime hour worked and based on regular rate of pay. If an employee's employment is terminated prior to using all accumulated comp time, the unused time must be paid in cash at a rate not less than the average regular rate received by such employee during the last 3 years of the employee's employment, or the final regular rate received by the employee, whichever is higher. Also, a "use it or lose it" policy is not allowed.

There are limits to the amount of comp time that can be accumulated. Public safety, emergency, and seasonal employees can accumulate up to 320 hours of overtime work (which results in 480 hours of comp time). Employees working in other areas can accumulate up to 160 hours of overtime (which results in 240 hours of comp time). These limits do not have to be reached in order for an employee to use accumulated comp time, and the time must be allowed on the date requested unless it creates undue hardship for the employer.

continued ▶

Related Overtime Matters, *continued*

Overview of "Comp Time": FLSA Rule for Compensatory Time in Lieu of Overtime, Continued

For public or private exempt employees, the FLSA does not require overtime pay. Therefore an employer may offer comp time as a form of overtime pay to exempt employees at the employer's own discretion.

Note: A few states allow comp time in lieu of overtime compensation for private sector employers. However, the FLSA, if applicable, preempts such laws. Local labor law counsel should be consulted regarding the requirements of state law or local ordinance when the FLSA is believed to be inapplicable. (Also review DOL Fact Sheet #7.)

The term "comp time" is sometimes used when hours of work are merely rescheduled. The rescheduling of hours within a workweek, work period, or pay period is an employer's prerogative. Examples of rescheduling of hours are:

1) Flex time arrangements involving, within the workweek, long days and short days, four ten-hour days, etc.
2) Within a biweekly pay period in which an employee receives 1.5 hours off work in one week, to offset each hour of overtime work paid at the proper overtime rate in the other week. The employer is not failing to pay overtime compensation, but is recouping that expense by rescheduling hours in the non-overtime workweek of the pay period. For example, if an employee, in the first week of a biweekly pay period, works 44 hours (and is being paid time and one-half for the 4 overtime hours), the employer may elect to schedule this employee to only work 34 hours in the next week. The result is the equivalent of paying 80 hours at straight time, but the records must reflect hours and pay for each workweek separately.

Partial Pay Periods

Partial pay period issues typically arise in the following circumstances:

- New employees
- Payroll period-end payroll accruals
- Terminating employees

In general, all previously discussed pay requirements and procedures apply to partial payroll periods. Typical issues that arise are: 1) For new and terminating employees, verify starting and ending compensation dates, including all benefits. 2) Payroll period-end accruals are an accounting issue (See Section 3) that requires unpaid payroll liabilities to be recorded.

Off the Clock Time

"Off-the-clock" time means that an employee spends time working when not requested by the employer. When an employer is aware or should have reason to know that an employee is doing this work, and the employer is benefitting from the work, off-the-clock hours are included in time worked.

continued ▶

Related Overtime Matters, *continued*

Off the Clock Time, Continued	It includes: 1) work at home 2) arriving early 3) working late 4) preparation time. Non-exempt employees who work off the clock must be paid at the regular rate for the time, and at the overtime rate for hours exceeding 40 per week. This is true even if the employer has a policy that prohibits this activity. To avoid this result an employer needs: 1) accurate time keeping 2) regular monitoring of time-keeping results 3) a clearly communicated disciplinary policy if off the clock work occurs.
Training Time	Training time for a non-exempt employee is included as part of paid weekly hours worked. In order for training time to not require regular compensation, the employer must demonstrate all four of these conditions: 1) Training time attendance is not within an employee's regular (shift) hours. 2) Attendance is voluntary 3) The training content is not directly related to the employee's job 4) The employee does not perform any productive work during attendance.
Travel Time	The kind of travel determines whether of not the time is included as part of compensation. 1) Regular travel between home and work location, in other words commute time, generally is not work time. 2) Travel between home and a special assignment location within a single day is work time, minus what would be regular commute time. 3) Travel as part of an employee's principal work activity is work time. 4) Travel away from home overnight is work time for the travel that occurs during what would be regular working hours, regardless of the day of the week. On the other hand, the DOL does not treat as work time that time spent in travel away from home outside of regular working hours as a passenger on an airplane, train, boat, bus, or automobile.
Meal and Rest Periods	The FLSA does not require an employer to provide meal or rest breaks. Bona fide meal periods that last 30 minutes or more are not work time if the employee is completely relieved from duty. However, if an employee continues to work and is not relieved of responsibility during a meal, that time is part of work time. When rest breaks are 20 minutes or less, those breaks are work time. Longer breaks might also be work time, depending on all of the facts. (See 29 CFR Part 785.)
Retroactive Pay	Retroactive pay (also called "retro pay") is pay for work performed but due to error should have been computed at a higher amount but was not, and is owed to an employee. For non-exempt employees, calculate the correct pay with correct hours and rates and then subtract what was actually paid. The difference is the retroactive amount. Keep in mind that if overtime hours were worked, the retroactive pay will increase the regular rate and the overtime pay. For exempt employees, the process

continued ▶

Related Overtime Matters, *continued*

Retroactive Pay, Continued	is to determine a retroactive amount as the difference in salary and allocate the difference to applicable pay periods. In the case of deferred amounts that cannot be determined until after a pay period(s), such as bonuses or commissions, a special rule allows late payment of the additional overtime premium pay. As soon as it can be calculated, the deferred amount then must be allocated to weeks as it was earned, or otherwise in some "reasonable and equitable manner", based on facts, to determine correct overtime for those weeks. Payment must be no later than the next pay period following the calculation. Retroactive pay cuts are not permissible.

TIP

If an employer is barely paying the weekly required salary level for exemption, and wishes to develop an equivalent annual salary, it is necessary to begin with the weekly salary and work to the annual salary by multiplying by 52. Starting with an anticipated annual salary and working backwards can yield a weekly equivalent that is below the required salary level, because of rounding down.

Example #1

Beatrice is a non-exempt employee and is paid biweekly at $20 per hour. For the work week beginning June 2 and ending June 9 she worked 40 hours. She worked 47 hours in the following week beginning June 10. Due to a processing error Beatrice was paid at a regular rate of only $18 per hour during the biweekly period. What is the retroactive pay to be added to her paycheck in the following weekly period after the error was discovered?

- Week 1 correct pay: 40 × $20 regular rate = 800
- Week 2 correct pay: (47 × $20) + (7 × $10) = $1,010
- Retroactive pay: $1,810 – [(40 × $18) + (47 × $18) + (7 × $9)] = $181

Example #2

James is an exempt employee and has semimonthly pay periods and is paid as of the 15th and last day of a month. He received a $5,000 raise to his annual salary rate of $78,000 to a new annual salary of $83,000, effective October 15 payroll period. However, the payroll department did not receive the raise information until its October 31 payroll processing. What is the amount of retroactive pay for James?

- Correct October 15 pay: $83,000/24 = $3,458.33
- Retroactive pay: $3,458.33 – ($78,000/24) = $208.33

Example #3

Marsha is an exempt employee and is paid in biweekly payroll periods, and received an annual salary rate increase from $91,000 to $95,000, effective May 1. However, the current biweekly pay period that started on April 25 did not record the salary change; therefore, 8 days of the biweekly period

continued ▶

Related Overtime Matters, *continued*

Example #3, Continued	should have been paid at the new rate. What is the amount of retroactive pay to be added to Marsha's pay for the next payroll?
	▪ Correct biweekly pay: $95,000 / 26 = $3,653.85 ▪ Prior biweekly pay: $91,000 / 26 = $3,500.00 ▪ Difference in biweekly pay: $3,653.85 − $3,500.00 = $153.85 ▪ $153.85 × 8/14 = $87.91 retroactive pay
Back Pay	Back pay has a different meaning than retroactive pay. Back pay refers to compensation owed because of never having been paid at all, despite being able to be calculated, where an employee is entitled to the payment or has been promised payment. Back pay is often associated with wage violations assessed by the DOL.
Shift Differential	A shift differential occurs when during a week an employee works more than one shift and is paid at a different rate for each shift. Other differential pay examples: hazard pay, on-call pay, and differential between civilian and military pay while on active duty. Overtime is based on a weekly regular rate that is total earned in all the shifts divided by total hours worked.
Example	Vivienne worked two shifts during the week. She worked three 10-hour day shifts at $20 per hour and two 8-hour evening shifts at $25 per hour.
	▪ 3 × 10 hours × $20 = $600 ▪ 2 × 8 hours × $25 = $400 ($5/hour shift differential) Total $1,000 ▪ ($1,000 / 46 hours worked) = $21.74 regular rate (rounded) ▪ ($21.74 × .5) = $10.87 overtime premium rate
	Total straight time pay for 46 hrs.: $1,000 Total overtime premium: 6 hrs. × $10.87 = $65.22 Total pay: $1,000 + $65.22 = $1,065.22
Multiple Rates	When an employee works in multiple positions with different rates of pay for the same employer and there is no overtime, to calculate total pay simply multiply each pay rate by hours worked at that rate, and add the results for the total. When there are overtime hours it is necessary to calculate a regular rate. This is done by multiplying each pay rate by the hours worked at that rate, and then dividing the total by total hours worked. This is called the weighted average regular rate (each pay rate "weighted" by hours worked at that rate) that is used to determine overtime.

continued ▶

Related Overtime Matters, *continued*

Example #1	Roger works as a manager in a hotel and sometimes fills in as a host that greets the guests at the same hotel. This week he worked 30 hours at $35 per hour as manager and 10 hours as host at $25 per hour.

- 30 hours × $35 = $1,050
- 10 hours × $25 = $250

Total pay: $1,050 + $250 = $1,300

Example #2	Assume in Example 1 that Roger worked 30 hours as manager and 20 hours as host.

- 30 hours × $35 = $1,050
- 20 hours × $25 = $500

Regular rate: $1,550 / 50 = $31 per hour.
Total pay: $1,550 + [10 hours (.5 × $31)] = $1,705

Involuntary Reductions in Gross Pay: Non-Exempt Employees

Reductions in gross pay for non-exempt employees are permitted if pay is not reduced below minimum wage (or required overtime–see Overtime). Deductions from wages or pay reductions in overtime workweeks are permitted only under certain very specific circumstances. In such instances, the regular rate is not affected. (29 CFR Part 531.) Reductions cannot be retroactive. Allowed deductions under the FLSA are:

- Legally required deductions such as FICA taxes, tax assessments, judgments, garnishments, child and spousal support.
- Items provided for the benefit or convenience of employer, provided that the deduction *does not* reduce pay below minimum wage and does not reduce overtime pay. Examples: uniforms, work tools, compensation for theft or damage to employer property.
- The employer cost of lodging, and transportation primarily provided for the benefit or convenience of the employer, provided that the deduction *does not* reduce pay below minimum wage and does not reduce overtime pay.

Voluntary Reductions

Voluntary reductions under federal law require request, preferably written, from employee or are allowed by contract (such as collective bargaining). Examples are:

- Voluntary reductions if for the benefit of the employee: these include meals, lodging, transportation savings plans, insurance, dues, and employee-added withholding. These voluntary deductions are permitted to reduce a *net* cash payment below minimum wage.
- Repayment of principal of employer loans.

continued ▶

Related Overtime Matters, *continued*

TIP

Offsets against wages for uniforms and tools primarily for benefit of employer, shortages, or disciplinary actions violate the FLSA if the resulting hourly rate for the workweek is less than the minimum wage requirement or overtime wages are reduced. The DOL treats employee job-related expenses as the equivalent of deductions from wages. For example, if an employee purchases safety shoes, uniforms, or uses his/her personal vehicle on the job (e.g., pizza or grocery delivery), these expenses reduce the effective rate of pay.

Deferred Compensation

Deferred compensation is compensation that has been earned, but payment has been deferred to a future date. This may take various forms such as regular withholding from wages as part of a retirement plan or in what are referred to as deferred compensation plans in which compensation is earned but not paid by the employer until a later date. Deferred compensation is included as part of the regular rate for non-exempt employees when earned.

Payroll Periods

Selecting a Payroll Period ("Payroll Cycle")

What is the best pay period (also called "payroll cycle") to use? The first consideration is to check state law. Most states have established minimum pay frequency, often called a "pay day requirement". Beyond this, there is no single best solution for selecting a payroll cycle. Some considerations are:

- **Monthly**: Financial reports, budgeting, and benefits are typically prepared on a monthly basis, so this correlates easily with monthly payroll costs and can minimize accounting accruals (see page 203) at period-end that are usually created by more frequent payrolls. Overtime calculations can be complicated and employees may want pay more often.
- **Semi-monthly**: This also correlates with financial reporting and benefits. Overtime calculations are also difficult with semi-monthly periods.
- **Bi-weekly**: Overtime is much easier to calculate with bi-weekly periods, and hourly employees may prefer to be paid more frequently at biweekly intervals. Biweekly can result in some months with three payrolls.
- **Weekly**: Overtime is easiest with a weekly payroll. As with bi-weekly payroll, some employees may prefer to be paid more frequently.
- **Earned Wage Access**: Companies especially in the gig, service, and transportation economies are beginning to make wage payments available daily or at end of shifts, possibly reducing expensive worker credit and increasing productivity, provided there are no fees.
- **Cost**: More frequent pay periods and multiple periods create higher cost. This is true for both internal payroll preparation and for

continued ▶

Payroll Periods, *continued*

Selecting a Payroll Period ("Payroll Cycle"), Continued

outsourcing payroll. Costs include timekeeping approvals, payroll calculations (including commissions, expense reimbursements, and incidental items), tracking credit card tips for next payday payment, irregular payments, and internal and external reporting.

- **Cash flow**: If cash flow will generally follow a pattern, an employer will want to consider this in order to have sufficient cash available to meet payroll requirements. More frequent payments might result in smoother cash flow.
- **Time considerations**: Are some times of a month or year predictably busy? Payrolls can create significant time demands.
- In some cases it might be more useful, although more expensive and time- consuming, to maintain two periods. For example, biweekly for non-exempt employees and monthly for exempt employees.

Similar-Sounding and Confusing Names

Payroll period: The time interval after which compensation is paid.
Pay date: The day on which compensation is paid.
Work period: An FLSA term of reference for a period of time used to determine minimum wage, regular compensation, and overtime.
Work schedule: A schedule for when work is to be performed.
Pay period: Usually means work period, sometimes payroll period, depending on context.

Other Work Schedules and Work Periods

Although monthly, semi-monthly, biweekly, and weekly are the typical payroll periods, a variety of work schedules and work periods are used that allow variable or flex hours.

- **9/80 period**: 9/80 is a work schedule within a biweekly work period in which employees work eight 9-hour days and one eight-hour day within the two week period. In this way, employees receive one day off every other week, usually for a 3-day weekend. For example, 9 hours are worked Monday –Thursday and Friday is either an 8-hour day or a day off. The first week in the period ends after the first 4 hours are worked on Friday and the second workweek begins with the second 4 hours. This is followed by 4 days at 9 hours, totaling 80 hours for the biweekly period. No overtime is incurred. There is no exception to FLSA weekly requirements. The staffing arrangement may require two different work groups.
- **4/40 period**: A 4/40 is a work schedule within a weekly period in which employees work four 10-hours days. The days do not need to be consecutive. If there are shifts, there are two shifts in a 24-hour period, with the next beginning on the 20th hour. A variation of this system uses more hours Monday –Thursday and Friday becomes a half-day, although for various reasons this is not as popular.

continued ▶

Payroll Periods, *continued*

<table>
<tr><td valign="top">

*Other Work
Schedules and
Work Periods,
Continued*

</td><td valign="top">

- **8/80 period**: An 8/80 system uses an FLSA biweekly work period and is an FLSA exception to measuring compensation on a weekly basis. The method applies only to hospitals and residential care establishments. See page 75.
- **Police and firefighters**: For certain public safety employees the FLSA allows public agencies to increase the standard from a weekly work period to between 7 to 28 days; usually the work periods are 14 or 28 days in biweekly payroll periods. Police officers receive overtime after 171 hours in a 28-day period and firefighters receive overtime after 212 hours in a 28-day period. If the period is shorter than 28 days, the hours are pro-rated to a lower amount. (See 29 CFR Part 553.)

</td></tr>
</table>

TIP

Late paychecks are not permissible. The DOL requires, and is upheld by courts, that paying employees their regular compensation after the regular payday is a violation of the FLSA; in other words, a late payment is treated the same as no payment. Interest and costs can be awarded to employees. Furthermore, liquidated damages (an add-on amount) may be imposed plus, when the employer's action was "willful" (intentional) or the employer has previously been found to be in violation, additional civil penalties apply. State penalties may apply. Prompt payment is therefore essential. In a situation of a brief cash flow problem, a temporary solution would be to at least pay the applicable minimum wage to non-exempt employees, and, with respect to overtime workweeks, pay (for overtime hours) the full regular rate plus the half-time premium. Exempt employees should be paid their full salary, in order to avoid loss of exemption, but withholding payment of commissions or bonuses should not be a compliance issue.

Payroll Processing

<table>
<tr><td valign="top">

Overview

</td><td valign="top">

A section on "Calculate the Payroll" would not be complete without some overview of actual processing. This is probably most useful for those who are new to payroll and/or have not already participated in processing a payroll. At best, this is a basic procedural summary because each organization will have its own variations and requirements. Complexity increases as the number of employee categories, job categories, deductions, and pay frequencies increase. Finally, processing details are often dictated in significant measure by the user guide of the payroll processing software being used. The illustration below provides a basic visual overview.

</td></tr>
</table>

continued ▶

Payroll Processing, *continued*

Illustration 2.1

```
┌──────────────────────────────────────────┐
│                    1.                      │
│  Receive salary, regular and overtime      │
│  hours, paid time off use, and other       │
│  compensation data input. Check and        │
│  verify.                                   │
└──────────────────────────────────────────┘
                      │
                      ▼
┌──────────────────────────────────────────┐
│                    2.                      │
│  Receive HR data. Make any needed up-      │
│  dates to pay and to withholding rates.    │
└──────────────────────────────────────────┘
                      │
                      ▼
┌──────────────────────────────────────────┐
│                    3.                      │
│  Process payroll trial run. Review output  │
│  and make any needed changes.              │
└──────────────────────────────────────────┘
                      │
                      ▼
┌──────────────────────────────────────────┐
│                    4.                      │
│  Process another trial run. Process final  │
│  payroll when the last trial run is correct.│
│  Generate paychecks and direct deposit file.│
└──────────────────────────────────────────┘
                      │
                      ▼
┌──────────────────────────────────────────┐
│                    5.                      │
│  Distribute signed paychecks and transmit  │
│  direct deposit file to bank.              │
└──────────────────────────────────────────┘
                      │
                      ▼
┌──────────────────────────────────────────┐
│                    6.                      │
│  After processing (See following sections):│
│   ▪ Prepare journal entries / review ledger.│
│   ▪ Calculate and remit payroll deposits.  │
│   ▪ Prepare and submit required payroll    │
│     forms.                                  │
│   ▪ Reconcile payroll bank account.        │
│   ▪ Submit management reports.             │
└──────────────────────────────────────────┘
```

Step 1

At this point we assume that there is a master file of individual employee information such as name, employee number, social security number, pay rate(s), exempt vs. non-exempt status, all withholding items, garnishments, and so on.

- Using active employees list from Human Resources, begin reminders to employees several days before timecards are due.
- Salaries are fixed amounts and timecards are not necessary for salaries.
- Check timecards for accuracy, employee signature, supervisor signature.

continued ▶

Payroll Processing, *continued*

Step 1, *Continued*	<ul><li>Check cards received against list from HR. Follow up as necessary for each employee time reporting not received. If time reporting is online, check against list and whatever verification system in place.</li><li>What if some timecards are not received in time for processing? Under the FLSA and state laws an employer must pay an employee for time worked, and payment cannot be delayed. However, an employer is allowed to make a good-faith estimate and adjust any difference as soon as reasonable. If there is established policy, employees may be disciplined as well as terminated for repeated violations.</li><li>Commission calculations require: 1) Invoices or other documentation to verify amount on which commissions will be calculated 2) Application of an approved formula(s) or calculation checklist to calculate the commissions. A spreadsheet with built-in formulas can be of great help, as well as keeping formulas and adjustments as simple as possible.</li><li>If tips are involved, employees must provide a form showing tips received.</li><li>Piecework calculations are checked and verified.</li><li>PTO compensation, including vacation time in current period, is verified.</li><li>Other (overtime, bonus, rewards): Each requires approval.</li><li>Employee expense reimbursement forms must be submitted with approvals if reimursement is to be made as part of payroll.</li><li>Obtain data for manual payroll checks that have been written. This data should be included in the payroll register, but without a check computer-generated.</li><li>Payroll supervisor reviews all data, calculations, and verifications. If all is correct supervisor approves proceeding to processing.</li><li>Determine if W-9s have been received from independent contractors. If not, apply backup withholding.</li></ul>
Step 2	At the same time as Step 1 above, communicate with Human Resources department to determine if there are any employee status changes. These can be: <ul><li>New employee</li><li>Terminated employee</li><li>Withholding changes (particularly retirement, medical insurance, garnishment)</li><li>Receive active employee status change update from Human Resources.</li><li>Enter any changes to master file from Human Resources department update data.</li></ul>

Payroll Processing, *continued*

Step 3	When using a payroll software system:

- Enter correct pay period.
- Enter hours and other compensation data from Steps 1 and 2.
- Enter manual paycheck information (see below).
- Trial run creates a payroll register (see page 196) and an exceptions report*.

*An exceptions report is a list of items created by comparing the payroll register to master file data and to other control parameters such as number of employees paid, maximum/minimum amounts, negative withholding, and other items that management wants to check.

Step 4	

- Carefully review the exceptions report.
- Enter any changes required by the exceptions report, after they have been verified.
- If there are new or terminated employees verify that the pay is correct for partial period worked.
- Process another trial run based on changes
- Process the final payroll run, including checks, when there are no further changes.
- "Final" payroll register and checks are inspected and approved if correct.
- If there is a period locking or finalizing function, use that function.
- All payments, including direct deposit, will have a remittance advice ("check stubs") that shows pay and withholding details.
- Perform backups and archive backups (online or with hardware such as flash dives) stored on and offsite.
- Close program (it should be password protected) and return unused checks to locked storage facility.
- All physical input data is archived and securely stored in locked facility.

Step 5	

- If checks are automatically signed, distribute checks; otherwise, deliver checks to employee responsible for signature.
- "Distribution" includes hand delivery of checks, mailing, and direct deposit. Pay cards can also be used.
- Send employee deposit file to bank as required.
- Send positive pay file to bank if this service is in use.
- Check with Accounts Payable department to ensure that required payroll deposits are timely made.
- A payroll register (page 196) is generated and delivered to accounting.

Internal Control	Internal control procedures reduce the possibility of fraud and error. See Section 7 for further details regarding applications to processing the payroll.

continued ▶

Payroll Processing, *continued*

TIP

A payroll feature growing in popularity is employee online access called self-service, which allows employees to view pay statements, W-2s, PTO data, garnishment data, update personal information, and change benefit elections. This both provides quick access for employees as well as relieves HR and Payroll of some manual work. Of course, the feature comes with the usual caution for online data breaches.

Manual Paychecks

The term "manual paycheck" can refer to different circumstances:

- A business outsources its payroll to a company that processes the payroll but does not download the various payroll amounts into the client's accounting system. In this case the client must either enter the data in the payroll functions module in its accounting software or make debit and credit journal entries into the system to record the payroll. Accounting systems often provide instructions on how to create payroll accounts and make entries. Note that if the payroll processer makes all payments, no liabilities will need to be entered, only cash is credited. Also see Section 4.

- Regardless of how the payroll is processed and recorded, occasionally a payroll check is either processed incorrectly or a payment is overlooked, or perhaps an unanticipated employee payment must be made. Therefore the company must prepare a separate paper check to pay the employee. It is not optimal to record and pay the amount of the check as a liability through the accounts payable department. If this is done the salaries or wages expense could be understated if only the net check amount is recorded. As well, the employee withholding and employer payroll tax expense may be overlooked unless the accounts payable department remembers to pass the information to the payroll department, or the payroll processor if payroll is outsourced. As well, the same information could be omitted from payroll reports and W-2 forms.

When an in-house payroll module or payroll system is available this should be used to process manual checks. The module or system normally has a feature expressly designed to process manual checks; look for a tab such as "manual check" or "unscheduled payroll". Using this will include the check in the payroll data without actually creating a physical check. The check amount and related accounts will be recorded, included in an updated payroll register, and posted into the ledger. (Note: If an incorrect check has been processed, a system usually allows a reversal of the check amount and related accounts. The employer should void the check or stop payment. If an error is not large, it also can be adjusted on the next check.)

Finally, if payroll checks are being recorded with manual debit and credit entries, there will have to be a process in place to ensure that all employee checks are always sent to a responsible person. This person reviews the checks and verifies that they are correctly recorded.

Outsourced Payroll Processing

Overview

"Outsourced" payroll processing means that a business uses a payroll service company to process payroll, instead of doing the processing on its own. These services are generally provided online. The cost, methods, and extent of the processing service can vary significantly.

Some basic-level service companies require that a client do its own time-keeping and then supply this data for every payroll period, for only processing checks with remittance advice and maintaining basic records. Alternatively, some full-service companies provide online time keeping, check processing and distribution, direct deposit/pay cards, timely filing of forms and reports, timely payroll tax deposit services, and benefit plan services. The decision to outsource and the extent of outsourcing usually depends on: 1) cost of wages, software, training, supplies, internal control, and overhead saved by not having to process designated parts of payroll, 2) the desire to avoid payroll law violations 3) any additional services that will be offered.

Note: **1) An employer remains responsible for full legal compliance,** regardless of who does processing (except on-site employee "CPEO" contracts). **2) Outsourcing does not relieve an employer from all payroll duties.** A review of the payroll process illustration on page 38 should illustrate the wide scope of payroll duties. An employer must properly classify workers, comply with fair employment laws and FLSA, maintain human resource data that is input to processing, payroll records, and related duties.

Basic Considerations

The first step in the decision process is to view the process in its entirety as illustrated on page 38. Consider which elements of the process are candidates for outsourcing, and why. The following list of basic considerations may help to further clarify the initial review:

- **Security**: We consider this issue before cost and other considerations because of the significance of potential damage. Compromised safety can result from inadequate evaluation of a payroll processor, and appears in several forms. These are: 1) weak data security, resulting in data breaches and employee and company data theft, 2) poor financial condition, resulting in poor service or outright business failure and suddenly terminated processing, 3) financial theft, in which funds intended for employees and/or payroll tax deposits are stolen, and 4) staffing and management inadequacy, resulting in processing errors. It behooves a potential client to evaluate these risks–all the above have occurred with payroll processors.

There are several means to help identify the reliable processors. These are: 1) Obtain a list of clients and contact the clients, 2) Obtain a referral from a trusted associate 3) Contact a CPA firm that outsources payroll for clients, 4) Obtain a service level agreement (SLA) that a client will be reimbursed for processor errors. 5) The American Institute of Certified

continued ▶

Outsourced Payroll Processing, *continued*

Basic Considerations, Continued

Public Accountants (AICPA) has developed a three-level *service organization compliance report* (SOC) protocol for evaluation of service providers. Can the processor provide a report? 6) Can the processor provide *ISO certification*? 7) Is the processor *CPEO certified* under the IRS program? (see: irs.gov/business/small-business-self-employed/third-party-arrangement-chart). 8) Can a fidelity bond be provided? 9) Legal actions?

- **Cost**: The array of price quotes for payroll processing services is large. The best way to be assured of optimizing cost is *having a clear understanding of exactly what functions are needed for outsourcing now and what they will be in the near future*, and then contacting a variety of providers to compare prices for these services.

Outsourcing companies have to make a profit. Advertised prices are usually for generic or the most basic services. Costs are added beyond these services; for example, set-up fees, commission calculations, particular overtime situations, special work schedules allowed (see page 85), payroll tax reports filed, systems integration, customer service, retroactive pay, shift differentials, and others, are services that often can be expected to increase costs. More customization means greater cost.

Second, price quotes may be for bundled services. Carefully evaluate whether all these services are needed. More expensive plans allow for selected services. Third, check if some in-house and outsourced system integration is required, or if employee files are updated in another way. Fourth, before agreeing on a service that includes automatic payments, an employer should verify if/when funds are transferred from the company bank account to the processor, particularly for payroll tax deposits. Funds withdrawn too far in advance result in interest and working capital lost to the employer and gained by the processor. Check regularly. Finally, generally be prepared for price increases with increases in processing activity or just the passage of time.

It is relatively easy to monitor outsourcing costs. Dividing monthly cost by employee average FTE results in a cost per employee. Also, examine details of each invoice and identify the following: 1) cost item not in prior invoice, 2) "one-time" cost, 3) which costs are fixed in total but change per unit (per employee, per paycheck etc.) with changes in volume, and 4) which costs are constant per unit but variable in total with changes in activity. This should help when estimating future processing costs.

- **Time saved:** Time is usually the biggest element of cost savings. Assume that specific functions of payroll are outsourced. What amount of company time is being saved by these outsourced functions? What is the cost of this time if it is not outsourced? What is the combined cost of outsourcing plus remaining payroll duties?

Outsourced Payroll Processing, *continued*

Basic Considerations, Continued

- **Protocol and control**: When payroll is outsourced from an existing in-house system, the in-house procedures will change–to a lesser or greater degree dictated by the procedures and requirements of the service company. Much of the employer responsibility will manifest as a need for accurate and timely data input to the service company. Prioritizing systems integration between employer and out-sourcing service helps with this. Outsourcing also will usually relieve an employer from part of internal control responsibilities (Section 7) because some of the processing is offsite.
- **Customer service**: Is customer service easily accessible and responsive? What is the cost? When corrections are needed, how quickly will the payroll service respond? What training is available?
- **Timing**: It is far easier to change to or from one system to another as of the first day of a calendar year, and not attempt to change data recording and storage methods before year-end reporting. Even more conservatively, some payroll elements might be outsourced incrementally at the beginning of each year and evaluated over two or more years.
- **Error rates**: Data on outsourced processing error rates are not readily available; however, if the suggestions in the paragraphs on security (above) are followed the cost of errors due to the processing should not be significant. As well, the larger processors may have greater staff resources that can deal with complex issues that would otherwise create a higher error rate if handled in-house.

Error discussion also raises the following question: Does an employer that outsources payroll assume that all processing is correct, or **will the employer regularly review the output, at least sampling for FLSA and reporting accuracy**? When no service level agreement (which also should be tracked for compliance) or other assurance is available, review may be a wise decision, even with the added time and cost.

The Big Picture– What Are Others Doing?

To assist in making an outsourcing decision, knowing the "big picture" and what other companies are doing may be useful. Payroll outsourcing use data by company size, type, location, and other parameters are available online at:

https://www2.deloitte.com/us/en/pages/human-capital/articles/payroll-operationssurvey. html ("Deloitte Global Payroll Benchmarking Survey": See pages 19-23 re. outsourcing.).

Withholding: FICA

Overview

What is Payroll Withholding?

Payroll withholding means that an employer withholds (deducts) amounts from an employee's gross pay, with each pay period. These amounts are then paid by the employer to taxing authorities and other third parties. The amounts withheld from an employee's pay are called "payroll deductions". The remaining amount of gross pay that an employee actually receives is called "net pay". The employer is simply acting as a collection agent. The two categories of payroll deductions are:

- Deductions required by law
- Voluntary deductions by agreement

Deductions Required by Law

The following items are imposed upon individuals classified as employees and must be withheld (deducted) by the employer from employee gross pay:

- Employee social security (FICA) tax, discussed in this part.
- Federal income tax
- State and local income/employment taxes (Search online)
- Other required deductions such as garnishment (See index)

Employment tax liability arises upon compensation payment. Also see "Constructive Receipt" pg. 216. In some circumstances, withholding may also be required for individuals who are not employees. See "backup withholding", pages 130–131.

Voluntary Deductions by Agreement

Optional deductions can consist of many different items. Some examples are:

- Savings and stock purchase plan contributions
- Retirement account contributions
- Union dues
- Charitable contributions

Employee Social Security (FICA)

Overview

The "social security tax" is a general term and is a result of a very dramatic and difficult time in American history. This period began in 1929 with the onset of a stock market crash and the "great depression". In 1935, the United States Congress enacted the Federal Insurance Contribution Act (*FICA*). This act imposed a tax on employees that is matched by employers to provide employees with a guaranteed minimum amount of old age and survivor's income, and disability insurance benefits (*OASDI*).

FICA was expanded in 1965 to provide limited medical benefits for people without medical insurance (*Medicare*), generally at age 65 and who oth-

continued ▶

Employee Social Security (FICA), *continued*

Overview,
Continued

erwise qualify for OASDI; **therefore, "FICA" really consists of two parts: OASDI and Medicare.** A .9% Medicare surtax applies only to employees on earnings above $200,000 single/$250,000 MFJ. An employer is required to determine an employee's FICA tax each payroll period, withhold the tax, and forward the amount to the Internal Revenue Service (IRS). To summarize: Here, when we use the general term "Social Security" we are referring to FICA, which consists of OASDI and Medicare.

The definitions of "employer" and "employee" for FICA purposes are generally the same as discussed on page 17/18. For FICA purposes most workers are considered employees based on common law; however, FICA both expands the definition of employee for some workers who would otherwise be considered as independent contractors ("statutory" employees) and exempts other workers, as explained below. Keep in mind that these designations are for FICA purposes.

Statutory
Employee
Categories

In some cases a worker does not qualify as an employee under common law, but that person will still be classified as a "statutory employee" ("statutory": law enacted by a legislature) as follows:

- An agent or commission driver. Duties are to deliver food, beverages (other than milk), laundry, or dry cleaning for the provider of these items.
- A full-time life insurance salesperson who works for one company.
- A worker who works at home according to the specifications of the person for whom the work is done, using materials furnished by that person with product and materials returned to that person or their agent (e.g. a "homeworker"). Note: there are some cases in which homeworkers are not deemed to be statutory employees.
- A traveling salesperson who works full time for one firm or person, taking orders for merchandise for resale or supplies for use in the customer's business. Additional incidental part-time work does change the worker's status.

Exception: If the workers either have a substantial interest in the facilities used to perform their services or the services are from a single transaction not part of a continuing relationship they are not covered by FICA.

Statutory
Non-Employees

Persons who perform the following activities are considered to be independent contractors for both income tax and employment tax purposes. This means that they are not subject to FICA withholding or income tax withholding. (They must make quarterly estimated tax payments for income tax and self-employment tax.) Non-employees file Schedule C.

- Direct sellers (no retail establishment)
- Licensed real estate agents
- Certain companion sitters (e.g. baby sitters, caretakers, nannies, cooks), are generally considered as self-employed for federal tax purposes.

Employee Social Security (FICA), *continued*

FICA Wages	For FICA, "wages" is a general term that includes all compensation, including reportable tips, except that which is exempt by law.
Payments Exempt From FICA	Social Security, or FICA, (referring to both OASDI and Medicare) exempts specific payment categories from the tax and from withholding. The table below shows typical employment categories and other types of payments (such as fringe benefits) that are exempt from FICA.

Table 2.2: Payments Exempt From FICA Taxes and Withholding

Exempt Item	Description
Achievement Awards	Exempt up to $1,600 for qualified awards and $400 for non-qualified awards for specified items. See Part V discussion.
Advances to Employees	Business-related expenses paid by an employee under an accountable plan that includes advances, reimbursements, and repayments of excess are exempt. See publications 535 and 463 and Part V.
Agricultural Labor	Non-cash payments are exempt. For each worker, annual cash payments of less than $150 are exempt. If total cash and non-cash compensation for all workers is less than $2,500 FICA tax is not required. Foreign agricultural workers temporarily admitted with H-2A visas and doing H-2A related-work are exempt from FICA; special rule for seasonal workers.
Athletic Facilities	Generally exempt if primarily used by employees. See discussion in Part V.
Cafeteria Plan Benefits	Generally exempt for excludable benefits; not exempt if cash received. 401(k) elective deferrals are subject to FICA withholding.
Deceased Worker	Not exempt on compensation accrued but unpaid at date of death and paid later in year of death. Include FICA on Form W-2, boxes 3 – 6. Not taxable and no withholding when paid after year of death. See Pub. 559.
Dependent Care Assistance	Employer payments to employees or by third parties for dependent care under a qualified dependent care assistance program and/or the value of employer-maintained dependent care facilities used to a maximum of $5,000 ($2,500 married filing separately) are exempt.

continued ▶

Employee Social Security (FICA), *continued*

Table 2.2: Payments Exempt From FICA Taxes and Withholding, *continued*

Exempt Item	Description
Disabled Worker: Sick Pay/ Disability Pay	Taxable for a period: when subject to income tax, also subject to FICA during the first six months after the day the employee became disabled, and exempt when not subject to income tax. Other specified FICA exempt payments: 1) Payments received by employee's estate or beneficiary after the calendar year of the employee's death aren't taxable. 2) Payments received according to a separate definite sick pay plan on or after an employee's death or disability retirement are not subject to FICA tax except for accrued compensation/vested PTO. 3) Employees entitled to disability payments under Social Security provided that the individual became entitled to the payments before the calendar year in which the payments are made and performs no services during period of payments. 4) Payments received more than six months after the last calendar month in which the employee worked 5) Payments attributable to employee contributions made with after-tax dollars are exempt. Also see Part V.
Education	Annual payments up to $5,250 made by an employer under an education assistance plan to maintain or improve employee job skills are exempt to both active and prior employees. Repayment of student loans is also included. Undergraduate and graduate (if teaching or performing research) tuition reduction by an educational institution is also generally exempt. International students and scholars are generally exempt; refer to F-1, J-1, M-1, Q-1/2 visa.
Emergency Workers	Exempt if hired on a temporary basis for major emergencies such as flood, fire, or earthquake
Employee Benefits ("Fringe Benefits")	Generally exempt for tax-excludable benefits while tax-deferred income benefit requires withholding. See Part V on employee benefits. Taxable benefits minus employee-paid portion require withholding. Taxable benefits to which FICA applies are reported on Form W-2, boxes 3 and 5 with withholding. An employer withholds .9% Medicare tax on calendar-year compensation in excess of $200,000.
Employee Business Expense Reimbursement	Exempt per government rates and guidelines if under an accountable plan and within guidelines. See Part V and Publication 535.
Employee Discounts	Subject to certain limitations, employer discounts on property other than real estate, stocks, and bonds purchased by employees are exempt.

continued ▶

Employee Social Security (FICA), *continued*

Table 2.2: Payments Exempt From FICA Taxes and Withholding, *continued*

Exempt Item	Description
Family Employee	1) Child employed by parent: exempt under age 18 for all services in a sole proprietorship trade or business or in a partnership in which each partner is a parent; exempt until 21 if not in parent's trade or business. 2) Parent employed by child: Exempt if services are *not* in the child's trade or business; however, may be subject to tax for certain domestic services (See Publication 15). 3) Spouse employed by spouse: exempt if services are *not* part of the employer spouse's trade or business.
Foreign Affiliates	Foreign affiliates of American employers.
Government Employee	1) Federal: Exempt if hired before 1984, but Medicare applies 2) State and local: Exempt if hired after March 31, 1986 and covered under a public employee retirement plan, but Medicare applies if hired after March 31, 1986. (For services after July 1, 1991 and not covered by a public employee retirement system or by social security, FICA coverage is required.). Military: Differential pay while on active service that is paid by employer is exempt.
Group-term life insurance	Employer-paid premiums for group-term life insurance to $50,000 are exempt.
Health/Medical/ Accident Insurance	Exempt
Health Savings Accounts	Employer payments under qualified plans exempt up to contribution limits.
Homeworker	Exempt if paid *less* than $100 per year in cash and is a statutory employee.
Household employee	■ Domestic service in private homes: exempt if paid less than $2,400 annually (excluding value of room, board, transportation and other noncash items). Also exempt if services are performed by a spouse, parent (subject to exceptions), person under age 18 at any time during the year and these services are not a principal occupation, or by employer's child who is under 21. ■ Domestic service in college clubs, fraternities, and sororities: exempt if payment is to a regular student; also exempt if the employee is paid less than $100 per year by a tax-exempt employer. Note that a household employee is not someone who works in your trade or business or is a home worker, or who is an independent contractor with his/her own business.

continued   ▶

Employee Social Security (FICA), *continued*

Table 2.2: Payments Exempt From FICA Taxes and Withholding, *continued*

Exempt Item	Description
Meals and Lodging	The value of meals provided for the convenience of the employer are generally exempt if furnished on employer's business premises. Lodging must be a condition of employment. Occasional light meals (coffee, snacks, etc.) are exempt. See Part V discussion of meals and lodging.
Military Service Differential Pay	The amount paid by an employer for the difference between military pay for activation to active service exceeding 30 days and regular employee compensation is exempt. (This applies to FICA, but not income tax.)
Ministerial Services	Exempt from withholding but subject to self-employment tax. Voluntary withholding is permitted, however. See Publication 517.
Moving Expense Reimbursement	Employer-paid moving expense reimbursements are exempt from tax and withholding only for members of the armed forces on active duty pursuant to an order for change of location.
Newspaper Carriers And Vendors	Exempt based on same rules as for income tax withholding
No-Additional Cost Services	Employer services provided to employees when no substantial additional cost will be incurred because of excess capacity are exempt.
Non-profit 501(c)(3)	Employee earning less than $100/calendar year
Railroad Retirement Act	Exempt for employees subject to this act
Religious Exemption	Services performed in connection with duties of an ordained ministry, a religious order, or Christian Science practitioner, including the fair value of housing, are exempt from FICA but are subject to self-employment tax under **SECA** (Self-Employment Contributions Act) with the following exceptions: 1) Membership in an order that takes a vow of poverty, 2) The IRS approves an exemption request (Forms 4361 and 4029), 3) A person who is subject only to the social security laws of a foreign country by treaty. Earnings separate from the above are generally subject to FICA or SECA. Otherwise exempt religious orders may request to be covered by filing SS-16. See also Publication 517.
Retirement Planning Services	Exempt
Retirement Plans	1) Exempt for employer non-elective/matching contributions. 2) Generally not exempt for employee elective deferrals. 3) Retirement plan employee distributions are generally exempt. See Part V discussion.
Sick Pay	See Disabled Worker, above

continued   ▶

Employee Social Security (FICA), *continued*

Table 2.2: Payments Exempt From FICA Taxes and Withholding, *continued*

Exempt Item	Description
Statutory Employees	Exempt if paid less than $100 per year.
Statutory Non-Employees	Exempt
Students Enrolled And Regularly Attending Classes	1) Exempt for domestic services in college clubs, fraternities, or sororities while working as a regular student. 2) Generally exempt when performing services for a school, college, or university unless organization has a special Social Security §218 agreement or work is for academic credit combining instruction with work experience as integral to program. 3) Student nurses performing part-time services at hospitals for nominal charge as part of training are exempt.
Transportation Benefits	Employee transportation benefits paid by an employer under a qualified compensation reduction plan are exempt to a monthly dollar limit of $280. This is for commuter travel, parking and transit passes. Bicycle commute payments are not exempt. Employer-provided local transportation tokens and passes discounted up to $21 and commuting cost reimbursement up to $21 are exempt if tokens/passes not available from employer.
Workers' Compensation	Employer payments for workers' compensation insurance, either into state funds or by private insurance contract, are exempt. Workers' compensation benefit payments are exempt unless simultaneously receiving Social Security disability payments, which may cause part of workers' compensation to become taxable.
Working Condition Benefits	Working condition benefits are services or property provided to an employee by an employer so that the employee is able to perform his or her duties. Examples are company-provided car, cell phone, computers, and training.

FICA Calculation   FICA tax is paid by the employee through withholding, with an equal amount paid by the employer. FICA is calculated using a tax rate that is applied to a wage base. A **wage base** is a maximum *calendar year* amount of gross pay that is subject to payroll tax. Gross pay that exceeds the annual base is not subject to OASDI tax. **The OASDI wage base usually increases each year**.

Employee Social Security (FICA), *continued*

The Social Security Tax Bases and Rates (OASDI and Medicare)	There is a separate wage base and tax rate for each part of the social security plan (OASDI and Medicare). Here are the components of FICA:

- The 2022 wage base for the OASDI part is $147,000. The tax rate is 6.2%. This means that during a calendar year, the first $147,000 of gross pay of each employee is subject to a 6.2% OASDI tax.
- The wage base for Medicare is unlimited. This means that all gross pay is subject to Medicare tax. The tax rate is 1.45%. (An additional Medicare surtax of .9% applies to high-income households: "High income" is annual compensation subject to Medicare exceeding: $250,000 for married, $125,000 for married filing separately, and $200,000 for a single person and other categories. The tax applies only to employees, and the employer must begin withholding in the payroll period that an employee's compensation exceeds these levels.)
- For wages not exceeding $147,000 (the OASDI wage base), the combined FICA rate (OASDI and Medicare) is 7.65%. The total FICA rate (combined employee and employer) is therefore 7.65% × 2 = 15.3%.
- Employee/employer combined OASDI is 6.2% × 2 = 12.4%. Combined Medicare is 2.9% (3.8% Medicare tax on investment income does not apply to payroll.)

Procedure With Examples	The table below illustrates the employee FICA tax calculation procedure by an employer. Suppose that a business has two employees, Adam and Amy who are paid monthly. The business needs to calculate the individual and total social security tax for the monthly payroll period ending November 30. During the current year prior to this period, Adam had gross pay of $98,000 and Amy had $133,000. Adam's November gross pay is $11,000 and Amy's November gross pay is $15,000. Assume a $140,000 wage base.

Step 1
Subtract the cumulative gross pay from the wage base.
IF the result is positive or zero, cumulative pay is still below the OASDI limit, so all of the current gross pay is taxable. Go to Step 3. **IF** the result is negative, cumulative pay has exceeded the limit, and this excess is not taxable for OASDI. Some or all of the current gross is excluded from the OASDI tax. Go to Step 2.

Adam		Amy	
Wage base	$140,000	Wage base	$140,000
Cumulative gross pay	109,000	Cumulative gross pay	148,000
Go to Step 3	$ 31,000	Go to Step 2	$ (8,000)

continued ▶

Employee Social Security (FICA), *continued*

Step 2
Offset the negative amount (the amount excluded) against the current gross pay to find the OASDI taxable portion of the current gross pay (but not less than zero). Then go to Step 3.

Adam	Amy
All current gross pay is fully taxable for FICA.	Current gross pay $15,000 Excluded portion (8,000) Taxable portion $ 7,000

Step 3

IF all the current gross pay is taxable, multiply the current gross pay by 7.65% combined rate.

IF some of the gross pay is excluded from OASDI:

- Multiply the taxable portion of current gross pay by 6.2% (OASDI tax)
- Multiply all the current gross pay by 1.45% (Medicare tax)
- Add the results

Adam	Amy
$11,000 × .0765 = $841.50	$ 7,000 × .062 = $434.00 (OASDI) $15,000 × .0145 = 217.50 (Medicare) $651.50

Employer and Employee Identification and Reporting

Employer Identification (EIN)
Every employer with one or more employees (including household employees) must have an employer identification number (EIN). An EIN is required on many forms and in employer correspondence with the Social Security Administration and employment-related matters with the Internal Revenue Service. An EIN can be obtained from the Internal Revenue Service by mailing or faxing a Form SS-4 or online at www.irs.gov.

Employee Identification (SSN)
Every employee and self-employed person must obtain a social security number (SSN). Application Form SS-5 is available from the Internal Revenue Service and the Social Security Administration and is filed with the Social Security Administration local office. The form is available online at www.ssa.gov/forms/ss-5.

Employer note: An ITIN (Individual Tax Identification Number) cannot be used as a substitute for a SSN for Form W-4. ITINs are used only for federal income tax reporting by foreign nationals and others who do not qualify for a SSN.

Employer and Employee Identification and Reporting, *continued*

Employer FICA
Reporting

- An employer annually reports Social Security wages and withholding as part of Form W-2 with copies to employees, IRS, and state taxing authorities. (See page 242.).
- An employer also files quarterly reports to the IRS on either Forms 941 or 943 or annually on Form 944 for Social Security and Medicare wages, withholding, deposit obligation, and deposits made. (See pages 237/238.).
- An employer is also required to make timely deposits of withheld income tax and social security taxes. We discuss deposit requirements on pages 218–221.

Over or Under Withholding

Employer Over-
Witholding

If an employer withholds excessive FICA from an employee, the employee can take the following actions:

1) During the current year, ask for a refund or reduced FICA withholding on the next paychecks. If after year-end, ask the employer for a refund of the excessive amount, as well as a corrected FormW-2c if needed, if there is a single employer.
2) If the employer does not provide the refund, an employee can file Form 843, *Claim for Refund and Request for Abatement.* Calculate individually for joint return filers. (Non-resident aliens should also include Form 8316, *Information Regarding Request for Refund of Social Security Tax Erroneously Withheld on Wages Received by a Nonresident Alien on an F, J, or M Type Visa.*)
3) If the over-withholding is the result of having multiple employers during a year, the employee can claim a credit against tax on an individual tax return. See Publication 505. The IRS provides a taxpayer assistance number: 1-800-829-1040.

A separate Form 941-X (or 943–X / 944-X / 945–X for those returns) is used by an employer to report corrections for each quarter previously filed needing a correction. An employer can either claim a refund or a credit for future payments; however, a refund must be given to the employee either through a payment or reduced withholding. The forms have detailed instructions. If an error is found after W-2s are filed, Form W-2c should be filed with correct FICA earnings and withholding.

Employer Under-
Witholding

By federal law, an employer is required to both withhold and remit the correct employee FICA and income tax. If an employer discovers that not enough FICA was withheld and paid, the employer should check the need to increase withholding in future paychecks, and use a 941-X (or 943–X / 944-X / 945–X for those returns) for each quarter previously filed needing a correction. The forms have detailed instructions on how to file. If discovered after W-2s are filed, a Form W-2c also should be filed that shows the correct FICA taxable earnings and withholding.

continued

Over or Under Withholding, *continued*

Employer Under-
Witholding,
Continued

If an employer pays the FICA on an employee's behalf in order to remit the correct withholding, there is an IRS procedure that allows the employer to recover the amount from the employee. If not recovered by year-end, the FICA paid on behalf of the employee becomes reportable compensation to the employee subject to income tax and FICA.

If an employer willfully under-withholds or fails to withhold FICA taxes and does not pay them to the government, serious penalties, including criminal, can apply to the employer, including to any and all individuals responsible for withholding. This does not affect an employee's right to claim credit for actually withheld FICA, even if not remitted by the employer. As well as not remitted withholding, the IRS also will seek to recover from the employer the amounts not withheld or under-withheld because of the employer's duty to withhold. However, if the employee has control of withholding, payment of FICA taxes becomes the employee's responsibility. Note that unpaid FICA can reduce future employee benefits. The IRS provides an employee assistance number at 1-800-829-1040.

Self-Employment Tax

Overview

Self-employed individuals pay the combined employee/employer FICA tax rate. This is called a "self employment tax", even though a sole proprietor is never considered to be an employee of his/her own business for accounting and legal purposes. Self-employment tax most often applies to sole proprietorship owners, although the applicable law (Self-employment Contributions Act, "SECA") also applies the tax to general partners, certain LLCs, commodity and option dealers, and church employees' wages exceeding $108.28. The tax is applied to taxable "self-employment income".

Taxable self-employment income is: (business net income) × .9235 (to adjust the business net income down by the FICA tax expense deduction an employer would ordinarily receive within the FICA wage base). If the taxable self-employment income in not greater than the annual FICA wage base, the tax rate is 15.3%. (7.65% × 2). Amounts above the base are taxed at 2.9% (1.45% × 2).

Example #1

Bill's business had net income of $170,000 for the current year. Assume a $140,000 wage base. Therefore taxable self-employment income is $170,000 × .9235 = $156,995. This is greater than the $140,000 wage base, so Bill's self-employment tax is: ($140,000 × .153) + ($16,995 × .029) = $21,912.86

Example #2

Bill's business had net income of $130,000 for the current year. Therefore taxable self-employment income is $130,000 × .9235 = $120,055. This is less than the $140,000 limit, so Bill's self-employment tax is: ($120,055 × .153) = $18,368.42

Self-Employment Tax, *continued*

Reporting and Paying

Self-employment tax is reported as additional tax on an individual's annual income tax return, Form 1040, calculated on schedule SE (which applies a 50% reduction). Self-employment net earnings less than $400 per year does not require reporting.

TIP

When a sole proprietor (or partner) draws cash from a business, it is not income. Income is determined as the net income from the business; in other words, total revenues minus total expenses. Draws are not taxable income. When a sole proprietor (or partner) removes cash or other assets from the business, this can be considered as nothing more than a kind of advance payment.

Withholding: Federal Income Tax

Employee Income Tax

Overview

As we have discussed, it is very important for an organization to correctly determine the distinction between an employee and an independent contractor. This is true not only for FLSA purposes, but also for income tax withholding purposes. For workers who qualify as employees based on common law, for income tax withholding purposes each pay period, an employer must:

- Correctly determine each employee's taxable compensation
- Estimate each employee's income tax for the period
- Withhold the income tax from the gross amount earned by an employee, thereby reducing the amount paid to the employee
- Regularly forward the withheld amounts to taxing authorities according to a required payment procedure.

If an employer fails to correctly identify an employee or fails to properly follow the above requirements, significant penalties will be imposed by federal, state, and local taxing authorities, as applicable.

The following discussion in this section addresses each of the above points.

General Rule: Taxable Compensation

The federal income tax code refers to taxable gross income as "from whatever source derived" (code §61). For example, included is payment in cash, other property, and virtual currency such as Bitcoin among the possibilities. Simply stated, what this means is that all income (even illegal income) is taxable unless it is otherwise excluded by law from taxation. State and local taxing authorities follow this same general procedure, using the federal approach as reference. Therefore, it follows that all employee compensation is taxable unless a specified form of compensation is otherwise excluded by law,

continued ▶

Employee Income Tax, *continued*

by a particular taxing authority. IRS Publications 525, 15, 15-A, and 15-B can provide more detailed federal guidance.

Employer Payments Exempt From Federal Income Tax Withholding

Overview   The table below shows a list of some common payments to or on behalf of employees that are exempt from employee federal income tax withholding. Most of the exempt withholding categories below are for nontaxable payments or benefits. In some cases such as qualified retirement plans, the benefits are generally taxable to the beneficiary upon distribution at a later date. These are called "tax-deferred plans". Additional details apply for many items in the table. Also see Publication 15-B related to fringe benefits. Statutory employees as described earlier are not subject to mandatory withholding. Finally, state rules may vary from federal.

Table 2.3: Payments Exempt From Income Tax Withholding

Exempt Item	Description
Achievement Awards	Exempt up to $1,600 for qualified awards and $400 for non-qualified awards for specified items. See Part V discussion.
Adoption Assistance	Employer-paid child adoption expenses under a qualified plan are exempt up to an annual limit. See benefits discussion, part V.
Accident Insurance	Employer-paid accident insurance premiums are not taxable or withheld for employees. Payouts if on employer-paid insurance are taxable, but not if employee-paid with after-tax dollars.
Advances to Employees	Business-related expenses paid by an employee under an accountable plan that includes advances, reimbursements, and repayments of excess are exempt. See publications 535 and 463.
Agricultural Employees	If H-2A visa worker provides valid taxpayer ID report wages of $600 or more in W-2 box 1, otherwise 1099-MISC. Withhold only if worker and employer agree, with Form W-4.
Athletic Facilities	Generally exempt if mostly employee use. See Part V.
Cafeteria Plan	Exempt for excludable benefits; cash received is not exempt.
Combat Zone Pay	Pay received while serving in a designated combat is non-taxable.
Compensatory Damages	Compensatory damages from personal injury are exempt.
"Concierge" Fringe Benefits (Not part of qualified plans)	Not exempt. There can be numerous types of fringe benefits, limited only by the creativity of the employer. Items such as dry cleaning, pet insurance, nutrition counseling, yoga classes, on-site child care, and so on are all desirable benefits. However, for a fringe benefit to be excluded from tax and/or withholding, the exclusion must be expressly allowed by law. Because none of these are expressly excluded, we classify them all as "concierge" (nice, but the value must be included as compensation on W-2). Because none are excluded, they are reported on Form W-2.

continued ▶

Employer Payments Exempt From Federal Income Tax Withholding, *continued*

Table 2.3: Payments Exempt From Income Tax Withholding, *continued*

Exempt Item	Description
Deceased Employee	Any accrued but unpaid compensation (including vacation pay) due an employee at date of death, and paid in the same calendar year is not reported in box 1 of W-2 (use boxes 3 and 5) and is exempt from withholding, unless constructively received before death (e.g. uncashed paycheck – new check issued to estate – box 1); $600 or more accrued gross amount is reported to employee's beneficiary or estate on Form 1099-MISC box 3. Amounts paid in years after death are reported on Form 1099 and not withheld.
Dependent Care Assistance	Employer payments to employees or by third parties for dependent care under a qualified dependent care assistance program and/or the value of employer-maintained dependent care facilities use to a maximum of $5,000 ($2,500 married filing separately) are exempt.
Disability Insurance Premiums	Pre-tax employee deductions and disability insurance premiums paid by employer are exempt unless employee chooses to include in compensation so benefits will not be taxed.
Disabled Worker: Sick Pay/Disability Pay	Employer-provided disability benefits may be subject to income tax for a period, depending on how insurance premiums were paid. See Part V discussion. (Direct employer disability payments are taxable and require withholding. Disability payments under Social Security are taxable and require withholding.)
Education	Annual employer payments up to $5,250 under an education assistance plan to maintain or improve employee job skills are exempt to both active and prior employees. Repayment of student loans is also included. Undergraduate and graduate (if teaching or performing research) tuition reduction by an educational institution are also generally exempt. See Benefits discussion.
Employee Benefits ("Fringe Benefits")	Tax-excluded employee benefits and tax-deferred income benefits are generally not subject to withholding when within limits. See Benefits section. Taxable benefits are added to taxable wages and reported on Form W-2 box 1 with withholding. Non-cash taxable benefits can be reported as per pay period, quarterly, or semiannually, or other basis, but at least annually. Cash benefits are reported and withheld for the pay period paid. Alternatively, taxable benefits can be reported as supplemental wages.
Employee Business Expense Reimbursement	Exempt per government rates and guidelines if under an accountable plan. See Part V and Publication 535.
Employee Discounts	Subject to guidelines, employer discounts on property other than real estate, stocks, and bonds purchased by employees are exempt.

continued   ▶

Employer Payments Exempt From Federal Income Tax Withholding, *continued*

Table 2.3: Payments Exempt From Income Tax Withholding, *continued*

Exempt Item	Description
Family Member Employment	1) Child employed by parent: Exempt if for domestic work in a parent's home, or work is for payments other than in a trade or business and less than $50 per quarter, or the child is not regularly employed in such work, otherwise taxable. 2) Parent employed by child: taxable. 3) Spouse employed by spouse: taxable.
Foreign Employment	Wages of a U.S. citizen or resident alien performing services for a foreign employer are exempt to the extent subject to income tax withholding by the foreign employer. Also exempt to the extent of the foreign earned income and housing exclusion under Internal Revenue Code §911.
Group-Term Life Insurance	Employer-paid premiums for group-term life insurance to $50,000 are exempt.
Health/Medical/ Accident Insurance	Employer-paid insurance premium payments for employees and their families are exempt, except for 2% shareholder-employees in S corporation.
Health Reimbursement Plans	Employer-paid contributions used to reimburse employee medical expenses are exempt to specified limits.
Health Savings Accounts	Employee pre-tax contributions and employer-paid contributions are exempt for qualified plans up to specified limits.
Homeworker	Exempt from withholding if a statutory employee. Generally receives Form 1099.
Household Employees	Employer is not required to withhold income tax unless requested by the employee and employer agrees. (Verify both household and employee status. Included are babysitters, caretakers, house cleaners and various other domestic workers who are not independent contractors. See Publication 926.)
Long-Term Care Insurance	Employer-paid contributions as part of an accident or health plan are generally exempt.
Meals and/or Lodging	The value of meals and/or lodging are not taxable to an employee if provided primarily for the benefit of the employer and are on the employment premises, and the lodging is a condition of employment. Occasional snacks are exempt.
Ministerial Services	Ordained clergy generally are exempt from wage withholding but pay income tax (and SECA – see page 99) using estimated tax. Fair value of housing allowance/parsonage and utilities are tax-exempt. Offerings, fees, etc. are self-employment income.
Newspaper Carriers/Vendors	Exempt if under 18; also, vendors buying at fixed prices and retaining receipts from retail sales to customers.

continued ▶

Employer Payments Exempt From Federal Income Tax Withholding, *continued*

Table 2.3: Payments Exempt From Income Tax Withholding, *continued*

Exempt Item	Description
No-Additional Cost Services	Employer services provided to employees when no substantial additional cost will be incurred because of excess capacity are exempt unless converted to cash.
Moving Expense Reimbursement	Employer-paid moving expense reimbursements are exempt from tax and withholding only for members of the armed forces on active duty pursuant to an order for change of location.
Retirement Planning Services	Employer-paid retirement planning services are exempt when an employer maintains a qualified retirement plan.
Retirement Plans	1) Employer non-elective/matching contributions to retirement plans are exempt (plans such as 401(k), 403(b), and 457(b)). 2) Employee elective contributions are generally exempt from income tax and withholding until distribution. See Part V retirement plans discussion.
Rewards Programs	Frequent-flyer mileage rewards resulting from travel and credit card rebates from purchases are not taxable and therefore not subject to withholding.
Sick Pay	See Disabled Worker above.
Transportation Benefits	Employee transportation benefits paid by an employer under a qualified compensation reduction plan are exempt to a monthly dollar limit of $280. This is for commuter travel, parking and transit passes. Bicycle commute payments are not exempt. Employer-provided local transportation tokens and passes discounted up to $21 and commuting cost reimbursement up to $21 are exempt if tokens/passes not available from employer.
Workers' Compensation	1) Employer payments for workers' compensation insurance, either into state funds or by private insurance contract, are exempt. 2) Workers' compensation benefits are also generally not taxable and not withheld unless received simultaneously with supplemental social security benefits.
Working Condition Benefits	Exempt if per guidelines. Working condition benefits are services or property provided to an employee by an employer so that the employee is able to perform his or her duties. See Part V discussion.
Exemption based on prior year tax liability	Employee is exempt from withholding if: ▪ For the prior tax year there was a right to a full refund because there was no tax liability for that year, and ▪ The employee expects the same condition to apply in the current tax year. The exemption is valid for one year. See IRS Publication 505 for further details.

Non-Employees

Statutory Non-Employees

Persons who perform the following activities are considered to be independent contractors for both income tax and FICA employment tax purposes. This means that they are not subject to withholding for income tax or for FICA. (However, they must make quarterly estimated tax payments for income tax and self-employment tax.)

- Direct sellers
- Real estate agents
- Household workers (e.g. baby sitters, caretakers, nannies, cooks), subject to specific requirements.

Review: Recall that specifically for FLSA employee designation purposes there are also certain exempt categories of activities. (See page 43/49)

Tip Income

Withholding on Tip Income

Employee tip income received either directly or indirectly (such as tip sharing or pooling) is includable as employee taxable income.

Employees are required to report tip income to the employer for any month in which tips exceed $20. Employees can use Form 4070-A or an equivalent daily written account for record keeping. Employees then report total monthly tips to the employer by the 10th day of the month following the month that is being reported, by using Form 4070. Fixed and required service charges added to bills and that are later distributed to employees are treated as wage income rather than tips.

Large food and beverage employers (normally more than 10 total employees on an average business day during the preceding year) must allocate tips to directly tipped employees. ***The amount to be allocated*** is the difference between 8% (or IRS approved lower rate) of gross receipts and total reported tips, when reported tips are less than 8% of the gross receipts. The allocation procedure is discussed below.

Allocated Tip Income

An employer annually reports total tips and tip allocation to the IRS on Form 8027 for each large food and beverage establishment by February 28 following the year being reported (April 2 for electronic filing). See Form 8027 instructions for definitions, detailed calculation examples, and protocol for application of an IRS approved lower rate. An employer will select one of three methods to allocate tip income:

1. Hours-Worked Method: Businesses with less than 25 full-time equivalent employees may use this method. (Fewer than 200 employee hours worked per day meets this test.) Each employee's share is calculated using the following ratio: the hours worked by a tipped employee divided by the hours worked by all tipped employees. Note: a drawback to this method is that the amount of tips may be different for different shifts and that hours will not measure tips received.

continued ▶

Tip Income, *continued*

*Allocated
Tip Income,
Continued*

2. Gross Receipts Method: Allocate tips based on gross receipts.

Step	Action
1	Calculate total direct tips as 8% (or a lower IRS-approved percentage) of gross receipts and subtract the amount of indirect tips.
2	Calculate each directly tipped employee's share of the Step 1 amount. For each directly tipped employee, multiply the Step 1 amount by the ratio (the fraction) of the gross receipts attributable to the employee to the gross receipts attributable to all employees.
3	For each directly tipped employee, determine if there is any reporting shortfall. Subtract the employee's reported tips from the result in Step 2.
4	Calculate total shortfall based on the 8% allocation. From the amount in Step 1, subtract all reported tips by both directly and indirectly tipped employees.
5	For each employee who had a shortfall from Step 3, allocate has/her share of the total shortfall from Step 4. Multiply the amount in Step 4 by the ratio of the employee's shortfall to the total of all employees with a shortfall.

3. Good-Faith Agreement: An allocation of the difference between 8% of gross receipts (no reduction for indirect tips) and total reported tips can be based on a written agreement between the employer and at least two-thirds of employees who receive tips.

There is no income or FICA tax withholding on allocated tips. An employer reports allocated tips on Form W-2, box 8 by January 31. Employees must use the box 8 amount to file Form 4137 with their tax returns. The IRS then uses the form to determine an employer's FICA tax on allocated / unreported tips, and notifies the employer by a "Section 3121(q) Notice and Demand" letter that shows the amount of tax due. The employer then includes the amount as part of the next payroll tax deposit. The employer reports the amount on line 5f of Form 941.

TIP

There is a tax credit for the employer for FICA tax paid by the employer on food and beverage tips. See Form 8846 instructions and file the form with annual tax return as part of the general business credit.

Income Tax Withholding: Employee Requirements

What Is a Withholding Allowance?

The underlying idea of income tax withholding is to make, during the course of a year, a prepayment that roughly approximates (within requirements) the total income tax that will be due at year-end. Before 2020, tax withholding tables based on compensation and withholding allowances were the primary means of accomplishing this for employee compensation. Each allowance is an estimate of a reduction in taxable income. For example, for those employees still permitted to use the allowance method, in 2022 each allowance equates to an estimated $4,300 reduction in an individual's taxable income, and therefore a withholding reduction.

Prior to 2018, allowances were connected to "personal exemptions". Generally each individual could claim at least one exemption that would act as a reduction in taxable income. For example, in 2017 each personal exemption reduced taxable income by $4,050. Additional exemptions also could be claimed for each dependent and to reduce income for additional deductions, losses, and credits. To reduce complexity, the amount of each allowance for withholding purposes was also the same amount as the personal exemption amount; however, an allowance would not actually appear as a deduction on an income tax return. An allowance is only for the purpose of determining withholding.

The connection to personal exemptions ceased with the Tax Cuts and Jobs Act of 2017, which set personal exemptions to a zero federal tax deduction through 2025. After a transition period during 2018-2019, use of a "withholding allowance" now depends on when an employee has submitted a Form W-4 (see below) to the employer. For existing employees who submitted a W-4 prior to 2020 and have not revised it, the withholding calculation still uses the number of allowances that were claimed, using the current amount of $4,300 for each allowance. These are allocated to the number of pay periods to determine what is called either a "wage amount" or "adjusted wage amount", depending on the method used, for withholding tables with a built-in standard deduction.

For employees hired beginning in 2020 and for existing employees hired before 2020 who submit a new W-4 to revise their data, the term "allowance" is no longer used in a W-4, although an amount does appear in Worksheet 1A, Table 3, and Worksheet 5, all to deal with pre-2020 withholding data, depending on method. Instead of allowances, the changed W-4 contains wage/salary adjustments for other sources of income and additional deductions resulting in what is called an "adjusted wage amount", used with withholding tables that contain a built-in standard deduction.

Income Tax Withholding: Employee Requirements, *continued*

Form W-4

- Employers use Form W-4 to calculate an employee's federal income tax withholding each pay period. An employee completes a W-4 when beginning employment. If an employee's income tax status changes, the employee should prepare a new W-4 for the employer. The new withholding then becomes effective not later than the beginning of the first payroll period ending on or after 30 days from the date the employer received the new form.

- An employer must retain the W-4 form on file for each employee until 4 years following employee departure. An employer does not file any W-4 forms with the IRS unless requested to do so by an IRS written notice. If a W-4 is not submitted by an employee, the employer must withhold as if the employee were single with no deductions or allowances.

- Employers can make online W-4 filing available, but also must make paper copies available to any employee who does not want to use the electronic system.

- If an employee does not have a social security number, he or she should apply for one by completing and mailing in Form SS-5, which is available online. The form can also be taken to a local Social Security office. A list of these offices are available at https://secure.ssa.gov/apps6z/FOLO/fo001.jsp

Assisting Employees With Form W-4

Because a revised Form W-4 for 2020 and later and the old W-4 forms are both in use, there is likely to be some confusion among employees, who probably will seek employer help and ask questions concerning the correct use and preparation of the form. As well, an employee may need to take the new form home for additional information instead of trying to complete it the first day on the job. The following discussion addresses the basic procedures concerning W-4 completion, without the intent or action of becoming a tax advisor.

Who has to prepare the new W-4 form? 1) All employees hired or rehired in 2020 and after must complete the new W-4. 2) Employees hired before 2020 that have a change in tax status that will affect their tax (such as marriage, divorce, change in dependents, other income, additional deductions, and tax credits) that wish to adjust their withholding will need to submit a new W-4. The new form is called "***Employee's Withholding Certificate***".

Are employees hired before 2020 required to submit a new W-4? No. If the new form is not submitted the same withholding method will continue based on the prior form. An employer cannot require a new form for these employees. The prior form is called "***Employee's Withholding Allowance Certificate***".

continued ▶

Income Tax Withholding: Employee Requirements, *continued*

Assisting Employees With Form W-4, Continued

What are the essential steps in completing the new W-4? The following discussion summarizes essential procedures for completing the form.

- The form is divided into five steps (see next page). Completion of Step 1 and Step 5 is mandatory. Steps 2, 3, and 4 are optional steps that increase the accuracy of the withholding by making adjustments.
- **Step 1** identifies the employee. An employee should check one of the boxes in Step 1c. This will indicate to the employer the correct tax table to use based on filing status.
- **Step 2** should be used if there are multiple jobs. This situation creates some added complexity that could result in insufficient withholding and possible year-end penalties if this section is not completed when there are multiple jobs. The employee can select any one of three choices. Generally, selecting choice (a) to use the IRS online withholding estimator at www.irs.gov/W4App will provide the most accurate results, but the most complex of the three. (The withholding estimator can also be used for any individual or filing status to estimate total tax and possible under or over withholding based on current withholding. For complex situations such as alternative minimum tax and capital gains, employees should review Publication 505 for withholding and estimated tax.)
- **Step 3** is used when there are tax credits. Tax credits reduce tax liability and therefore reduce withholding. The first line in Step 3 is for the child tax credit. The second line is used for both: 1) tax credits for dependents, and 2) any other tax credits, such as for education. Both can be added together. The total Step 3 amount is an annual withholding reduction. Dependents are explained in Publication 17.
- **Step 4** allows for: a) other *annual* income for which there is no withholding, b) additional *annual* deductions beyond the standard deduction, and c) any additional withholding *per payroll period*. Item c can result from using the online calculator, the W-4 worksheets, or can simply be a flat amount added by the employee. Note that Step 4 reveals additional information to an employer that an employee may wish to keep private.

Below line 4c in Step 4, non-resident aliens indicate that status by writing in capital letters "NRA" if they are subject to the supplemental withholding rules. As well, an exempt employee indicates exempt status by writing in capital letters "EXEMPT". Exempt status must be claimed by February 15th of each year.

Income Tax Withholding: Employee Requirements, *continued*

Illustration 2.2: Form W-4

Form **W-4** Department of the Treasury Internal Revenue Service	**Employee's Withholding Certificate** ▶ Complete Form W-4 so that your employer can withhold the correct federal income tax from your pay. ▶ Give Form W-4 to your employer. ▶ Your withholding is subject to review by the IRS. OMB No. 1545-0074 2022

Step 1:
Enter Personal Information

(a) First name and middle initial   Last name

(b) Social security number

Address

▶ **Does your name match the name on your social security card?** If not, to ensure you get credit for your earnings, contact SSA at 800-772-1213 or go to *www.ssa.gov.*

City or town, state, and ZIP code

(c) ☐ **Single** or **Married filing separately**
☐ **Married filing jointly** or **Qualifying widow(er)**
☐ **Head of household** (Check only if you're unmarried and pay more than half the costs of keeping up a home for yourself and a qualifying individual.)

Complete Steps 2–4 ONLY if they apply to you; otherwise, skip to Step 5. See page 2 for more information on each step, who can claim exemption from withholding, when to use the estimator at *www.irs.gov/W4App*, and privacy.

Step 2:
Multiple Jobs or Spouse Works

Complete this step if you (1) hold more than one job at a time, or (2) are married filing jointly and your spouse also works. The correct amount of withholding depends on income earned from all of these jobs.

Do **only one** of the following.

(a) Use the estimator at *www.irs.gov/W4App* for most accurate withholding for this step (and Steps 3–4); **or**

(b) Use the Multiple Jobs Worksheet on page 3 and enter the result in Step 4(c) below for roughly accurate withholding; **or**

(c) If there are only two jobs total, you may check this box. Do the same on Form W-4 for the other job. This option is accurate for jobs with similar pay; otherwise, more tax than necessary may be withheld   .   .   ▶ ☐

TIP: To be accurate, submit a 2022 Form W-4 for all other jobs. If you (or your spouse) have self-employment income, including as an independent contractor, use the estimator.

Complete Steps 3–4(b) on Form W-4 for only ONE of these jobs. Leave those steps blank for the other jobs. (Your withholding will be most accurate if you complete Steps 3–4(b) on the Form W-4 for the highest paying job.)

Step 3:
Claim Dependents

If your total income will be $200,000 or less ($400,000 or less if married filing jointly):

Multiply the number of qualifying children under age 17 by $2,000 ▶ $ _____

Multiply the number of other dependents by $500   .   .   .   . ▶ $ _____

Add the amounts above and enter the total here   .   .   .   .   **3** $ _____

Step 4 (optional):
Other Adjustments

(a) **Other income (not from jobs).** If you want tax withheld for other income you expect this year that won't have withholding, enter the amount of other income here. This may include interest, dividends, and retirement income   .   .   .   .   **4(a)** $ _____

(b) **Deductions.** If you expect to claim deductions other than the standard deduction and want to reduce your withholding, use the Deductions Worksheet on page 3 and enter the result here   .   .   .   .   **4(b)** $ _____

(c) **Extra withholding.** Enter any additional tax you want withheld each **pay period**   .   .   **4(c)** $ _____

Step 5:
Sign Here

Under penalties of perjury, I declare that this certificate, to the best of my knowledge and belief, is true, correct, and complete.

▶ _____   ▶ _____
Employee's signature (This form is not valid unless you sign it.)   **Date**

Employers Only

Employer's name and address

First date of employment

Employer identification number (EIN)

For Privacy Act and Paperwork Reduction Act Notice, see page 3.   Cat. No. 10220Q   Form **W-4** (2022)

Source: Internal Revenue Service

Income Tax Withholding: Employee Requirements, *continued*

Assisting Employees With Form W-4, Continued

An employee is qualified for exempt status if:

- For the prior tax year there was a right to a full refund because there was no tax liability for that year, and
- The employee expects the same condition to apply in the current tax year.

In some cases the employer and employee may receive a follow-up notice from the Internal Revenue Service requiring additional information. A new W-4 must be completed each year.

Employees that do not submit a W-4 must have withholding calculated as single, with no adjustments.

Prior W-4

For reference, the prior Form W-4 that uses withholding allowances is illustrated below. It is no longer in use for new employees or for withholding revisions.

Illustration 2.3: Prior Form W-4

Form **W-4**	**Employee's Withholding Allowance Certificate**	OMB No. 1545-0074
Department of the Treasury / Internal Revenue Service	▶ Whether you're entitled to claim a certain number of allowances or exemption from withholding is subject to review by the IRS. Your employer may be required to send a copy of this form to the IRS.	2019

1 Your first name and middle initial   Last name   2 Your social security number

Home address (number and street or rural route)

3 ☐ Single ☐ Married ☐ Married, but withhold at higher Single rate.
Note: If married filing separately, check "Married, but withhold at higher Single rate."

City or town, state, and ZIP code

4 If your last name differs from that shown on your social security card, check here. You must call 800-772-1213 for a replacement card. ▶ ☐

5 Total number of allowances you're claiming (from the applicable worksheet on the following pages) **5**
6 Additional amount, if any, you want withheld from each paycheck . . . . **6** $
7 I claim exemption from withholding for 2019, and I certify that I meet **both** of the following conditions for exemption.
 • Last year I had a right to a refund of **all** federal income tax withheld because I had **no** tax liability, **and**
 • This year I expect a refund of **all** federal income tax withheld because I expect to have **no** tax liability.
 If you meet both conditions, write "Exempt" here . . . . ▶ **7**

Under penalties of perjury, I declare that I have examined this certificate and, to the best of my knowledge and belief, it is true, correct, and complete.

Employee's signature
(This form is not valid unless you sign it.) ▶   Date ▶

8 Employer's name and address (**Employer:** Complete boxes 8 and 10 if sending to IRS and complete boxes 8, 9, and 10 if sending to State Directory of New Hires.) | 9 First date of employment | 10 Employer identification number (EIN)

For Privacy Act and Paperwork Reduction Act Notice, see page 4.   Cat. No. 10220Q   Form **W-4** (2019)

Source: Internal Revenue Service

Note: Many states have their own W-4 equivalent forms, using allowance method. Also, states have different withholding methods for multi-state employees; it is important to **check each relevant state**.

Income Tax Withholding: Employee Requirements, *continued*

Estimated Tax Payments	Employees with other income that does not involve employer withholding can also make estimated tax payments. This is usually needed for individuals with other sources of income that are big enough to affect tax liability. These payments increase tax payments, but are not in lieu of withholding. Estimated tax payments are made by completing Form 1040-ES worksheet and vouchers with payment. States have similar forms.
Non-Resident Alien Withholding	Apart from tax treaties and special provisions (such as for non-resident alien students from India and business apprentices from India), non-resident aliens' wage income is taxed at a flat 30% rate. Employee withholding is required at the time a person realizes income whether or not cash or property is received, as long as the payment is made for the person's benefit. Employers are required to add an amount to wages only for the purpose of determining the withholding. See Section 6. (Also refer to Publication 15, Chapter 9, for table and instructions.) As indicated above, federal withholding is generally required at a 30% rate unless exceptions such as tax treaties apply. If these apply, the employee must submit a Form 8233 to the employer.
Determination by the IRS	In some cases, an employer may receive a written notice from the IRS called a *lock-in letter* to increase income tax withholding on a particular employee; the letter will specify a minimum amount of withholding. A copy of this should be given to the employee. An employee may submit additional information to the IRS to request a revision of the withholding; however, an employer cannot change the required withholding without IRS approval. An employer will wait at least 60 days from the letter date before implementing the lock-in letter, using the date specified in the letter. If the person is no longer an employee, no further action is required. An employer who does not implement the withholding becomes liable for paying the additional amount of tax that should have been withheld. If an employee had been using a pre-2020 W-4 and submits a new form, the withholding still cannot be less than required by the lock-in letter.

Income Tax Withholding: Employer Requirements

Overview	At this point, we have discussed what compensation is subject to income tax withholding and the W-4 form prepared by an employee that is used to calculate the employee's federal income tax withholding. The next part of our discussion of the withholding process is to explain an employer's responsibilities and methods of withholding. An employer's withholding process begins by obtaining the required employee data that is provided on Form W-4. An employer uses this data in one of two ways: 1) Employers with automated payroll systems initially input the annual gross pay and the W-4 data when an employee

continued ▶

Income Tax Withholding: Employer Requirements, *continued*

Overview, Continued

is hired, and then whenever the W-4 data changes or the gross pay or pay periods change. Therefore, data entry is relatively infrequent, and once the data are in the system withholding and pay calculations are automatic. 2) Employers manually record employee pay and/or W-4 data with each payroll to manually calculate withholding. This occurs with either a more limited or not-updated payroll software system or a procedure that is entirely manual.

Withholding Procedure With an Automated System

The IRS provides a worksheet called "Worksheet 1" (and also a related withholding rate table) in Publication 15-T that can be used to understand the data input and calculation procedure in an automated system. Of course, in practice the worksheet and withholding table wouldn't regularly be needed because the automated system would be using the W-4 and withholding table data already entered and applied in a programmed calculation procedure, as illustrated in the worksheet steps. However, the worksheet is useful to help understand the procedure and to occasionally check system output results. Withholding procedure: Step 1: Use the worksheet to calculate the *annual* adjusted wage amount from W-4 data. The worksheet can use either a 2020 or later W-4 or pre-2020 W-4 data. Step 2: Use the Step 1 result in the withholding table titled "2022 Percentage Method Tables for Automated Payroll Systems" to calculate tentative withholding. Step 3: Enter any tax credits, divide by the payroll periods,

Example #1

The adjusted annual wage amount from Worksheet 1A in Publication 15-T for Rosemary Davis is $78,000. She is married, files jointly, and earns about the same as her husband so they each checked box 2c in their 2020 W-4 forms. The employer should then use the right section of the withholding table (next page - read the heading carefully). $78,000 falls between $54,725 and $102,025. The withholding calculation in Step 2 of the worksheet is: $4,807.50 + [($78,000 − $54,725) × .22] = $9,928.00. This is Mary's annual withholding amount. Dividing this by the number of pay periods is the tentative withholding amount for the pay period before any tax credits. Step 3: Enter any annual tax credits from the W-4, divide by the pay periods, and subtract from the tentative withholding amount. This is the final withholding amount unless there is additional withholding to add from Step 4c of the W-4.

Example #2

The adjusted annual wage amount from the Worksheet 1A for James Winston, who is single, is $111,000. James has not revised or updated his W-4 that he submitted in 2016. The total annual withholding amount from the withholding table is: $15,213.50 + [($111,000 − $93,425) × .24] = $19,431.50. If James is paid monthly his monthly withholding is $19,431.50/12 = $1,619.29. Rounding to the nearest dollar is permitted.

Income Tax Withholding: Employer Requirements, *continued*

Illustration 2.4: Withholding table for automated systems and Worksheet 1A

2022 Percentage Method Tables for Automated Payroll Systems and Withholding on Periodic Payments of Pensions and Annuities

STANDARD Withholding Rate Schedules
(Use these if the Form W-4 is from 2019 or earlier, or if the Form W-4 is from 2020 or later and the box in Step 2 of Form W-4 is **NOT** checked. Also use these for Form W-4P from any year.)

Form W-4, Step 2, Checkbox, Withholding Rate Schedules
(Use these if the Form W-4 is from 2020 or later and the box in Step 2 of Form W-4 **IS** checked)

If the Adjusted Annual Wage Amount on Worksheet 1A or the Adjusted Annual Payment Amount on Worksheet 1B is:		The tentative amount to withhold is:	Plus this percentage—	of the amount that the Adjusted Annual Wage or Payment exceeds—	If the Adjusted Annual Wage Amount on Worksheet 1A is:		The tentative amount to withhold is:	Plus this percentage—	of the amount that the Adjusted Annual Wage exceeds—
At least—	But less than—				At least—	But less than—			
A	B	C	D	E	A	B	C	D	E
Married Filing Jointly					**Married Filing Jointly**				
$0	$13,000	$0.00	0%	$0	$0	$12,950	$0.00	0%	$0
$13,000	$33,550	$0.00	10%	$13,000	$12,950	$23,225	$0.00	10%	$12,950
$33,550	$96,550	$2,055.00	12%	$33,550	$23,225	$54,725	$1,027.50	12%	$23,225
$96,550	$191,150	$9,615.00	22%	$96,550	$54,725	$102,025	$4,807.50	22%	$54,725
$191,150	$353,100	$30,427.00	24%	$191,150	$102,025	$183,000	$15,213.50	24%	$102,025
$353,100	$444,900	$69,295.00	32%	$353,100	$183,000	$228,900	$34,647.50	32%	$183,000
$444,900	$660,850	$98,671.00	35%	$444,900	$228,900	$336,875	$49,335.50	35%	$228,900
$660,850		$174,253.50	37%	$660,850	$336,875		$87,126.75	37%	$336,875
Single or Married Filing Separately					**Single or Married Filing Separately**				
$0	$4,350	$0.00	0%	$0	$0	$6,475	$0.00	0%	$0
$4,350	$14,625	$0.00	10%	$4,350	$6,475	$11,613	$0.00	10%	$6,475
$14,625	$46,125	$1,027.50	12%	$14,625	$11,613	$27,363	$513.75	12%	$11,613
$46,125	$93,425	$4,807.50	22%	$46,125	$27,363	$51,013	$2,403.75	22%	$27,363
$93,425	$174,400	$15,213.50	24%	$93,425	$51,013	$91,500	$7,606.75	24%	$51,013
$174,400	$220,300	$34,647.50	32%	$174,400	$91,500	$114,450	$17,323.75	32%	$91,500
$220,300	$544,250	$49,335.50	35%	$220,300	$114,450	$276,425	$24,667.75	35%	$114,450
$544,250		$162,718.00	37%	$544,250	$276,425		$81,359.00	37%	$276,425
Head of Household					**Head of Household**				
$0	$10,800	$0.00	0%	$0	$0	$9,700	$0.00	0%	$0
$10,800	$25,450	$0.00	10%	$10,800	$9,700	$17,025	$0.00	10%	$9,700
$25,450	$66,700	$1,465.00	12%	$25,450	$17,025	$37,650	$732.50	12%	$17,025
$66,700	$99,850	$6,415.00	22%	$66,700	$37,650	$54,225	$3,207.50	22%	$37,650
$99,850	$180,850	$13,708.00	24%	$99,850	$54,225	$94,725	$6,854.00	24%	$54,225
$180,850	$226,750	$33,148.00	32%	$180,850	$94,725	$117,675	$16,574.00	32%	$94,725
$226,750	$550,700	$47,836.00	35%	$226,750	$117,675	$279,650	$23,918.00	35%	$117,675
$550,700		$161,218.50	37%	$550,700	$279,650		$80,609.25	37%	$279,650

Source: Internal Revenue Service

Withholding Procedure With a Manual System

Manual withholding calculation requires the availability of four different withholding tables. This is because manual calculation does not have the flexibility of an automated system programmed to produce correct results with a variety of calculation procedures that depend on data input.

There are two basic table formats for calculating withholding. One format uses percentage withholding rates applied to wages. This type of table can accept any amount of income, and is the type of table we used above (although that table is only for annual amounts). It is generally called a "percentage method" table. The second type of format calculates withholding based on specific wage ranges per payroll period. This is called the "wage bracket" method. If pay exceeds the limit of a wage bracket table, the calculation must be switched to a percentage method table.

continued ▶

Income Tax Withholding: Employer Requirements, *continued*

Withholding Procedure With a Manual System, Continued

Manual calculation offers the choice between using either a percentage method table or a wage bracket table. However, we have to keep in mind that two types of W-4s are now in use: pre-2020 and 2020 (and beyond). Because the type of W-4 data dictates the type of withholding table to use, there must be two withholding table types for each format, a total of four manual method tables. The result is:

Format Type	IF W-4 IS:	THEN USE THE WITHHOLDING TABLE:
Wage bracket method	2020 & later	Wage bracket method table with forms W-4 from 2020 and later (Table 2 in Pub. 15-T)
	Pre-2020	Wage bracket method table with forms W-4 from 2019 and earlier (Table 3 in Pub. 15-T)
Percentage method	2020 & later	Percentage method table with forms W-4 from 2020 and later (Table 4 in Pub. 15-T)
	Pre-2020	Percentage method table with forms W-4 from 2019 and earlier (Table 5 in Pub. 15-T)

There is an employer worksheet for each table, just as with the automated system, that calculates the correct amount of adjusted wages to use in a withholding table; however, here the adjusted wages amount is *per payroll period*. With manual calculation a worksheet is essential; it must be used prior to using its associated withholding table. Each worksheet is designed specifically for its withholding table. For example, a worksheet for a 2020 & later W-4 uses wage adjustments and credits, while a worksheet for a pre-2020 W-4 uses the number of allowances.

Example #1

Frank Delano is single and earns $1,950 biweekly. He completes only part 1 and part 5 of a 2020 W-4. His adjusted wage amount on the worksheet for the manual wage bracket method is $1,950. On the biweekly wage bracket withholding table (Illustration 2.5), $1,950 is in the bracket $1,950 – $1,970. Therefore, his biweekly withholding is $168.

Example #2

Same facts as Example #1, but the calculation is made using the percentage method table. The calculation for this withholding table (Illustration 2.6), using the left section of the table for single filing status: $39.50 + [($1,950 – $893) × .12] = $166.34, which conforms to the answer for the same facts in Example 1.

Income Tax Withholding: Employer Requirements, *continued*

Illustration 2.5: Wage bracket method withholding table for manual systems and Worksheet 2 (partial)

2022 Wage Bracket Method Tables for Manual Payroll Systems with Forms W-4 From 2020 or Later
BIWEEKLY Payroll Period

If the Adjusted Wage Amount (line 1h) is		Married Filing Jointly		Head of Household		Single or Married Filing Separately	
		Standard withholding	Form W-4, Step 2, Checkbox withholding	Standard withholding	Form W-4, Step 2, Checkbox withholding	Standard withholding	Form W-4, Step 2, Checkbox withholding
At least	But less than			The Tentative Withholding Amount is:			
$1,130	$1,150	$14	$69	$39	$86	$69	$112
$1,150	$1,170	$16	$72	$41	$89	$72	$116
$1,170	$1,190	$18	$74	$43	$91	$74	$121
$1,190	$1,210	$20	$76	$45	$94	$76	$125
$1,210	$1,230	$22	$79	$47	$96	$79	$129
$1,230	$1,250	$24	$81	$49	$98	$81	$134
$1,250	$1,270	$26	$84	$51	$101	$84	$138
$1,270	$1,290	$28	$86	$53	$103	$86	$143
$1,290	$1,310	$30	$88	$55	$106	$88	$147
$1,310	$1,330	$32	$91	$58	$108	$91	$151
$1,330	$1,350	$34	$93	$60	$110	$93	$156
$1,350	$1,370	$36	$96	$62	$113	$96	$160
$1,370	$1,390	$38	$98	$65	$115	$98	$165
$1,390	$1,410	$40	$100	$67	$118	$100	$169
$1,410	$1,430	$42	$103	$70	$120	$103	$173
$1,430	$1,450	$44	$105	$72	$122	$105	$178
$1,450	$1,470	$46	$108	$74	$126	$108	$182
$1,470	$1,490	$48	$110	$77	$130	$110	$187
$1,490	$1,510	$50	$112	$79	$135	$112	$191
$1,510	$1,530	$52	$115	$82	$139	$115	$195
$1,530	$1,550	$54	$117	$84	$144	$117	$200
$1,550	$1,570	$56	$120	$86	$148	$120	$204
$1,570	$1,590	$58	$122	$89	$152	$122	$209
$1,590	$1,610	$60	$124	$91	$157	$124	$213
$1,610	$1,630	$62	$127	$94	$161	$127	$217
$1,630	$1,650	$64	$129	$96	$166	$129	$222
$1,650	$1,670	$66	$132	$98	$170	$132	$226
$1,670	$1,690	$68	$134	$101	$174	$134	$231
$1,690	$1,710	$70	$136	$103	$179	$136	$235
$1,710	$1,730	$72	$139	$106	$183	$139	$239
$1,730	$1,750	$74	$141	$108	$188	$141	$244
$1,750	$1,770	$76	$144	$110	$192	$144	$248
$1,770	$1,790	$78	$146	$113	$196	$146	$253
$1,790	$1,810	$81	$148	$115	$201	$148	$257
$1,810	$1,830	$83	$151	$118	$205	$151	$261
$1,830	$1,850	$85	$153	$120	$210	$153	$266
$1,850	$1,870	$88	$156	$122	$214	$156	$270
$1,870	$1,890	$90	$158	$125	$218	$158	$275
$1,890	$1,910	$93	$160	$127	$223	$160	$279
$1,910	$1,930	$95	$163	$130	$227	$163	$283
$1,930	$1,950	$97	$165	$132	$232	$165	$288
$1,950	$1,970	$100	$168	$134	$236	$168	$292
$1,970	$1,995	$103	$170	$137	$241	$170	$297
$1,995	$2,020	$106	$173	$140	$246	$173	$303
$2,020	$2,045	$109	$176	$143	$252	$176	$309
$2,045	$2,070	$112	$179	$146	$257	$179	$315
$2,070	$2,095	$115	$182	$149	$263	$182	$321
$2,095	$2,120	$118	$185	$152	$269	$185	$327
$2,120	$2,145	$121	$191	$155	$275	$191	$333
$2,145	$2,170	$124	$196	$158	$281	$196	$339
$2,170	$2,195	$127	$202	$161	$287	$202	$345
$2,195	$2,220	$130	$207	$164	$293	$207	$351
$2,220	$2,245	$133	$213	$167	$299	$213	$357
$2,245	$2,270	$136	$218	$170	$305	$218	$363
$2,270	$2,295	$139	$224	$173	$311	$224	$369
$2,295	$2,320	$142	$229	$176	$317	$229	$375
$2,320	$2,345	$145	$235	$179	$323	$235	$381
$2,345	$2,370	$148	$240	$182	$329	$240	$387
$2,370	$2,395	$151	$246	$185	$335	$246	$393
$2,395	$2,420	$154	$251	$188	$341	$251	$399
$2,420	$2,445	$157	$257	$191	$347	$257	$405
$2,445	$2,470	$160	$262	$194	$353	$262	$411
$2,470	$2,495	$163	$268	$197	$359	$268	$417
$2,495	$2,520	$166	$273	$200	$365	$273	$423
$2,520	$2,545	$169	$279	$203	$371	$279	$429

Source: Internal Revenue Service

Note: All IRS wage bracket tables are available online in Publication 15-T.

continued ▶

Income Tax Withholding: Employer Requirements, *continued*

Illustration 2.6: Percentage method withholding table for manual systems and Worksheet 4

2022 Percentage Method Tables for Manual Payroll Systems With Forms W-4 from 2020 or Later
BIWEEKLY Payroll Period

STANDARD Withholding Rate Schedules (Use these if the box in Step 2 of Form W-4 is **NOT** checked)					Form W-4, Step 2, Checkbox, Withholding Rate Schedules (Use these if the box in Step 2 of Form W-4 **IS** checked)				
If the Adjusted Wage Amount (line 1h) is:		The tentative amount to withhold is:	Plus this percentage—	of the amount that the Adjusted Wage exceeds—	If the Adjusted Wage Amount (line 1h) is:		The tentative amount to withhold is:	Plus this percentage—	of the amount that the Adjusted Wage exceeds—
At least—	But less than—				At least—	But less than—			
A	B	C	D	E	A	B	C	D	E
Married Filing Jointly					**Married Filing Jointly**				
$0	$996	$0.00	0%	$0	$0	$498	$0.00	0%	$0
$996	$1,787	$0.00	10%	$996	$498	$893	$0.00	10%	$498
$1,787	$4,210	$79.10	12%	$1,787	$893	$2,105	$39.50	12%	$893
$4,210	$7,848	$369.86	22%	$4,210	$2,105	$3,924	$184.94	22%	$2,105
$7,848	$14,077	$1,170.22	24%	$7,848	$3,924	$7,038	$585.12	24%	$3,924
$14,077	$17,608	$2,665.18	32%	$14,077	$7,038	$8,804	$1,332.48	32%	$7,038
$17,608	$25,913	$3,795.10	35%	$17,608	$8,804	$12,957	$1,897.60	35%	$8,804
$25,913		$6,701.85	37%	$25,913	$12,957		$3,351.15	37%	$12,957
Single or Married Filing Separately					**Single or Married Filing Separately**				
$0	$498	$0.00	0%	$0	$0	$249	$0.00	0%	$0
$498	$893	$0.00	10%	$498	$249	$447	$0.00	10%	$249
$893	$2,105	$39.50	12%	$893	$447	$1,052	$19.80	12%	$447
$2,105	$3,924	$184.94	22%	$2,105	$1,052	$1,962	$92.40	22%	$1,052
$3,924	$7,038	$585.12	24%	$3,924	$1,962	$3,519	$292.60	24%	$1,962
$7,038	$8,804	$1,332.48	32%	$7,038	$3,519	$4,402	$666.28	32%	$3,519
$8,804	$21,263	$1,897.60	35%	$8,804	$4,402	$10,632	$948.84	35%	$4,402
$21,263		$6,258.25	37%	$21,263	$10,632		$3,129.34	37%	$10,632
Head of Household					**Head of Household**				
$0	$746	$0.00	0%	$0	$0	$373	$0.00	0%	$0
$746	$1,310	$0.00	10%	$746	$373	$655	$0.00	10%	$373
$1,310	$2,896	$56.40	12%	$1,310	$655	$1,448	$28.20	12%	$655
$2,896	$4,171	$246.72	22%	$2,896	$1,448	$2,086	$123.36	22%	$1,448
$4,171	$7,287	$527.22	24%	$4,171	$2,086	$3,643	$263.72	24%	$2,086
$7,287	$9,052	$1,275.06	32%	$7,287	$3,643	$4,526	$637.40	32%	$3,643
$9,052	$21,512	$1,839.86	35%	$9,052	$4,526	$10,756	$919.96	35%	$4,526
$21,512		$6,200.86	37%	$21,512	$10,756		$3,100.46	37%	$10,756

Source: Internal Revenue Service

Example #3

Annie Nguyen earns a $7,385 monthly salary, and has a filing status of married. Her 2015 W-4, which uses 3 withholding allowances, has not been changed. To calculate withholding, her employer uses manual wage bracket tables. In the monthly payroll period, married filing status table, with three allowances for a manual payroll with forms W-4 from 2019 or earlier, her monthly withholding is $594.

Income Tax Withholding: Employer Requirements, *continued*

Illustration 2.7: Wage bracket method withholding table for manual systems and Worksheet 3 (partial)

2022 Wage Bracket Method Tables for Manual Payroll Systems With Forms W-4 From 2019 or Earlier												
MONTHLY Payroll Period												
If the **Wage Amount** (line 1a) is		**MARRIED** Persons										
		And the number of allowances is:										
At least	But less than	0	1	2	3	4	5	6	7	8	9	10
		The Tentative Withholding Amount is:										
$6,285	$6,345	$594	$551	$508	$465	$422	$379	$336	$293	$250	$207	$165
$6,345	$6,405	$601	$558	$515	$472	$429	$386	$343	$300	$257	$214	$171
$6,405	$6,465	$608	$565	$522	$479	$436	$393	$350	$307	$264	$221	$178
$6,465	$6,525	$615	$572	$529	$486	$443	$400	$357	$314	$271	$228	$185
$6,525	$6,585	$622	$579	$536	$493	$450	$407	$364	$321	$278	$235	$192
$6,585	$6,645	$630	$587	$544	$501	$458	$415	$372	$329	$286	$243	$200
$6,645	$6,705	$637	$594	$551	$508	$465	$422	$379	$336	$293	$250	$207
$6,705	$6,765	$644	$601	$558	$515	$472	$429	$386	$343	$300	$257	$214
$6,765	$6,825	$651	$608	$565	$522	$479	$436	$393	$350	$307	$264	$221
$6,825	$6,885	$658	$615	$572	$529	$486	$443	$400	$357	$314	$271	$228
$6,885	$6,945	$666	$623	$580	$537	$494	$451	$408	$365	$322	$279	$236
$6,945	$7,005	$673	$630	$587	$544	$501	$458	$415	$372	$329	$286	$243
$7,005	$7,065	$680	$637	$594	$551	$508	$465	$422	$379	$336	$293	$250
$7,065	$7,125	$687	$644	$601	$558	$515	$472	$429	$386	$343	$300	$257
$7,125	$7,185	$694	$651	$608	$565	$522	$479	$436	$393	$350	$307	$264
$7,185	$7,245	$702	$659	$616	$573	$530	$487	$444	$401	$358	$315	$272
$7,245	$7,305	$709	$666	$623	$580	$537	$494	$451	$408	$365	$322	$279
$7,305	$7,365	$716	$673	$630	$587	$544	$501	$458	$415	$372	$329	$286
$7,365	$7,425	$723	$680	$637	$594	$551	$508	$465	$422	$379	$336	$293
$7,425	$7,485	$730	$687	$644	$601	$558	$515	$472	$429	$386	$343	$300
$7,485	$7,545	$738	$695	$652	$609	$566	$523	$480	$437	$394	$351	$308
$7,545	$7,605	$745	$702	$659	$616	$573	$530	$487	$444	$401	$358	$315
$7,605	$7,665	$752	$709	$666	$623	$580	$537	$494	$451	$408	$365	$322
$7,665	$7,725	$759	$716	$673	$630	$587	$544	$501	$458	$415	$372	$329
$7,725	$7,785	$766	$723	$680	$637	$594	$551	$508	$465	$422	$379	$336
$7,785	$7,845	$774	$731	$688	$645	$602	$559	$516	$473	$430	$387	$344
$7,845	$7,905	$781	$738	$695	$652	$609	$566	$523	$480	$437	$394	$351
$7,905	$7,965	$788	$745	$702	$659	$616	$573	$530	$487	$444	$401	$358
$7,965	$8,025	$795	$752	$709	$666	$623	$580	$537	$494	$451	$408	$365
$8,025	$8,085	$803	$759	$716	$673	$630	$587	$544	$501	$458	$415	$372
$8,085	$8,155	$818	$767	$724	$681	$638	$595	$552	$509	$466	$423	$380
$8,155	$8,225	$833	$776	$733	$690	$647	$604	$561	$518	$475	$432	$389

Source: Internal Revenue Service

2022 standard deduction amounts incorporated in the tables are:

- Married filing jointly: $25,900
- Head of household: $19,400
- Unmarried and married filing separately: $12,950

TIP

Income Tax Withholding: Employer Requirements, *continued*

Relief From Manual Calculations:

The Income Tax Withholding Assistant

The Income Tax Withholding Assistant is an online application provided by the IRS that is designed to help small business employers that calculate withholding manually. This tool can be used instead of completing individual worksheets. Employers that use automated systems do not need the Income Tax Withholding Assistant. The tool can be accessed by searching for the name (or at https://www.irs.gov/businesses/small-businesses-self-employed/income-tax-withholding-assistant-for-employers) and then clicking the download button on the page that appears (available until 2023). The following screen will appear with a step-by-step prompt:

Illustration 2.8: Income tax withholding assistant

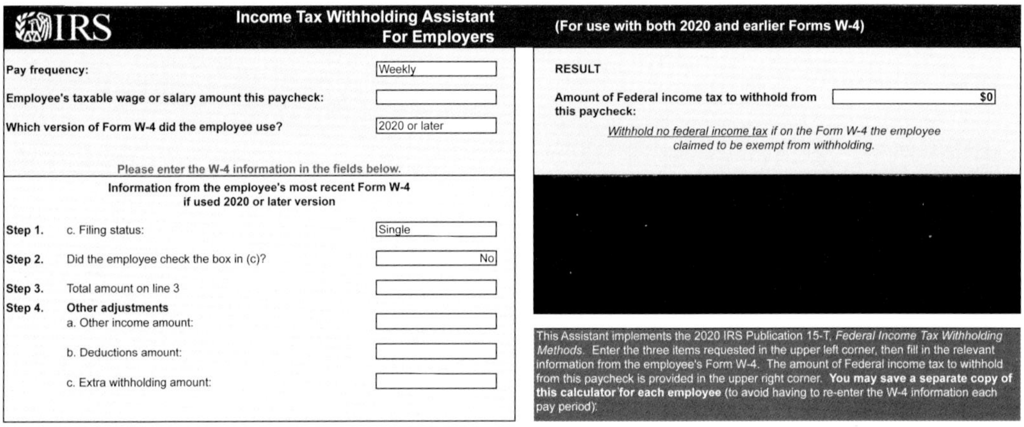

This is used to calculate withholding for each employee for whom the employer would otherwise use the tables in Publication 15-T. Each employee's completed calculation should be saved and filed. (Publication 15-T also provides an optional method to convert pre-2020 W-4s into equivalent current W-4s. It's easier to just use the tables.)

Withholding Ordering Rule

Sometimes tipped employees receive a very small wage in comparison to tips, both of which are taxable. If there are insufficient employee funds to deduct all employee taxes, then withhold in this order: 1) Regular wages/compensation. 2) Social Security /Medicare on tips 3) Income tax on tips. Continue collecting unpaid income tax until calendar year-end. If insufficient funds for Social Security/Medicare by the 10th of the month following the month of reported tips, they don't need to be collected. Report on line 9 of Form 941 (or line 6 of Form 944) and box 12, M, N on W-2. Employees are liable for their uncollectable taxes on tips; employee either pays employer or makes estimated tax payments.

Income Tax Withholding: Employer Requirements, *continued*

Withholding on Part-Year Earnings

For an employee who works only part of a year, either full-time or part-time, the employer has two choices:

- Calculate withholding in the normal manner as previously discussed.
- If the employee requests in writing to withhold tax by the "part-year employment method" to prevent over-withholding, then complete the procedure below. The request (in writing) must detail:
    - Last day of employment with previous employer
    - A declaration that the employee uses a calendar accounting method
    - A declaration that he or she expects no more than 245 days of continuous employment during the current calendar year (counting all days in the continuous period except layoffs more than 30 days).

Example: Mark Williams was last employed on September 14 in 2022. He begins employment with the new employer on November 4, 2022. Mark is paid weekly and earns $1,400 per week. His 2022 W-4 shows single with no adjustments or credits. The employer makes a manual payroll calculation. The tax withheld in the previous week was $16. For the second week ending November 18, the income tax withholding would be calculated as follows:

Step	Procedure	Example
1	Add current period wages to wages already paid in the current term of continuous employment by the same employer.	$1,400 + $1,400 = $2,800
2	Add the number of payroll periods in step 1 to the number of payroll periods from last employment to the beginning of current employment. To find this second amount, divide the days between the last day of the previous employment (or the last December 31, if later) by the number of days in the current payroll period.	2 + (50/7) = 9 (disregarding fractional periods)
3	Divide the step 1 amount by the total payroll periods calculated in step 2 (Average wages per period)	$2,800/9 = $311.11
4	Find the tax on step 3 using a withholding table for the appropriate filing status, period and W-4.	See Illustration 2.9 below: $6
5	Multiply Step 4 by total payroll periods from step 2.	9 × $6 = $54
6	Subtract from step 5 the tax already withheld in previous periods of the current continuous employment.	$54 – $16 = $38

continued ▶

Income Tax Withholding: Employer Requirements, *continued*

Illustration 2.9: Wage bracket method weekly withholding table for manual systems (partial)

2022 Wage Bracket Method Tables for Manual Payroll Systems with Forms W-4 From 2020 or Later
WEEKLY Payroll Period

If the **Adjusted Wage Amount** (line 1h) is		Married Filing Jointly		Head of Household		Single or Married Filing Separately	
		Standard withholding	Form W-4, Step 2, Checkbox withholding	Standard withholding	Form W-4, Step 2, Checkbox withholding	Standard withholding	Form W-4, Step 2, Checkbox withholding
At least	But less than			The Tentative Withholding Amount is:			
$0	$125	$0	$0	$0	$0	$0	$0
$125	$135	$0	$0	$0	$0	$0	$1
$135	$145	$0	$0	$0	$0	$0	$2
$145	$155	$0	$0	$0	$0	$0	$3
$155	$165	$0	$0	$0	$0	$0	$4
$165	$175	$0	$0	$0	$0	$0	$5
$175	$185	$0	$0	$0	$0	$0	$6
$185	$195	$0	$0	$0	$0	$0	$7
$195	$205	$0	$0	$0	$1	$0	$8
$205	$215	$0	$0	$0	$2	$0	$9
$215	$225	$0	$0	$0	$3	$0	$10
$225	$235	$0	$0	$0	$4	$0	$11
$235	$245	$0	$0	$0	$5	$0	$12
$245	$255	$0	$0	$0	$6	$0	$13
$255	$265	$0	$1	$0	$7	$1	$14
$265	$275	$0	$2	$0	$8	$2	$15
$275	$285	$0	$3	$0	$9	$3	$17
$285	$295	$0	$4	$0	$10	$4	$18
$295	$305	$0	$5	$0	$11	$5	$19
$305	$315	$0	$6	$0	$12	$6	$20
$315	$325	$0	$7	$0	$13	$7	$21
$325	$335	$0	$8	$0	$14	$8	$23
$335	$345	$0	$9	$0	$16	$9	$24
$345	$355	$0	$10	$0	$17	$10	$25
$355	$365	$0	$11	$0	$18	$11	$26
$365	$375	$0	$12	$0	$19	$12	$27
$375	$385	$0	$13	$1	$20	$13	$29
$385	$395	$0	$14	$2	$22	$14	$30
$395	$405	$0	$15	$3	$23	$15	$31
$405	$415	$0	$16	$4	$24	$16	$32
$415	$425	$0	$17	$5	$25	$17	$33
$425	$435	$0	$18	$6	$26	$18	$35
$435	$445	$0	$19	$7	$28	$19	$36
$445	$455	$0	$20	$8	$29	$20	$37
$455	$465	$0	$21	$9	$30	$21	$38
$465	$475	$0	$23	$10	$31	$23	$39
$475	$485	$0	$24	$11	$32	$24	$41
$485	$495	$0	$25	$12	$34	$25	$42
$495	$505	$0	$26	$13	$35	$26	$43
$505	$515	$1	$27	$14	$36	$27	$44
$515	$525	$2	$29	$15	$37	$29	$45
$525	$535	$3	$30	$16	$38	$30	$47
$535	$545	$4	$31	$17	$40	$31	$49
$545	$555	$5	$32	$18	$41	$32	$51
$555	$565	$6	$33	$19	$42	$33	$54
$565	$575	$7	$35	$20	$43	$35	$56
$575	$585	$8	$36	$21	$44	$36	$58
$585	$595	$9	$37	$22	$46	$37	$60
$595	$605	$10	$38	$23	$47	$38	$62
$605	$615	$11	$39	$24	$48	$39	$65
$615	$625	$12	$41	$25	$49	$41	$67
$625	$635	$13	$42	$26	$50	$42	$69
$635	$645	$14	$43	$27	$52	$43	$71
$645	$655	$15	$44	$28	$53	$44	$73
$655	$665	$16	$45	$29	$54	$45	$76
$665	$675	$17	$47	$30	$55	$47	$78
$675	$685	$18	$48	$31	$56	$48	$80
$685	$695	$19	$49	$32	$58	$49	$82
$695	$705	$20	$50	$34	$59	$50	$84
$705	$715	$21	$51	$35	$60	$51	$87
$715	$725	$22	$53	$36	$61	$53	$89
$725	$735	$23	$54	$37	$63	$54	$91
$735	$745	$24	$55	$38	$65	$55	$93
$745	$755	$25	$56	$40	$67	$56	$95
$755	$765	$26	$57	$41	$70	$57	$98

Source: Internal Revenue Service

Income Tax Withholding: Employer Requirements, *continued*

Withholding for Part-Time Employment	Part-time employment should not be confused with part-year employment. If someone works part-time for more than 245 days in a calendar year, withholding is not reduced for a shorter period of employment.
Withholding Based on Quarterly Average Estimated Wages	An employer may withhold income tax by estimating total quarterly gross wage earnings, including any necessary adjustments. The employer divides the total gross amount by the number of payroll periods in the quarter to determine average earnings per period, and calculates withholding based on this amount. If the withholding is not equal to the amount that should have been withheld based on actual earnings, a withholding adjustment will be necessary at some point during the quarter. This method is not available for tip earnings; however, a similar method is available for tip earnings.
Withholding Based on Cumulative Wages	When an employee's gross wages varies significantly during a year, the employee may want to prevent annual under-withholding or over-withholding by requesting the cumulative wages method of withholding. An employee must make the request in writing, the employee's payroll periods must remain constant during the year, and the method applies for the remainder of the calendar year.
	Example: John Taylor is married and files jointly, is paid monthly, and checked box 2c on Form W-4. He had adjusted gross wages of only $500 per month in January and February, but then earned $5,700 in March and $6,200 each month in April and May. In June, he requests that his employer use the cumulative wages withholding method for the rest of the year. His June adjusted gross wages are $6,100. His total withholding through May 31 using the wage bracket method was $2,186. The table below illustrates an employer's withholding calculation procedure.

Step	Procedure	Example
1	Determine the number of wage periods to-date, including the current period.	January–June = 6
2	Calculate the average wages per payroll period by dividing all wages to date by Step 1.	$25,200/6 = $4,200
3	Calculate the withholding on the amount in Step 2. (Here, the percentage method table is used.)	$85.60 + [($4,200 – $1,935) × .12] = $357.40
4	Multiply the withholding from Step 3 by number of Step 1 periods.	$357.40 × 6 = $2,144.40
5	Withholding for June: Subtract withholding to-date from the amount in Step 4. (Note: A negative result means over-withholding to-date and no withholding is required for the current period.)	$2,144.40 – $2,186 = No June withholding

continued ▶

Income Tax Withholding: Employer Requirements, *continued*

Illustration 2.10: Percentage method monthly withholding table for manual systems (partial)

2022 Percentage Method Tables for Manual Payroll Systems With Forms W-4 from 2020 or Later
MONTHLY Payroll Period

STANDARD Withholding Rate Schedules (Use these if the box in Step 2 of Form W-4 is **NOT** checked)					Form W-4, Step 2, Checkbox, Withholding Rate Schedules (Use these if the box in Step 2 of Form W-4 **IS** checked)				
If the Adjusted Wage Amount (line 1h) is:		The tentative		of the amount that the Adjusted Wage	If the Adjusted Wage Amount (line 1h) is:		The tentative		of the amount that the Adjusted Wage
At least—	But less than—	amount to withhold is:	Plus this percentage—	exceeds—	At least—	But less than—	amount to withhold is:	Plus this percentage—	exceeds—
A	B	C	D	E	A	B	C	D	E
Married Filing Jointly					**Married Filing Jointly**				
$0	$2,158	$0.00	0%	$0	$0	$1,079	$0.00	0%	$0
$2,158	$3,871	$0.00	10%	$2,158	$1,079	$1,935	$0.00	10%	$1,079
$3,871	$9,121	$171.30	12%	$3,871	$1,935	$4,560	$85.60	12%	$1,935
$9,121	$17,004	$801.30	22%	$9,121	$4,560	$8,502	$400.60	22%	$4,560
$17,004	$30,500	$2,535.56	24%	$17,004	$8,502	$15,250	$1,267.84	24%	$8,502
$30,500	$38,150	$5,774.60	32%	$30,500	$15,250	$19,075	$2,887.36	32%	$15,250
$38,150	$56,146	$8,222.60	35%	$38,150	$19,075	$28,073	$4,111.36	35%	$19,075
$56,146		$14,521.20	37%	$56,146	$28,073		$7,260.66	37%	$28,073
Single or Married Filing Separately					**Single or Married Filing Separately**				
$0	$1,079	$0.00	0%	$0	$0	$540	$0.00	0%	$0
$1,079	$1,935	$0.00	10%	$1,079	$540	$968	$0.00	10%	$540
$1,935	$4,560	$85.60	12%	$1,935	$968	$2,280	$42.80	12%	$968
$4,560	$8,502	$400.60	22%	$4,560	$2,280	$4,251	$200.24	22%	$2,280
$8,502	$15,250	$1,267.84	24%	$8,502	$4,251	$7,625	$633.86	24%	$4,251
$15,250	$19,075	$2,887.36	32%	$15,250	$7,625	$9,538	$1,443.62	32%	$7,625
$19,075	$46,071	$4,111.36	35%	$19,075	$9,538	$23,035	$2,055.78	35%	$9,538
$46,071		$13,559.96	37%	$46,071	$23,035		$6,779.73	37%	$23,035
Head of Household					**Head of Household**				
$0	$1,617	$0.00	0%	$0	$0	$808	$0.00	0%	$0
$1,617	$2,838	$0.00	10%	$1,617	$808	$1,419	$0.00	10%	$808
$2,838	$6,275	$122.10	12%	$2,838	$1,419	$3,138	$61.10	12%	$1,419
$6,275	$9,038	$534.54	22%	$6,275	$3,138	$4,519	$267.38	22%	$3,138
$9,038	$15,788	$1,142.40	24%	$9,038	$4,519	$7,894	$571.20	24%	$4,519
$15,788	$19,613	$2,762.40	32%	$15,788	$7,894	$9,806	$1,381.20	32%	$7,894
$19,613	$46,608	$3,986.40	35%	$19,613	$9,806	$23,304	$1,993.04	35%	$9,806
$46,608		$13,434.65	37%	$46,608	$23,304		$6,717.34	37%	$23,304

Source: Internal Revenue Service

Other Methods

The withholding methods discussed here are not exhaustive. Other methods are permitted as follows:

Any other methods and tables for withholding taxes can be used, as long as the amount of tax withheld is consistently about the same as it would be as discussed under the *Percentage Method* in Publication 15.

Withholding on Supplemental Payments

Supplemental payments are payments to employees that are not paid as part of regular pay. Examples include bonuses, commissions, overtime, awards, taxable fringe benefits, back pay, severance pay, tips treated as wages, vacation pay, accumulated sick pay, and employer payment of non-deductible moving expenses. Use the following table to determine withholding. Also see page 226 for "grossing up" a payment if the intent is that an employee receives a specified amount after withholding.

Income Tax Withholding: Employer Requirements, *continued*

Table 2.4: Supplemental Withholding Procedure

IF	THEN
Total supplemental payments exceed one million dollars during a calendar year,	withhold the excess (above one million) at the top marginal individual tax rate.
The payment(s) is (are) one million or less.	see the table below.

IF	THEN
The supplemental payment is combined with regular wages (not separately identified),	withhold income tax in the normal manner used for regular payments in the payroll period, based on the applicable method.
The supplemental payment is paid separately or identified separately from regular wages,	the employer can do either one below, provided that the employer withheld income tax on regular wages in the current year or the immediately preceding year: 1) Withhold 22% of the supplemental amount OR: 2) If the supplemental payment is made concurrently with regular wages, combine the two and withhold as a single payment in a regular payroll period. If there are no regular concurrent wages, combine the supplemental amount with regular wages paid or to be paid in the current period or previously paid in the preceding pay period, figure the withholding on the total, and subtract the tax already withheld or to be withheld on the regular wages. Withhold the remainder from the supplemental payment. Method "2" must be used if no income tax was withheld in the current year or immediately preceding calendar year.

Note: Supplemental wage and salary payments are also subject to FICA and FUTA taxes.

Example #1 William Watson is paid biweekly and earns gross pay of $2,800. He was last paid on March 31 and his next check will be April 14. In the first April payroll period, he received a $500 bonus that was paid separately but at the same time (concurrently) as his regular paycheck on April 14. William files using head of household status. He completed a W-4 in 2020 with only parts 1 and 5 completed, so there is no additional income or deductions or credits; therefore, his adjusted wage amount is also $2,800. His employer uses the manual wage bracket withholding method. Because the payment was concurrent with his regular April paycheck, the employer calculates withholding as a single payment in a regular payroll period. The withholding amount is $337 on the combined amount of ($2,800 + $500 = $3,300).

Income Tax Withholding: Employer Requirements, *continued*

Illustration 2.11: Wage bracket method biweekly withholding table for manual systems (partial)

2022 Wage Bracket Method Tables for Manual Payroll Systems with Forms W-4 From 2020 or Later BIWEEKLY Payroll Period							
If the **Adjusted Wage Amount** (line 1h) is		Married Filing Jointly		Head of Household		Single or Married Filing Separately	
		Standard withholding	Form W-4, Step 2, Checkbox withholding	Standard withholding	Form W-4, Step 2, Checkbox withholding	Standard withholding	Form W-4, Step 2, Checkbox withholding
At least	But less than	The Tentative Withholding Amount is:					
$2,545	$2,570	$172	$284	$206	$377	$284	$435
$2,570	$2,595	$175	$290	$209	$383	$290	$441
$2,595	$2,620	$178	$295	$212	$389	$295	$447
$2,620	$2,645	$181	$301	$215	$395	$301	$453
$2,645	$2,670	$184	$306	$218	$401	$306	$459
$2,670	$2,695	$187	$312	$221	$407	$312	$465
$2,695	$2,720	$190	$317	$224	$413	$317	$471
$2,720	$2,745	$193	$323	$227	$419	$323	$477
$2,745	$2,770	$196	$328	$230	$425	$328	$483
$2,770	$2,795	$199	$334	$233	$431	$334	$489
$2,795	$2,820	$202	$339	$236	$437	$339	$495
$2,820	$2,845	$205	$345	$239	$443	$345	$501
$2,845	$2,870	$208	$350	$242	$449	$350	$507
$2,870	$2,895	$211	$356	$245	$455	$356	$513
$2,895	$2,920	$214	$361	$249	$461	$361	$519
$2,920	$2,945	$217	$367	$255	$467	$367	$525
$2,945	$2,970	$220	$372	$260	$473	$372	$531
$2,970	$2,995	$223	$378	$266	$479	$378	$537
$2,995	$3,020	$226	$383	$271	$485	$383	$543
$3,020	$3,045	$229	$389	$277	$491	$389	$549
$3,045	$3,070	$232	$394	$282	$497	$394	$555
$3,070	$3,095	$235	$400	$288	$503	$400	$561
$3,095	$3,120	$238	$405	$293	$509	$405	$567
$3,120	$3,145	$241	$411	$299	$515	$411	$573
$3,145	$3,170	$244	$416	$304	$521	$416	$579
$3,170	$3,195	$247	$422	$310	$527	$422	$585
$3,195	$3,220	$250	$427	$315	$533	$427	$591
$3,220	$3,245	$253	$433	$321	$539	$433	$597
$3,245	$3,270	$256	$438	$326	$545	$438	$603
$3,270	$3,295	$259	$444	$332	$551	$444	$609
$3,295	$3,320	$262	$449	$337	$557	$449	$615
$3,320	$3,345	$265	$455	$343	$563	$455	$621
$3,345	$3,370	$268	$460	$348	$569	$460	$627
$3,370	$3,395	$271	$466	$354	$575	$466	$633
$3,395	$3,420	$274	$471	$359	$581	$471	$639
$3,420	$3,445	$277	$477	$365	$587	$477	$645
$3,445	$3,470	$280	$482	$370	$593	$482	$651
$3,470	$3,495	$283	$488	$376	$599	$488	$657
$3,495	$3,520	$286	$493	$381	$605	$493	$663
$3,520	$3,545	$289	$499	$387	$611	$499	$671
$3,545	$3,570	$292	$504	$392	$617	$504	$679
$3,570	$3,595	$295	$510	$398	$623	$510	$687
$3,595	$3,620	$298	$515	$403	$629	$515	$695
$3,620	$3,645	$301	$521	$409	$635	$521	$703
$3,645	$3,670	$304	$526	$414	$642	$526	$711
$3,670	$3,695	$307	$532	$420	$650	$532	$719
$3,695	$3,720	$310	$537	$425	$658	$537	$727
$3,720	$3,745	$313	$543	$431	$666	$543	$735
$3,745	$3,770	$316	$548	$436	$674	$548	$743
$3,770	$3,795	$319	$554	$442	$682	$554	$751
$3,795	$3,820	$322	$559	$447	$690	$559	$759

Example #2

Assume the same facts as in Example #1 except that William received the supplemental payment on April 5, which is not a payment that is concurrent with a regular paycheck. The employer can add the $500 bonus to either the prior March 31 regular gross pay amount or the current period April 14 amount (In this example they are the same at $2,800.), before calculating the tax. Assume that the employer chooses the March 31 payment, on which $243 of federal income tax was withheld. The withholding for the supplemental payment is is $337 – $243 = $94.

Example #3

Assume the same facts as in Example #1 except that the employer withholds at a flat 22% rate. Withholding for the supplemental payment is $500 × .22 = $110.

Backup Withholding

Income tax backup withholding is a 24% rate and required when: 1) Taxpayer fails to provide a correct TIN to the payor, or 2) The payor receives a notice from the IRS to begin backup withholding. It applies to rents, independent contractor payments, commissions, royalties, gambling winnings, interest and dividends, broker payments, 3rd-party network transactions, and certain other payment types. Withholding for these payment types are reported annually on forms 1099 (page 252) that include withholding and on Form 945.

Income Tax Withholding: Employer Requirements, *continued*

State/Local Requirements	States and localities have different requirements, but the methods are similar to federal. Search online by name for details.
Withholding on Tips	Generally required as with federal taxes. Employers are required to withhold both income tax and FICA taxes on employees' net cash tips, received directly or indirectly, reported by employees on Form 4070 or equivalent, as well as on their wages. If an employee reports tips and also earns wages, the amounts are combined for income tax withholding calculation. Withholding on allocated tips is not required.
	Wages for tipped employees are often minimal. As a result, when an employee receives a paycheck for wages, the withholding will be calculated on both reported tips plus wages; however, because the wages are a small amount, they may not be sufficient to cover the required withholding. In this case, the withholding shortfall carries over to subsequent payroll periods. The employer is required to apply withholding in a specific order. See page 124 for a discussion of the withholding ordering rule.
	If this situation occurs, the employer should notify the employee that to avoid year-end underpayment and tax penalties he or she can: 1) Give the employer cash in order to make the additional withholding payments, or 2) Make his or her own estimated tax payments using Form 1040-ES.
Other Recurring Income	Withholding applies to more than just salary and wages. It also applies to recurring taxable income related to employees: pensions, annuities, and other deferred compensation income. A recipient should submit a Form W-4P to designate the amount, if any, of withholding on this type of recurring income. If a W-4P is not submitted, withholding should automatically be made based on a filing status of married with three allowances. A W-4P remains in effect until the recipient revokes or changes it. Finally, if a person submits an incorrect W-4P or fails to submit a W-4, withholding status is single, with no allowances.

TIP

For non-employee payments, how does a business obtain a taxpayer identification number (called a "TIN") as an alternative to 24% backup withholding? The business requests that a Form W-9 (see Illustration 2.12) be completed by the party being paid by the business. A W-9 request is a valid request only for non-employee income. For non-resident aliens or foreign businesses, use a Form W-8 (various types depending on entity). Note: for persons ineligible for a social security number, an individual uses Form W-7 to obtain an Individual Tax Identification Number (called an "ITIN") used only for tax filing and other identification, but not withholding.

continued   ▶

Income Tax Withholding: Employer Requirements, *continued*

Illustration 2.12: Form W-9

Form W-9
(Rev. October 2018)
Department of the Treasury
Internal Revenue Service

Request for Taxpayer Identification Number and Certification

▶ Go to *www.irs.gov/FormW9* for instructions and the latest information.

Give Form to the requester. Do not send to the IRS.

Print or type. **See Specific Instructions on page 3.**

1 Name (as shown on your income tax return). Name is required on this line; do not leave this line blank.

2 Business name/disregarded entity name, if different from above

3 Check appropriate box for federal tax classification of the person whose name is entered on line 1. Check only **one** of the following seven boxes.

☐ Individual/sole proprietor or single-member LLC ☐ C Corporation ☐ S Corporation ☐ Partnership ☐ Trust/estate

☐ Limited liability company. Enter the tax classification (C=C corporation, S=S corporation, P=Partnership) ▶ _____

Note: Check the appropriate box in the line above for the tax classification of the single-member owner. Do not check LLC if the LLC is classified as a single-member LLC that is disregarded from the owner unless the owner of the LLC is another LLC that is **not** disregarded from the owner for U.S. federal tax purposes. Otherwise, a single-member LLC that is disregarded from the owner should check the appropriate box for the tax classification of its owner.

☐ Other (see instructions) ▶

4 Exemptions (codes apply only to certain entities, not individuals; see instructions on page 3):

Exempt payee code (if any) _____

Exemption from FATCA reporting code (if any) _____

(Applies to accounts maintained outside the U.S.)

5 Address (number, street, and apt. or suite no.) See instructions.

Requester's name and address (optional)

6 City, state, and ZIP code

7 List account number(s) here (optional)

Part I | **Taxpayer Identification Number (TIN)**

Enter your TIN in the appropriate box. The TIN provided must match the name given on line 1 to avoid backup withholding. For individuals, this is generally your social security number (SSN). However, for a resident alien, sole proprietor, or disregarded entity, see the instructions for Part I, later. For other entities, it is your employer identification number (EIN). If you do not have a number, see *How to get a TIN,* later.

Note: If the account is in more than one name, see the instructions for line 1. Also see *What Name and Number To Give the Requester* for guidelines on whose number to enter.

Social security number

☐☐☐ – ☐☐ – ☐☐☐☐

or

Employer identification number

☐☐ – ☐☐☐☐☐☐☐

Part II | **Certification**

Under penalties of perjury, I certify that:

1. The number shown on this form is my correct taxpayer identification number (or I am waiting for a number to be issued to me); and

2. I am not subject to backup withholding because: (a) I am exempt from backup withholding, or (b) I have not been notified by the Internal Revenue Service (IRS) that I am subject to backup withholding as a result of a failure to report all interest or dividends, or (c) the IRS has notified me that I am no longer subject to backup withholding; and

3. I am a U.S. citizen or other U.S. person (defined below); and

4. The FATCA code(s) entered on this form (if any) indicating that I am exempt from FATCA reporting is correct.

Certification instructions. You must cross out item 2 above if you have been notified by the IRS that you are currently subject to backup withholding because you have failed to report all interest and dividends on your tax return. For real estate transactions, item 2 does not apply. For mortgage interest paid, acquisition or abandonment of secured property, cancellation of debt, contributions to an individual retirement arrangement (IRA), and generally, payments other than interest and dividends, you are not required to sign the certification, but you must provide your correct TIN. See the instructions for Part II, later.

Sign Here | Signature of U.S. person ▶

Date ▶

General Instructions

Section references are to the Internal Revenue Code unless otherwise noted.

Future developments. For the latest information about developments related to Form W-9 and its instructions, such as legislation enacted after they were published, go to *www.irs.gov/FormW9*.

Purpose of Form

An individual or entity (Form W-9 requester) who is required to file an information return with the IRS must obtain your correct taxpayer identification number (TIN) which may be your social security number (SSN), individual taxpayer identification number (ITIN), adoption taxpayer identification number (ATIN), or employer identification number (EIN), to report on an information return the amount paid to you, or other amount reportable on an information return. Examples of information returns include, but are not limited to, the following.

• Form 1099-INT (interest earned or paid)

• Form 1099-DIV (dividends, including those from stocks or mutual funds)

• Form 1099-MISC (various types of income, prizes, awards, or gross proceeds)

• Form 1099-B (stock or mutual fund sales and certain other transactions by brokers)

• Form 1099-S (proceeds from real estate transactions)

• Form 1099-K (merchant card and third party network transactions)

• Form 1098 (home mortgage interest), 1098-E (student loan interest), 1098-T (tuition)

• Form 1099-C (canceled debt)

• Form 1099-A (acquisition or abandonment of secured property)

Use Form W-9 only if you are a U.S. person (including a resident alien), to provide your correct TIN.

If you do not return Form W-9 to the requester with a TIN, you might be subject to backup withholding. See What is backup withholding, *later.*

Source: Internal Revenue Service

Over or Under Withholding

Over Withholding   Excessive withholding of income tax usually results in an employee receiving a refund when the annual federal income tax Form 1040 (and in some cases, state) is filed. This is less than optimal for an employee because not only has there been less cash available during the year for purchases or for investments, but the employee also has made an interest-free loan to the government. The issue can be corrected by the employee revising Form W-4 for the employer, using more deductions or possibly credits to reduce withholding.

However, "excessive" withholding (following Form W-4) is not the same as employer over withholding, which is withholding more than is correct for an employee's Form W-4 or other IRS rules. To correct over withholding, an employer uses Form 941-X (or 943–X / 944-X / 945–X for those returns) for each quarter previously filed needing a correction within the current calendar year in which the wages were paid. An employer can either claim a refund or a credit for future payments; however, a refund must be given to the employee either through a payment or reduced withholding. The employer can receive only a credit adjustment (not a refund) for 941 et al. forms filed in a prior year. The forms have detailed filing instructions. If an error is found after W-2s are filed, Form W-2c should be filed with correct earnings and withholding.

Under Withholding   By federal law, an employer is required to both withhold and remit the correct employee income tax. If an employer discovers that too little was withheld and deposited, the employer should check the need to increase withholding in future paychecks in the current year. If there are employer errors, use a 941-X (or 943–X / 944-X / 945–X for those returns) for a quarter previously filed needing a correction within the current calendar year in which the wages were paid. The forms have detailed instructions on how to file. If errors are discovered after W-2s are filed, a Form W-2c also should be filed that shows the correct taxable earnings and withholding.

If an employer willfully under withholds or fails to withhold income taxes and does not pay them to the government, serious penalties, including criminal, can apply to the employer, including to any and all individuals responsible for withholding. This does not affect an employee's right to claim credit for actually withheld tax, even if it was not remitted by the employer. As well as not remitted withholding, the IRS also will seek to recover from the employer the amounts not withheld or under withheld; it is the employer's duty to withhold. However, despite inadequate income tax withholding, payment of correct annual income tax is still the employee's responsibility. (This does not prevent penalties and interest from being assessed against the employer.) The IRS provides an employee assistance number at 1-800-829-1040.

Employer Payroll Tax Expenses

Overview

Summary and Types

In addition to gross pay expense, employers also incur a second type of payroll expense: employer payroll taxes. These kinds of payroll taxes apply only to an employer and add to an employer's total employment costs. Employer payroll taxes are assessed on a calendar-year basis. The types of employer payroll tax expenses are:

- Employer Social Security taxes
- Federal and state unemployment taxes: "FUTA": Federal Unemployment Tax Act and "SUTA": State Unemployment Tax Act
- Other state and local payroll taxes

These are taxes paid only by an employer; they should not be confused with payroll taxes that an employee pays and that are withheld from an employee's gross pay.

Social Security Tax (FICA)

Employer Matching

As indicated in Part 1, Social Security Tax (we refer to as "FICA" for the OASDI and Medicare components) is paid both by employee and employer. The amounts are equal; in other words, an employer matches the tax paid by an employee. An exception to the matching requirement is the .9% additional Medicare tax on high-income employees. Only the employee pays this tax; it is *not* matched the employer.

The OASDI and Medicare tax calculations were discussed on pages 94–102.

Unemployment Taxes

Overview

Both federal and state authorities have passed unemployment tax laws. At the federal level, the Federal Unemployment Tax Act (FUTA) was created by Congress in 1939. This law, imposed only on employers, is intended to ensure unemployment benefits to workers who lose jobs even though the workers are able and qualified. The annual FUTA wage base is currently $7,000 of gross pay (per employee) and the FUTA tax rate is 6%. However, the law allows a 5.4% credit against the FUTA tax for employers that pay state unemployment tax. (See below). All states currently impose unemployment taxes, so the effective federal rate therefore is generally .6%, subject to certain exceptions (See below). The .6%

continued ▶

Unemployment Taxes, *continued*

Overview, Continued	tax goes to the federal unemployment trust fund that is used to cover administrate expenses of federal and state unemployment programs and to make loans to states whose unemployment insurance funds have become depleted. §501(c)(3) non-profits are exempt from FUTA.
Employers Covered by FUTA	The general definition of "employer" for FUTA purposes is the same as we have previously discussed (See page 18). However, FUTA also has three specific tests for employers to determine if they are "FUTA employers"; that is, responsible for meeting FUTA requirements. An employer qualifies if any of the below apply:

- **General test**: The employer has paid wages of $1,500 or more in any calendar quarter during the current or preceding year to employees who are not farmworkers or household workers, or

  The employer had one or more employees for at least some part of a day in any 20 or more different calendar weeks (7 consecutive days beginning on Sunday) in the current or preceding year. The employees can be the same or different persons and they can be full time, part-time or seasonal.
- **Household employer test**: At least $1,000 was paid to household employees in any calendar quarter in the current year or preceding year. A "household employee" for this purpose is an employee who performs domestic services work such as cooking, cleaning, gardening, caretaking, etc. in a private home, college club, fraternity, or sorority.
- **Farmworker employer test**: 1) The employer paid at least $20,000 to farmworkers during any calendar quarter in the current year or preceding year, or 2) The employer employed 10 or more farmworkers during at least some part of a day during any 20 or more different calendar weeks in the current year or preceding year.

Upon satisfying a "FUTA employer" test, an employer retains that status for FUTA purposes during the entire calendar year in which the test was satisfied. Check state unemployment tax requirements.

Example: FUTA and SUTA Calculation Procedure	Assume that a business has three employees: John, Bill, and Mary. From January 1 to March 31 John had total gross pay of $5,100, Bill had $6,500 and Mary had $7,200. John's April gross pay is $1,700, Bill's is $1,700 and Mary's April gross pay is $3,150. The table below shows the three calculation steps to calculate FUTA and state unemployment tax (SUTA) for the April payroll. The SUTA rate is 5.4% on the first $7,000 of wages and the FUTA wage base is $7,000.

continued ▶

Unemployment Taxes, *continued*

Step 1

For each employee, subtract the cumulative gross pay from the wage base.
IF the result is **zero or positive**, cumulative gross pay is still below the annual limit, so all of the current gross pay is taxable. Go to Step 3. **IF** the result is **negative**, cumulative gross pay has exceeded the limit and this excess is not taxable. Some or all of the current gross pay is excluded. Go to Step 2.

John		Bill	
Wage base	$7,000	Wage base	$7,000
Cumulative gross pay	6,800	Cumulative gross pay	8,200
Go to Step 3	$ 200	Go to Step 2	$ (1,200)

Mary	
Wage base	$7,000
Cumulative gross pay	10,350
Go to Step 2	$ (3,350)

Step 2

Offset the negative amount (the amount excluded) against the current gross pay to find the taxable portion of the current gross pay (but not less than zero). Then go to Step 3.

FUTA	SUTA
John: current wages all taxable	John: current wages all taxable
Bill: $1,700 – $1,200 = $500 taxable	Bill: $1,700 – $1,200 = $500 taxable
Mary: $3,150– $3,350 = $0 taxable	Mary: $3,150– $3,350 = $0 taxable

Step 3

Multiply the taxable portion of the current gross pay times the tax rate, and add the results.

FUTA		SUTA	
John: $1,700 × .006 =	$10.20	John: $1,700 × .054 =	$91.80
Bill: $500 × .006 =	$ 3.00	Bill: $500 × .054 =	$27.00
Mary: $0 × .006 =	– $0 –	Mary: $0 × .054 =	– $0 –
Total FUTA	$13.20	Total SUTA	$118.80

Employees Covered by FUTA

The definition of "employee" for FUTA purposes is essentially the same as we have previously discussed; that is, for FUTA purposes most workers are considered employees based on common law. However, FUTA expands the definition of "employee" to include the following:

- An agent or commission driver. Duties are to deliver food, beverages (other than milk), laundry, or dry cleaning for the provider of these items.

continued ▶

Unemployment Taxes, *continued*

Employees Covered by FUTA, Continued	■ A traveling salesperson who works full time for one firm or person, taking orders for merchandise for resale or supplies for use in the customer's business. Additional incidental part-time work does change the worker's status.

Notice that these are the same as two of the four statutory employee categories under FICA. The other two categories of life insurance sales persons and home workers (not the same thing as domestic/household employees) are not included for FUTA.

FUTA Wages	As with FICA, "wages" is a general term that means any form of earned compensation including tips, unless specifically exempt by law.
Payments Exempt From FUTA	FUTA exempts specific payment categories. The table below shows common employment categories and types of payments that are exempt from FUTA.

Table 2.5: Payments Exempt From FUTA Tax

Exempt Item	Description
Achievement Awards	Exempt up to $1,600 for qualified awards and $400 for non-qualified awards for specified items. See Part V discussion.
Advances to Employees	Business-related expenses paid by an employee under an accountable plan that includes advances, reimbursements, and repayments of excess are exempt. See publications 535 and 463 and Part V.
Agricultural Labor	Farmworkers may or may not be exempt. An employer of agricultural employees must pay tax under FUTA if: ■ The employer paid cash wages of $20,000 or more to farmworkers in any calendar quarter in the current or preceding year, OR ■ The employer employed at least 10 farmworkers for part of at least one day during any 20 or more different calendar weeks during the current of preceding calendar year. The above requirements do not apply to exempt services from family members.
Athletic Facilities	Generally exempt if mostly used by employees. See discussion in Part V.
Deceased Worker	Taxable for wages paid in year of death; exempt for wages paid to estate after calendar year of worker's death.
De minimis (minimal) benefits	Exempt
Dependent Care Assistance	Employer payments to employees or by third parties for dependent care under a qualified dependent care assistance program and/or the value of employer-maintained dependent care facilities use to a maximum of $5,000 ($2,500 married filing separately) are exempt.

continued ▶

Unemployment Taxes, *continued*

Table 2.5: Payments Exempt From FUTA Tax, *continued*

Exempt Item	Description
Disabled Worker: Sick Pay/ Disability Pay	Taxable for a period: when subject to income tax, also subject to FUTA during the first six months after the day the employee became disabled, and exempt when not subject to income tax. Other specified FUTA exempt payments: 1) Payments received by employee's estate or beneficiary after the calendar year of the employee's death aren't taxable. 2) Payments received on or after an employee's death or disability retirement according to a separate definite sick pay plan are not subject to FUTA tax except for accrued compensation. 3) Payments received more than six months after the last calendar month in which the employee worked 4) Payments attributable to employee contributions made with after-tax dollars are exempt. Also see Part V.
Education	Annual payments up to $5,250 made by an employer under an education assistance plan to maintain or improve employee job skills are exempt to both active and prior employees. Undergraduate and graduate (if teaching or performing research) tuition reduction by an educational institution is also generally exempt.
Emergency Workers	Exempt
Employee Benefits ("Fringe Benefits")	Many employer-provided employee benefits are designated as "qualified" and are not subject to unemployment tax. See Part V on employee benefits.
Employee Business Expense Reimbursement	Exempt per government rates and guidelines if under an accountable plan.
Employee Discounts	Subject to certain limitations, employer discounts on property other than real estate, stocks, and bonds purchased by employees are exempt.
Family Employee	1) Child employed by parent: exempt under age 21 if work is for a sole proprietorship or partnership is which each partner is a parent 2) Parent employed by child: exempt 3) Spouse employed by spouse: exempt if services are *not* in a trade or business
Foreign Affiliates	Foreign affiliates of American employers are exempt.
Government Employer	Exempt (including public schools)
Group term life insurance	Exempt

continued ▶

Unemployment Taxes, *continued*

Table 2.5: Payments Exempt From FUTA Tax, *continued*

Exempt Item	Description
Health/Medical/ Accident Insurance	Employer contributions are exempt.
Health Savings Accounts	Employer payments under qualified plans exempt up to contribution limits.
Homeworker	Exempt if a statutory employee.
Hospital Employee	Exempt
Household Employee	▪ Domestic service in private homes: exempt if paid less than $1,000 in cash in any quarter in the current or preceding year; spouse, child under 21, and parent are exempt. ▪ Domestic service in college clubs, fraternities, and sororities exempt if paid less than $1,000 in cash in any quarter in the current or preceding year Note that a household employee is not someone who works in your trade or business or is a homeworker, or who is an independent contractor with his/her own business.
Meals and Lodging	The value of meals provided for the convenience of the employer are generally exempt if furnished on employer's business premises. Lodging also must be a condition of employment. Occasional light meals (coffee, snacks, etc.) are exempt. See Part V discussion of meals and lodging.
Military Service Differential Pay	The amount paid by an employer for the difference between military pay for employees called to active service exceeding 30 days and regular employee compensation is exempt. (This applies to FUTA and FICA but not income tax.)
Non-profit organizations	Non-profits qualifying under §501(c)(3) exempt from income tax are exempt from FUTA (but not SUTA, unless they self-insure, depending on the state).
Newspaper Carriers And Vendors	Exempt based on same rules as for income tax withholding
No-Additional Cost Services	Employer services provided to employees when no substantial additional cost will be incurred because of excess capacity are exempt.
Railroad Retirement Act	Exempt for employees subject to this act

continued ▶

Unemployment Taxes, *continued*

Table 2.5: Payments Exempt From FUTA Tax, *continued*

Exempt Item	Description
Retirement Planning Services	Exempt
Retirement Plans	1) Exempt for employer contributions to a qualified plan but not under a SIMPLE or SEP salary reduction agreement or employee elective contributions. 2) Exempt for distributions from qualified retirement plans. Also see Part V.
Sick Pay	See Disabled Worker
Statutory Employees and Non-Employees	Exempt
Students Enrolled And Regularly Attending Classes	1) Exempt when performing services for a school, college, or university–limited exceptions may apply when receiving academic credit combined with instruction and work experience. 2) Student nurses performing part-time services at hospitals for nominal charge as part of training are exempt. 3) Students employed by an organized camp are exempt.
Transportation (commuting) benefits	Exempt up to exclusion limits
Workers' Compensation	Employer payments for workers' compensation insurance, either into state funds or by private insurance contract, are exempt. Workers' compensation benefit payments are also exempt.
Working Condition Benefits	Working condition benefits are services or property provided to an employee by an employer so that the employee is able to perform his or her duties are exempt. Examples are company-provided car, cell phone, computers, and training.

Unemployment Taxes, *continued*

Overview:
State
Unemployment
Tax

As previously discussed, individual states are the direct payers of unemployment benefits to their residents.

Employers pay state unemployment insurance (usually referred to as "SUTA", for "State Unemployment Tax Act" or "SUI" for "State Unemployment Insurance"), which assesses a tax on at least the first $7,000 of wages (a "wage base") that a worker has received during a calendar year; this tax is also paid by the employer*, as is FUTA. Most states have a higher wage base. The wage base applies to each employee for each employer.

All states maintain an unemployment compensation experience rating system. This means that a state maintains a record of each employer's contributions* into the state unemployment compensation fund (maintained in an account with the U.S. Treasury) as well as the fund's expenditures on behalf of employees from the employer. Employers with stable employment that requires lower fund expenditures are charged a lower percentage tax rate, and vice versa. In some states employers can make voluntary contributions to increase their fund balances and thereby reduce their tax rates. Nonprofit, religious, educational and government employers are either exempt or can self-insure, depending on the organization.

---

*Three states–Alaska, New Jersey, and Pennsylvania–also require SUTA contributions from employees.

Determining the
FUTA Credit

An employer can receive up to a maximum of 5.4% (90% × 6%) credit against the 6% FUTA tax. This is a fixed percentage (except for Title XII advances–see below). If an employer pays a lower SUTA rate than 5.4% into a state fund (because stability of employment history lowers the state rate), the 5.4% will not decrease (except for a credit reduction state – below). Likewise, if an employer pays a higher SUTA rate to a state than 5.4%, the FUTA 5.4% credit does not increase.

The $7,000 wage base is used for the FUTA calculation; however, most states have a higher wage base for calculating contributions into their state unemployment insurance funds. Even though these higher bases will often result in a higher dollar tax (than using a $7,000 base) at the state rate, this does not affect the FUTA 5.4% credit or $7,000 wage base.

Title XII
Advances and
FUTA Credit
Reduction

In the event that a state does not have sufficient funds to make unemployment benefit payments to workers, it can borrow the funds from the federal government trust fund. The funds loaned to a state for this purpose are called "Title XII advances", from Title XII (12) of the Social Security Act.

continued ▶

Unemployment Taxes, *continued*

Title XII Advances and FUTA Credit Reduction, Continued

In general, a state has until November 10 of the second year following the loan to repay the borrowed funds; if it does not, beginning in the second year after the loan, the FUTA tax credit is reduced by .3% per year, subject to a maximum reduction depending on state solvency (a "credit reduction state"). In this way, the loan funds are indirectly repaid through a higher effective FUTA tax rate on employers in the state.

SUTA Wages

For the purpose of SUTA, "wages" are for the most part defined the same as for FUTA. However, individual states do have variations and may consider certain additional activities as taxable wages and exempt other activities. Review state guidelines.

Interstate Employees: SUTA

In some situations an employee will work in more than one state for the same employer. Many states conform to a reciprocal system that provides the criteria to determine to which state unemployment tax should apply. Otherwise, (and including any disability withholding) the criteria as applied in sequence if a prior test is not determinative, are:

1) Where the work primarily, not incidentally, takes place
2) The base of operations to which the employee regularly begins and ends his/her work and to which he/she reports.
3) The location from which directions are issued.
4) The employee's state of residence.

Interstate Employees: Income Tax

The basic rule is to withhold tax for the state in which an employee performs work. However, some states have reciprocity agreements with other states to avoid dual income taxation (which also occurs). Relief often takes the form of credits for other state taxes or withholding allocation rules based on location work days. It is essential that a business contact non-resident employee state tax agencies to determine rules, especially if any business activity in another state (called "nexus") takes place.

TIP

What is your true payroll cost? Consider the following: Gross wages (includes bonuses, commissions, overtime, sick leave, vacation and compensatory time), employer payroll taxes, workers' compensation, and fringe benefits. Ancillary costs would include payroll services and software and–hopefully not–penalties.

TIP

SUTA "Dumping"? Some dishonest employers obtain multiple state SUTA employer experience numbers or buy a business with a low experience number. (Lower employee turnover is associated with a low experience number, and therefore the SUTA tax rate is lower.) Then high-turnover employees are moved to the lower rate business. Serious penalties apply.

Benefits Expenses

Employee Benefits Overview

Definition

Employee benefits are often called "fringe benefits". A benefit/fringe benefit is a form of employee compensation from an employer that is in addition to wages for the services performed by an employee. Benefits can be services or property.

Overview

The dollar value consequences of providing employee benefits appear when a payroll is recorded; however, before that occurs an employer should be aware of the variety of benefit choices, their financial effects, and qualification requirements. In a larger business, a human resources staff manages benefits and answers employee questions. Businesses also can use professional benefits administrators to help. In addition to the dollar cost, several important tax-related issues arise from benefits choices. They are: 1) What amount is taxable to the employee? 2) What amount is a tax deduction for the employer? 3) What should be the recordable amount. 4) When should a benefit be recognized (recorded)? Also see Publication 15-B.

General Rule: Employee Taxable Compensation

Federal tax law (the Internal Revenue Code) both generally and specifically provides guidance for the taxation of employee benefits. The general rule is that a benefit is taxable compensation to an employee unless: 1) the benefit is of a type or is based on a qualified plan specifically excluded from tax in the Internal Revenue Code or, 2) the employee pays for the benefit. Specifically identified benefits can be fully exempt, exempt up to a designated limit, or some portion exempt. (Amounts shown here are as of 2022.) The value of a benefit received in excess of what a recipient pays to obtain it is taxable unless otherwise excluded. The qualified benefit types that the Internal Revenue Code specifically identifies are listed and discussed below.

General Rule: Employer Expense Deduction

The general rule for employers (other than non-profit) is that employee expenses are tax-deductible operating expenses because the tax law considers these expenditures to be ordinary and necessary for the operation of a business. However, the Internal Revenue Code also identifies some types of benefit expenses that are not tax deductible or are only partially deductible by an employer (even though the expenses may be fully deductible for financial accounting purposes).

General Rule: Valuation

The general rule for recording the value (dollar amount) of a benefit is to use the fair market value of the benefit that would be paid to a 3rd party in an arm's-length transaction. In most cases this is easy to determine when cash is involved; however, other types of property such as stock benefits can be more subjective and take longer to value. In some cases the IRS may set valuation guidelines such as cents-per-mile vehicle use or group-term life insurance rates.

Employee Benefits Overview, *continued*

General Rule: When to Report Taxable Benefits

Benefits are normally reported as paid in the calendar year in which a benefit is received. An employer usually adds taxable benefits to regular wages on Form W-2 and calculates withholding based on this total. Taxable benefits also can be reported as supplemental wages (see supplemental wages) and withheld per those rules. The reasonably estimated value of non-cash taxable benefits can be reported as per pay period, or any other interval without a fixed pattern, but at least once per calendar year. A special rule allows non-cash taxable benefits within the last two calendar months to be reported in the next 10 months of the following calendar year, if applied consistently. Cash benefits are reported and withheld in the period paid.

Benefits Non-Discrimination

Non-Discrimination Rules

Because the idea of equity and fairness is deeply embedded in much of American culture, the requirement for non-discrimination appears in most of the sections of the Internal Revenue Code that provide for non-taxable qualified plans and benefits. It makes no difference if the sponsoring organization is a business, charity, or church. Generally, the plans/benefits can be categorized into "health and welfare", "retirement", and "certain others." In fact, each code section that describes benefits refers to non-discrimination testing, as well as the "cafeteria plan" description that includes various non-taxable benefits. Unfortunately, there is some variation in the rules between sections that is confusing; however, there are some commonalities that can be used as a starting point. These are:

1) There are prohibited groups of individuals who discriminated benefits cannot favor
2) Eligibility testing to confirm that enough employees not in the prohibited group are eligible for benefits
3) A test that contributions and benefits are available equally to those eligible.
4) An overall test that members of the prohibited group are not benefitting disproportionately.
5) Who can be excluded from testing.

Discrimination testing is really a job for specialists (done at calendar year-end). Various benefits publications discuss the issue, but not thoroughly.

Tax-Exempt Employee Benefits Summary

Specifically Identified Qualified Benefits in the Federal Tax Code

- Achievement awards
- Adoption assistance
- Athletic facilities provided by employer
- Cafeteria plans
- *De minimis* benefits
- Dependent care assistance

continued ▶

Tax-Exempt Employee Benefits Summary, *continued*

Specifically Identified Qualified Benefits in the Federal Tax Code, Continued

- Educational assistance plans and tuition reduction
- Employee discounts
- Employee stock option plans / stock purchase plans
- Group term life insurance
- Health, accident, long-term care, and disability benefits
- Meals and lodging for convenience of employer
- Military base closure and realignment
- Moving expenses
- No additional-cost services
- Retirement planning services
- Transportation (commuting) expenses
- Working condition fringe benefits

Achievement Awards

- **Overview:** These are awards for safety and length of service.
- **Tax effect for employee:** Generally not taxable for income tax or FICA to $1,600 annually for qualified plan awards and $400 for a non-qualified plan, based on employer's cost. Awards must be tangible personal property other than cash, cash equivalents, or gift cards (except certain limited cards), and subject to other limitations. "Nominal value" (probably less than $50) is also exempt. Non-profit and government organization programs for volunteer public safety employee length of service accruals for any year are exempt to $6,000 increased by $500 annually, i.e. taxed only when paid, not when accrued/vested.
- **Tax effect for employer:** Payments are deductible in year paid. There is no FICA or FUTA tax on exempt amounts.

Adoption Assistance

- **Overview:** There is a plan and is subject to eligibility requirements, generally excluding former employees, self-employed individuals, highly compensated management and certain shareholders. There is an additional provision for special needs children. Also see IRS tax topic No. 607 and Form 8839 instructions.
- **Tax effect for employee:** Reimbursed amounts are excluded from tax up to $14,890 per child subject to phaseout beginning at about $223,000 of modified adjusted gross income. (Note that for unreimbursed expenses, a tax credit up to the limit amount is also available for adoption expenses; however, reimbursed expenses cannot be used for the credit, and exclusion must be claimed first if applicable). All qualifying expenses reimbursed are reported on Form W-2, box 12, code T. Payments are excluded from income tax but subject to FICA tax, and are reported in boxes 3 (subject to limit) and 5 and subject to withholding.
- **Tax effect for employer:** Payments/reimbursements are deductible in the year paid. An employer is responsible for FICA and for FUTA.

Tax-Exempt Employee Benefits Summary, *continued*

Athletic Facilities Provided by Employer

- **Overview:** To exclude the value from employee income: 1) substantially all use of an athletic facility during a calendar year is by employees, spouses, and dependent children, 2) the facility is operated on premises owned or leased by the employer and cannot include residential use. The facility cannot be made available to the general public through membership, rental, or some similar arrangement.
- **Tax effect for employee:** Benefit value is exempt from income and FICA taxes.
- **Tax effect for employer:** Costs are deductible in year paid. There is no FICA or FUTA payroll tax on exempt amounts.

Cafeteria Plan

- **Overview:** A cafeteria plan, also called a flexible benefit plan, is set up by an employer who does not provide paid medical benefits, but who still wants to provide employees tax savings when they pay for medical expenses. Also, employers who want to include tax-exempt benefits with a cash opt-out and other taxable benefits must use a cafeteria plan. Subject to eligibility, non-discrimination, and other rules, a cafeteria plan includes employee choices (the "cafeteria" analogy) among specific ("qualified") benefits that permit using pre-tax wages for payment. A cafeteria plan allows employees to pay for allowable benefits with pre-tax dollars. An employer deducts amounts from gross wages and the amount accumulated is used to pay for the benefits. An IRS-qualified (Internal Revenue Code "Section 125") cafeteria plan is the means by which an employer can offer employees the alternative of either receiving cash (salary or lump sum) and/or other taxable benefits that might otherwise be included in "constructive receipt" (page 216).

  A key feature is that a cafeteria plan is needed in order to allow pre-tax employee salary/wage deductions to pay for certain benefits. These benefit choices are: 1) group medical, dental, vision, and disability insurance, 2) adoption assistance program, 3) COBRA (see group health insurance below for COBRA explanation), medical-related insurance continuation, 4) flexible spending accounts (FSA: discussed next), 5) health savings accounts (HSA: page 159), 6) group-term life insurance (page 156), and 7) 401(k) retirement plan contributions (the only deferred tax retirement plan included). A cafeteria plan also allows benefits purchased with after-tax employee dollars.

  The simplest and most popular cafeteria plan feature is a direct payment plan called a "premium only plan" ("POP") in which insurance premiums are paid directly by deducting a portion of an employee's gross wage during a plan's calendar year. An employee's check stub (remittance advice) should indicate the deduction and reference it, such as "cafe code section 125".

continued ▶

Tax-Exempt Employee Benefits Summary, *continued*

Cafeteria Plan,
Continued

- **Tax effect for employee:** Adoption contributions are exempt from income tax but are taxable for FICA purposes. Disability benefit payments may or may not be exempt from tax depending on who pays for them and whether payments were before or after tax. See the discussion on disability benefits. Group-term life insurance premiums for more than $50,000 coverage are taxable for income tax and FICA purposes. Subject to plan qualification requirements, and except for cash and taxable benefits, the other cafeteria plan employee contributions are exempt from income tax and FICA. Employer reporting for exempt cafeteria plan contributions is optional on Form W-2, box 14 with notation, except for HSA payments. Both employee/employer HSA plan contributions will appear in box 12, code W. The benefits classified as wage income are included in boxes 1, 3 (subject to limit), and 5. Also note that for an HSA an employee must include Form 8889 with the annual 1040 tax return to identify deductible contributions.

  Example of employee tax savings: During the year, an eligible employee earning $90,000 gross pay that pays 22% average income tax and also pays FICA tax, had $3,000 pre-tax dollars withheld for HSA medical payments. The employee pays tax on $87,000, which is $87,000 × (.22 + .0765) = $25,795.50. After paying for the insurance the employee has $90,000 – $25,795.50 – $3,000 = $61,204.50 net pay. If the employee had paid for the insurance with after-tax dollars, the total tax would be $90,000 × (.22 + .0765) = $26,685 which is an $889.50 increase in tax and reduction in net pay. Earnings in the fund are exempt from federal income tax.

- **Tax effect for employer:** Wages allocated by employees for benefits remain as deductible employer business expenses. Employer contributions on behalf of employees (sometimes called "flex credits") are deductible as business expenses. Except for adoption assistance, FICA and FUTA tax don't apply to pre-tax wages used for benefits, and possibly SUTA and workers' compensation insurance, depending on state rules. FICA and FUTA also don't apply to employer contributions. Also there are "simple" Sec. 125 plans, requiring some employer contributions.

TIP

Keep in mind that that although a cafeteria plan reduces recognized gross wages and therefore income tax and social security taxes for an employee, it can also reduce future employee benefits that are based on income level, such as social security and retirement benefits.

Tax-Exempt Employee Benefits Summary, *continued*

Flexible Spending Account (FSA)

- **Overview:** An FSA, a type of cafeteria plan benefit, allows pre-tax wage deductions. Subject to annual limits, the employer allocates pre-tax wages as determined by the employee into an FSA account; the employee then submits bills for tax-free reimbursement from the account. Employer matching is permitted. FSA plan types: **1) medical** (also called health) for medical expenses. (Note that an FSA cannot be used to pay for long-term care insurance or long-term care expenses but an HSA or HRA (later discussion, page 159) can.) **2) dependent care, 3) adoption assistance**, and **4) limited purpose** that includes dental, vision, and some over-the-counter items. Annual limits are: 1) medical $2,600/employer and limited employer match; 2) dependent (to age 13) care $5,000/household ($2,500 married filing separately); 3) adoption assistance $14,890/child; 4) limited purpose $2,850/individual. See Pub. 15-B.

  A medical FSA is pre-funded at the beginning of a year by the employer, so bills can be immediately paid; however, dependent care and adoption FSA accounts are funded only as an employee is paid during the year.

  Each expense type can only be used for the associated account type. For example, dependent care expenses cannot be paid by a medical FSA. An important issue with an FSA is the "**use-it-or-lose-it**" **requirement**, which means that funds not spent at the end of a plan year are lost and transferred to the employer. However, an employer has the option of offering either one of the following to employees: 1) carry over up to full 2021 health care balance into 2022 and $570 for the 2022 plan year if enrolled in a 2022 health care plan (limit is unaffected), 2) allow a grace period for medical costs incurred in the first 2.5 months of the next calendar year (employer may extend to December 31, 2022). The 2.5 month limitation does not apply if there is a change in an employee's marital status, number of dependents, or employer that has an effect on FSA-allowed expenditure types.

  An FSA cannot favor either highly compensated or key employees. See Publication 15-B for definitions.

- **Tax effect for employee:** An employee does not pay income tax or FICA tax on FSA-allocated amounts. Because pre-tax dollars are being deducted from employee pay and allocated for FSA use, an employee saves the amount of tax that would have been imposed on the deducted amounts. For example, assuming no state tax, if an employee pays 24% average income tax and also pays 7.65% FICA tax, an FSA allocation of $1,000 that is fully used will save 31.65% × $1,000 = $316.50.

- **Tax effect for employer:** Wages expense allocated to employee FSA accounts are excluded from FICA and FUTA tax. Reporting cafeteria plan deductions on Form W-2 is optional, in box 14. Small business cafeteria plans are also available.

Tax-Exempt Employee Benefits Summary, *continued*

De Minimis
Benefits

- **Overview:** The term *de minimis* means small or immaterial. (The IRS has ruled that items exceeding $100 are not *de minimis*.) Some *de minimis* benefits examples are: incidental personal use of company-provided cell phone (if non-compensatory benefit), personal copy machine use (less than 15% of total use), some minimal group-term life insurance, snacks, and holiday and birthday gifts.
- **Tax effect for employee:** Small/incidental benefits only occasionally received, less than $100, are exempt from income tax and FICA tax. Cash or equivalent are not excluded, except for cash for local transportation fare unrelated to hours worked and for meals when working overtime, which are allowed when *de minimis*.
- **Tax effect for employer:** All business-related items are deductible expenses.

Dependent
Care Assistance
Program

- **Overview:** Subject to eligibility, non-discrimination, and other IRS rules, a dependent care assistance written plan provides for household and dependent care services paid directly or indirectly (including value of onsite facilities use) by an employer to an employee so that the employee is able to work. The services must be for the care and well being of a qualifying person: children, disabled spouse, and legally dependent parents (Note that a dependent care program also is accessible in a cafeteria plan FSA; however, this is for a pre-tax earnings exclusion.). Exclusion does not apply to highly-compensated or key employees. (See page 158.)
- **Tax effect for employee:** The amount that can be excluded from income tax and FICA tax is the lesser of: 1) the value of dependent care benefits received, 2) the earned income of the lowest earning spouse, or 3) $5,000 per household ($2,500 if married filing separately). W-2 box 10 shows total plan benefits paid by employer. Employee also files Form 2441 with tax return. An employee also should check to see if services received makes him/her a household employer, in which case an EIN is required. Excluded amount is exempt from income and FICA tax and withholding. Excess amount is in W-2 boxes 1,3, and 5 but a non-taxable carryover from 2021 to 2022 is allowed.
- **Tax effect for employer:** Expenditures are deductible, including all facilities costs. FICA and FUTA don't apply up to exclusion limits.

Educational
Assistance Plans
and Tuition
Reduction

- **Overview**: Subject to eligibility and non-discrimination rules, an employee education assistance written plan provides reimbursement for tuition, books, fees, supplies, and student loan repayment as well as use of tools and equipment for an employee to maintain or improve job skills. Skills developed to meet minimum job qualification requirements do not qualify. Benefits do not apply to employee family members but do apply to former employees who retired, left on disability or were laid off and sole proprietors and partners. An employer may add requirements such as a minimum grade or continued employment.

continued ▶

Tax-Exempt Employee Benefits Summary, *continued*

Educational Assistance Plans and Tuition Reduction, Continued	Undergraduate tuition reduction by an educational institution is also exempt for current employees, retired employees on disability, a widow or widower of an employee who died while employed, retired, or disabled, and a dependent child or spouse of the above. Graduate student tuition is exempt if performing teaching or research for the organization reducing the tuition. See Publications 15-B and 970.

- **Tax effect for employee**: Annual payments up to $5,250 made by an employer under a written education assistance plan to maintain or improve employee job skills are exempt from income and FICA tax and withholding. Payments above this amount are taxable unless they are working condition fringe benefits (See later discussion). Meals, lodging, transportation, and retained tools are not exempt.
- **Tax effect for employer:** Expenses are deductible. FICA and FUTA don't apply.

Employee Discounts	

- **Overview**: These are free or reduced cost property or services provided from an employer to employees. The property and services must be offered to customers in the ordinary course of business. The discounts don't apply to real estate or investment personal property such as stocks and bonds. The exclusion is available to a current employee, spouse, dependent children, retired or disabled employee, widow or widower of an employee who died while an employee or retired or left on disability, and leased employees on the job full time for at least one year.
- **Tax effect for employee:** The value of the discount received generally is excluded from employee income as follows: 1) For services: a maximum of 20% of the price charged non-employee customers. 2) For property: the gross profit percentage (based on the year before the discount became available for all property offered to all employee and non-employee customers) times the price charged non-employee customers. However, if the benefit is not offered on the same terms to all other employees, then the exclusion does not apply to highly compensated employees. Excluded amounts are not taxed for income tax or FICA and there is no withholding.
- **Tax effect for employer**: Employer actual cost (excludes discount) is a deductible operating expense. FICA and FUTA do not apply to excluded amounts.

Employee Stock Options: Incentive Stock Options *("ISO"/ "Qualified")*	

- **Overview:** A employee qualified stock option, also called an "Incentive Stock Option" or "ISO" or "statutory" option, is a right granted to an employee to purchase company stock at a designated price, called the "exercise price". Options are granted from the employer, and to be qualified, stock options must be part of a written plan subject to eligibility, non-discrimination, and other IRS rules.

continued ▶

Tax-Exempt Employee Benefits Summary, *continued*

*Employee
Stock Options:
Incentive Stock
Options*

*("ISO"/
"Qualified"),
Continued*

- **Tax effect for employee:** Usually there is no reportable compensation income when an option is granted to an employee because the exercise price will be at or above the stock value. (There are special rules if this is not the case.) Also, there is no reportable compensation income when an employee exercises an option and buys stock. If the option is held at least one year from date of exercise and two years from offering (grant) date, gains are long-term capital gains, which is a favorable tax rate. Losses are long-term capital losses. This is called a "qualifying disposition". There is also a continuous employment requirement. Gain or loss on the stock sale is the difference between the sale price and the purchase (exercise) price. (However, an employee must calculate alternative minimum tax on his/her individual tax return in the year an option is exercised unless the stock is sold in that year.)

  If the stock is sold without meeting these time requirements (a "disqualifying disposition") or without making a special election to recognize the income at time of exercise, called an "83(b)" election (best done when there is only little gain), compensation income is created when the stock is sold. This is the difference between the option exercise price and the stock's fair market value at the time the option was exercised. If the stock is sold for less than that fair market value, generally the compensation is the difference between the sales price and exercise price, but not less than zero. (A loss creates a capital loss). If the stock is sold for more than the fair market value at time of exercise, there is capital gain for any excess above the purchase (exercise) price plus the compensation income recognized (see following examples). Compensation income is reported to the employee on Form W-2, box 1. There is no withholding for stock sales. FICA and FUTA taxes do not apply. Capital gain or loss is reported to the employee on Form 1099-B. An employee should receive Form 3921 from the employer each time an option is exercised. See Publication 525. (Note: For income to be recognized and taxed, an employee's rights to stock must be "vested", which means acquisition cannot be subject to restrictions.)

- **Tax effect for employer:** An employer does not receive a deduction when a sale is qualified. If a sale is not qualified, an employer receives a deduction in the same period and the same amount as taxed to the employee; FICA and FUTA taxes do not apply.

*Employee Stock
Options:
Non-Qualified*

- **Overview:** If a company grants a stock option that does not conform to IRS qualified plan requirements, the option is called a "nonqualified" or "non-statutory" ("NSO" or "NQSO") stock option. These options do not have the same favorable tax treatment for an employee as incentive stock options. The options can have certain advantages to an employer, such as less complexity and cost, more deductibility, and ability to be offered to non-employees such as independent contractors.

continued   ▶

Tax-Exempt Employee Benefits Summary, *continued*

Employee Stock Options: Non-Qualified, Continued

- **Tax effect for employee:** Generally there is no reportable compensation income when an option is granted to an employee because the exercise price will be at or above the stock value. (There are special rules if this is not the case.) Also, usually a non-qualified option doesn't meet certain other conditions when granted, so tax occurs later when an option is exercised. When a non-qualified option is exercised to purchase stock, compensation income is reported as the difference between the stock's fair market value and the option exercise price.

  Income is reported to an employee on Form W-2, boxes 1, 3 (subject to limit), 5 and box 12, code V when an option is exercised. For non-employees, a Form 1099-NEC is issued. Withholding or payment is required for income tax and FICA. After stock is acquired, later sales result in capital gain or loss, which is the difference between sales price and any excess above the purchase price plus compensation income recognized. An employee should receive Form 1099-B for these sales. Employer should also send a Form 3921 each time an option is exercised. (Note: For income to be recognized and taxed, an employee's rights to stock must be "vested", which means acquisition cannot be subject to restrictions.)

- **Tax effect for employer:** An employer receives a deduction in the same period and generally the same amount as compensation taxed to the employee. An employer is also responsible for its share of FICA and for FUTA taxes on employee compensation.

Example #1 ISO: Qualifying Sale

Offering date: 5/1/20	Market price: $20
Purchase date: 12/1/20	Market price: $30
Sale date: 6/20/22	Market price: $40
Number of shares: 100	Option exercise price $25

This is a qualifying disposition because the holding period requirements have been satisfied. As well, the gain is long-term capital gain because the stock has been held more than a year from the purchase date. The gain is: ($40 × 100) – ($25 × 100) = $1,500 in 2022. If the stock had been sold for $22 dollars instead of $40, there would be a $300 long-term capital loss. In either case, the employee must calculate alternative minimum tax on ($30 × 100) – ($25 × 100) = $500 in 2020, because the stock is held after 2020, even if there may be a capital loss in a subsequent year.

continued ▶

Tax-Exempt Employee Benefits Summary, *continued*

Example #2
ISO: Disqualifying
Sale

Offering date: 5/1/20	Market price: $20
Purchase date: 12/1/21	Market price: $30
Sale date: 6/20/22	Market price: $40
Number of shares: 100	Option exercise price $25

This is a disqualifying disposition because the holding period requirements have not been satisfied. The compensation (wages) income is: ($30 × 100) – ($25 × 100) = $500 in 2022. Capital gain (here, short-term) is: ($40 × 100) – [$500 + ($25 × 100)] = $1,000 in 2022. (Or simply, sales price minus fair market value at time of purchase.)

Example #3
NSO: Sale

Offering date: 5/1/20	Market price: $20
Purchase date: 12/1/20	Market price: $30
Sale date: 6/20/22	Market price: $40
Number of shares: 100	Option exercise price $25

The calculation for the NSO is the same as a disqualifying disposition of an ISO. However, the sale requires withholding for income tax, FICA and FUTA in year of exercise that an ISO does not. ($30 × 100) – ($25 × 100) = $500 in 2020. Capital gain (here, long-term) is: ($40 × 100) – [$500 + ($25 × 100)] = $1,000 in 2022. (Or simply, sales price minus fair market value at time of purchase.)

Employee Stock
Purchase Plan
(ESPP): Qualified

▪ **Overview:** An employee stock purchase plan allows employees to purchase company stock at a discount. (Technically its called a purchase plan option.) A qualified plan has the following general requirements: 1) The plan is voted in by a majority of shareholders during the preceding 12 months before the planned start date, 2) Employees who own more than 5% of voting stock are excluded, but all other employees not specifically excluded according to plan rules are eligible 3) Discount on stock purchases cannot exceed 15%, 4) All participants have equal rights except that a purchase amount can be as a percentage of income, 5) no employee can purchase more than $25,000 of stock (the number of shares determined by using the closing price on the offering date), and 6) The maximum term of offering periods generally cannot exceed 27 months. Also see Publication 525 and IRC Regulations §1.143.

Typically, employees elect to have a designated amount withheld after-tax from each paycheck. The withheld amounts accumulate until a designated purchase date at which time the company makes purchases on behalf of the employees. Depending on the plan, a purchase is made by: 1) an automatic percentage discount from the market price on the purchase date at the end of a period, and/or 2) a lookback period that applies the discount to the stock price at a designated point or lowest price over a period of time, according to the plan rules.

continued ▶

Tax-Exempt Employee Benefits Summary, *continued*

Employee Stock Purchase Plan (ESPP): Qualified, Continued

- **Tax effect for employee:** There is no reportable compensation income until the stock is sold. A "qualifying disposition" requires that: the stock is held for at least one year from the purchase date, and the stock is held for at least two years from its offering (grant) date. If these requirements are met, the per-share compensation income is the value of the discount on the offering date (or less if the difference between the stock's sales price and the discounted purchase price is smaller when the stock is sold–but not less than zero.) If the total gain on sale exceeds the compensation income, the remainder of the gain is capital gain, which is the sale price minus stock purchase price plus the amount recognized as compensation income. If the stock is sold at a loss (sales price minus purchase price), the loss is capital loss.

  If the holding period requirement is not met, the sale is a "disqualifying disposition". The per-share compensation income is the difference between the stock's market value and the discounted purchase price when the stock is purchased.

  If the total gain on sale exceeds the compensation income, the remainder of the gain is capital gain, which is the sale price minus the market price of the stock when it was purchased. If the stock is sold at loss, the loss is capital loss. Withholding is not required for a qualifying disposition. Compensation income is reported on Form W-2, box 1, but if not reported the employee still includes the income on line 7 of Form 1040. FICA does not apply. Employee should receive Form 1099-B for any capital gain or loss on sale of stock. Employee should also receive Form 3922 from the employer when the stock sold/transferred. This form is for informational purposes only, and similar information may be reported on the W-2, box 14.

- **Tax effect for employer:** An employer does not receive a deduction when a disposition is qualified. If a disposition is not qualified, an employer receives a deduction in the same period and the same amount as taxed to the employee; FICA and FUTA taxes do not apply.

Employee Stock Purchase Plan (ESPP): Non-Qualified

- **Overview:** Stock purchase plans that do not meet the requirements described above for qualified stock purchase plans are called "non-qualified", and do not provide the same tax benefits as qualified plans.
- **Tax effect for employee:** The excess of the stock fair market value at the time of purchase above the discounted purchase price is compensation income. Any further gain is capital gain, and a sales price below purchase price is capital loss. Withholding is not required for a disqualifying disposition. Compensation income is reported in Form W-2, box 1; however, if not reported the employee still includes the income on line 7 of Form 1040. FICA applies to non-qualified

continued ▶

Tax-Exempt Employee Benefits Summary, *continued*

Employee Stock Purchase Plan (ESPP): Non-Qualified, Continued

purchases. Employee should receive Form 1099-B for any capital gain or loss on sale of the stock. Employee should also receive Form 3922 from the employer when the stock sold/transferred. This form is for informational purposes only, and similar information may be reported on the W-2, box 14.

- **Tax effect for employer:** An employer receives a deduction in the same period and generally the same amount as compensation taxed to the employee. An employer is also responsible for its share of FICA and for FUTA taxes on employee compensation.

Example #1 ESSP: Qualifying Sale

Offering date: 5/1/20	Market price: $20
Purchase date: 12/1/20	Market price: $30
Sale date: 6/20/22	Market price: $40
Number of shares: 100	Discount percentage: 15%

This is a qualifying disposition because the holding period requirements have been satisfied. The compensation income is $300 which is the lesser of:

1) ($20 × 100 × .15) = $300 and
2) ($40 × 100) – ($30 × .85 × 100) = $1,450

Capital gain is also recognized in the year of sale. Here, this is:
($40 × 100) – [($300) + ($30 × .85 × 100)] = $1,150.

Example #2 ESSP: Disqualifying Sale

Offering date: 5/1/20	Market price: $20
Purchase date: 12/1/21	Market price: $30
Sale date: 6/20/22	Market price: $40
Number of shares: 100	Discount percentage: 15%

This is a disqualifying disposition because the holding period requirements have not been satisfied. The compensation income is:

($30 × 100) – ($30 × .85 × 100) = $450

Capital gain (in this case short-term capital gain because stock is not held more than a year from purchase date) is also recognized in the year of sale. Here, this is:

($40 × 100) – [($450) + ($30 × .85 × 100)] = $1,000

continued ▶

Tax-Exempt Employee Benefits Summary, *continued*

TIP

Caution: Both ISOs and employee stock purchase plans can create situations that result in "***phantom income***", in which there is taxable income but an actual loss has occurred, and in a worst case, insufficient cash to cover the tax. With an ISO, if stock is not sold in the year that an option is exercised, alternative minimum tax (called an "AMT") income is calculated for that year. The amount subject to the tax is the difference between the market value of the stock and the option exercise price on the exercise date. If it happens that the stock declines and is sold at a loss in a later year, AMT will have been paid and an actual loss on the stock sale will have occurred, plus the loss may not be fully deductible due to capital gain/loss rules. Hopefully, if there are no restrictions on selling the stock, it is usually wise to sell some shares when an option is exercised in order to provide cash.

With an ESPP a disqualifying disposition results in compensation income calculated as of the purchase date. This is the difference between the stock's market value and the purchase price, regardless of when the stock is sold. Thus, if the stock is sold later than the purchase date at less than the market value on the purchase date, tax for compensation income is still calculated on the earlier higher value that no longer exists. Furthermore, a loss on the stock sale may not be fully deductible due to capital gain/loss rules.

Group Term Life Insurance

- **Overview:** Group-term life insurance is provided for an employee, but not spouse or children, under a policy carried directly or indirectly by an employer. Additional rules apply, such as the 10-employee rule and key employee rule. See IRS Publication 15-B for details.
- **Tax effect for employee:** Insured employees can exclude from income the cost of employer-paid insurance premiums to a maximum of $50,000; there is no income tax or FICA tax or withholding on the first $50,000. *De minimis* employer-paid coverage for spouse or dependent is also exempt if it does not exceed $2,000. Cost of coverage exceeding $50,000 (minus any amount paid by employee): This is employee compensation income unless the employer is a beneficiary and is subject to income tax and FICA tax; withholding is optional for income tax and is required for FICA. Taxable amounts are included on Form W-2 boxes 1, 3 (subject to limit), 5 and box 12, code C.
- **Tax effect for employer:** Cost is fully deductible. The cost above $50,000 is subject to FICA, but entire cost is exempt for FUTA. To determine the cost of insurance in excess of $50,000 refer to the group-term uniform premiums table in IRS Publication 15–B, available online.

Tax-Exempt Employee Benefits Summary, *continued*

Group Health and Accident Insurance Plans

- **Overview:** Aside from its tax benefits under a qualified plan, medical insurance is probably the most valuable employee benefit an employer can offer. Major medical costs can be financially devastating and force individuals into bankruptcy. Without insurance, even recurring medical costs can be challenging because uninsured individuals pay a "retail" price for medical services that is often significantly more than the discounted prices paid by insurance companies.

  Subject to IRS rules, group insurance plans provide specified payments to cover medical costs in the event of injury or sickness. They are now sometimes referred to as "traditional health plans." Typically an employer pays most, sometimes all, of the premium cost with any balance paid by the employee through payroll withholding. A plan can apply to employees and their spouses, dependents, and children under the age of 27 at the end of a tax year. Depending on plan provisions, "employee" includes current common-law employees, retired employees, former employees, widow or widower of a deceased employee, and leased employees who have provided full-time services for at least a year under the direction of the employer.

  According to plan provisions, the insurance either pays medical costs directly to providers or reimburses the insured employee. The term "provider" refers to the doctor, hospital, clinic, lab, or other source providing medical services. Three basic types of provider arrangements are covered by insurance:

- Health maintenance organization ("HMO"): This is a network of providers who have agreed with the insurance company to offer their medical services and receive payment according to the terms of the insurance plan. The insured employee is limited to these providers.
- Preferred provider ("PPO"): This is usually the most expensive plan. It allows employees to use providers both within and outside a designated network.
- Point of service plan ("POS"): This is a combination of HMO and PPO features. An insured employee selects a single primary in-network care doctor but may also use services outside the plan's designated network at a higher cost, if the primary doctor refers these services.

  Some employers use group health insurance as a backup to cover major medical costs. These employers pay an employee's medical expenses up to a certain limit; if expenses exceed this limit, the insurance takes over. These companies are said to be partially "self-insured." Fully self-insured employers assume the entire responsibility for employee medical expenses. Although this permits greater control and possible cost reduction, it requires very good cash flow.

continued ▶

Tax-Exempt Employee Benefits Summary, *continued*

Group Health and Accident Insurance Plans, Continued

- **Tax effect for employee**: Insurance benefits are generally excluded from employee wages and therefore not subject to income tax or FICA or withholding. These benefits also include employer premiums paid to maintain COBRA (see below) coverage. *Also see discussion on cafeteria plans, page 146.* The cost of employer-provided major medical, COBRA coverage, and hospital or specified illness paid via an FSA are required to be reported on Form W-2, box 12, code DD for employee information purposes, not tax calculation.
- **Tax effect for employer**: Cost of contributions is deductible by an employer as a business expense. Contributions are exempt from FICA and FUTA.

Highly-compensated employees are any one of the following:

- The highest paid 25% of non-excludable employees
- The five highest paid officers
- More than 10% shareholders

If an employer meets any one of three tests a plan does not discriminate. The simplest eligibility test is that a plan must benefit at least 70% of all non-excludable employees. The benefits test is essentially that all non-excludable employees must receive benefits that are as good or better than highly compensated employees. If an employer does not satisfy both tests, some or all of the benefit value for the highly compensated employees are included in their income, based on formulas.

Note: Discrimination testing is done only for self-insured plans.

Discrimination Test Example

As an example, the cafeteria plan – commonly used – requires three discrimination tests:

The prohibited group: "**Highly-compensated employees (participants) (HCE) (#1 and #2)**" and "**Key**" employees (#3). For 2022, an HCE is an employee who, for the preceding year: Earned greater than $135,000 (or can elect to be in top 20% of earners) OR is or was a greater than 5% owner during the plan year or prior year, including a spouse or dependent.

1) Eligibility test: The plan must be offered to all employees except union employees and non-resident aliens and not favor HCEs, and the waiting period is less than three years.
2) Contributions/benefits: The available terms of the plan are the same for all and don't favor HCEs.
3) Concentration test: Key employees (for 2022, a key employee is an officer who earns greater than $200,000 OR is or was a greater than 5% owner during the plan year or prior year, OR earns more than $150,000 and owns a greater than a 1% interest.) do not receive more than 25% of pre-tax benefits actually going to all employees. (A 401(k) retirement plan has a similar "top heavy" rule for plan assets.)

Failure to meet tests 1, 2, or 3 results in benefits becoming fully taxable to HCEs and key employees. "Simple" plans are available that automatically meet the tests.

continued ▶

Tax-Exempt Employee Benefits Summary, *continued*

What is COBRA?

When an employee leaves an employer (except churches and church-related tax-exempt organizations), a federal law called the Consolidated Budget Reconciliation Act (COBRA) gives the employee the right to continue group health plan medical insurance from the former employer for a period of 18 months, sometimes up to 36 months. This is not free or low-cost insurance coverage. An employer has no obligation to share the cost and often an employee pays full price plus a small administrative fee. An employer must provide continuing coverage with COBRA when three conditions are met:

1) The health plan/ medical arrangement is covered by COBRA: This occurs with plans sponsored by employers with at least 20 full-time equivalent employees on more than 50% of typical business days in the previous calendar year. Part-time employees are counted for their hours as a fraction of full-time weekly 40 hours, on a daily, weekly, quarterly, annual or other consistent basis. E.g. 15-hours/ week equals 15/40 =.375 full-time equivalent. Note: state laws may apply that increase benefits.

2) A "qualifying event": A qualifying event is an event that would cause the employee to lose coverage under their group health plan: 1) termination of employment (except for gross misconduct), 2) reduction in hours, 3) qualifying for Medicare coverage, 4) divorce or separation, 5) death of employee, and 6) loss of dependent child status. Covered employee/beneficiary must provide notice of events 4 or 6 within 60 days.

3) The beneficiary is qualified: employee, spouse, former spouse, and dependent children, if they were covered by an active plan the day before a qualifying event occurred. Retired employees, spouses, and dependent children are covered if the employer goes bankrupt.

An employer must notify the plan administrators within 30 days of the qualifying event, the plan administrator has 14 days to notify an employee after receiving notice, and an employee has 60 days to decide following that notice. Employer should regularly check with plan administrator to avoid COBRA violations and penalties.

Health Savings Account ("HSA")

■ **Overview**: An HSA permits an employer, former employer, or an individual, including a self-employed or unemployed person, to create a bank account with a qualified trustee, such as a bank or insurance company, to reimburse IRS-allowed out-of-pocket medical expenses. Unlike an FSA, any person can contribute to an HSA for a beneficiary: employer, employee-beneficiary, both, employee family members, or any other person. For employees, the employee-beneficiary, not the employer, owns an HSA. An HSA, along with an FSA are sometimes referred to as "account-based plans." "Account-based" refers to medical expense reimbursement accounts created on behalf of an individual. "Consumer-driven" is another, more general, term that means individuals will have to share more health care costs and are required to make more cost-related decisions, which requires access to reliable information.

continued ▶

Tax-Exempt Employee Benefits Summary, *continued*

Health Savings Account ("HSA") Continued

An HSA requires that a beneficiary also be enrolled in an HSA high-deductible (see IRS guidelines) medical insurance plan–unlike an FSA. The insurance plan protects employees from the more costly medical expenses. Because the employee out-of-pocket expenses (deductibles and co-pays) are higher, the medical insurance premiums are usually lower. Lower premiums are always a cost-reduction benefit for an employer, who pays much or all of the premiums (and for employees if they incur some premium cost). Also, to be an eligible beneficiary or for *contributions*, a person cannot be: 1) enrolled in or eligible for Medicare or other health coverage, with certain exceptions, and 2) a dependent on another person's tax return. The current total contribution limit is $3,650 for individuals and $7,300 for families and a $1,000 catch-up for families. See Publication 969.

To avoid tax, HSA account withdrawals must be for IRS-qualified medical expenses. (Eligible medical-related expenses are similar for both an HSA and an FSA medical plan, except that an FSA does not allow health insurance premium reimbursements but an HSA allows Medicare A/B/ health premium *reimbursement* at 65 from a balance.) Often an employer will include a debit card or checks for employee payments; also, an employee can simply transfer amounts from an HSA account to a regular checking account. In practice, an HSA might require beneficiaries to carefully decide which medical costs they will incur and/or possibly limit medical services. This is because potentially they could be paying significant costs out-of-pocket for recurring medical issues despite some costs being paid with their pre-tax dollars. IRS rules specify "except for preventive care," the annual deductible must be met first, before other medical expenses are allowed. This is a greater burden on lower-income employees.

An HSA is the property of the beneficiary, so it is portable between jobs. Beneficiaries keep all unused funds at the end of a year or can roll them over to the next year, subject to the annual limit. A beneficiary is also allowed a range of choices for how funds in the account can be invested. Account earnings are tax-exempt. See IRS publications 15-B and 969 for further rules and details.

TIP

If an employer makes contributions, it may want to contribute a lump-sum portion such as 40-50% at the start of a year so employees have funds available for use. Any remainder can be contributed equally during the rest of the year.

- **Tax effect for employee**: There are several HSA variations:

  1) An employer uses payroll to withhold pre-tax employee wages: This is excluded from income and is a tax savings for employee and a deduction for the employer. A cafeteria plan with a pre-tax deduction provision is needed to do this. See the HSA discussion and example in

continued ▶

Tax-Exempt Employee Benefits Summary, *continued*

Health Savings Account ("HSA") Continued

the cafeteria plan discussion, earlier. This reduces taxable compensation and FICA as reported on Form W-2, boxes 1, 3, 5 if the contribution is made through a cafeteria plan. FICA is not reduced if the contribution is via a pay reduction plan. An HSA cannot be used with an FSA, unless the FSA is "limited purpose" or "post-deductible."

2) The employee contributes to his/her HSA account with after-tax dollars: This can be done by employee payroll withholding using after-tax dollars or with by a personal payment. The employee/beneficiary uses these contributions to reduce adjusted gross income directly (without itemizing) on Form 1040 annual individual tax return; however, there is no FICA tax savings as via an employer plan.

3) An employer contributes: Employer contributions per IRS guidelines, with or without a cafeteria plan, are not taxable for income or FICA purposes if it is reasonable to believe at the time of payment the contribution will be excludable.

4) Employer and employee combine contributions in a cafeteria plan: This results in combined tax savings as described above.

The total employee and employer combined contributions are reported on Form W-2, box 12, code W. At year-end an employee should receive Form 5498–SA for contributions and Form 1099-SA for distributions from the account. ***An employee must include Form 8889 as part of the annual 1040 tax return to identify deductible contributions***. Note that if an employer makes contributions that pay long-term care insurance premiums, these amounts cannot be excluded from employee income tax if the same coverage is provided by an HSA. However these payments are excluded from payroll taxes.

- **Tax effect for employer**: Both employer contributions and employee wages allocated to an HSA are deductible business expenses. An employer avoids FICA and FUTA taxes and possibly state employment taxes and workers' compensation insurance on employer HSA contributions and employee pre-tax plan deductions provided that it can be reasonably believed an employee qualifies for exclusions (up to contribution limits).

Medical Savings Account (MSA)

"Medical Savings Account" is sometimes used as a general term for any medical-related tax-favored account, but more specifially refers to either an Archer MSA or a Medicare MSA. Both plans require a high deductible (see IRS guidelines online) insurance plan. The Archer MSA was designed for self-employed persons and employees in small businesses. It was phased out in 2007 but some plans are still active (a 1099-SA goes to employees); however, it led to the development of the HSA plan. The Medicare MSA is for people who enroll in Medicare with a high deductible Medicare Advantage plan. Medicare pays an amount tax-free each year into a trustee account; if that is used up the deductible applies until the limit is reached. Other plans are generally not allowed.

Tax-Exempt Employee Benefits Summary, *continued*

Health Reimbursement Arrangement ("HRA")

- **Overview:** An HRA is popular with employers because of flexibility in plan design and because the employer only reimburses employees, and does not assume the responsibilities for selecting or managing a health care plan. Subject to eligibility and other IRS rules, an HRA is a written employer-funded plan, and only the employer can contribute to an HRA, and it is not part of a cafeteria plan; the self-employed are not eligible. An employer sets the contribution amount and makes monthly fixed contributions. An employer may not offer employees the choice between a traditional employer group health plan and an HRA; employees enroll in individual coverage such as major medical. An employer owns an HRA; therefore, it is not portable. Within the IRS guidelines of qualified medical expenses, an employer controls what categories are eligible for reimbursement, disposition of account funds at the end of a year, when claims need to be submitted, and other factors. Employees pay for health care premiums and other benefits and then must submit proof for reimbursement from the employer.

  The following are some common types of health reimbursement accounts:

  - One-person/stand alone HRA: A business offers a fixed monthly HRA contribution to only one employee. There is no group insurance plan requirement.
  - Group coverage ("integrated") HRA: This HRA requires a *group* health care plan that employees must use. The HRA is offered to employees as a supplement to help with out-of-pocket expenses (but not individual insurance premiums). Special provisions permit employers to provide up to $1,800 per year, inflation adjusted, for an employee who does not enroll in group coverage.
  - Retiree HRA (one person): An HRA available only to an employer's retired employees who converted from an existing plan, with special provisions to pay for *individual* health insurance premiums, copays, and Medicare costs.
  - Qualified small employer HRA (QSEHRA): for businesses with less than 50 employees and no group insurance policy, and therefore not subject to group health plan requirements. Also, the employer cannot offer an FSA. An employer can allocate different amounts to individuals, families, and full and part-time employees, subject to annual funding limits for individuals and families. However, several different exclusions are allowed. Subject to guidelines, funds can be used by individual employees for their own *individual* health insurance plans and uncovered out-of-pocket expenses. Contribution limits are $5,450 for individuals and $11,050 for families.
  - Individual coverage HRA ("ICHRA"): There is no limit on employer size. There is also no annual funding limit. This HRA allows employees to purchase their own *individual* health insurance and pay uncovered out-of-pocket expenses. Also see ACA.

continued ▶

Tax-Exempt Employee Benefits Summary, *continued*

Health Reimbursement Arrangement ("HRA"), Continued	■ **Tax effect for employee:** Subject to allowable reimbursement categories, reimbursed payments to employees are tax-exempt and not subject to income or FICA taxes. There is no W-2 reporting requirement. ■ **Tax effect for employer:** Reimbursements are a fully deductible business expense. FICA and FUTA do not apply to amounts reimbursed to employees.

Affordable Care Act (ACA)

Employers should also be aware of the federal Affordable Care Act (also called the "ACA" or "Obama Care". Full name: Patient Protection and Affordable Care Act). The ACA does not require employers to provide employee medical insurance; however, it imposes penalties on larger employers (At least 50 full-time equivalent employees in the previous year) who do not provide employee medical insurance coverage. Illustration 2.13 provides a basic employer compliance outline.

The purpose of this complex law is to create a large insurance pool that is sufficient to provide widespread medical coverage. In effect, this means medical insurance coverage for most people, particularly directed to people who are otherwise unable to obtain coverage, generally because they do not work for an employer who provides medical insurance, or because they cannot afford to pay for medical insurance, or because they do not qualify for Medicare.

Employee Meals

Employer-provided meals with or without charge can be excluded from an employee's income if any of the below apply:

■ The meals are during working hours and are furnished at the employer's business premises and are for the convenience of the employer so that the employee can properly perform his/her duties. Examples are: being available for emergencies, short meal breaks making it too difficult to eat elsewhere, meeting customer demands, or overtime for meeting project deadlines. (This is a potentially gray area that depends on facts and circumstances, and best practice is to create and follow a written policy.) If an employee was unable to eat an employer-offered meal during work hours because of duties, the meal provided immediately work hours is excludable.

■ For restaurant employees, meals immediately before or after a shift, or after work if work duties prevented an employee from eating are excludable.

■ Meals are furnished to more than half of the employees on premises for convenience of the employer, then exclusion applies to all employees.

■ Meals are part of occasional parties or picnics open to employees and guests.

continued ▶

Tax-Exempt Employee Benefits Summary, *continued*

Illustration 2.13: Affordable Care Act Employer Health Insurance Compliance Procedure

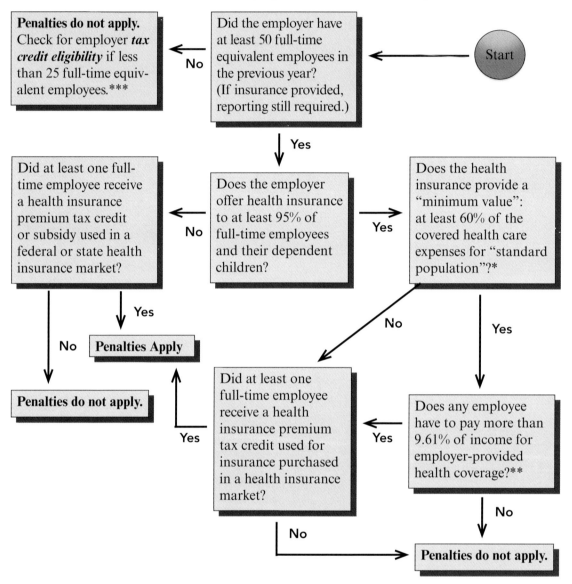

*Minimum value for a standard population can be determined by: 1) Using the Health and Human Services (HHS) website calculator, 2) Contacting an employee benefits insurance company

**Refers to employee household income. Check current rate and guidelines. For 2022, employer can apply 9.61% against these guidelines to determine household income for self-coverage: 1) Current federal poverty level for a single person calculated monthly as of six months before start of plan year, 2) Employee's W-2 box 1 current year-end reported wages, per month (however, difficult to determine before year-end), 3) Hourly rate of pay at 130 monthly hours or regular salary at beginning of coverage period. Note that percentage is annually inflation adjusted.

***See https://www.healthcare.gov/small-businesses/provide-shop-coverage/small-businesstax-credits/ for details.

continued ▶

Tax-Exempt Employee Benefits Summary, *continued*

Employee Meals, Continued	Small food amounts, such as snacks during short breaks and occasional small meals and/or meal money to allow an employee to work overtime are excluded from taxable income.

- **Tax effect for employee:** Subject to the guidelines, the value of meals is generally excludable from employee income tax and withholding and FICA. A meal exclusion does not apply to a cash payment in lieu of a meal or a choice between additional pay and meals. Also exclusions do not apply to highly compensated employees.
- **Tax effect for employer**: Except for employee recreation, picnics, and holiday parties that are 100% deductible, employee meal costs are 50% deductible by an employer (100% only at restaurants for only 2022). Beginning in 2026 these meals will not be deductible. Meals for social, recreational, or similar events open to all employees that don't discriminate in favor of highly-compensated employees are 100% deductible – for example, an annual holiday party or picnic. Also, shift meals (before, during, or after shift) for restaurant employees are 100% deductible.

Voluntary Employees Beneficiary Association (VEBA)	A VEBA is a type of tax-exempt organization that provides health reimbursement benefits that are similar to an HSA plan. (A VEBA can also provide life, disability, and accident insurance and other benefits. Also, a properly structured VEBA term life policy offers estate tax benefits.) An employer or multiple employers typically contribute(s) funds into VEBA with a tax-exempt trust that reimburses eligible employees' out-of-pocket medical expenses. Employees can be active or retired. Employees can also contribute. Key differences between an HSA and VEBA:

- Generally there is no VEBA annual contribution limit
- A VEBA is designed to help multiple employees, not just one or two.
- A high-deductible insurance plan is not required.
- A VEBA must qualify for ERISA, and assets in the trust are protected from creditors
- Dual coverage is allowed with other health plans; some qualified plan requirements do not apply.
- **Tax effect for employee:** Contributions and account earnings are tax-free to employees. There is no income tax or FICA withholding on contributions.
- **Tax effect for employer:** Contributions are deductible as operating expenses within IRS rules. FICA and FUTA do not apply.

Employee Lodging	- Employer-provided lodging can be excluded from an employee's income if: 1) the lodging is furnished at the employer's business premises, and 2) is for the convenience of the employer so that the employee can properly perform his/her duties, and 3) the employee must accept the lodging as a condition of employment. As with employer-furnished

continued ▶

Tax-Exempt Employee Benefits Summary, *continued*

Employee Lodging, Continued	meals, "convenience of employer" is a matter of facts and circumstances. Cash allowances for lodging or an employer offer of cash lieu of the above are not excludable. Also see the discussion of working conditions fringe benefits. ■ **Tax effect for employee:** Subject to the guidelines, the value of lodging is generally excludable from employee income tax, FICA, and withholding. ■ **Tax effect for employer**: Fully deductible by employer. Not subject to FICA or FUTA
Military Base Closure/ Realignment	These are payments made to members of the military to offset the price of housing when a military base closes or is downsized. For further information see https://www.usace.army.mil/Missions/Military-Missions/Real-Estate/HAP/.
Moving Expense	The 2017 Tax Cuts and Jobs Act has suspended the exclusion of qualified moving expense reimbursement from employee income until 2026, except for members of the U.S. Armed Forces on active duty who move because of a permanent change in station. See IRS Publication 3 for details.
No Additional Cost Services	These are free or reduced cost services provided from an employer to employees at no additional cost and/or no loss of revenue to the employer. The same services must be offered to customers in the ordinary course of business. What is provided to employees are excess capacity; typical employers are transportation companies that have unused seat space. The provision also applies to services provided for a spouse, dependent children, parents, retired or disabled employee, widow or widower of an employee who retired or who left on disability, and leased employees on the job full time for at least one year. Non-discrimination rules apply. ■ **Tax effect for employee:** The value of services received are generally excluded from income and FICA tax and withholding. However, if the benefit is not offered on the same terms to all other employees, then the exclusion does not apply to highly compensated employees. ■ **Tax effect for employer**: The cost of services is a fully deductible operating expense. Not subject to FICA or FUTA
Retirement Planning Services	■ **Overview:** Subject to eligibility, non-discrimination, and other rules, services that help employees plan for retirement are a qualified benefit if the employer maintains a qualified retirement plan. ■ **Tax effect for employee:** Excluded from income and FICA tax and withholding. ■ **Tax effect for employer**: Cost is fully deductible. Not subject to FICA or FUTA.
Transporation: (Commuting, Bicycle, Parking)	■ **Overview:** In this context, "transportation" refers to qualified commuting activity to and from work and to incidental cost ("*de minimis*") commuting and local travel. "Qualified" here refers to: 1) a

continued ▶

Tax-Exempt Employee Benefits Summary, *continued*

Transporation:
(Commuting,
Bicycle, Parking),
Continued

commuter highway vehicle with at least 80% of mileage between home and place of work, with seating for at least six adults and driver, 2) a transit pass, 3) qualified parking: a location at or near an employer's worksite or at a commute transit location for public transit, vanpool, or carpool. Benefits can be in the form of salary allocation that uses pre-tax payments for transportation costs or benefits can be in the form of employer reimbursement of substantiated employee expenditures. Generally, except for a bicycle transportation benefit, which is taxable, total qualified transportation benefits up to $280 per month are excludable. See Publication 15-B for further details. Some states may require a cafeteria plan to exclude the benefits.

- **Tax effect for employee:** Benefits are excludable from wages subject to guidelines. Any excess amounts are taxable wages for income tax and withholding purposes, and FICA, reported on Form W-2, boxes 1, 3, (subject to limit) and 5. Exclusions do not apply to self-employed persons.
- **Tax effect for employer:** No employer deduction is allowed for qualified transportation benefits or for providing transportation, except as follows: 1) ensuring the safety of an employee, or 2) qualified bicycle commuting reimbursements. A deduction is allowed for employee taxable transportation benefits.

TIP

The following transportation *de minimis* benefits are excludable from an employee's income: 1) discounted public transit passes, tokens, and fare cards furnished by the employer if the discount doesn't exceed $21 per month, 2) vouchers from an employer for the above items if the discount doesn't exceed $21 per month, 3) a bona fide reimbursement plan for an employer to reimburse an employee up to $21 per month for substantiated commuting costs on a public transit system.

TIP

Local transportation benefits provided to an FLSA non-exempt hourly employee (and making less than $130,000 per year), because of unusual circumstances or unsafe travel conditions resulting from a history of crime around the workplace or residence, is taxable to an employee up to $1.50 each way. The employee walks and/or uses public transportation. Any additional amount is excludable from income.

continued   ▶

Tax-Exempt Employee Benefits Summary, *continued*

*Working
Condition Fringe
Benefits*

▪ **Overview:** A working condition fringe benefit is any property or service provided from employer to employee that the employee uses to facilitate his/her job performance in the employer's business. Employer reimbursements under an accountable plan for specified or prearranged business activities are also included as a working condition fringe benefit if: 1) expenses are verified, and 2) any excess payments are returned to the employer. The following are specifically identified as not working condition fringe benefits: 1) FSA employer-provided noncash benefits with a predetermined cash value 2) employer-provided physical examinations 3) a working condition fringe benefit that the employee uses in a different business. Some examples of working condition fringe benefits are:

Cell phones: Cell phones qualify if provided as a non-compensatory benefit such as maintaining contacts for business reasons, but not if for goodwill, morale, or to attract a potential employee. Incidental personal use is not taxable to employee.

Vehicles: The amount excludable is determined by the proportion of use in the employer's business; therefore, personal use is not excluded from wages. Demonstrator vehicles use qualifies as long as their use is primarily to help full-time sales staff perform duties and personal use is substantially restricted. Finally, certain types of vehicles that are designated for non-personal use, or other vehicles that have been specially modified for business will qualify. Examples are vans modified for business use, ambulances, heavy trucks, cranes and derricks, forklifts, tractors, and pickup trucks with added hydraulic lift gates or for transport of certain loads. See Publication 15-B.

Tools: Employer-provided tools specifically for work and not personal use qualify as working condition fringe benefits.

Education: Education designed to improve employee performance qualifies as a working condition fringe benefit. At least one of the following tests must be met: 1) The education is required by the employer or by law to maintain salary, status, or job, and it serves a bona fide business purpose. 2) The education maintains or improves current job skills. In either case, the education does not qualify if it is needed for the minimum educational requirements for the employee's present trade or business or for a new trade or business. Note that an employer's education assistance plan exceeding the plan limit can qualify as a working condition benefit.

Local lodging: Sometimes it may be important for an employee to temporarily remain close to work overnight. The employee stays in lodging near work instead of going to his/her home at night and returning to work next morning. The overnight lodging can be treated as a working condition fringe benefit if the lodging cost: 1) is incurred for a bona fide condition of employment imposed by the employer, 2) is for a business purpose and not primarily to provide a personal benefit to the employee,

continued ▶

Tax-Exempt Employee Benefits Summary, *continued*

*Working
Condition Fringe
Benefits,
Continued*

3) is not lavish or extravagant for the circumstances, and 4) does not pro-vide a significant element of personal pleasure or recreation. The IRS also provides a "safe harbor" test if certain specific conditions exist. This type of expense is discussed in Internal Code Regulations §1.162-32.

Outplacement services: These services qualify if: 1) the employer pro-vides them on the basis of need, 2) the employer receives a business benefit (such as employee morale) apart from paying wages, and 3) the employee is seeking employment in the same trade or business.

Product testing: Under certain guidelines employee product test will qualify as a working condition fringe benefit. See Publication 15-B for guidelines.

- **Tax effect for employee (and partner performing services for a partner-ship, director, and independent contractor)**: Working condition fringe benefits per guidelines are excluded from compensation and are ex-empt from income and FICA taxes and withholding.
- **Tax effect for employer**: Working condition fringe benefits are deduct-ible expenses that are exempt from FICA taxes and from FUTA.

TIP

Except for product testing, discrimination is allowed among em-ployee categories, even if the benefits are provided only to officers, highly compensated employees, board members, and independent contractors.

TIP

The 2017 Tax Cuts and Jobs Act eliminated employees' ability to deduct unreimbursed business expenses. This makes an accountable employer reimbursement plan all the more necessary and working condition fringe benefits all the more valuable.

*Sick Pay and
Disability
Payments*

- **Overview**: The IRS defines sick pay as "...any amount paid under a plan because of an employee's temporary absence from work due to injury, sickness, or disability." The IRS treats sick pay and disability insurance in the same manner. The insurance is designed to replace lost income as a result of sickness or disability and therefore is treated as wages. However, the income payments may or may not be taxable as discussed below. Benefits are often calculated based on a percentage of gross pay. (Note: sick pay and disability payments are not any of the following: 1) disability retirement payments, 2) workers' compensa-tion, 3) medical insurance payments under a medical insurance plan, 4) accident insurance payments relating to permanent loss of use of member or function of body if not determined by absence from work. Items 2,3, &4 are generally not taxable for income tax, and FICA and FUTA don't apply. Disabled persons should read Publication 907.

continued ▶

Tax-Exempt Employee Benefits Summary, *continued*

Sick Pay and Disability Payments, Continued

■ **Tax effect for employee**: Sick pay and disability benefits income that result from insurance *paid by an employee* with after-tax dollars or *paid by an employer and included in employee income* is *not taxable to the employee*. Conversely, if the insurance premium payments have been made by the employee *using pre-tax dollars* or *paid by the employer and not included in employee income*, the income *is taxable to the employee and subject to withholding*. If given a choice, an employee must decide what is best, *based on his/her risk tolerance and income level*. If both employee and employer pay premiums, the taxable income is pro-rated using the above guidelines based on the ratio for the prior 3 years' contributions. Payments received at any time after an employee's death by an employee's estate or beneficiary are not subject to income tax and withholding.

FICA: 1) To the extent payments are taxable as discussed in the paragraphs above, payments received in the first six months after the last month of employment are taxable and subject to FICA. Payments received after the calendar year of an employee's death aren't taxable. 2) Payments received on or after an employee's death or disability retirement according to a definitive sick pay plan are not subject to FICA tax except for accrued compensation. 3) Payments attributable to after-tax premium payments by employee are not taxable. FUTA: The same rules apply.

Pre-tax employee compensation and employer contributions used to pay disability insurance premiums are not taxable for income tax or FICA and are not included on Form W-2. Taxable disability benefits income (sick pay benefits) are subject to tax and reported on Form W-2, boxes 1, 3 (subject to limit), and 5 as well as withholding. Some employers prepare a separate W-2 for disability income payments and sick pay.

When a person separates from service before retirement age due to disability, the income is treated as described above. However, when that person reaches (normal) minimum retirement age, beginning on the day after reaching minimum retirement age the payments are treated as a taxable pension or annuity income. Minimum retirement age is generally the age at which a person would receive a pension or annuity from the employer, or other source if there is no employer plan, without being disabled. Veterans' disability pensions and related grants as a result of military service are not taxed.

■ **Tax effect for employer:** The cost of the insurance premiums is a fully deductible business expense. When sick pay/disability pay is paid by an employer or an agent of the employer, the employer is responsible for withholding and remitting employee/employer FICA and FUTA, unless there is an agreement that the agent assumes some portion of responsibility; however, this does not relieve the employer of liability

continued ▶

Tax-Exempt Employee Benefits Summary, *continued*

*Sick Pay and
Disability
Payments,
Continued*

for payment. An employer must prepare a W-2 reporting sick/disability pay even if payments are not taxable. Non-taxable payments are reported in box 12, code J. Employers should check requirements for filing Form 8922.

Third party payers other than agents of the employer, such as insurance companies, are responsible for reporting and for withholding income tax if requested by the employee, and are fully responsible for FICA and FUTA withholding and reporting. Employees should note that insurance companies might not withhold income tax on taxable amounts unless requested. Employers deposit their share of OASDI, Medicare, and FUTA. Both employer and third party report on Form 941 with an adjustment on line 8.

Finally, employers should keep in mind that a qualified written sick pay/disability plan must be in place for payments to be tax-deductible. Simply continuing to pay compensation to sick or disabled employees will result in non-deductible payments by the employer and taxable income to the recipient. A sick pay/disability plan can be funded by insurance to reduce out-of-pocket payments.

TIP

A tax credit is available for persons who were permanently and totally disabled when they retired. See Publication 524. Also, earned income tax credit may apply.

*Workers'
Compensation*

In all but one state (Texas), workers' compensation insurance is a compulsory employer expense, although some states require it only when there are a minimum number of employees. With some variation in policies, employees' compensation insurance coverage pays workers who are injured, disabled, or killed on the job. Although coverage in most states is mandatory, the method of purchasing insurance varies. Most states permit employers to either purchase private insurance (provided coverage and insurance company rating meet state requirements) or purchase the insurance through a state fund. The cost of the insurance is generally calculated as a rate per $100 of annual gross compensation of individual job categories, based on a risk rating of each job category. This in turn may be adjusted by an experience loss rating based on loss history. The method of payment varies. A common procedure is for the employer to make an initial payment based on a beginning of the year estimate. At year-end the cost is finalized based on actual employment and the premium cost is adjusted, requiring either an additional payment or a rebate.

Example: ABC company has two job categories: office and construction. The actual annual gross wages are: office category, $185,000 and repair services, $500,000. The rate for office is $.22 per $100 and the rate for

continued   ▶

Tax-Exempt Employee Benefits Summary, *continued*

Workers' Compensation, Continued	repair services is $2.75 per $100. The company has had minimal losses, so has a .9 overall loss rating. The annual cost is:

$$[(\$185,000 / 100) \times \$.22] + [(\$500,000 / 100) \times \$2.75]$$
$$= \$14,157 \times .9 = \$12,741.30$$

In return for providing this insurance, the insurance becomes the sole remedy for work-related injury, with certain exceptions depending on state law. Employees do not need to incur the cost and substantial risk of suing employers for job-related injuries, and employers do not become parties to lawsuits. Workers' compensation premiums paid by employer are not taxable to an employee and the benefits are not taxable. The premiums are tax-deductible operating expenses for an employer.

TIP

Check with your state workers' compensation. Some dollar payroll calculation states don't include overtime. Also check for other exemptions and exclusions. For examples of these, see: https://workcompconsultant.com/remuneration-workers-compensation-payroll.htm.

ABLE Accounts	An Achieving a Better Life Experience (ABLE) account is designed to accept contributions for an eligible disabled individual who is the beneficiary of the account. Account distributions are used to help defray expenses related to an individual's disability and these distributions are not included in income. Earnings in an ABLE account are excluded from income unless the distributions exceed qualified disability expenses. Various state governments have ABLE accounts accessible online. ABLE contributions are not tax-deductible and must be in cash or cash equivalents; however, anyone can contribute. See IRS publication 907.

Special Vehicle Use Valuation Rules

Overview	As discussed at the beginning of this section, benefits are generally valued at their fair market value. This is the value (dollar amount) that would be paid to a 3rd party in an arm's-length transaction. However, because the business use of vehicles is widespread among employees with a significant potential for personal use, the IRS has developed special rules to value business vehicle use. The purpose of these rules is to provide clear guidelines that determine the value of any personal vehicle use, and therefore employee taxable wage/salary income, that is included in an employee's Form W-2 boxes 1, 3, and 5. (There are also rules for aircraft.). There are three specified valuation methods that can be applied: 1) Annual lease value, 2) Cents-Per-Mile, and 3) Commuting rule. An employer does not have to use the same method for all vehicles

Special Vehicle Use Valuation Rules, *continued*

Keeping a Record   The common necessity for each of these methods is record keeping. The best method is to maintain a contemporaneous log that records the date, mileage, travel locations, and business purpose. If adequate records are not maintained that substantiate business use, the mileage will be treated as personal use.

Annual Lease Value   The annual lease value of an automobile is determined as the basis for valuation. Use the IRS table in Publication 15-B available online that converts a vehicle fair market value (FMV) into annual lease value. The FMV of the vehicle is what a person would pay to buy it from a 3rd party in an arms-length transaction at the present time. Fair market value is reduced by any amount used as a working condition fringe benefit.

Safe harbor rule: The lease value of a purchased automobile will be accepted if it is determined by the documented cost, sales tax, title, and other acquisition expenses. (Note that this may be a high value compared to a later sale to a 3rd party.) For a leased vehicle, any of the following can be used: 1) manufacture cost plus 4%, 2) manufacturer retail price including purchase costs less 8% or 3) Retail price as listed by a nationally recognized source if price is "reasonable".

Calculation of personal use: Multiply the percentage of personal use mileage by the annual lease value.

Applying lease value: 1) Use the lease value on the first day a vehicle is made available for any personal use. 2) Use lease value method annually for all remaining years if circumstances remain the same. 3) If an employee uses the vehicle for at least 30 days but less than a year, divide the lease value by 365 for a daily rate. This is then multiplied by days of use. 4) If use is less than 30 days, use the lower of: #3 rate × 4 × days of use, or the daily rate of #3 multiplied by 30 days. Periods of unavailability, such as PTO periods, cannot be used in the calculation. If employer provides fuel, add 5.5¢ per mile personal use. See Publications 463 and 15-B.

Cents-Per-Mile   Personal use of an employer-provided vehicle can be calculated at a standard rate of 58.5¢ per mile times the number of personal use miles under either of the following conditions:

1) The employer reasonably expects the vehicle to regularly be used in its trade or business during the calendar year. At least 50% of total annual mileage as business use satisfies this requirement. So does sponsoring a commuting pool that generally uses the vehicle each workday with at least three employees.
2) The vehicle meets the mileage test:

- The vehicle is actually driven at least 10,000 miles during the year. If owned or leased only part of a year, reduce the 10,000 proportionately for time owned or leased and
- The vehicle is used during the year primarily by employees. Being used consistently for commuting satisfies this requirement.

continued ▶

Special Vehicle Use Valuation Rules, *continued*

Cents-Per-Mile, Continued	Consistency requirements:

- The method must be used on the first day it is available to any employee for personal use.
- The method must be used for all later years in which the vehicle is available to any employee for personal use and the vehicle qualifies, except that the commuting rule can be used for any year in which the vehicle qualifies for that rule. If the vehicle ceases to qualify for the cents-per-mile rule, any other rule can be used for that year and later years.

Value requirement: The maximum value to which the cents-per-mile method may apply for cars, vans and trucks is $56,100.

Commuting Rule   An employer can provide an employer vehicle to an employee that is used exclusively for the purpose of commuting to and from work. The value to include as taxable to an employee is $1.50 per one-way trip per employee. The commuting rule can be used if all the following requirements are satisfied:

- Employer provides the vehicle to an employee for use in employer's trade or business and, for bona fide non-compensatory business reasons, requires the employee to commute in the vehicle. Employer also qualifies if the vehicle is generally used each workday to carry at least three employees to and from work in an employer-sponsored commuting pool.
- Employer establishes a written policy under which employer doesn't allow the employee, nor any individual whose use would be taxable to the employee, to use the vehicle for personal purposes other than for commuting or de minimis personal use (such as a stop for a personal errand on the way between a business delivery and the employee's home).
- The employee doesn't use the vehicle for personal purposes other than commuting and de minimis personal use.
- The employee is not a control employee. A control employee is any of the following in a nongovernmental employer: 1) officer with pay of at least $120,000, 2) A director, 3) an employee with pay at least $245,000, 4) an employee who owns 1% or more in equity, capital, or profits. Alternatively, a control employee may be defined as a highly compensated employee: 5% owner in current or preceding year and received more than $135,000 pay in the prior year, unless this is not in top 20%.

Reporting   Personal vehicle use (including using the vehicle to commute) is reported as wages on Form W-2. If the employer provides fuel for personal use, add $.055/mile to the wages. Employee/employer payroll taxes apply. Report on form 941, 943, or 944 as applicable. Noncash fringe benefits can be reported in the period deemed by the employer as paid, but at least annually.

Tax-Deferred Benefits Summary: Employer Plans

Overview

Employers can create retirement plans for employees. If an employer retirement plan meets government requirements, it is called a "qualified" retirement plan and provides valuable employee and employer benefits (often called a "tax-advantaged" plan). The tax benefits allow employees to annually contribute part of their wages before tax (called "pre-tax") into investment accounts in which the earnings are also tax-free until later, when the account is distributed. Therefore tax on wages and earnings are deferred, not eliminated. Employers can currently deduct all the wages and even make additional contributions, which are deductible. (Note: a deferral is different than a salary reduction agreement in which an employee agrees to a salary decrease or forgoes a salary increase.)

A plan is "qualified" in two respects. First, the tax benefits result from an employer creating a written plan that complies with a certain part of the federal Internal Revenue Code. The second qualification results from a written plan that complies with the federal Employee Retirement Security Income Act, called "ERISA" which is designed to protect employees with retirement plans (see later ERISA discussion). ERISA applies to certain retirement plans (and some health plans) offered by a private-sector (non-governmental and non-church) employer. Therefore, whenever a private-sector employer offers a "qualified" tax-advantaged retirement plan, this means that the plan qualifies for both Internal Revenue code and ERISA purposes, although sometimes the word "qualified" is used to refer to only the tax-advantaged aspect. Government sector, church, and individual (IRA) tax-advantaged plans are often referred to as "non-qualified" for ERISA purposes. Our discussion focuses on the various tax-advantaged aspects of plans.

Plan names such as "401(k)" or "403(b)" may seem confusing at first, but the names are nothing more than quick references to the numbered sections of the Internal Revenue Code that describe the plans and set the rules. These plans are either ***defined contribution plans***, which means the contributions are specified but the ultimate benefits are not, or ***defined benefit plans***, in which future benefits are specified, and contributions can change to meet the required benefit. Most companies have moved away from defined benefit plans because of generally higher cost and to avoid the financial responsibility of providing recurring future benefits following employee retirements.

All qualified benefit plans require some form of at least annual compliance testing. Administrative costs can vary considerably by type of plan. ERISA requires annual reports and full disclosure to employees, called a ***summary plan description*** for new employees and a ***summary of benefits coverage*** annually and for new employees.

continued ▶

Tax-Deferred Benefits Summary: Employer Plans, *continued*

Overview,
Continued

Both the IRS and the Department of Labor regularly audit retirement plans and assess penalties for various types of non-compliance. For example, the ERISA penalty for failure to file a timely and completed Form 5500 is $250/day (IRS) and about $2,500/day (DOL). A good plan administrator will regularly assist in evaluating all compliance and stay in touch with the Human Resources to help avoid expensive penalties.

401(k) Plan:
Traditional

This is a defined contribution retirement plan that allows an employee (and self-employed persons) to direct the employer to deduct a pre-tax amount from paychecks, up to an annual limit, and have the funds placed in an employee's account that is part of a special supervised trust. (The technical tax jargon sometimes used for this process is "elective deferral", referring to a participant's election to defer receipt of some of his/her income to a later time when it will be taxed.)

A plan may also allow after-tax contributions. An employer may contribute (called "non-elective" and "matching" contributions) either alone or with the employee. To encourage savings, some employers have a matching program in which the employer will match an employee's contributions up to a certain limit of wages, such as 3% to 4%. Matching can be dollar for dollar or at a fixed rate, such as 50%.

Often employer contributions will have a vesting provision that phase in employee ownership of employer contributions based on years of employment. Non-elective and matching contributions are also tax-deferred for an employee–i.e., funds are not taxed until distributed from the retirement account. Traditional 401(k) plans require strict non-discrimination; there are potentially serious IRS penalties to prevent a greater proportion of contributions from being made by highly compensated employees.

Many 401(k) plans also allow borrowing by a participant. Generally the dollar limit is the lesser of 50% of the account vested amount or $50,000. Unless a loan was used to help buy a primary residence, it must be repaid in regular installments with interest determined by plan rules within 5 years or by date taxes due if leaving employer; otherwise, unpaid amounts are treated as a taxable distribution of income. Unless for personal emergencies, home purchase, or to pay high interest rate debt, these loans are generally not recommended. Some plans permit hardship withdrawals while still working. There are specific rules for these withdrawals. Also see the IRS *401(k) resource guide.*

The annual participant elective contribution limit for all regular 401(k) plans is the lesser of $20,500 or 100% of compensation unless a plan specifies a lower amount; however, for participants (both employees and self-employed) age 50 and older a plan may permit an annual additional $6,500 catch-up to a limit of $27,000 except for highly compensated employees. Also see IRS Publications 560, 4222, and 4531 for further 401(k) information.

continued ▶

Tax-Deferred Benefits Summary: Employer Plans, *continued*

401(k) Plan: Traditional, Continued

Tax effect on employee: An employee is not taxed on pre-tax and non-elective and matching contributions until funds are distributed after age 59 ½. As well, income earned in the investment account is not taxed while funds remain in the account. Except for hardship or severance from current employer at age 55 or later, a 10% early withdrawal penalty will apply. After-tax contributions are not taxed when funds are withdrawn at any time. Current employee 401(k) elective deferrals are reported in box 12, Code D on Form W2. Box 13 is checked. (A box 13 check indicates an "active participant": there are contributions or forfeitures by an eligible employee.) FICA tax applies to employee elective deferrals. Elective deferrals are included in box 3 (subject to limit) and box 5. This may make boxes 3 and 5 greater than box 1. Distributions are reported on Form 1099-R and Form 945 for non-payroll withholding.

Tax effect on employer: Employee elective deferrals are tax-deductible expenses as are employer contributions. Employer maximum tax-year deduction is 25% of all plans participants' compensation that is not greater than $305,000 per employee, plus employee elective deferrals. Employer FICA and FUTA apply to elective deferrals but not to employer contributions except for SIMPLE and SEP salary reduction agreements.

401(k) Plan: Safe Harbor

A 401(k) safe harbor plan is similar to a traditional plan. The key difference is that when an employer adopts a safe harbor plan, the requirements and risks of non-discrimination rules and most other compliance testing in a traditional plan are eliminated. However, a safe harbor plan requires mandatory minimum annual employer contributions, and the plan must provide that all contributions are immediately fully vested; i.e., funds are immediately owned by employees. All employer contributions are subject to a percentage limit of an employee's compensation. Employees can contribute. Loans are permitted. A 10% penalty applies to withdrawals before 59 ½. Employee and employer tax effects are the same as the traditional 401(k).

401(k) Plan: SIMPLE

A SIMPLE (Savings Incentive Match Plan for Employees) 401(k) plan is similar to a safe harbor plan, but is for small employers: 100 or fewer employees in the prior year who each earned at least $5,000 and sometimes less in either of two prior calendar years. Employers ceasing to meet this requirement are treated as meeting it for two calendar years following the year of non-compliance. Employers cannot maintain other plan types for eligible employees, but can offer other plans to ineligible employees. Mandatory minimum employer contributions are required (vested) using dollar-for-dollar matching or employee earnings. A primary attraction for employers is the simplicity and minimal cost to set up and maintain the plan. In most circumstances an employer can use a single form

continued ▶

Tax-Deferred Benefits Summary: Employer Plans, *continued*

401(k) Plan: SIMPLE, Continued	available from the IRS to set up the plan (Form 5305-S); however an annual Form 5500 is required for ERISA. The maximum annual employee contribution is $14,000 and the additional annual catch up provision is $3,000 for age 50 or older; however, when an employee participates in other plans the limit becomes $20,500. Loans may be permitted. A 10% penalty applies to withdrawals before 59 ½ and 25% if within two years of participation. Employee and employer tax effects are the same as the traditional 401(k). The employer deduction is limited to the maximum contribution. Annual ERISA Form 5500 is required.
401(k) Plan: Roth IRA	See the later discussion concerning an individual retirement account (IRA). A Roth IRA is a plan in which an employer can withhold a designated amount of an employee's after-tax earnings and deposit that amount into the employee's IRA. The contribution limit is the same as the traditional 401(k), and there are no income limits as with a traditional Roth IRA. Employer matching is allowed; however, this must be with pre-tax dollars placed into the 401(k) account, not the Roth. Form W-2, box 12, code AA, will indicate employee Roth contributions. Trustee should provide reporting Form 5498.
Other 401(k) Plans	There are other 401(k) variations. A "self directed" feature allows wider investment choices for the employees in a plan. A "tiered" profit sharing 401(k) is designed for very profitable companies with 50 or less employees. Employees are classified into working groups and profit sharing varies according to a group's contribution to profitability. A "Pooled" 401(k) allow small employers to join together to offer a 401(k) plan to their employees for administrative cost-sharing.
403(b) Plan	■ **Overview:** A 403(b) plan is very similar to a 401(k) plan, except that a 403(b) is specifically designed for public school districts and tax-exempt organizations. It has fewer compliance rules such as nondiscrimination testing. In some plans there may be fewer investment choices that sometimes involve high fee annuity contracts (that should be avoided). A 403(b) is sometimes called a "tax sheltered annuity" plan. A 401(k) plan generally is not used for the above organizations because it is actually a modified profit sharing, stock bonus, or similar plan that becomes a "401(k)", and these plan types do not really apply to public and nonprofit organizations. As well, administrative costs are much higher. A 403(b) allows a Roth IRA. The maximum annual employee 403(b) contribution limit is $20,500; however, both age 50 and 15-year catch-ups can increase the limit by $6,500 and $3,000 respectively. The annual employer/employee limit is the lesser of compensation or $61,000 ($67,500 if age 50 or older). See IRS Publications 4483 (sponsors) 4482 (participants) and 571. **Tax effect on employee:** An employee's elective deferrals are subject to OASDI and are included on Form W-2 box 3 (subject to limit) if the employee is not otherwise covered by a qualified state or local public

continued ▶

Tax-Deferred Benefits Summary: Employer Plans, *continued*

403(b) Plan, *Continued*	retirement system. Medicare may apply in many cases. Employee contributions are reported in box 12, code E on Form W-2. Box 13 will also be checked if there were current contributions or forfeitures. Form W-2, box 12, code BB, will indicate Roth contributions. Distributions are reported on Form 1099-R and Form 945 for non-payroll withholding. **Tax effect on employer:** Employer FICA taxes apply on employee deferrals if an employee is not otherwise covered as indicated above. FUTA does not apply to state and local governments; employer contributions are not subject to FICA.
457(b) Plan	■ **Overview:** A 457(b) plan is similar to a 403(b) plan because a 457(b) is a tax-advantaged, defined contribution, deferred compensation plan. However, a 457(b) is designed for state and local government employees (and to certain nonprofit organizations with special rules); a 457(b) is not covered by ERISA, and so is called "non-qualified", but is "eligible" to be tax-advantaged. A 457(b) allows larger annual contributions when nearing retirement. The financial hardship withdrawal options while still working are more limited in a 457(b) plan, although unlike qualified plans, there is no penalty for early distribution with severance of employment. The annual employee contribution limit is $20,500. Employees age 50 and older are permitted an annual additional $6,500 catch-up to a limit of $27,000 Loans are not permitted. 457(b) Roth IRAs are allowed for only government employees. An employee can contribute to both a 401(k) and 457(b) simultaneously. Also see Publication 4484. **Tax effect on employee:** As with the other plans, the deferred income is not subject to income tax until the employee withdraws funds. An employee's elective deferrals are subject to FICA and are included on Form W-2 boxes 3 (subject to limit) and 5 if the employee is not otherwise covered by a state or local public retirement system. All employee/employer contributions are reported in box 12, code G, Form W-2. Box 13 will not be checked. Form W-2, box 12, code EE indicate Roth contributions. Distributions: 1099-R and Form 945 for non-payroll withholding. **Tax effect on employer:** State and local governments generally do not pay federal income tax. Employer FICA taxes apply. FUTA does not apply for state and local governments.
Profit-Sharing *Plan*	■ **Overview:** This is another defined contribution plan, and as the name indicates, a profit-sharing plan is designed to allow an employer to make contributions into employee retirement accounts based on a share of company profits, although except for self-employed persons, a profit in any given year is not required in order to make a contribution. There are four allowed methods a company may use to determine allocations to employees. A common method is to multiply the total contribution amount by each employee's wages as a fraction of

continued   ▶

Tax-Deferred Benefits Summary: Employer Plans, *continued*

Profit-Sharing Plan, Continued

all wages. Only employer contributions are allowed, and these are discretionary. If a provision is added to a profit-sharing plan that allows employee contributions, the profit-sharing plan becomes a 401(k) plan. An employer may use this plan with other retirement plans.

The annual contribution limit per individual currently is the lesser of 25% of employee compensation or $61,000; a catch up amount of $6,500 is allowed for employees over age 50. Vesting schedules are allowed. Employee loans are permitted. See IRS Publications 4806 and 560 for more details.

Tax effect on employee: An employee is not taxed until funds are distributed after age 59 ½, or age 55 if no longer employed by current employer. As well, income earned in the investment account is not taxed while funds remain in the account. Early withdrawals may result in penalties. FICA does not apply. No amounts are reported on Form W-2 but box 13 will be checked if there was an allocation. Distributions are reported on Form 1099-R and Form 945 for non-payroll withholding.

Tax effect on employer: Employee deferrals are deductible as are employer contributions. Employer maximum deduction is 25% of all plans participants' compensation that is not greater than $305,000 per employee, plus employee deferrals. FICA and FUTA do not apply to contributions.

Thrift Savings Plan (TSP)

A TSP is designed for federal employees and for members of the armed services. It is similar to a 401(k) plan. Investment choices may be somewhat more limited than under some 401(k) plans but costs are low. A TSP Roth IRA is available.

TIP

The annual combined employee/employer limit for all above defined contribution plans except stand-alone SIMPLE plans is the is the lesser of $61,000 ($67,500 if 50 or older) or 100% of an employee's compensation. **Contribution limits** for 401(k)/403(b)/457(b) before catch-up: 1) Annual elective total of all plans: $20,500 or 100% of compensation if less 2) Total elective + non-elective/matching per plan: $61,000. **Compensation limits:** 1) Employer: 25% of aggregate earned income of plan beneficiaries 2) Individual compensation exceeding $305,000 is ineligible for contribution calculations.

TIP

Matching: Although the annual employee pre-tax 401(k) contribution is limited to $20,500 (before any catch-up), employer matching can equal this, also as a pre-tax contribution and payroll taxes don't apply to employer matches. The combined pre- and after-tax employee/employer contribution limit is $61,000.

Tax-Deferred Benefits Summary: Employer Plans, *continued*

SEP-IRA

■ **Overview:** See the later discussion concerning an individual retirement account (IRA). A simplified employee pension plan (SEP) is a defined contribution plan set up by an employer of any size on behalf of employees or by a self-employed person. Only an employer can make contributions and these contributions are discretionary, but equal percentages, go into regular IRA accounts owned by each eligible employee. No other qualified retirement plan can be in place. The annual limit is the lesser of 25% of employee compensation or $61,000 with a $6,500 catch-up for age 50 or over. Employee must earn at least $600 in the year, and worked for the employer 3 of 5 last years

A primary attraction for an employer is the simplicity and minimal cost to set up and maintain the plan because it does not need to qualify for ERISA. Generally, a provider can use a single IRS form to set up the plan (Form 5305-A-SEP) or prototype with no filing thereafter. Another desirable feature is the relatively large amount of tax-free compensation that potentially can be saved, which is particularly attractive to self-employed persons. Loans are not permitted. See IRS Publication 560. Also see later discussion of an IRA (Individual Retirement Account).

Tax effect on employee: Contributions are reported in box 12, code F. Box 13 is also checked. An IRA reporting Form 5498 should be provided by trustee. FICA does not apply. Other distributions are reported on Form 1099-R and Form 945 for non-payroll withholding.

Tax effect on employer: Employer maximum deduction is 25% of all plans participants' compensation (except sole proprietors) that is not greater than $305,0000 per employee. FICA and FUTA don't apply except for salary reduction agreements.

TIP

To promote more enrollment, savings, and to spread benefits, plans that allow employee elective contributions–401(k), 403(b), 457(b), SIMPLE IRAs–permit an automatic enrollment feature in which employees must opt out or they are automatically enrolled in contributions based on a default percentage of compensation. Also, plans permit an automatic escalation feature in which contributions are increased by a fixed percent amount at intervals, typically annually, or when pay increases. An automatic rebalancing feature can be available that annually reallocates investment accounts to their initial relative percentages. (However, an employee should check that this does not create significant additional commissions, fees, or "loads" from sales/purchases.) Finally, the 2019 SECURE ACT provides a $500 small employer (up to 100 employees) tax credit for automatic enrollment to new employees in 401(k) and SIMPLE IRAs for 3 years.

continued ▶

Tax-Deferred Benefits Summary: Employer Plans, *continued*

Limits

The annual **limit on combined employee and employer** *contributions* (also called "annual additions") is $61,000 plus any catch-up amounts for a plan participating employee for any one employer. The annual limit for elective contributions out of salary ("pre-tax") for an employee is: • For 401(k) and 403(b): $20,500/or catch-up to $27,000; SIMPLE 401(k) and IRA plan: $14,000 and $17,000 catch-up. For SEP plans the limit is the smaller of $61,000 or 25% of compensation. Excess contributions are subject to a penalty if not withdrawn by April 15 of the following year. Both pre-tax and after-tax contributions are subject to the combined limit.

The annual **limit on** *compensation* is $305,000. For example, an employee enrolled in a 401(k) who earned $400,000 with a 3% elective deferral could only calculate a contributions on a limit of $305,000, for $9,150 (employer can match to that limit). If the plan permits, the employee could switch to flat amounts to the limit of $20,500/$27,000 as well as after-tax amounts subject to the combined limit. Employer tax-year limit: 25% of all compensation.

SIMPLE-IRA

- **Overview**: A SIMPLE IRA is attractive to self-employed persons because of the relatively large amount of income that can be saved tax-free. As well, set-up is straightforward and can be completed by using IRS forms 5304-SIMPLE and 5305-SIMPLE. An employer is required to make at least a minimum contribution to employees' IRA accounts according to guidelines and employees can also contribute. This plan is also for small employers: 100 or fewer employees in the preceding year who each received at least the employer's-designated amount (generally $5,000) in any two preceding calendar years and can reasonably be expected to earn the same amount in the current calendar year. Employers ceasing to meet this requirement in any subsequent year are treated as meeting it for two calendar years following the year of non-compliance. Other plan types are not allowed except those under collective bargaining agreements. Loans and hardship withdrawals are not allowed as with the 401(k) SIMPLE plans. No discrimination testing.

  Self-employed persons with earned income and leased employees are included. An employee can withdraw funds before age 59 ½ but the withdrawal is subject to a 10% penalty (25% if within first two years). Annual contribution limit is $14,000 or age 50/older catch-up to $17,000.

  Tax effect on employee: Elective deferrals are subject to FICA and Form W-2 will include contributions in boxes 3 (subject to limit) and 5. Employee contributions are reported in box 12, code S on Form W-2. (Code D if part of a 401(k).) Box 13 is also checked. An IRA reporting Form 5498 should be provided by trustee. Distributions are reported on Form 1099-R and Form 945 for non-payroll withholding.

continued ▶

Tax-Deferred Benefits Summary: Employer Plans, *continued*

SIMPLE-IRA,
Continued

Tax effect on employer: Employee elective deferrals are deductible and employer FICA and FUTA apply. Employer contributions are deductible to above limits and FICA and FUTA do not apply except for salary reduction agreements. ERISA Form 5500 not required.

TIP

For a sole proprietor or a single-member LLC, qualified and SEP plan limits are determined differently. The procedure is: 1) Determine net earnings from self-employment (SE), which is generally .9235 of business net income; 2) determine SE tax (See page 104 for self-employment tax.) 3) multiple SE by ½ ; 4) Subtract from net income; 5) Multiply by the amount of contribution, determined as a percentage of income before the contribution. For example, assume a self-employed person's business net income is $120,000 and the retirement contribution plan percentage is 10%.1) $120,000 × .9235 = $110,820 net earnings from self-employment; 2) Self-employment tax is $110,820 × .153 = $16,955; 3) $16,955 × .5 = $8,478 one-half of self-employment tax. 4) $120,000 – $8,478 = $111,522 net income reduced by one-half of self-employment tax; 5) $111,522 × 10%/110% (which is .0909) = $10,138. The IRS provides worksheets in Publication 560.

ESOP

■ **Overview**: An Employee Stock Ownership Plan (ESOP) is a qualified written plan that invests primarily in the stock of the company that sponsors the plan. The main purpose of an ESOP is to create significant employee ownership in the sponsoring company. This creates a sense of participation, motivation, and productivity among employees. At the same time, it serves as a defined contribution retirement plan for employees who accumulate shares of the stock. ESOPs are used by companies of all sizes, but generally not smaller than about 15 to 20 employees and that have reliable cash flow. Plan setup-costs can be $50,000 - $100,000.

To set up an ESOP a company creates a trust and contributes cash for one or a period of years (and sometimes its stock) into the trust so that the trust can buy shares of company stock from current public or private owners. As the trust acquires more shares it becomes a larger owner of the company. Often a trust will obtain a loan (called a "leveraged" ESOP), guaranteed by the company, to purchase the shares.

As the trust purchases the stock at its discretion, it allocates the shares to individual employee accounts in the trust for all eligible employees. Typically there is a vesting period for up to six years before an employee obtains full ownership of the shares. The longer an employee remains with a company, the more shares are accumulated and owned, without the employee having to pay anything for the shares. The plan is particularly helpful for employees who cannot

continued ▶

Tax-Deferred Benefits Summary: Employer Plans, *continued*

ESOP,
Continued

afford to contribute to retirement plans. The shares accumulate until employment terminates. The trust or the company then pays the employee for the value of the shares as determined by appraisal if there is no public market; otherwise, an employee may receive cash for the shares, shares, or a combination of both. The timing and method of payment varies depending on several factors. A company with an ESOP can also set up other retirement plans.

Tax effect on employee: Current allocations to an employee account are not taxable to the employee, and there is no W-2 reporting. Distributions are reported on Form 1099-R and Form 945 for non-payroll withholding. Increases in account value are also tax-free. Cash distributions are generally taxed as ordinary income; if shares are received, a plan can provide an election for the ESOP acquisition cost be taxed as ordinary income and any later stock appreciation is taxed at lower capital gains rates. Also, distributions may rolled over into an IRA or other qualified retirement plan without tax (except Roth IRA). Early withdrawals before age 59 ½ are subject to a 10% penalty as with other employer retirement plans.

An attractive alternative is available to shareholders who sell their shares of corporate stock (except "S" corporations) to the ESOP. Shares may be sold without tax if: 1) after the transaction the ESOP owns at least 30% of company stock and, 2) the proceeds are invested in ownership of another company, typically publicly traded stock in other companies. This defers tax until the shares are sold later and also improves diversification (IRC §1042 "rollover").

Although an ESOP can be a valuable plan, employees must be careful not to concentrate too much of their retirement resources, depending heavily on a single company. There are some ESOP diversification requirements that allow older employees to purchase other assets within their accounts before the distribution.

Tax effect on employer: Contributions of cash or stock to an ESOP by the sponsoring company are tax-deductible generally up to 25% of eligible employee pay including other plans, capped currently at an annual $305,0000 as with other employer plans. Also repayments of ESOP loan principal are tax-deductible within this limit. Interest on the loan for certain corporations are not subject to the limit. Note that an ESOP itself is not subject to income tax; therefore, a company owned by an ESOP does not pay federal income tax.

Money Purchase
Plan

A money purchase plan is similar to a profit-sharing plan, except that in a money purchase plan employer contributions are not discretionary. Employers must set a contribution level amount at the beginning of a plan year, based as a percentage of employee wages. The annual individual contribution limit is 25% of compensation or $61,000 whichever is less.

Tax-Deferred Benefits Summary: Employer Plans, *continued*

TIP

How are my funds invested? When an employee is asked if he or she has made any investments, it is not unusual to hear a response such as "Yes, I have a 401(k)" or "I have a 403(b)". When asked again to describe the investments, often the answer again is "I have a 401(k)" or "I have a 403(b)". This indicates that there is little awareness of exactly how the money has been invested and the risks, returns, fees, and possible penalties involved. What kind of funds, bonds/fixed income, annuities, accounts, or other things are in the account? What fees are being charged and how do they compare to alternatives? The best plans offer employees a wide choice of investment alternatives. Thoughtful employers provide help or encourage employees to do at least a little financial homework before making investment choices, and to periodically check performance.

What is a "CHIP"?

CHIP stands for the **Children's Health Insurance Program**. This program provides low-cost children's health insurance to families that earn too much for Medicaid. Every state has a CHIP program. To determine if they qualify, families can call 1-800-318-2596 (TTY 1-855-889-4325) or go to healthcare.gov, search for CHIP, and use the "create an account" link.

ERISA requires that every company that is ERISA qualified inform employees of the availability of CHIP. Failure to comply will result in daily penalties per employee.

Traditional Defined Benefit Plan

- **Overview:** In a traditional qualified defined benefit plan (sometimes called a "pension" or "pension plan"), the employer makes contributions and upon retirement (usually about age 65) a beneficiary employee is generally guaranteed a lifetime annuity (regular equal payments) or might have the option of a lump sum amount. This is in effect additional deferred compensation, not a deferral of income. The amount of the benefit received is usually calculated as a percentage of pay over a designated period multiplied by the years of service. Each year a professional actuary must estimate a high/low range to achieve the desired benefit, based on multiple variables and assumptions such as investment return, amount in the retirement fund, employee age, benefit payment method, and so on*. For example, if an employee will receive 3% of average annual pay based on the last 5 years of employment, which is $75,000, and worked 25 years for the employer, the annual annuity benefit would be: $75,000 × .03 × 25 = $56,250 for life. Alternatively, based on lifetime expectancy tables, the employee might

---

*As of January 1, 2020 the 2019 SECURE Act permits annuities to also be included in 401(k) plans; the act also places fiduciary liability on insurance companies offering the plan, rather than on the employer. Historically, annuity fees are the highest among plans.

continued ▶

Tax-Deferred Benefits Summary: Employer Plans, *continued*

Traditional Defined Benefit Plan, Continued

receive the value of that annuity at retirement as a lump sum. The maximum annual contribution limit is annual benefit of $245,000. In some plans employees can make elective contributions. A variation is a "cash benefit plan" in which the objective is a cash balance upon retirement. Qualified defined benefit plans are the most expensive and complex to administer. (Non-qualified plans are sometimes an alternative.)

As indicated earlier defined benefit plans are the most complex and expensive plans to set up, manage, and fund, and the employer assumes full responsibility* for meeting the defined benefit. Perhaps counter-intuitively, defined benefit plans also can be very beneficial to older high-income sole owners and very small business owners. This is because of the high defined benefit annual employer deduction limit.

Tax effect on employee: An employee's elective contributions are included in income and also subject to FICA, which are included on Form W-2 boxes 3 (subject to limit) and 5. Box 13 will be checked if an employee is eligible to participate. Distributions are reported on Form 1099-R and Form 945 for non-payroll withholding.

Tax effect on employer: Employer contributions are deductible based on actuarial assumptions. Employee elective contributions are subject to FICA and FUTA. FICA and FUTA do not apply to employer contributions in qualified plans.

Group Annuity Contracts

Some employers fund their defined benefit obligations by purchasing annuity contracts from large and reliable insurance companies. These contracts cover benefits for all eligible employees. The employer pays the insurance company premiums, usually as regular payments over a period of years, and in return the insurance company is responsible for providing the necessary funds to employees when benefits are due. The insurance company may assume all legal responsibilities and pay the employees directly or reimburse an employer that still retains payment obligation. Reserves and funding levels are often higher than in an employer managed plan. (Note: individual employee annuities also are often part of the investment choices in 403(b) plans.)

Tax effect on employee and employer: Same as traditional plan.

Cash Balance Plans

A cash balance plan also offers a guaranteed benefit; however, instead of an annuity the target benefit is a guaranteed cash balance. Each eligible employee is assigned an account and the account is credited each year with a percentage of pay. In addition the account is also receives and interest credit, which may be fixed or variable depending on the plan. In a sense, the account is just a calculation of the employer's growing obligation to an employee, a sort of hypothetical account, because it may not reflect the actual results of the employer's underlying investment

continued ▶

Tax-Deferred Benefits Summary: Employer Plans, *continued*

Cash Balance Plans, Continued	fund results. However, regardless of changes in the actual funding, the employer is obligated to provide the employee with guaranteed amount upon retirement. Sometimes this lump sum amount can be converted into its equivalent annuity value.

Tax effect on employee: Same as traditional plan.
Tax effect on employer: Same as traditional plan.

Target Benefit Plan	A target benefit plan is similar to a defined benefit plan in that the benefit is defined as a certain distribution of funds to an employee; however, unlike a defined benefit plan the defined benefit is not guaranteed. This is similar to a money purchase plan. However, instead of uniform percentages, with a target benefit plan contributions to individual accounts are based on actuarial variables needed to obtain the desired benefit. So although an employer is required to make contributions to an employee account according to a formula, the results are on a "best efforts" basis only. The benefit target for each employee is adjusted up or down as conditions change, which creates greater employee uncertainty, particularly for older employees.
HR10 Plan (Keogh Plan)	This plan is the legacy of a plan that was first created in the early 1960s. It is a qualified employer plan. It applies generally to self-employed persons who operate as a business and to other small business owners. The plan can be either a defined contribution plan that is a profit sharing or money purchase plan, or a defined benefit plan. Only the owner can make contributions; however, the plan benefits must be made available to both owner and all eligible employees. Because of extensive paperwork and contribution restrictions, the plan is no longer popular in comparison to SEP and SIMPLE plans for small businesses. A Keogh plan is used primarily because contribution limits are much higher than other plans. A Keogh plan is really for high-income sole proprietors and small business owners in businesses with significant cash flow. A final important point to note is that these plans are not covered by ERISA and are therefore not protected from creditors, unless protected under state laws.
ERISA *(Employee Retirement Plan Protection)*	ERISA (Employee Retirement Income Security Act of 1974) is a federal law that sets minimum standards primarily for non-governmental and non-church employer retirement and health plans. ERISA also does not generally apply to voluntary contribution and to non-U.S. plans that are primarily for the benefit of non-resident aliens. ERISA was created to ensure that plans are properly funded and that workers who are retirement plan participants would receive the proper amount of benefits in accordance with their years of service and particular plan features.

As well, ERISA can provide protection from lawsuit judgments for employer-sponsored ERISA-qualified retirement plans and some medical plan assets such as 401(k), HSAs, defined benefit pensions, and profit-sharing, except for spousal and child support, qualified domestic

continued ▶

Tax-Deferred Benefits Summary: Employer Plans, *continued*

ERISA

(Employee Retirement Plan Protection), Continued

relations orders, and the IRS for unpaid taxes. (Generally non-ERISA-qualified plans protection depends on state law. These types of plans include 403(b), 457(b), SEP, IRAs, Keogh, government and church plans.)

The key ERISA requirements are:

- Plan information: Participants must receive plan information that explains the features of the plan, minimum standards for participation, how the plan will be funded, information on plan assets and investment results, how benefits accrue, how the plan will be managed, the responsibilities of managing the plan and grievance and appeals procedures.
- Vesting: "Vesting" means the right of an employee to receive payment if the employee terminates employment prior to retirement. Vesting is based on years of service required in order to receive full or partial payment. Upon full vesting, an employee has the right to full retirement benefits, regardless of whether the employee at that time is working for the same or a different employer.
- Termination of a defined benefit plan: If a defined benefit plan is terminated, ERISA guarantees designated benefit payments through the Pension Benefit Guarantee Corporation (below) created by ERSISA.
- Reporting: The plan administrator must file either Form 5500 or 5500-SF depending on the number of participants in a plan. The due date is the last day of the seventh month following the end of a plan year. Note: one-participant plans and foreign plans not subject to ERISA file form 5500-EZ. It should be noted that other reporting requirements exist as well. Further information is available at: https://webapps.dol.gov/elaws/elg/erisa.htm and at https://www.dol.gov/sites/dolgov/files/EBSA/about-ebsa/our-activities/resource-center/publications/reporting-and-disclosure-guide-for-employee-benefit-plans.pdf for reporting on employer benefit plans.

Pension Benefit Guarantee Corporation (PBGC)

The Pension Benefit Guarantee Corporation (PBGC) is an independent federal agency created by ERISA for the primary purpose of guaranteeing that workers receive at least a basic pension for defined benefit pension plans that have been terminated without sufficient funds to pay promised benefits ("distress" termination). The amount that a worker receives depends on age or service time and other factors. The current annual maximum benefit amount for a single-employer worker at 65 is about $75,000 and lower (higher) for younger (older) workers or with fewer years of service. The PBGC also supervises payouts of financially sound funds ("standard" termination) by lump sum or annuity.

The PBGC is funded by insurance premiums paid by employers with defined benefit pension plans. The amount of the premium depends on the number of participants in a plan. Because companies have been shifting to defined contribution plans, there is substantially less insurance premium funding, and in the future the PBGC may require taxpayer funds to remain solvent and continue operating.

Tax-Deferred Benefits Summary: Individual Plans

Overview

A person can establish his or her own individual retirement plan for savings and investments that is not part of an employer plan. This is done by working with a bank, insurance company, or other qualified financial institution to establish an individual retirement account, called an "IRA". This is also called a "self-directed IRA". Payroll deduction plans are also allowed. The two IRA types are a traditional IRA and Roth IRA. (Note: sometimes an IRA can be part of an employer plan as previously described with the SIMPLE IRA and the SEP-IRA.)

Traditional IRA

A traditional IRA allows individuals with earned income to make deductible contributions into a savings or investment account in which the wage and account income is tax deferred. The IRA contributions are reported as deductions from an individual's taxable gross income when the annual individual income tax return is filed. For individuals under age 50 the current annual contribution limit is the lesser of 100% of earned income (salary, wages, commissions, self-employment income, spousal support, and non-taxable combat pay) or $6,000; for age 50 and above there is a catch-up provision that allows an additional annual $1,000 contribution. There are income limits for an employee who also makes contributions to an employer plan (box 13 is checked on Form W-2). Non-deductible after-tax dollars can also be contributed to a traditional IRA and are reported on Form 8606 (this keeps a record of after-tax dollars so they will not be taxed later upon distribution). These contributions are subject to the same annual IRA limit. Contributions are subject to FICA and FUTA.

If funds are withdrawn from an IRA account before age 59 ½, the withdrawal is included in taxable income; additionally, a 10% penalty is assessed on the amount withdrawn. A penalty exception is allowed for hardship needs, first-time home purchase, death or disability, IRS levy, and several other items.

Per 2019 SECURE act, distribution of benefits must begin at the earlier of April 1 of the year following age 72 or plan requirements for persons reaching 70 ½ as of January 1, 2020. A minimum amount is required. This is called a "required minimum distribution" and uses a calculation based on life annuity tables. (This is frequ ently referred to as an "RMD", which also applies to employer qualified plans.) Annual distributions are taxed as ordinary income and reported on an annual individual tax return. A final point: an IRA is not covered and protected by ERISA. For further information on IRAs see IRS Publications 590-A (contributions) and 590-B (withdrawals and distributions).

Roth IRA

A Roth IRA allows non-deductible after-tax contributions, subject to annual income limits depending on filing status (regardless of whether there is participation in an employer plan) into a savings or investment account

continued

Tax-Deferred Benefits Summary: Individual Plans, *continued*

Roth IRA,
Continued

in which the account earnings are never taxed, provided that when earnings are withdrawn: 1) at least 5 years have passed since January 1 of the year in which contributions began and, 2) age 59 ½ has been reached. If these requirements are not met, a 10% penalty applies in addition to ordinary income tax on the earnings. There are penalty exceptions. Penalty and tax apply only to earnings; withdrawals of after-tax contributions are always tax-free. The contribution limit is the same as regular IRA. Withdrawals at age 59 ½ or later are tax-free. An account balance–from both pre and after-tax contribution–in a regular IRA may be converted to a Roth IRA subject to conversion rules, including tax possibly due.

Rollovers

A "rollover" means directing a distribution from one employer tax-deferred plan into another employer tax-deferred plan or into an IRA, or from one IRA into another IRA. Some employer plans allow rollovers from an IRA into the plan. Required minimum distributions and some other specified distributions do not qualify. Rollovers most often occur when an employee leaves one employer and begins work with a new employer (although not usually mandatory, depending on plan rules), but also can be done for purposes of greater investment choices, lower fees, estate planning, or other reasons. Rollovers are tax-free if allowed procedures are correctly followed; however, rollovers from pre-tax accounts into Roth IRAs incur tax with special rules. A Roth works best when funds are kept for an extended period after a rollover to compensate for taxes paid. When rollover funds are directed into an IRA, that IRA is sometimes called a "Rollover IRA"; either an existing IRA or a new IRA can be used for this purpose. (Note: when simply moving IRA balances between financial institutions a process called a direct "trustee-to-trustee" transfer is easier and should be used.) See Publications 560 and 590-B for further rollover details.

TIP

To attract higher-earning employees motivated by saving, an employer should consider adopting or revising a qualified plan so that it allows rollovers to Roth IRAs while an employee is still in-service, and also to permit employee after-tax contributions. For example, this would mean that when a 401(k) pre-tax contribution limit of $20,500 is passed ($27,000 for after age 50), an employee can continue saving with after-tax dollars to the annual limit of $61,000 ($67,500 for after age 50). While still employed, these additional contributions beyond the pre-tax limit can then be rolled over into a Roth IRA in which, unlike the 401(k), the earnings are tax-free when withdrawn, plus much more has been saved beyond the annual Roth IRA contribution limit.

Tax-Deferred Benefits Summary: Employer Plans, *continued*

TIP

A common assumption in most employee retirement planning is that an employee's tax rate will be lower after retirement when distributions are made, because income will be less. This may not always be the case for several reasons: 1) successful retirement planning may result in income not materially lower, 2) tax rates can increase as taxing authorities require more revenue, 3) The surviving spouse will pay higher tax on the same income at single rates. Therefore planning for a tax-free and a secure retirement income should be considered, with methods such as: 1) Roth IRAs, including annuities purchased in a Roth IRA if fees are reasonable, 2) permanent life insurance (whole life, universal life) contract that can be used for tax-free cash out, 3) Municipal bonds, 4) reduction of state taxes by relocating, 5) least desirable–life insurance tax-free payout at death of insured.

Managing Benefits

Overview

Benefits management involves a number of important tasks, some of which are discussed below. As well, employers incur an ongoing cost when providing benefits. Why spend the time and incur the costs and responsibilities? The answer is simple – to attract and keep the best employees. Benefit choices are initially made by management with input from the human resources department; however, continuing benefits management is a joint effort between human resources and payroll departments.

Initial Analysis

Before a benefits plan is created, an employer must understand both the alternatives available and the details involved with any plan of possible interest. Management also should try to identify what benefits similar companies are providing to their employees. Usually the human resources department assists management with benefits choices and analysis. Working with a benefits advisory consultant also is a good idea and can provide valuable help with the evaluation, but in the end management must do its own evaluation of the information, which requires time and effort. As part of this, benefits budgets that identify the significant plan costs should be developed for each plan of interest.

Audit the Plans

Qualified benefit plans have compliance rules; usually each plan has multiple rules. These are Internal Revenue Code requirements and ERISA requirements. An employer should self-audit each type of benefit plan at least annually, checking compliance requirements for both IRS and ERISA purposes. Compliance failures can result in fines, loss of favorable tax treatment to certain employees, or plan disqualification

continued ▶

Managing Benefits, *continued*

Audit the Plans, Continued	that potentially results in retroactive loss of plan benefits with income tax and possible payroll tax assessment for all enrolled employees, and a disallowance of past rollovers. For employers with 100 or more employees, ERISA requires that outside auditors perform an audit at the beginning of each plan year; the audit evaluates both IRS and ERISA compliance.
Human Resources Department	Within the scope of benefits management, the human resources department has the ongoing responsibility of informing employees about available benefits features, updating insurance carriers and 3rd parties, maintaining records and updating each employee's benefits choices, checking compliance, and timely informing the payroll department of changes. A working knowledge of compliance requirements and the ability to ask questions and understand professional guidance when necessary are essential. The following solutions (not mutually exclusive) may help to address these responsibilities:

1) Numerous training seminars and programs are available. Online training is generally less expensive than in-person.
2) Various kinds of in-house and cloud-based benefits software systems are available that can support and automate many levels of complexity, including the responsibilities described above. As benefits become more numerous and employment increases, a good system can save many hours. Examples: Facilitating compliance, including reporting requirements records updates with job changes, open enrollment, new enrollments, and terminations tools that assist employees in making benefits decisions and allow direct access to personal benefits status.

   • Paid time off (PTO) tracking • updating performance appraisal
   • Facilitating employee communication, such as garnishment and contribution limit notices (be sure that a system has validation checks to ensure limit compliance) • interface to payroll processing.

3) Use a benefits advisory or consulting firm. The level and type of assistance can be pre-defined in many cases. Some firms can be particularly helpful in monitoring changes in benefits legislation.
4) Use a staffing agency to provide experienced individuals to help at busy times or to help the department transition into additional responsibilities.

Payroll Department Interface	A key responsibility is to provide the payroll department with accurate and current employee benefits information with each payroll run. At minimum a checklist should be employed; combining this with benefits software helps streamline and optimize the procedures.

Managing Benefits, *continued*

Accounts Payable Department Interface	The human resources department must verify and approve different types of payments and notify the accounts payable department of the approval in order to begin a payment process. Examples include: changes in insurance premiums, approval of other HR-related vendor bills, and employee reimbursements.

Other Operational Suggestions and Tips

- **The DOL has a useful employer guide at**: https://www.dol.gov/sites/default/files/ebsa/about-ebsa/our-activities/resource-center/publications/reporting-and-disclosure-guide-for-employee-benefit-plans.pdf.
- **The IRS has the following useful resources**: 1) "Retirement Plan Operation and Maintenance" (has numerous useful topics and checklists): https://www.irs.gov/retirement-plans/retirement-plan-operation-and-maintenance 2) "Fix It Guides": https://www.irs.gov/retirement-plans/plan-sponsor/fix-it-guides-common-problems-real-solutions
- Frequent employee plan changes can become overwhelming. Limit plan changes to a once-per-year time period with limited exceptions.
- Develop a method or system that tracks both current and former employees with stock options and stock purchase plans so future exercises and dispositions can be reported to payroll as it becomes necessary.
- When feasible try to cross train duties. This provides a more flexible departmental resource and develops a greater understanding of departmental processes.

Reporting Compliance

Depending on the type of benefit, regular reporting to taxing authorities and/or employees may be required. For example, the Department of Labor and IRS have numerous reporting requirements for qualified retirement plans. A checklist of reporting requirements will be useful for avoiding non-compliance problems.

CAUTION! Federal Contracts Change

Remember: Federal contracts entered into or extended after January 30, 2022 require a federal minimum wage of $15/hour.

TIP

For employers paying periodic pension and retirement income, use Worksheet 1B in Publication 15-T (available online) for automated systems. Optional tables are also available. Form W-4P for pension recipients has been redesigned; optional tables will work with earlier and current forms. Non-periodic payments are subject to a flat 10% withholding on taxable amounts except rollovers at 20%.

The Payroll Process

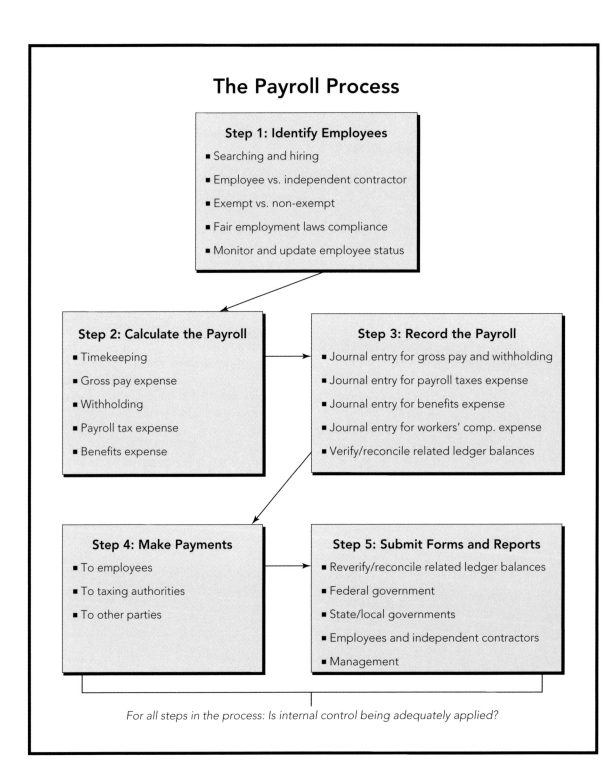

Step 1: Identify Employees
- Searching and hiring
- Employee vs. independent contractor
- Exempt vs. non-exempt
- Fair employment laws compliance
- Monitor and update employee status

Step 2: Calculate the Payroll
- Timekeeping
- Gross pay expense
- Withholding
- Payroll tax expense
- Benefits expense

Step 3: Record the Payroll
- Journal entry for gross pay and withholding
- Journal entry for payroll taxes expense
- Journal entry for benefits expense
- Journal entry for workers' comp. expense
- Verify/reconcile related ledger balances

Step 4: Make Payments
- To employees
- To taxing authorities
- To other parties

Step 5: Submit Forms and Reports
- Reverify/reconcile related ledger balances
- Federal government
- State/local governments
- Employees and independent contractors
- Management

For all steps in the process: Is internal control being adequately applied?

Introduction	Recording payroll is primarily an accounting function, rather than involving compliance questions, as in Section 2. This section discusses the typical accounting procedures that are required each time that a payroll is calculated. Additionally, conforming to the application of ***internal control*** procedures is essential for reducing the chances of fraud and error. (See Section 7 on internal control.)

Overview

General Procedures	After the correct gross wages, employee withholding, employer payroll taxes, and benefits for a payroll period have been processed, these amounts must be permanently recorded in the accounting system. This requires an understanding of basic accounting procedures such as the use of debits and credits, journals, and ledgers. The content presented in this section assumes an understanding of these topics. The journal illustrations here use a general journal format. Many companies use a payroll journal that records only payroll transactions, although this may not appear in some payroll software. Methods illustrated conform to the application of generally accepted accounting principles (GAAP) using accrual basis accounting. (In a cash basis accounting system, accrual entries, receivables, and payables are not used. See page 350.)
Four Basic Parts	The process of recording a payroll involves four basic parts:

- Journal entry to record the gross wages expense and related accounts
- Journal entry to record employer payroll taxes expense and related accounts
- Journal entry to record benefits expenses and related accounts
- Update each employee's earnings record

In our examples we show journal entries as they would appear in a general journal format. Some companies might use a special journal designed specifically to show individual payroll transactions with gross wages, withholding, net pay, and totals.

Summarize the Information	Before the recording process, the payroll department must first summarize and organize the payroll information. This is usually accomplished by producing a ***payroll register*** (sometimes called a payroll record). A payroll register is an informal summary tool that is created each time

continued ▶

Summarize the Information, Continued

payroll is processed to show the individual and total amounts of gross earnings, deductions, and net pay for that particular payroll period. A payroll register also facilitates analysis of wages and withholding.

TIP

For best practices, use a **separate payroll cash account**. When we record "Cash" in the following entries, we assume that the Cash entry refers to a payroll cash account, not the general cash account. There are several key advantages of a separate payroll cash account: 1) It is easier to reconcile two smaller cash accounts than one large account. 2) All cash payroll transactions are in a single source. 3) After payroll is calculated, the exact amount of cash can be deposited into the account, and overdrafts should not occur. 4) A layer of security is provided–payroll checks do not show the general cash account number and if a payroll account is hacked, the general cash account is protected.

The Payroll Register Illustrated

Example

On this page and the next page is an example of a completed payroll register.

Illustration 3.1: Payroll Register

		1		2		Current Gross Taxable For... 3	
		Earnings					
Employee Name	Total Hours	Regular	Overtime	Current Gross	Year to Date Gross	FUTA/ SUTA	OASDI
Acevedo, Baxter	40	600.00		600.00	7,200.00	400.00	600.00
Dunston, Walt	40	1,400.00		1,400.00	14,500.00	-0-	1,400.00
Heintz, Marilyn	44	600.00	90.00	690.00	7,150.00	540.00	690.00
Onishi, James	–	1,800.00		1,800.00	18,800.00	-0-	1,800.00
Sanders, Emily	40	480.00		480.00	5,350.00	480.00	480.00
Van Arsdale, R.	42	720.00	54.00	774.00	7,900.00	-0-	774.00
Washington, E.	–	1,900.00		1,900.00	19,900.00	-0-	1,900.00
Totals	–	7,500.00	144.00	7,644.00	80,800.00	1,420.00	7,644.00

Payroll Register for the

The Payroll Register Illustrated, *continued*

Detailed Explanation

Each of the following items relates to the numbered highlighted boxes shown in the payroll register above.

1) **Earnings:** For wage employees, earnings are calculated at an hourly rate; for salaried employees (Onishi and Washington), earnings are a fixed amount. Gross earnings in the current period include both the regular and overtime pay. For example, Marilyn Heintz earned $600 regular pay, so her regular rate must be $15 per hour ($600 regular pay/40 hours). Therefore, her combined regular plus overtime premium rate is $15 × 1.5 = $22.50 per hour. Because she worked 4 hours in excess of 40, she earns overtime of $22.50 × 4 = $90.

2) **Year to date gross:** This is an optional column that helps identify the cumulative amount of employee gross pay that includes the current payroll. Cumulative amounts are part of each employee's individual earnings record.

3) **Current gross taxable FUTA/SUTA and OASDI:** This is the amount of the gross pay in the current period that is subject to these taxes. *Example*: The FUTA/SUTA limit is $7,000. Baxter Acevedo's current period gross pay is $600 and this amount exceeded the limit by $200. This means that only $400 of his current gross pay ($600 – $200) is subject to FUTA/SUTA tax this period. The 2022 OASDI limit of $147,000 is much greater than his cumulative gross pay, so it is easy to see that all of his current gross pay is taxable for OASDI.

Week Ended March 11, 2022

4		Deductions				**5** Payment		Acct. Debited **6**	
Federal Inc. Tax	State Inc. Tax	OASDI/ Medicare	Health Insur- ance	Union Dues	Total	Net Pay	Ck. #	Office Salaries	Wages
89.00	18.00	45.90	12.00	5.25	170.15	429.85	857		600.00
169.00	92.00	107.10	9.00	5.25	382.35	1,017.65	858		1400.00
104.00	21.00	52.79	15.00	5.25	198.04	491.96	859		690.00
250.00	124.00	137.70	11.00	-0-	522.70	1,277.30	860	1,800.00	
48.00	10.00	36.72	18.00	5.25	117.97	362.03	861		480.00
116.00	23.00	59.21	12.00	5.25	215.46	558.54	862		774.00
280.00	130.00	141.55	10.00	-0-	561.55	1,338.45	863	1,900.00	
1,056.00	418.00	580.97	87.00	26.25	2,168.22	5,475.78	–	3,700.00	3,944.00

continued ▶

The Payroll Register Illustrated, *continued*

Detailed Explanation, Continued	4) **Deductions:** These are the withholding deductions for each employee. For example, Baxter Acevedo has a total of $170.15 of deductions, consisting of federal and state income taxes, FICA (OASDI/Medicare), health insurance contributions, and union dues. 5) **Net pay:** This shows the net amount of pay each employee will receive and, when paid, the check number of the payroll check written to the employee. Net pay is the current gross pay minus the total deductions. 6) **Account debited:** These columns classify the gross wage expense. In this case, gross wages are classified as either office salaries or wages. Different companies use different classifications.
Register Format	Payroll registers can vary somewhat in format and design. Some companies produce a single integrated payroll register, some split the register in separate sections, while smaller companies might use a system that incorporates a payroll register into a cash payments journal. In general, the point to keep in mind is that although the design may vary, a payroll register is a useful summary device for a completed payroll period that includes gross amounts earned, withholding, and net amounts for a completed payroll. Accruals of unpaid and owed amounts are generally not part of a payroll register.

Journal Entry to Record Gross Wages Expense and Related Accounts

Overview	The first step in recording payroll is the journal entry for the gross pay expense. This journal entry consists of recording gross pay, the related deductions, and the net pay. *The payroll register totals are the sources of information for this journal entry.* In an automated system, even when using account codes, verify that the totals in a payroll register produced by the system correspond to the amounts in the journal entry. As well, a reconciliation between payroll amounts posted into ledger accounts and payroll register totals should be performed every payroll.

Example	March 14	Office Salaries Expense	3,700.00	
		Wages Expense	3,944.00	
		Federal Income Tax Payable		1,056.00
		State Income Tax Payable		418.00
		FICA Payable		580.97
		Medical Insurance Payable		87.00
		Union Dues Payable		26.25
		Salaries and Wages Payable		5,475.78

Journal Entry to Record Gross Wages Expense and Related Accounts, *continued*

Withholding Liabilities

Salaries and Wages Payable is the total net pay for all employees after withholding. All the other credits are totals of employee withholding deductions for various liability items. The liabilities are current liabilities; the employer is required to act as a collection agent and is obligated to remit the withheld amounts to other parties in a timely manner. For example, the federal income tax and FICA withheld must be paid to the U.S. Treasury Department within a prescribed period of time.

The journal entry above records a Salaries and Wages Payable liability for a completed payroll period; actual payment to employees may be some days later when checks are written or direct deposits made. Also, some companies use an accounting system that requires all potential cash payments to first be recorded as liabilities that are reviewed and authorized before payment. If this is not the case, an alternative is to credit Cash instead of Salaries and Wages Payable. This can be done when the completed payroll period and the cash payment occur within the same accounting period

The specific tax amounts actually become obligations (and reportable on payroll tax forms) at the time employees receive their payroll checks or have full access to funds (see "constructive receipt," page 216); however, they should be recorded as part of the journal entry as you see above because they are probable and measurable liabilities, which are recorded per GAAP.

Journal Entry to Record Employer Payroll Tax Expense

Overview

The second step in recording payroll is the journal entry for the employer payroll tax expense. This journal entry consists of recording the employer FICA matching, FUTA, and SUTA payroll taxes, plus any other state and local payroll taxes, if applicable. The dollar amounts subject to these taxes are the totals shown in the payroll register in "Current Gross Taxable For..." columns. Remember that these taxes only apply to the employer; there are no employee deductions. (Note: some companies might combine this entry with the one above for a single large entry.)

Example

The example below shows a journal entry for the employer payroll tax expense. FICA (consisting of OASDI and Medicare) is the same as employee withholding = \$379.75. FUTA is .006 × \$1,420 = \$8.52; SUTA is .054 × \$1,420 = \$76.68.

March 14	Payroll Tax Expense	666.17	
	FICA Payable		580.97
	FUTA Payable		8.52
	SUTA Payable		76.68

Journal Entry to Record Benefits Expenses

Overview

When an employer pays benefits, the third step in recording payroll is the journal entry (or entries) for all benefits expenses. This journal entry consists of accruing an expense and liability for each type of benefit.

Example

The example below shows the accrued benefits expenses consisting of vacation, health insurance, and workers' compensation.

March 14	Vacation Pay Expense	300.00	
	Medical Insurance Premiums Expense	350.00	
	Workers' Compensation Expense	150.00	
	Medical Insurance Payable		350.00
	Workers' Compensation Insurance Payable		150.00
	Vacation Pay Payable		300.00

Note: Benefits obligations such as medical and other insurance are often recorded separately in the accounts payable department as bills are received from providers. Often workers' compensation insurance is prepaid. It is then expensed during the accounting periods during which it is used. In that case there would be a credit to Prepaid Workers' Compensation Insurance instead of the Workers' Compensation Insurance Payable as shown above.

What is the Total Payroll Cost?

The total employer cost for this payroll is the gross pay expense, the employer payroll taxes, and the employer-paid benefits expense (excludes overhead, processing, etc.) For the three examples above this is $4,964.00 + $464.95 + $800.00 = $6,228.95

Employee Earnings Records

Overview

Every employer is required by the Department of Labor to maintain payroll records for at least three years, and by the IRS generally for at least 4 at years. The primary purpose of these earnings records is to provide the information necessary to report the annual gross pay and withholding to each employee at year-end on **Form W-2**. Employees also use the W-2 information for preparing their annual individual income tax returns as well as for other purposes such as loan applications. The employer must also provide the same information to government taxing authorities.

Example

The example below is a partial *employee earnings record* that shows information for the month of March. Notice that the record is updated after each completed payroll period. Think of each record as a kind of subsidiary ledger for each employee's earnings history. The example you see here has a cumulative gross pay column so the wage base limits can be identified. It also provides information for required quarterly payroll reports.

continued ▶

Illustration 3.2: Employee Earnings Record

Tropics Travel Company
Employee Earnings Record
For the Year 2022

Employee: Van Arsdale, Robert
S.S. #: 123-45-6789
Employment Date: July 11, 2015
Termination Date:
Address: 80 Sunshine Ct., Denver, CO. 80229

Filing Status Single
Dependents: 1
Pay rate: $18 hourly
Job Title: Staff Assistant

2022 Week Ended	Total Hrs.	Earnings					Deductions							
		Reg. Pay	O.T. Pay	Gross Pay	Cum. Gross Pay	Fed. Income Tax	State Income Tax	OASDI Medicr.	Health Ins.	Union Dues	Total	Net	Chk No.
3/4	40	720.00		720.00	7,126.00	108.00	22.00	55.08	12.00	5.25	202.33	517.67	755
3/11	42	720.00	54.00	774.00	7,900.00	116.00	23.00	59.21	12.00	5.25	215.46	558.54	862
3/18	44	720.00	108.00	828.00	8,728.00	133.00	26.00	63.34	12.00	5.25	239.59	588.41	912
3/25	43	720.00	81.00	801.00	9,529.00	129.00	25.00	61.28	12.00	5.25	232.53	568.47	988
March		2,880.00	243.00	3,123.00		486.00	96.00	238.91	48.00	21.00	889.91	2,233.09	
First Quarter		8,719.00	810.00	9,529.00		1,590.00	312.00	731.34	144.00	63.00	2,840.34	6,688.66	

Note: The source of this information is the payroll register. For example, the March 11 (highlighted) entry comes from the March 11 payroll register example.

Employee Earnings Records, *continued*

Reconciling the Payroll Register and Earnings Records

Even in an automated system, the totals of all individual earnings records should be checked or system verified to ensure they are the same as the payroll register totals, related ledger accounts, the totals recorded in quarterly (or annual) employer reports, and Form W-2 totals.

Each payroll period the payroll department must reconcile the totals on the payroll register to the total amounts on the employee earnings records. For example, if the gross pay on the payroll register is $4,964.00, then adding the gross pay shown on all of the employee earnings records for all the employees for the same date should also result in a total of $4,964.00. This reconciliation is also completed for each deduction item and net pay. A payroll software system with internal verification should perform this function automatically.

Medical Insurance Shared Expense

Overview

In many businesses, employees share the cost of medical insurance, and sometimes other benefits, with the employer. Usually the employee share is recorded as an amount withheld from paychecks as you see with the account "Medical Insurance Premiums Payable" on page 198. There are several possible procedures and types of accounts that can be used to record these arrangements, generally depending on whether the employer pays premiums in advance or is billed as benefits are provided. However, the key point is that the proper amount of employer net expense must be recorded in the accounting period that will be reported by financial statements.

For example, let's say that on May 4 the Park Place Company paid $24,000 in advance for the next 8 months of medical insurance. If the company's current quarter ends on June 30, then 2 months, or $24,000 × 2/8 = $6,000 of insurance expense must be recorded in that quarter so that it appears on the income statement for the quarter ended June 30. In turn, if employees also contribute towards the cost of the insurance, then the $6,000 of expense must be reduced by the employees' contribution. Assume there was $2,000 of medical insurance withholding for May and June ($2,000 credit). First, the employer's cash payment would then be recorded as:

May 4	Prepaid Medical Insurance	24,000	
	Cash		24,000

The quarter's medical insurance expense would then be recorded as:

June 30	Medical Insurance Premium Expense	4,000	
	Medical Insurance Premiums Payable	2,000	
	Prepaid Medical Insurance		6,000

continued ▶

Medical Insurance Shared Expense, *continued*

Overview, *Continued*	Some companies might credit Medical Insurance Premium Expense as part of the withholding, instead of Medical Insurance Premiums Payable. This would temporarily create a $2,000 negative balance in the expense account until the prepaid account is credited and the insurance expense is debited for the period for $6,000, leaving a net $4,000 expense. The June 30 insurance expense account balance would then show the correct net amount, although the procedure isn't typical.

A different example would occur if the Park Place Company had received a $6,000 bill on July 3 for May and June medical insurance premiums. Assume the bill was paid on July 11. When the bill is received, the following accrual journal entry would be dated June 30 to include the expense in the June quarter:

June 30	Medical Insurance Premium Expense	6,000	
	Medical Insurance Premiums Payable		6,000

From withholding, the following entry would be made, resulting in a net $4,000 balance in the Medical Insurance Premium Expense account:

June 30	Medical Insurance Premiums Payable	2,000	
	Medical Insurance Premiums Expense		2,000

Payment would then be recorded:

July 11	Medical Insurance Premium Payable	6,000	
	Cash		6,000

If as described above the company had credited Medical Insurance Premium Expense as part of the withholding entries, then the second June 30 entry above would not be needed because the Medical Insurance Premium Expense account would have the correct $4,000 balance after the first June 30 entry.

Payroll Accruals at the End of an Accounting Period

Overview	It often happens that a financial period ends part way through a payroll period. Generally accepted accounting principles (GAAP) require that an expense be recorded in the same accounting period in which it helped to create revenues, even if no cash has yet been paid. Therefore, the amount of accrued (in the accounting sense, meaning earned but unpaid) salaries and wages must be recorded as of the end of the accounting period. This is sometimes called an accrual entry.
Example	Billings Company's current accounting period ends on April 30. The payroll periods are biweekly. The current payroll period began on April 24 and will end on May 7. As of April 30, $44,000 hourly wages were

continued ▶

Payroll Accruals at the End of an Accounting Period, *continued*

Example,
Continued

earned. From May 1 to May 7, $48,000 of wages were earned. Biweekly salaries are $60,000. Income tax is assumed to be 20% and state tax is assumed to be 5%. All salaries and wages are within the FICA wage base and $40,000 per week are within the FUTA/SUTA wage base. The April 30 accrual entry to record one week of salaries and wages that are earned but unpaid is:

April 30	Salaries Expense	30,000	
	Wages Expense	44,000	
	Salaries and Wages Payable		74,000

One approach is to record individual withholding credit entries and a lower amount of Salaries and Wages Payable; however, the withholding totals for the full payroll period can be recorded later at the end of the completed payroll period (as illustrated below, in the first May 7 entry). The April 30 total expense and total liability are still correct. Because employer payroll tax expense for FICA, FUTA, and SUTA will be incurred in addition to employee salaries and wages, an accrual for employer payroll tax is also made for April 30. There are no benefits in this example.

April 30	Payroll Tax Expense	8,061	
	Accrued Payroll Tax Payable		8,061
	[(74,000 × .0765) + (40,000 × .06 FUTA/SUTA) = 8,061]		

Later, to complete the current payroll period from May 1 – May 7:

May 7	Salaries Expense	30,000	
	Wages Expense	48,000	
	Employee Federal Income Tax Payable		30,400
	(152,000 × .2 = 30,400)		
	Employee State Income Tax Payable		7,600
	(152,000 × .05 = 7,600)		
	FICA Tax Payable (152,000 × .0765 = 11,628)		11,628
	Salaries and Wages Payable		28,372

May 7	Payroll Tax Expense	8,367	
	[(78,000 × .0765) + (40,000 × .06 FUTA/SUTA) = 8,367]		
	Accrued Payroll Tax Payable	8,061	
	FICA Payable (matches employees)		11,628
	FUTA Payable (80,000 × .006 = 480)		480
	SUTA Payable (80,000 × .054 = 4,320)		4,320

continued ▶

Payroll Accruals at the End of an Accounting Period, *continued*

Example, *Continued*	This approach saves time by calculating all employee withholding at the end of the completed payroll period. Therefore, the final Salaries and Wages Payable ledger account balance for the completed payroll period is $152,000 (total salaries and wages) − $30,400 − $7,600 − $11,628 = $102,372 credit balance, the net pay due to employees after all their withholding is subtracted. The May 7 entry for Salaries and Wages Payable (here, $28,372) will be a reconciling, or "plug", amount (can be credit or debit) that brings that account balance to the total of $102,372 for the completed payroll period. Here, this is calculated as: $102,372 − $74,000 (recorded on April 30) = $28,372.

The total $102,372 of Salaries and Wages Payable liability as well as withholding liabilities will later be debited and Cash (payroll account) will be credited when employees are paid and other payments made. Also, the payroll tax liabilities of $11,628 + $480 + $4,320 will be debited and $16,428 Cash credited.

For FICA, each employee and employer share is calculated on the total gross wages for the payroll period as. $152,000 × .0765 = $11,628. Total FUTA liability is ($40,000 × 2) for both periods × .006 = $480, and SUTA liability is ($40,000 × 2 for both periods) × .054 = $8,208. Federal income tax is 20% and state income tax is 5%. **Note:** Although this is a workable method and might be a matter of preference, there is a quick and more common technique called "***reversing entries***" that we will illustrate in the next section.

Other Accruals

Bonus Expenses	If a bonus is likely to occur, an employer should accrue the bonus in the accounting period in which the bonus is determined to be likely. If necessary the expense and payable can be adjusted as circumstances become clearer. For example, if it is determined on October 30 that an employee will receive a $5,000 bonus:

Oct. 30	Bonus Expense	5,000	
	Bonus Payable		5,000

Commission *Expenses*	A commission expense and liability should be recorded in the accounting period in which the related sale item has been delivered to a customer who appears to have the ability to pay. For example, an art gallery salesperson who earns a 15% commission obtains a customer promise to buy a $10,000 painting. The customer agrees in November, but the painting is not delivered until January 12. The journal entry is:

Jan. 12	Commission Expense	1,500	
	Commission Payable		1,500

continued ▶

Other Accruals, *continued*

Benefits Expenses Advance Payment, Not an Accrual

Employers make payments to providers of benefits. Assume that on August 3 ABC Company pays $8,000 for medical insurance coverage through December 31. The current quarter reporting period ends on September 30. 2/5 (two of five months) of the $8,000 is a current period expense. The rest is an asset that will be used up by the end of the next period.

Aug. 3	Medical Insurance Premium Expense		3,200	
	Prepaid Medical Insurance		4,800	
	Cash			8,000
Dec. 31	Medical Insurance Premium Expense		4,800	
	Prepaid Medical Insurance			4,800

More on Vacation Pay

Overview

Vacation pay is a common form of compensation. In the example on page 200, we can see that $300 of vacation pay expense was accrued for the March 14 payroll period. However, this does not fully explain how the vacation pay was calculated, which is discussed below.

Vacation Pay Earned

Vacation pay normally is earned according to the amount of time an employee has worked and paid at the regular rate of pay. Some organizations require that an employee work full time for a minimum period of time, such as six months or a year, before vacation pay begins to be earned. However, if during a probationary period an employee earns vacation pay that is vested, an expense and liability must be recorded. Using a worksheet, an employer maintains a record of vacation pay as it accrues. This reflects the amount of time earned and the value of the time. The total employee accrual each pay period is recorded with a debit to vacation pay expense (or a similar name) and a credit to Vacation Pay Payable, as you see in the page 200 journal entry. (It is also acceptable to record the accrued amounts for all pay periods within a single accounting period at one time immediately prior to a financial statement date for that accounting period.) Be sure to check state and local law to determine the requirements relating to vacation pay.

Example

Beautiful Designs Company gives two weeks of paid vacation to each employee per year. Therefore, the annual cost of the vacation pay is accrued over 50 weeks of employment, or 4% per week (2 weeks/ 50 weeks = .04). Dave Smith works 5 days per week and earns gross pay of $6,500 per month, or $78,000 per year, including his two weeks of paid vacation. ($78,000/52 weeks) × 2 = $3,000 for two weeks. This vacation pay is earned over 50 weeks of work: $3,000/50 = $60/week. (Or: ($78,000/52) × .04 = $60/week.)

More on Vacation Pay, *continued*

Rate Change

If an employee's pay rate is changed, for example by receiving a raise, the difference is recorded at the time of payment as an additional expense; in other words, a change in an accounting estimate. The new rate is applied to all accrued vacation time, which is also the rate of pay the employee expects to receive. Note: If vacation pay is paid at a different rate than regular pay supplemental pay rules apply (Section 2).

Example

Assume that Dave Smith in the example above had worked 30 weeks and earned 30 × $60 = $1,800 of vacation pay. As of Monday, March 1, he then received a 5% raise, which is $78,000 × .05 = $3,900 annually. His weekly vacation pay is now calculated as: annual pay of $81,900 divided by 26 biweekly periods equals $3,150 accrued vacation pay per year. This $3,150 divided by 50 weeks of regular pay (while not on vacation) equals $63 per week of vacation pay accrual

Five weeks later Dave takes off 7 workdays for vacation and uses all of his vacation pay. His total vacation pay at that point consists of his accrued vacation pay prior to March 1 plus his vacation pay after his March 1 raise accrued until he takes his vacation. Prior to March 1, the accrued account becomes ($1,800 × 1.05) = $1,890. Notice that this results in an additional $90 expense to the employer that will be recorded when Dave is paid his vacation pay (change in accounting estimate). After March 1, vacation pay accrual is ($63 per week × 5 weeks) = $315. When Dave is paid his vacation pay he will receive the gross amount of $2,205 minus related taxes as illustrated below.

Journal Entries Example

April 7	Vacation Pay Payable	2,115.00	
	Vacation Pay Expense	90.00	
	Federal Income Tax Payable		441.00
	State Income Tax Payable		110.25
	FICA Payable		168.68
	Cash		1,485.07

This transaction also creates another current period expense that must be recorded so it can be matched against current period revenues, as well as recording the related probable and measurable liabilities, recorded as follows:

Payroll Tax Expense	300.98	
FICA Payable		168.68
FUTA Payable		13.23
SUTA Payable		119.07

Vacation Pay Liability

Organizations may have different policies on vacation pay use by employees. If vacation pay accrues as long as an employee continues to work, then the liability continues to grow larger, and remains a current liability if there are no limitations as to the time and amount that the accrued amount may be used.

continued ▶

More on Vacation Pay, *continued*

Vacation Pay Liability, Continued	Some organizations have a "use it or lose it" vacation pay policy, meaning that the full amount of vacation pay must be used within a designated period or will be forfeited. This adds complexity because the employer will have to adjust the total amount of accrued expense down based on a percentage from past experience. The method will vary among employers.
	Note that in some states (e.g. California, Montana, Nebraska) vacation pay use-it-or-lose-it policy is prohibited because vacation pay is considered to be earned compensation and cannot be reduced after it has been earned. Many businesses simply set a vacation pay limit and discontinue accrual when the limit is reached, until vacation pay is used.
Vacation Hours Deficit	A company may allow employees to use vacation time and create a negative balance of cumulative vacation time earned, up to a limit. This allows flexible use of vacation time during a year. However, if an employee leaves the company with a negative balance this will be offset against the final paycheck, using the same rate at which it was paid.

TIP

Are unpaid year-end salary and wage expense accruals deductible for employer income tax? The answer is yes if the following conditions are met by year-end: 1) all events needed to establish the liability with reasonable accuracy have occurred (for example, bonuses and commissions can be dependably calculated and are vested obligations to employees), 2) The employee has performed the services, and 3) For unrestricted bonuses and vacation pay, the accrued liabilities are paid within 2 ½ months of year-end. This does not apply to S corporation shareholders or LLC members (except for guaranteed payments) or greater than 50% C corporation shareholders. 4) A year-end deduction for payroll tax on the accrual is allowed if a "recurring item exception" is elected. Cash-basis employers can deduct expenses only in year of payment.

Sick Leave and Other PTO

Overview	Sick leave is another frequently offered type of PTO. Similar to vacation pay, a sick leave worksheet for each employee is maintained that shows sick leave time earned, used, and the remaining balance. However, a journal entry to accrue sick leave is required only if the sick leave is vested; that is, the employer is obligated to pay the employee regardless of the employee's future services. If that is the case the journal entry would be similar to the examples above for vacation pay, except that the account names would identify the transaction as for sick pay. Otherwise, the journal entry is optional. Other types of PTO expense resulting in payments to employees would be treated in the same manner.

continued ▶

Sick Leave and Other PTO, *continued*

Table Example The partial table below illustrates a format for accumulating vacation pay and sick leave. Other formats are also used. In this example vacation and sick leave hours are accumulated hourly except when being used. For example, vacation pay is earned at a rate of 80 hours per year. Allocated over 2,000 annual working hours the rate is 80/2,000 = .04 hours of vacation time per hour worked, or .04 × 8 = .32 hours per day.

Example **Illustration 3.3:** Vacation and sick leave hours record

Employee Vacation and Sick Leave Record

Employee Name: Davis, Albert
Employee Number: 145

Vacation accrual rate: .04/hour   Max. allowed: 120 hours
Sick leave accrual rate: .02/hour   Max. allowed: 160 hours

Current pay rate: $21.50/hour   Pay period: Biweekly

	Hours Earned		Hours Used		Cumulative Balance	
Pay Period	V	SL	V	SL	V	SL
8/1/22-8/14/22	3.200	1.600			26.800	157.500
8/15/22-8/28/22	3.200	1.600			30.000	159.100
8/29/22-9/11/22	2.240	.90	24.000		8.240	160.000
9/12/22-9/25/22	3.200	00.00			11.44	160.000
9/26/22-10/9/22	3.200	1.600		5.000	14.64	156.600

Severance Accrual Policy

Severance Pay If an employer has a severance policy in place for the amount and type of severance payments to employees, or has a regular history of severance payments to employees, an expense is accrued when the severance decision has been made, the payment is probable, and the amount of the payment can be estimated. Example: assume that the accounting period ends December 31 and the severance decision is made on December 12. The payment will be three monthly $7,500 payments in January, February and March. The severance is recorded as follows,

continued ▶

Severance Accrual Policy, *continued*

Severance Pay,
Continued

regardless of the extent that the employee is still performing services after the decision:

Dec 12	Severance Expense	22,500	
	Severance Payable		22,500

If the decision is made after the December 31 period end, the expense can be recorded with the payments in the next year.

If an employer does not have a severance policy in place or a regular history of severance payments, the method of recording is different. In the above example, but with no policy or regular history, if the employee were to continue working after the severance decision, the severance expense would be pro-rated over the period of time of continued service, following the severance decision per the same guidelines in the first paragraph. If there is no future service the expense is recorded at the time of the decision, per the guidelines. Severance pay is treated as a supplemental payment taxable for income tax (page 128) and employment tax.

Summary of Accounts Used

Overview

The following lists show the accounts that are typically used (if both federal and state income tax applies) when recording each of the three elements of payroll transactions. Account names may vary somewhat in practice. **Reconcile** each payroll liability account balance in the ledger by reviewing: 1) debit/credit entries, 2) non-zero balances, 3) accrual calculations worksheet(s), 4) final payroll register totals.

Recording Gross
Wages and
Withholding

Account	Description
▪ Wages Expense/Salaries Expense (Appears on income statement)	An operating expense that is the gross amount earned by employees. See Form 941 lines 5a -5d categories to create specific ledger accounts as applicable.
▪ Federal Income Tax Payable (Appears on balance sheet)	A current liability resulting from amounts withheld from employees for federal income tax
▪ State Income Tax Payable (Appears on balance sheet)	A current liability resulting from amounts withheld from employees for state income tax
▪ FICA Payable (Appears on balance sheet)	A current liability from withholding for OASDI and Medicare.
▪ Medical Insurance Premiums Payable (Appears on balance sheet)	A current liability that records a medical (health) insurance premium obligation.

continued ▶

Summary of Accounts Used, *continued*

Recording Gross Wages and Withholding, Continued	Account	Description
	■ Union Dues Payable* (Appears on balance sheet)	A current liability resulting from amounts withheld from employees and payable to their union
	■ Salaries and Wages Payable	A current liability for the net amount due employees after subtracting withholding

*(There may be other voluntary withholding items)

Recording Employer Payroll Tax Expense	Account	Description
	■ Payroll Tax Expense (Appears on income statement)	An operating expense resulting from all the payroll tax obligations of the employer
	■ FICA Payable (Appears on balance sheet)	A current liability resulting from amounts withheld from employees for OASDI and Medicare
	■ FUTA Payable (Appears on balance sheet)	A current liability resulting from the employer's federal unemployment tax obligation
	■ SUTA Payable (Appears on balance sheet)	A current liability resulting from the employer's state unemployment tax obligation

Recording Benefits Expense	Account	Description
	■ Vacation Pay Expense (Appears on income statement)	An operating expense that records the vacation pay accrued to employees
	■ Medical Insurance Premium Expense (Appears on income statement)	An operating expense that records the cost of medical insurance premiums paid by the employer
	■ Workers Compensation Insurance Expense (Appears on income statement)	An operating expense that records the cost of workers compensation insurance
	■ Sick Pay Expense (Appears on income statement)	An operating expense that records the sick pay accrued to employees
	■ Vacation Pay Payable (Appears on balance sheet)	A current liability that records the amount of vacation pay due employees.
	■ Medical Insurance Premium Payable (Appears on balance sheet)	A current liability that records a medical (health) insurance premium obligation.
	■ Workers Comp. Insurance Payable (Appears on balance sheet)	A current liability that records the amount of workers compensation insurance premiums obligation

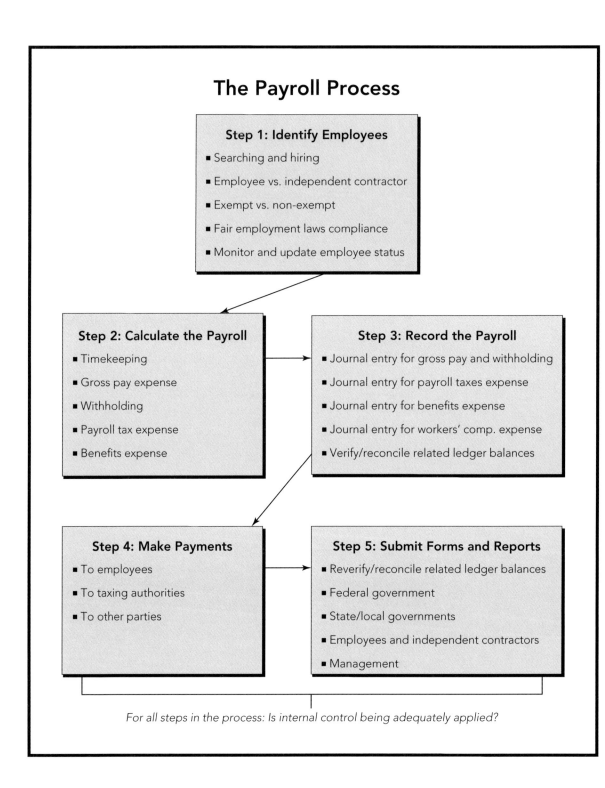

The Payroll Process

Step 1: Identify Employees

- Searching and hiring
- Employee vs. independent contractor
- Exempt vs. non-exempt
- Fair employment laws compliance
- Monitor and update employee status

Step 2: Calculate the Payroll

- Timekeeping
- Gross pay expense
- Withholding
- Payroll tax expense
- Benefits expense

Step 3: Record the Payroll

- Journal entry for gross pay and withholding
- Journal entry for payroll taxes expense
- Journal entry for benefits expense
- Journal entry for workers' comp. expense
- Verify/reconcile related ledger balances

Step 4: Make Payments

- To employees
- To taxing authorities
- To other parties

Step 5: Submit Forms and Reports

- Reverify/reconcile related ledger balances
- Federal government
- State/local governments
- Employees and independent contractors
- Management

For all steps in the process: Is internal control being adequately applied?

Section 4 Make Payments

Payments related to payroll generally consist of making the following payments discussed in the previous section:

- To employees,
- For liabilities resulting from deductions from gross pay,
- For employer payroll taxes,
- For benefits providers and to other third parties.

  Note: The constant application of **internal control** procedures is essential to reduce the chances of fraud and error. This is especially true when cash payments are involved. See Section 7 for a procedures checklist.

Payments to Employees

A Completed Payroll

In the previous section we discussed how to record a fully completed payroll period, using the following example:

March 14	Office Salaries Expense	3,700.00	
	Wages Expense	3,944.00	
	Federal Income Tax Payable		1,056.00
	State Income Tax Payable		418.00
	FICA Payable		580.97
	Medical Insurance Payable		87.00
	Union Dues Payable		26.25
	Salaries and Wages Payable		5,475.78

In this example the total net pay owing to employees is $5,475.78 because there was no immediate cash payment at the time of recording the payroll. When checks are later prepared and/or direct deposits are made, the following entry records the payment:

March xx	Salaries and Wages Payable	$5,475.78	
	Cash		$5,475.78

We also recorded the employer's payroll tax expense for the full payroll period, which was:

March 14	Payroll Tax Expense	666.17	
	FICA Payable		580.97
	FUTA Payable		8.52
	SUTA Payable		76.68

continued ▶

Payments to Employees, *continued*

A Completed Payroll, Continued	The payment for these is recorded as:		

March xxx	FICA Payable	580.97	
	FUTA Payable	8.52	
	SUTA Payable	76.68	
	Cash		666.17

(*Note:* payroll tax deposits might be made at intervals. The deposits would debit each Tax Payable and credit Cash.)

Accrued Payroll

We also previously discussed the need to accrue salaries and wages for an accounting period that ended part way through a payroll period. In the example: "Billings Company second quarter accounting period ends on April 30. The payroll periods are biweekly. The current payroll period began on April 23 and will end on May 7. As of April 30, $44,000 hourly wages were earned in this payroll period. From May 1 to May 7, $48,000 of wages were earned. Biweekly salaries are $60,000. Federal income tax is rate is 20% and state tax is 5%." We made the following April 30 accrual entry:

April 30	Salaries Expense	30,000	
	Wages Expense	44,000	
	Salaries and Wages Payable		74,000

Example: Reversing Entry for Accrued Payroll

Instead of making the next entries as previously discussed (page 204), a reversing entry can be used to save time and reduce potential errors. The April 30 accrual entry is reversed as of the first day of the *next* accounting period. This eliminates the liability and temporarily places credit balances in the expense accounts:

May 1	Salaries and Wages Payable	74,000	
	Salaries Expense		30,000
	Wages Expense		44,000

To simplify the example, we ignore withholding for the moment. When employees are paid for the completed payroll, we make the following entry as if the expenses were all recorded in a single cash payment:

May 7	Salaries Expense	60,000	
	Wages Expense	92,000	
	Cash		152,000

The result is that $74,000 of salaries and wages have been correctly recorded in the accounting period ending April 30 and $78,000 have been

continued ▶

Payments to Employees, *continued*

Example: Reversing Entry for Accrued Payroll, Continued	correctly recorded in the accounting period beginning on May 1. The salaries and wages expense accounts for the these periods will show:			

Salaries Expense			**Wages Expense**	
April 30	**30,000**		April 30	**44,000**	
May 1		30,000	May 1		44,000
May 7	60,000		May 7	92,000	
	30,000			**48,000**	

Completed Payroll With Cash Payment

The journal entry below now includes the withholding amounts. The reversal and allocation to the expense accounts are the same. The only difference now is that the credit to cash has been reduced because of the employee withholding accounts.

Example: Completed Payroll With Cash Payment

The entry for the completed payroll is:

May 7	Salaries Expense	60,000	
	Wages Expense	92,000	
	Employee Federal Income Tax Payable		30,400
	Employee State Income Tax Payable		7,600
	FICA Tax Payable		11,628
	Cash		102,372

Employee Payment Format

The credit to cash such as the $102,372 above represents the total net pay on payroll checks that employees receive. Each physical payroll check should have a detachable portion called a ***statement of earnings***, also called a "check stub", or "remittance advice" that shows the gross pay, withholding detailed by type and amount, and net pay for the stated payroll period. Employees should understand that they need to retain the statement of earnings. Check amounts and distribution should be confidential.

Payment can be electronic by **direct deposit** to an employee's bank account. This is quicker, saves time, reduces cost, and eliminates lost checks. The employee may still receive an earnings statement. Federal law (Electronic Funds Transfer Act) and state laws control the procedures, fees, and if this can be mandatory.)

Finally, debit cards, also called "**pay cards**", are being used increasingly as a means of payment. An employer transfers funds from its bank to the bank that issues the cards for employees. The cards are used in the same way as any other debit card. They are especially useful for employees who do not have bank accounts. Also, they are a lower cost procedure than issuing checks. A statement of earnings is still sent to each employee for every payroll. Fees should not reduce net pay below minimum wage; federal law requires at least one other method.

Payments on Accruals

Employer Payroll Tax Expense

In our previous example with Billings Company in Section 3 we accrued employer payroll taxes as shown below:

| April 30 | Payroll Tax Expense | 8,061 | |
| | Accrued Payroll Tax Payable | | 8,061 |

$[74,000 \times .0765) + (40,000 \times .06) = \$8,061]$

Using the reversing method, we can make the following entries:

| May 1 | Accrued Payroll Tax Payable | 8,061 | |
| | Payroll Tax Expense | | 8,061 |

| May xx | Payroll Tax Expense | 16,428 | |
| | Cash | | 16,428 |

$[152,000 \times .0765) + (80,000 \times .06) = 16,428]$

(*Note:* payroll tax deposits might be made at intervals. The deposits would debit Payroll Tax Expense and credit Cash.)

Other Expense Accruals

Use the same reversal method to record other accruals involving expenses that span two or more accounting periods as you see above. As above, reverse the accrual at the beginning of the next period and then record an expense for the entire amount of the cash payment. A simpler situation occurs when an accrued expense item belongs entirely in the period in which it was accrued, and is just paid in the next period. No reversal is needed (although it is still OK if you want to reverse all accruals); the entry in the next period is:

| Date xxx | Payable | $$$ | |
| | Cash | | $$$ |

Constructive Receipt

The day that income is received is important. For wages, consequences most often appear at the end of a calendar year when tax rates or wage bases change for a new year. An employee's wages are considered received when the employee is paid, or are "constructively received", meaning an accessible paycheck that could be cashed or unrestricted funds that are credited to the employee's account. Check date does not affect this rule. The rule also applies to cash-equivalent PTO and wage overpayments.

For example, an employee performs services in December of 2022, and the employer makes the payroll check available on Friday, December 30. The employee picks up the check the following week in January 2023. The employee's income was constructively received in 2022. The employer/employee 2022 payroll tax and deposit rules apply and income is taxable to the employee in 2022. If payment had not been available until Tuesday, January 3, 2023, the 2023 tax and deposit rules apply and the payment is taxable to the employee in 2023 even though the service was performed in 2022. (Also see "Tip" on page 208.)

continued ▶

Payments on Accruals, *continued*

Constructive Receipt, Continued	These are cash basis tax rules. For financial reporting, a company using accrual accounting would still record the cost of the 2022 employee services in 2022 to match against 2022 revenues. (Also see pages 208 and 350.)

Manual Paychecks and Outsourced Payroll

Manual Paychecks	Occasionally it may be necessary to write manual checks even though a computerized payroll system is being used. Recording a manual check will depend on if/how the check has already been recorded and the manual check recording procedure required by the payroll software system. The key point is that a manual paycheck's information should be recorded as part of a payroll computer check run to ensure that the check data is recorded in the system. A physical check output can be voided but the: 1) gross wages, 2) related payroll taxes and 3) net pay must be recorded by the software. If the software cannot do this automatically, the payroll staff will manually calculate gross wages, withholding, and net pay and enter this into the system. The system should be able to calculate employer payroll tax expense. If the cash payment was made in the regular checking account instead of the payroll checking account, the above entry can be made using the regular checking account; this requires careful review of the account for payroll transactions.

For example, assume that $4,000 of wages expense incurred with a 20% federal tax rate and 7.65% FICA withholding. The $2,894 check was written on the regular checking account but not yet recorded. The employee has not exceeded any payroll wage base. The journal entry is:

Date xxx	Wages Expense	4,000	
	Income Tax Payable		800
	FICA Payable		306
	Cash		2,894
	Payroll Tax Expense	546	
	FICA Payable		306
	FUTA Payable		24
	SUTA Payable		216

If just $4,000 of wages expense and cash paid is recorded, wages expense must be grossed up. See pages 227 and 235. If only the net check amount was recorded as payroll expense, the first entry is:

Date xxx	Wages Expense	1,106	
	Income Tax Payable		800
	FICA Payable		306

Manual Paychecks and Outsourced Payroll, *continued*

Outsourced Payroll	When payroll is outsourced and payment is made, the only accounts to record are the gross wages expense, employer tax expense, and cash paid, plus any other liabilities not handled by the outsourcing company. Payment has been made so there are no liabilities to record. Assume the above amounts had occurred as an outsourced transaction:	

Date xxx	Wages Expense	4,000	
	Payroll Tax Expense	546	
	Cash		4,546

Payments to Taxing Authorities

Overview	A journal entry that is a debit to Payroll Tax Expense and a credit to Cash for total payroll taxes is an example of recording a payment to taxing authorities for employer taxes. An example of recording a payroll tax payment for payroll tax liabilities is:

Date xxx	FICA Payable	$$$	
	FUTA Payable	$$$	
	SUTA Payable	$$$	
	Cash		$$$

Whatever the recording, there are additional important considerations that involve making the actual payments to taxing authorities. The following discussion reviews these considerations.

Overview of Deposit Procedures	Federal tax authorities require regular and timely payroll deposits for FICA, and employee income tax, reported quarterly by employers on Form 941. (Also similar but slightly different rules apply to filers of Forms 943, 944, and 945. See next Section for a discussion of payroll forms.) The first step in determining deposit requirements is to create a "lookback" period. FUTA deposits are similar – see Table 4.2. States also have similar rules for state taxes.

FICA and Employee Income Tax: Lookback Period	On the first business day of a calendar year, an employer determines a 4-quarter lookback period by referring to the 941 forms previously filed as follows:

- 3rd and 4th quarters of the second preceding calendar year, plus
- 1st and 2nd quarter of the preceding calendar year.

Example: for 2022 the lookback period is July 1–September 30 and October 1–December 31 of 2020, plus January 1–March 31 and April 1–June 30 of 2021.

continued ▶

Payments to Taxing Authorities, *continued*

Table 4.1: Payroll Tax Deposit Rules (Forms 941, 944, 945), Except FUTA

Step	IF	THEN
1	Form 941 total tax originally due excluding refundable credits is less than $2,500 for the current quarter or was less than $2,500 in the prior quarter, AND there was not a $100,000 or more undeposited tax liability on any day in the current deposit period OR Form 944/945 total tax liability for the year is less than $2,500 (or 4th required deposit is less than $2,500)	**Pay the amount due with a timely filed Form** 941 (or 944 or 945 if applicable). Also use the 941-V payment voucher (or 944-V or 945-V if applicable). Note: If the employer is not qualified from the prior quarter and unsure about current quarter, it is safer to make monthly or semi-weekly deposits.
2	The employer reported tax due of $50,000 or less* during the lookback period OR the employer is in the first year of a new business,	The employer is a **monthly** depositor. Tax for a month must be deposited by the 15th day of the following month.
3	The employer reported tax due of more than $50,000* during the lookback period,	The employer is a **semi-weekly** depositor. The following schedule applies: ■ Payday is on Wednesday, Thursday, and/or Friday: Deposit is on the **next Wednesday**. ■ Payday is on Saturday, Sunday, Monday, and/or Tuesday: Deposit is on the **next Friday**. (Also 945-A if applicable)
4	Regardless of the above schedules, on any day in the current deposit period there is a $100,000 or more under-deposited tax liability,	■ The tax must be deposited by the **next business day** AND ■ The employer becomes a semiweekly depositor for the remainder of the current calendar year and all of the next calendar year.
5	Any deposit day falls on a non-business day,	The deposit is considered timely if made by the next business day (Any weekday except Saturday, Sunday, or a federal holiday).
—	**New Employers**	A new depositor becomes a **monthly** depositor until a lookback period is established after the first calendar year.

*For a 944 filer in the current or either of previous two years, the lookback period to determine deposit schedule is two years prior to the current year for deposits. For Form 945 the lookback is also the second previous year. Note: NEVER mix fund types to determine which return to file or deposit rules.

Payments to Taxing Authorities, *continued*

FUTA Deposits   FUTA (and SUTA) employer payroll taxes require separate reporting and have their own deposit requirements. The FUTA deposit requirements are shown below.

Table 4.2: FUTA Tax Deposit Rules

Step	IF	THEN
1	The cumulative unpaid FUTA tax is more than $500 by the end of a calendar quarter,	Deposit the tax no later than the last day of the month following the quarter.*
2	No deposit results from Step 1	Carry the liability forward until it is more than $500 and return to Step 1, unless it is the last quarter of the year, then go to Step 3.
3	If it is the last calendar quarter of the year and the amount due is $500 or less,	Deposit the amount with filing of Form 940 by January 31.

*As with other payroll tax deposits, electronic deposit is generally required. The electronic federal tax payment system (EFTPS) can be used at no charge. Information is available at www.eftps.gov and customer service at 800-555-4477 and 800-733-4829, and Publications 966 and 4990.

Accuracy of Deposit Rule (A "Safety Net")   In general, the IRS requires that 100% of every required deposit amount be made in full on or before the required date in order to avoid a penalty. But there is an exception, if both of these conditions are met:

- A deposit shortfall does not exceed greater of $100 or 2% of the amount due,
- The deposit shortfall is deposited by the applicable shortfall makeup deposit date.

Deposit shortfall makeup dates:

- For monthly depositors: No later than the due date of the return for the period for which the shortfall occurred.
- For semi-weekly depositors: The earlier of:

  1) The first Wednesday or Friday on or after the 15th of the month following the month in which the shortfall occurred, or
  2) The due date of the return to which the shortfall is related.

How to Make Deposits   Except for payments that can be made with filing of a return, employment taxes must be deposited by EFT (Electronic Funds Transfer). This is a system that will electronically transfer amounts from an employer's bank account to the Treasury Department.

With this system payments can be made online, by phone (a voice-response and touch-tone system) or by batch software processing for

continued ▶

Payments to Taxing Authorities, *continued*

How to Make Deposits, Continued

tax professionals. The system used is called "EFTPS". It is a free service for all types of federal government tax payments; to obtain more information go to www.eftps.gov or call 800-555-4477, or 800-733-4829.

Enrollment in the system can be completed online at www.eftps.gov or with Form 9779. Payment can also be made through third-party processors, but this may involve fees. For a new business, if deposits are required and the employer has applied for but not yet received an EIN (Employer Identification Number) deposits can be mailed to the IRS with a copy of the application and a brief explanation.

CARES Act Deferral Payment

Employers who deferred FICA payments are required to pay the remaining 50% of the deferral by December 31, 2022 (first payment December 31, 2021.)

Payments That Can Be Made With a Return

Payments below certain limits are permitted to be made with a timely filed tax return instead of being filed electronically using EFTPS, as follows:

- For Form 941, if total amount due is less than $2,500 in current and prior quarter and there was not greater than a $100,000 liability on any day in the current deposit period; for Form 943, if total taxes are less than $2,500; for Form 944, if total 4th quarter (prior quarters were timely paid) or total year's tax is less than $2,500.
- For Form 940, less than $500 total liability

First Quarterly Deposit Penalty Waiver

Summary

The IRS may waive deposit penalties applicable to a first quarter in the following circumstances:

- If an employer timely filed the applicable employment tax return, the IRS may waive deposit penalties if the employer inadvertently failed to make a timely deposit and it was the first quarter that the employer was required to deposit any employment tax.
- If an employer inadvertently failed to timely make the first deposit after the deposit frequency changed, the IRS may also waive penalties.

Limitations: A business cannot have more than 500 employees or a net worth exceeding $7 million.

Deposit Penalties

As previously mentioned, payroll deposits are an important source of cash flow to federal, state, and some local governments. As with all types of filing and tax payment requirements, penalties are imposed if deposit requirements are not met. See page Section 5 for a summary of payroll-related penalties.

Garnishment

Overview "Wage garnishment" or "garnishment" means that an employer has been ordered to make a deduction – usually recurring – from an employee's compensation, typically because of a creditor winning a lawsuit to collect an upaid debt. Some obligations that result in garnishment do not require a creditor to win a lawsuit, such as awards of child or spousal support, an upaid student loan, or unpaid taxes. A garnishment requires that an employer make a deduction from an employee's compensation and then pay the deducted amount as instructed to a third party. A requirement to send an amount to a Chapter 13 bankruptcy trustee is called an ***income deduction order***. An income deduction order also is used for child/spousal support and is sometimes called an ***income withholding order***, or "***IWO***". Technically, "garnishment" refers to other kinds of debt payment orders. However, the word "garnishment" is often used as a general term for all the above items.

First Garnishment for an Employee It is vitally important that an employer immediately and correctly respond to official orders, because an employer is liable if it fails to garnish the ordered payments. When an employer receives a first garnishment order for an employee, the employer should perform the following steps immediately upon receipt:

1) Verify authenticity. Agency and court orders are written, not verbal, and should not be confused with official-looking documents from collection agencies or private law offices seeking information. When an order comes from a court, or federal or state agency, it can be verified online before using any contact information in the order. Also distinguish between a "notice" and an "order". In the case of an IWO, there is a standardized order document. Also, if a document is from a source other than a court or a child support agency, it could be only a "notice" that would not require immediate action.

2) Create a permanent file for documents. Record the date an order is received. Maintain a log showing names, dates of correspondence, and identification of items. Verify that an order is not a duplicate.

3) Verify that the order contains all information needed to properly calculate the deduction and to remit payments to the correct party. If not, contact the sender and explain the problem that prevents the employer from garnishing funds.

4) Immediately contact the affected employee and inform him/her of the order. Provide: 1) a garnishment notification form, 2) a copy of the order and accompanying forms for the employee. • It is essential to make clear to the employee that an employer has no choice in the matter and must follow instructions, regardless of what the employee may say about the validity of the obligation.• Provide contact information to the employee. Make clear that only the employee can dispute an order; the employer is merely a collection agent.• Respect employee confidentiality. This includes distribution of paychecks. Never discuss garnishment with co-workers; keep files confidential.

continued ▶

Garnishment, *continued*

First Garnishment of an Employee, Continued

5) Immediately follow response requirements. For example:

- Child support order: An employer will receive a standard form OMB 09700154. If this is not the case or there are other questions use contact information provided in the order or contact the Office of Child Support Enforcement at 1-800-258-2736 or csportal@acf.hhs.gov. **There will be withholding and response instructions and a deadline for both employee and employer.**
- Federal tax levy: A tax levy is an administrative action used by the IRS and state governments to seize property in order to satisfy unpaid taxes. A levy also includes the right to garnish wages. An employer will receive form 668-W from the IRS. **There will be specific response and withholding instructions and response deadline for both employee and employer.**

6) Give the order to the payroll department for calculation and withholding start date.

7) Garnishment payments should be regularly checked to verify accuracy and timeliness, if any limit has been reached, or if a release was received. The person conducting the review should be different than the person initiating the process.

Multiple Garnishment Orders

If an employer receives more than one garnishment order for an employee, the correct employer response becomes a more complex issue because there are various and sometimes conflicting federal and state priority requirements. Although the steps in the prior paragraph still apply, in this situation it would be prudent for an employer to contact local labor law counsel or a knowledgeable human resources professional. The table below shows a general overview of priorities.

Table 4.3: Garnishment Priorities

Item	IF...	THEN...
1) Child support/ spousal support	a child/spousal support income withholding order is received,	the order is first priority and items below follow, unless a federal or state tax levy was ordered prior to the child/spousal support order date. Multiple child/spousal support orders are allocated among each other.
2) IRS levy for unpaid tax as garnishment	an IRS garnishment order is received,	the order is second priority unless the order is issued prior to a child/spousal support order; IRS levy then becomes first priority.
3) Other: federal agency orders (can have priority before tax levy if order is an earlier date), state taxes, local taxes, unsecured debt. General rule: the first orders in time have priority over later orders.		
4) When one debt is fully paid or otherwise terminates, payment begins on the next remaining item in order of priority.		

Garnishment, *continued*

Bankruptcy (Chapter 13)	A court-ordered Chapter 13 bankruptcy payment plan eliminates or reduces many obligations and eliminates garnishments. A Chapter 13 bankruptcy plan generally determines how much debt can be repaid within a maximum of five years. Child/spousal support, income tax levies for unpaid tax within three years prior to bankruptcy filing, and student debt except for extreme hardship cannot be eliminated and must be repaid 100% as part of the payment plan, and after if necessary. Therefore, in place of the garnishment(s), an employer will be required to withhold an amount from employee compensation according to terms of a federal bankruptcy income deduction order.
Garnishment Limits	There are laws that limit the portion of an employee's pay that can be deducted for a garnishment payment. These are generally calculated as a percentage of "disposable income". Disposable income means gross pay including vacation pay and PTO minus mandatory deductions including health insurance required by law and higher priority orders. For tipped employees, gross pay is federal $2.13/hr. cash wage plus any additional amounts such as a share of service charges; tips are excluded from gross pay. Where state law is more favorable to the employee, that law takes priority. Garnishment limits include the following:

Table 4.4: Garnishment Limits

Item	Limit of Disposable Income
Child/spousal support	Up to 50% for employee supporting a second family, 60% for no second family, plus 5% for each case past due greater than 12 weeks.
Bankruptcy Chapter 13	No specified limit. Bankruptcy court sets payment.
Federal tax levy (Form 668-W)	See IRS Publication 1494 for exemption tables. This indicates the *portion of pay that an employee is permitted to keep after calculating "take-home pay."* Generally **take-home pay** is gross pay minus: all taxes, involuntary deductions, voluntary deductions in effect before levy, condition of employment deductions, and increases in deductions beyond employee control such as health care premium increases. A 3-day response from employee after receiving statement is required or exempt amount is reduced. Employers have one payroll period to begin payments.
General unsecured creditor debt	Lesser of 25% of disposable earnings or the amount of disposable earnings that exceeds 30 times the minimum wage. (Weekly: $7.25 × 30 = $217.50; 25% on $290 or more. Use multiples for longer periods.) See DOL Fact Sheet #30 for "disposable earnings".

continued ▶

Garnishment, *continued*

Table 4.4: Garnishment Limits *continued*

Item	Limit of Disposable Income
Federal student loans	Lesser of 15% of weekly disposable earnings or the amount that exceeds 30 times the weekly minimum wage.
State guaranteed student loans	10% of disposable earnings
Other federally guaranteed loans	15% of disposable earnings
State taxes	See state law.

Employer Fees   Because of the time and paperwork involved, many states permit an employer to charge a garnished employee an administration fee. Usually this is a nominal amount per paycheck; in some cases it can be a percentage of the amount garnished.

Retaliation/ Termination   Federal law prohibits an employer from firing an employee for a single debt, regardless of how many orders. However, there is no prohibition if multiple debts are garnished. Employees cannot be fired for declaring bankruptcy.

Examples   The following examples are provided by the Department of Labor.

1. An employee's gross earnings in a particular week are $263. After deductions required by law, the disposable earnings are $233.00. In this week, $15.50 may be garnished, because only the amount over $217.50 may be garnished where the disposable earnings are less than $290.
2. An employee receives a bonus in a particular workweek of $402. After deductions required by law, the disposable earnings are $368. In this week, 25% of the disposable earnings may be garnished. ($368 × 25% = $92).
3. An employee paid every other week has disposable earnings of $500 for the first week and $80 for the second week of the pay period, for a total of $580. In a biweekly pay period, when disposable earnings are at or above $580 for the pay period, 25% may be garnished; $145.00 (25% × $580) may be garnished. It does not matter that the disposable earnings in the second week are less than $217.50.
4. An employee on a $400 weekly draw against commissions has disposable earnings each week of $300. Commissions are paid monthly and result in $1,800 in disposable earnings for July after already-paid weekly draws are subtracted and deductions required by law are made. Each draw and the monthly commission payment are separately subject to the law's limitation. Thus, 25% of each week's disposable earnings from the draw ($75 in this example) may be garnished. Additionally, 25% of the disposable earnings from the commission payment may be garnished, or $450 ($1,800 × 25% = $450).

continued ▶

Garnishment, *continued*

Examples,
Continued

5. Pursuant to a garnishment order (with priority) for child support, an employer withholds $90 per week from the wages of an employee who has disposable earnings of $295 a week. Title III allows up to 50% or 60% of disposable earnings to be garnished pursuant to court orders for child support. A garnishment order for the collection of a defaulted student loan is also served on the employer. If there was no garnishment order (with priority) for child support, Title IIIs general limitations would apply to the garnishment for the defaulted student loan, and a maximum of $73.75 (25% × $295) would be garnished per week. However, the existing garnishment for child support means in this example that no additional garnishment for the defaulted student loan may be made because the amount already garnished is more than the amount (25%) that may be generally garnished. Additional amounts could be garnished to collect child support, delinquent federal or state taxes, or certain bankruptcy court ordered payments.

"Grossing Up" a Net Amount

Overview

There are occasions when a payment is not treated as gross pay, but rather is made with the intention that the employee receives a designated net amount as take-home pay, without payroll taxes subtracted. However, the avoided payroll taxes are a taxable benefit. The employer therefore pays a larger gross amount to cover both the net amount and tax withholding. Indirectly, the employer is paying the payroll taxes for the employee as well as the net amount. This payment requires both: 1) a calculation of the gross amount before withholding, and 2) checking if supplementary payment rules apply (page 128), as with a discretionary bonus. (Although often a supplementary payment is intended to be a gross rather than a net amount.).

The following examples illustrate a variety of situations and provide a reliable calculation of gross pay and approximate federal income tax for these types of transactions. As well, the examples illustrate concepts that support the calculations. These payments become part of total annual taxable income for an employee. However, keep in mind that determining the resulting total annual income tax is subject to a variety of factors including progressive tax rates (examples here assume a single rate), pay frequency, other income, deductions taken, and tax credits. To achieve a more accurate federal income tax estimate before year-end filing that includes all payments, use the IRS online calculator at www.irs.gov/W4App.

"Grossing Up" a Net Amount, *continued*

Example #1: Below OASDI Limit

When an employee receives a net amount and the employer pays a higher gross amount to cover tax withholding, the following formula can be used to determine the equivalent taxable gross amount:

[Desired Take-Home Amount/(1 – Total Withholding Percentage)].

The key to applying the formula is to remember that the stated amount received is a *net* amount; the formula restates this to its equivalent gross amount.

Example: Macon Enterprises is giving its star salesperson, Mary Smith, a discretionary bonus (See page 76). Mary receives a monthly salary and her employer withholds taxes. The employer wants her to receive a separate take-home amount of $10,000, and needs to determine the correct amount of gross pay before withholding so that she receives the $10,000 as take-home pay (net amount). Mary's year-to-date gross pay will be below the OASDI limit. The employer uses a federal income tax rate of 22% and a state rate of 7%.

Step	Procedure	Example
1	Combine the withholding percentages.	FICA: .0765 FIT: .2200 SIT: .0700 Total .3665
2	Subtract from 1.	1 – .3665 = .6335
3	Divide desired take-home amount by the result from Step 2 for gross pay.	$10,000/.6335 = $15,785.32 equivalent gross pay
4	Determine withholding amounts.	FICA: $15,785.32 × .0765 = $1,207.58 FIT: $15,785.32 × .22 = $3,472.77 SIT: $15,785.32 × .07 = $1,104.97
5	Verify net payment amount.	$15,785.32 – $1,207.58 – $3,472.77 – $1,104.97 = $10,000

The $15, 785.32 is included in boxes 1, 3, 5, and 16 on Form W-2. $3,472.77 is included in box 2 and $1,104.97 is included in box 17. For FICA: Social Security of $978.69 (6.2%) is included in box 4 and Medicare of $228.89 (1.45%) is included in box 6. Note that this method can also be used for irregular manual net check amounts to determine gross.

If this were a net supplemental payment Mary should request that her employer make a separate bonus payment, use 22% as the federal tax rate, and not use tax tables to calculate a gross amount that is added into her regular paycheck. This could result in using a higher tax rate and excess income tax withholding. (Also, if her tax rate were greater than 22%, receiving a separate payment applying the 22% alternative would result in less withholding.)

"Grossing Up" a Net Amount, *continued*

Example #2: *Above OASDI* *Limit*		Macon Enterprises is giving its star salesperson, Mary Smith, a bonus separate from her regular pay. The company wants Mary to receive an amount of $10,000 (a net amount), but needs to determine the correct amount of gross pay before withholding so that she receives the $10,000 as a net amount. Mary's cumulative regular year-to-date gross pay is already above the OASDI limit before the bonus. The employer uses a federal income tax rate of 22% and a state tax rate of 7%.

Step	Procedure	Example
1	Combine the applicable withholding percentages.	FICA (Medicare only): .0145 FIT: .2200 SIT: .0700 Total .3045
2	Subtract from 1.	1 – .3045 = .6955
3	Divide desired take-home amount by the result from Step 2 for gross pay.	$10,000/.6955 = $14,378.15 equivalent gross pay
4	Determine withholding amounts.	FICA: $14,378.15 × .0145 = $208.49 FIT: $14,378.15 × .22 = $3,163.19 SIT: $14,378.15 × .07 = $1,006.47
5	Verify net amount.	$14,378.15 – $208.49 – $3,163.19 – $1,006.47 = $10,000

Effect of OASDI Wage Base

Example 1 is designed to be used when the total gross pay does not exceed the annual OASDI wage base limit (after which only the 1.45% Medicare rate applies). However, there are circumstances in which the prior year-to-date gross pay is below, but near, the OASDI limit, which then would be exceeded because of the supplemental payment. This creates a more complex situation and a few more steps are required.

Example 1 should not be applied in this circumstance. It will result in a gross pay amount that is too high, resulting in OASDI overwithholding, and excess withholding for other items connected to gross pay, such as federal/state income tax. In addition, an overstated gross wage will overstate average regular rate calculation used for overtime (except for discretionary payments, to which overtime does not apply) and possibly the calculation for workers' compensation

Example #3:
Exceeding the
OASDI Limit

When the prior year-to-date gross wages (that is, before the net payment) are below but near the OASDI limit, and you are not sure if the gross equivalent of the net payment will exceed the limit, you can use the table below. Part I of the table determines which procedure to apply. Part II shows the procedure to use if the supplemental payment's gross

continued ▶

"Grossing Up" a Net Amount, *continued*

Example #3,
Continued

equivalent amount starts below and then passes above the OASDI limit. Sometimes just part of the payment will be subject to OASDI and sometimes all will.

Assume that the OASDI wage base limit is $160,000 and that Millie's prior year-to-date (YTD) gross wages before a bonus are $135,000. Millie's employer wants her to receive a $24,000 supplemental payment as a net take-home amount.

Step	Procedure	Example	
	Part I		
1	Calculate these withholding percentages columns: 1. With total FICA rate 2. With only Medicare rate	<u>1</u> FICA: .0765 FIT: .2200 SIT: <u>.0700</u> Total .3665	<u>2</u> FICA: .0145 FIT: .2200 SIT: <u>.0700</u> Total .3045
2	IF prior YTD gross wages exceed the OASDI limit, use same procedure as Examle #2, otherwise continue.	$135,000 < $160,000. so continue here	
3	Determine if current payment will exceed wage base for FICA tax purposes: ▪ Divide payment by (1 – net of FICA %) ▪ Add result to prior YTD gross wages IF result does not exceed wage base, use Example #1. IF result is > wage base AND prior YTD gross wages don't exceed wage base limit, go to step 4.	▪ $24,000/.9235 = $25,988.09 ▪ $135,000 + $25,988.09 = $160,988.09 ($160,988.09 > the OASDI wage base limit of $160,000.)	
	Part II		
4	Calculate OASDI up to limit: (Wage base limit – prior YTD gross wages) × .062	$25,000 × .062 = $1,550.00	
5	Add step #4 result to payment amount	$24,000 + $1,550.00 = $25,550	
6	Calculate equivalent gross amount of payment for other taxes: divide Step #5 result by (1-column 2 total)	$25,550/.6955 = $36,736.16	
7	Determine withholding amounts.	FICA: (OASDI $1,550 above) + (Medicare $36,736.16 × .0145) = $2,082.67 FIT: $36,736.16 × .22 = $8,081.96 SIT: $36,736.16 × .07 = $2,571.53	
8	Verify net amount	$36,736.16 – $2,082.67– $8,081.96 – $2,571.53 = $24,000.	

continued ▶

"Grossing Up" a Net Amount, *continued*

Example #3, Continued	Federal reporting that is included on Form W-2 for this transaction: The $25,000 OASDI (Social Security) wages are included in box 3 on Form W-2; however, $36,736.16 become part of Medicare wages for box 5. Box 1 wages are $36,736.16. Federal withholding amounts (row 7) are included in boxes 2, 4, and 6. The FICA taxable amount and equivalent FICA withholding are reported on Form W-2 as well as reported on Form 941 or 944 and the employer also pays the employer share.
Example #4: Fixed Dollar Amount Part of Withholding	If there is a fixed dollar amount that is part of withholding such as a recurring membership payment, this amount is included as an additional amount in the gross pay calculation.

Example: Atwater Company is making a supplemental payment to Walter Thompson for a production enhancement. The company wants Walter to receive $20,000 after all amounts are deducted. After the bonus, Walter's cumulative regular gross pay will be under the OASDI wage base limit. His federal tax rate is 22% and his state rate is 4%. $50 of union dues must also be paid by Walter. |

Step	Procedure	Example
1	Combine the applicable withholding percentages.	FICA: .0765 FIT: .2200 SIT: .0400 Total .3365
2	Subtract from 1.	1 – .3365 = .6635
3	Calculate total gross pay.	$20,050/.6635 = $30,218.53
4	Determine withholding amounts.	FICA: $30,218.53 × .0765 = $2,311.72 FIT: $30,218.53 × .22 = $6,648.08 SIT: $30,218.53 × .04 = $1,208.74 Dues: $50.
5	Verify net amount.	$30,218.53 – $2,311.72 – $6,648.08 – $1,208.74 – $50.00 = $20,000 (rounded)

Federal reporting included on Form W-2 for this transaction: Box 1: $30,218.53, box 2: $6,648.08, boxes 3 and 5: $30,218.53; FICA: box 4: social security $1,873.55 (6.2%) and Medicare box 6: $438.17 (1.45%).

Example #5a: Payment Includes a Tax Deferred Plan	It is possible in some payment situations (although probably not common) that an employer wants to pay an employee a fixed net amount that also included payment to the employee's qualified tax deferred retirement or savings plan.

continued ▶

"Grossing Up" a Net Amount, *continued*

Example #5a,
Continued

Assume the same facts as in Example #1, and that the employee also has a pre-tax 5% qualified tax deferred retirement plan contribution deducted from gross pay that is excluded from income tax. The employer wants to calculate a gross amount that will include the pre-tax (tax-deferred) 5% qualified retirement plan contribution and still provide the net $10,000 supplemental payment.

Step	Procedure	Example
1	Add the withholding percentages, with income tax percentages adjusted to a rate net of the deferral percentage.	FICA: .0765 FIT: (.22 × .95) = .2090 SIT: (.07 × .95) = .0665 Total .3520
2	Subtract Step 1 result from the net taxable rate (here, 1.00 − .05).	.95 − .3520 = .5980
3	Divide the desired take-home amount by the result from Step 2 for gross pay.	$10,000/.5980 = $16,722.41
4	Determine contribution and withholding amounts.	Contribution: $16,722.41 × .05 = $836.12 FICA: $16,722.41 × .0765 = $1,279.26 FIT: $16,722.41 × .2090 = $3,494.98 SIT: $16,722.41 × .0665 = $1,112.04
5	Verify net amount.	$16,722.41 − $836.12 − $1,279.26 − $3,494.98 − $1,112.04 = $10,000 (rounded)

Federal reporting included on Form W-2 for this transaction: The amounts of ($16,722.41 × .95) = $15,886.29 (wages for income tax) and $16,722.41 (FICA-taxable wages) create a difference of $836.12 between boxes 1 and 3 on form W-2. The $16,722.41 is also used for employer payroll taxes calculation (FICA, FUTA, SUTA). For accounting purposes, the total debit to wages expense is $16,722.41 before withholding liabilities to arrive at net pay payable of $10,000. Federal withholding amounts are reported in boxes 2, 4, and 6.

Example #5b:
Payment Includes
a Tax Deferred
Plan

These are the same facts as Example #5a except that the employer will not pay for the retirement plan contribution. Instead, in this case, assume that a fixed pre-tax $500 retirement plan contribution will be paid by the employee out of the net amount received from the employer. Therefore the remaining net cash proceeds for the employee are $9,500.

continued ▶

"Grossing Up" a Net Amount, *continued*

Step	Procedure	Example
1	Calculate FICA tax on retirement plan deferred amount	$500 × .0765 = $38.25
2	Combine row 1 amount with the after-tax cash proceeds because row 1 represents additional net proceeds to the employee, since these are FICA taxes the employee did not have to pay.	$38.25 + $9,500 = $9,538.25
3	Add the withholding percentages, with income tax percentages adjusted to a rate net of the deferral percentage.	FICA .0765 FIT: .2200 SIT: .0700 Total .3665
4	Subtract Step 3 result from 1.	1.00 – .3665 = .6335
5	Divide the net proceeds amount by the result from Step 4 for the gross income taxable amount.	$9,538.25/.6335 = $15,056.43
6	Determine withholding amounts. (Note that income taxable amount is $500 less.)	FICA: $15,556.43 × .0765 = $1,190.07 FIT: $15,056.43 × .22 = $3,312.41 SIT: $15,056.43 × .07 = $1,053.95
7	Verify net amount.	$15,556.43 – $500.00 – $1,190.07 – $3,312.41 – $1,053.95 = $9,500

Federal reporting included on Form W-2 for this transaction: $15,056.43 is included in box 1 of Form W-2. $15,556.43 is reported in boxes 3 and 5. Box 2: $3,312.41, box 4: $964.50, and box 6: $225.57.

Example #6a: Employer Regularly Pays Withholding: FICA

In some situations an employer directly pays some or all employment tax; in other words, the employee is receiving a net amount and there is also no withholding. This is different than earlier examples in which a gross amount was calculated in order to determine a larger gross payment needed to cover withholding and the net amount. When an employee is below the OASDI limit, Example #1 is an illustration of this. In the following examples, the employer makes the tax payment.

A common example of this occurs when an employer agrees to pay an employee's share of FICA (OASDI and Medicare) tax, so there is no withholding for these items. Except for agricultural and household employees (see below), the net amount is grossed up in order to determine FICA "withholding amounts" (as well as income tax). There is no actual FICA withholding for the employee; however, the employer reports the taxable FICA amount and the calculated "withholding" on Form W-2 so the employee receives credit. Also, the employer reports the FICA

continued ▶

"Grossing Up" a Net Amount, *continued*

Example #6a, Continued

"withholding" plus the employer's share on Form 941, which determines the employer payment for total payroll taxes.

Example: John is a short-term employee. John's employer has regularly been paying John's FICA. So far, John has received $1,500 and the current payment to John is $500. The current FICA wage base is $147,000. FIT rate is 22%. There is no SIT.

Step	Procedure	Example
1	Calculate percentage factor for the FICA wage base.	1 – .0765 = .9235 (.062 OASDI + .0145 Medicare = .0765)
2	Multiply current FICA wage base by Step 1 to determine FICA in net terms.	$147,000 × .9235 = $135,754.50
3	If employee cumulative net pay is at or below this amount, continue, otherwise go to example #6b.	$1,500 + $500 = $2,000 which is less than $135,754.50. Go to step 4.
4	Divide the current net pay by the result from Step 1. This is gross pay subject to FICA; also subject to income tax and FUTA to applicable limit.	$500 / .9235 = $541.42
5	Determine withholding reported.	FICA: (OASDI and Medicare): $541.42 × .0765 = $41.42 FIT: $541.42 × .22 = $119.11
6	Verify net pay (for FICA gross-up).	$541.42 – $41.42 = $500

Federal reporting included on Form W-2 for this transaction: $541.42 is included in box 1 of Form W-2 and in boxes 3 and 5. Federal income tax withholding of $119.11 is included in box 2; for FICA: Social Security of $33.57 (6.2%) in box 4, and Medicare of $7.85 (1.45%) in box 6.

Example #6b: FICA Paid Above FICA Wage Base

Assume that John's current net pay for the period is $3,500. John's prior net pay for the year is $150,000. The employer pays John's FICA tax (OASDI and Medicare). The current FICA wage base is $147,000. FIT rate is 22%. There is no SIT.

continued ▶

"Grossing Up" a Net Amount, *continued*

Step	Procedure	Example
1	Calculate percentage factor for the FICA wage base.	1 – .0765 = .9235 (.062 OASDI + .0145 Medicare = .0765)
2	Multiply current FICA wage base by Step 1 to determine FICA in **net** terms.	$147,000 × .9235 = $135,754.50
3	Subtract the result in Step 2 from cumulative **net** pay.	$153,500 – $135,754.50 = $17,745.50
4	Calculate a percentage factor for wages above the wage base. (This is for Medicare only – there is no cap on Medicare).	1 – .0145 = .9855 (Medicare rate is 1.45%)
5	Divide the result in Step 3 by the result in Step 4. This is Medicare **gross** wage above the OASDI wage base.	$17,745.50 / .9855 = $18,006.60
6	Add the result in Step 5 to the wage base. This is gross wage that includes taxable Medicare wages.	$18,006.60 + $147,000 = $165,006.60.
7	Calculate tax to report.	On FICA wage base: [($147,000 × .0765) + Medicare above base: ($165,006.60 – $147,000) × .0145)] = $11,506.60 FIT: $165,006.60 × .22 = $36,301.45
8	Verify total net (for FICA gross-up).	$165,006.60 – $11,506.60 = $153,500

Federal reporting included on Form W-2 for this transaction: $165,006.60 is included in box 1 and in box 5. $147,000 is reported in box 3. Federal withholding amounts are included in boxes 2, 4, and 6.

Agricultural and Household Employees

For agricultural and household employees, a special provision applies. In this case the employer payment is treated differently. FICA is calculated on the net payment amount and added to the employee payment for income tax purposes.

Example #7: Household Employee Payments

Angela hires Constance (an unrelated person over 18) as a household employee to help with child care and pays Constance $225 per week with no withholding; Angela pays the FICA. Constance does not request income tax withholding. For FICA purposes, taxable wages are $225. Employee FICA tax is $225 × .0765 = $17.21 (and employer FICA tax is the same amount). Wages for income tax purposes are $225 + $17.21 = $242.21.

continued ▶

"Grossing Up" a Net Amount, *continued*

Example #7, Continued	(As a review, annual cash wages of less than $2,400 to any one household employee are not subject to FICA tax and withholding is not required. If unsure of annual total, employer can withhold; if total turns out to be less than $2,400 the employer must repay the employee the withheld total and not report the repayment. If less than $1,000 per calendar quarter is paid to all household employees, FUTA is not required. See earlier discussion of who is a household employee and Publication 926.)

Grossing Up Example for Page 217

Calculation: $4,000/[1 − (.20 + .0765)] = $5,528.68 gross wage
$5,528.68 − $4,000 = $1,528.68 addition to gross wage
Federal income tax and FICA: calculate on total gross wage

Journal entry:

Date xxx	Wages Expense	1,528.68	
	Federal Income Tax Payable		1,105.74
	FICA Payable		422.94

The Payroll Process

Step 1: Identify Employees

- Searching and hiring
- Employee vs. independent contractor
- Exempt vs. non-exempt
- Fair employment laws compliance
- Monitor and update employee status

Step 2: Calculate the Payroll

- Timekeeping
- Gross pay expense
- Withholding
- Payroll tax expense
- Benefits expense

Step 3: Record the Payroll

- Journal entry for gross pay and withholding
- Journal entry for payroll taxes expense
- Journal entry for benefits expense
- Journal entry for workers' comp. expense
- Verify/reconcile related ledger balances

Step 4: Make Payments

- To employees
- To taxing authorities
- To other parties

Step 5: Submit Forms and Reports

- Reverify/reconcile related ledger balances
- Federal government
- State/local governments
- Employees and independent contractors
- Management

For all steps in the process: Is internal control being adequately applied?

Section 5 Submit Forms and Reports

Introduction	Submitting federal, state, and sometimes local required tax forms and reports is a regular and required part of the payroll process. This section primarily discusses federal reporting and requirements.

Quarterly Reporting

Overview	Employers are generally required to file regular quarterly reports to the Internal Revenue Service to report wages, salaries, tips, employer and employee FICA obligation, income tax withheld from employees, and amount of deposits. The report used by most employers is Form 941, filed quarterly. We discuss Form 941 below.

Note: Other withholding, such as backup withholding (employer has not received employee social security number) and non-employee withholding (pensions, annuities, investments, etc.) is annually reported on Form 945.

Who Files Form 941?	The purpose of these reports is to inform tax authorities each designated period of: 1) FICA: employer and employee liability 2) Employee income tax: how much was withheld 3) Any related adjustments or credits 4) Deposits: All deposits made and when they were made.

Employers must file Form 941 if any of the below items apply, unless one of the exceptions below apply:

- There are employees who receive wages and/or tips subject to federal income tax or social security taxes
- Form 941 was previously filed, even if there are no current wages or withholding amounts, unless a final return was previously filed.

Exceptions:

- Employers of farm workers subject to federal income tax and/or FICA must file annual Form 943 for the farm workers instead of the quarterly Form 941 used for non-agricultural workers.
- If employer believes the annual deposit obligation will be $1,000 or less, and with written approval offered by the IRS, Form 944 is filed annually instead of filing Form 941.
- Employers of household employees generally file Schedule H with their own annual Form1040, individual tax return. (See Publication 926).
- Seasonal employers may not have to file Form 941 every quarter. (See Form 941 instructions)

TIP

Federal forms resource: All current federal forms can be accessed online at http://www.irs.gov/formspubs/.

continued ▶

Quarterly Reporting, *continued*

| *Form 941 Due Dates* | Form 941 reports are required for calendar quarters, as follows: |

Form 941 Due Dates

Form 941 reports are required for calendar quarters, as follows:

- 1st quarter: January, February, March
- 2nd quarter: April, May, June
- 3rd quarter: July, August, September,
- 4th quarter: October, November, December

IF...	THEN...	OTHERWISE...
If the filing due date falls on a Saturday, Sunday, or legal holiday,	File on the next business day.	File by the last day of the month following the end of the quarter.

Sources of Form 941 Information

The employee earnings records (page 201) and reconciled ledger accounts are primary sources of Form 941 information. Forms 4070, and supplemental records will provide tips information if not incorporated into individual earnings records. "(Also see Form 8974, Qualified Small Business Payroll Tax Credit for Increasing Research Activities.)"

An employer must be aware of the importance of reconciling accounting records and reporting. Assuming that amounts on the payroll register are correct, it must reconcile: 1) line items to individual earnings records, 2) totals to ledger account balances. Review journal entries for payroll related items. Payroll ledger balances, 941 (or 944) forms, W-2/W-3 forms must all reconcile with each other. The Social Security Administration verifies W-2s and the annual total of quarterly reports for consistency. The IRS matches the annual totals on Form W-3 with the annual totals of quarterly reports.

TIP

IRS Electronic Payment and Filing Systems

- For payment: EFTPS (Electronic Federal Tax Payment System) is a free system offered by the U.S. Treasury Department. Go to www.eftps.gov to enroll. Also see Publications 966 and 4990. EFTPS customer service is 800-555-4477 and 800-733-4829.
- For filing: Employment tax returns (and many other types) can be filed online using the IRS e-file "MeF" system. An employer can either purchase commercially available software (https://www.irs .gov/e-file-providers/94x-mef-providers) to apply for a PIN number (Form 8543-EMP is also required) or use a 3rd party professional for the process (See https://www.irs.gov/e-file-providers /authorized-irs-e-file-providers-for-individuals for IRS-approved professionals). **For filing W-2 forms see page 249.**
- For filing and payment: FIRE system is an IRS electronic system only for business filers of certain information tax forms. For employers, the forms applicable for FIRE would be: W-2G, 1042-S, 1097, 1098, 1099, 3921, 3922, 8027, and 8955-SSA. See form 4419. (Search form numbers online for full names.)

continued ▶

Quarterly Reporting, *continued*

Illustration 5.1: Form

Form 941 for 2022: Employer's QUARTERLY Federal Tax Return
(Rev. March 2022)

Department of the Treasury — Internal Revenue Service

950122

OMB No. 1545-0029

Employer identification number (EIN) ☐☐ – ☐☐☐☐☐☐☐

Name (*not your trade name*)

Trade name (*if any*)

Address

Number   Street   Suite or room number

City   State   ZIP code

Foreign country name   Foreign province/county   Foreign postal code

Report for this Quarter of 2022
(Check one.)

☐ **1:** January, February, March

☐ **2:** April, May, June

☐ **3:** July, August, September

☐ **4:** October, November, December

Go to *www.irs.gov/Form941* for instructions and the latest information.

Read the separate instructions before you complete Form 941. Type or print within the boxes.

Part 1: Answer these questions for this quarter.

1 Number of employees who received wages, tips, or other compensation for the pay period including: *Mar. 12* (Quarter 1) . . . . **1** ☐

2 Wages, tips, and other compensation . . . . **2** ☐

3 Federal income tax withheld from wages, tips, and other compensation . . . . . . **3** ☐

4 If no wages, tips, and other compensation are subject to social security or Medicare tax ☐ Check and go to line 6.

	Column 1		Column 2
5a Taxable social security wages* . .	☐	× 0.124 =	☐
5a (i) Qualified sick leave wages* . .	☐	× 0.062 =	☐
5a (ii) Qualified family leave wages* .	☐	× 0.062 =	☐
5b Taxable social security tips . .	☐	× 0.124 =	☐
5c Taxable Medicare wages & tips .	☐	× 0.029 =	☐
5d Taxable wages & tips subject to Additional Medicare Tax withholding	☐	× 0.009 =	☐

*Include taxable qualified sick and family leave wages paid in 2022 for leave taken after March 31, 2021, and before October 1, 2021, on line 5a. Use lines 5a(i) and 5a(ii) **only** for taxable qualified sick and family leave wages paid in 2022 for leave taken after March 31, 2020, and before April 1, 2021.*

Line-by-line Form 941 instructions are available online.

5e Total social security and Medicare taxes. Add Column 2 from lines 5a, 5a(i), 5a(ii), 5b, 5c, and 5d **5e** ☐

5f Section 3121(q) Notice and Demand—Tax due on unreported tips (see instructions) . . **5f** ☐

Line 5f: Also see page 111.

6 Total taxes before adjustments. Add lines 3, 5e, and 5f . . . . **6** ☐

7 Current quarter's adjustment for fractions of cents   Line 7: Rounding difference between withholding and column 2. **7** ☐

8 Current quarter's adjustment for sick pay . . . .   Line 8: Explained in instructions. **8** ☐

9 Current quarter's adjustments for tips and group-term life insurance . . . . **9** ☐

Line 9: Negative adjustment for uncollected employee share of FICA (OASDI and Medicare). Also see W-2 general instructions for box 12, codes M, N.

10 Total taxes after adjustments. Combine lines 6 through 9 . **10** ☐

11a Qualified small business payroll tax credit for increasing research activities. Attach Form 8974 **11a** ☐

11b Nonrefundable portion of credit for qualified sick and family leave wages for leave taken before April 1, 2021 . . . . **11b** ☐

11c Reserved for future use . . . . **11c** ☐

▶ You MUST complete all three pages of Form 941 and SIGN it. Next ▶

For Privacy Act and Paperwork Reduction Act Notice, see the back of the Payment Voucher. Cat. No. 17001Z Form **941** (Rev. 3-2022)

Source: Internal Revenue Service.

continued ▶

Quarterly Reporting, *continued*

Illustration 5.1: Form 941, continued

```
                                                                                    950222
```

Name *(not your trade name)*	Employer identification number (EIN)

Part 1: **Answer these questions for this quarter.** *(continued)*

11d Nonrefundable portion of credit for qualified sick and family leave wages for leave taken after March 31, 2021, and before October 1, 2021 . . . . **11d** [▪]

11e Nonrefundable portion of COBRA premium assistance credit (see instructions for applicable quarter) . . . . **11e** [▪]

11f Number of individuals provided COBRA premium assistance [ ]

11g **Total nonrefundable credits.** Add lines 11a, 11b, 11d, and 11e . . . . **11g** [▪]

12 **Total taxes after adjustments and nonrefundable credits.** Subtract line 11g from line 10 . **12** [▪]

13a Total deposits for this quarter, including overpayment applied from a prior quarter and overpayments applied from Form 941-X, 941-X (PR), 944-X, or 944-X (SP) filed in the current quarter **13a** [▪]

13b Reserved for future use . . . . **13b** [▪]

13c Refundable portion of credit for qualified sick and family leave wages for leave taken before April 1, 2021 . . . . **13c** [▪]

13d Reserved for future use . . . . **13d** [▪]

13e Refundable portion of credit for qualified sick and family leave wages for leave taken after March 31, 2021, and before October 1, 2021 . . . . **13e** [▪]

13f Refundable portion of COBRA premium assistance credit (see instructions for applicable quarter) . . . . **13f** [▪]

13g **Total deposits and refundable credits.** Add lines 13a, 13c, 13e, and 13f . . . . **13g** [▪]

13h Reserved for future use . . . . **13h** [▪]

13i Reserved for future use . . . . **13i** [▪]

14 **Balance due.** If line 12 is more than line 13g, enter the difference and see instructions . . . **14** [▪]

15 **Overpayment.** If line 13g is more than line 12, enter the difference [▪] Check one: ☐ Apply to next return. ☐ Send a refund.

Part 2: **Tell us about your deposit schedule and tax liability for this quarter.**

If you're unsure about whether you're a monthly schedule depositor or a semiweekly schedule depositor, see section 11 of Pub. 15.

16 Check one: ☐ **Line 12 on this return is less than $2,500 or line 12 on the return for the prior quarter was less than $2,500, and you didn't incur a $100,000 next-day deposit obligation during the current quarter.** If line 12 for the prior quarter was less than $2,500 but line 12 on this return is $100,000 or more, you must provide a record of your federal tax liability. If you're a monthly schedule depositor, complete the deposit schedule below; if you're a semiweekly schedule depositor, attach Schedule B (Form 941). Go to Part 3.

☐ **You were a monthly schedule depositor for the entire quarter.** Enter your tax liability for each month and total liability for the quarter, then go to Part 3.

Tax liability: Month 1 [▪]

Month 2 [▪]

Month 3 [▪]

Total liability for quarter [▪] **Total must equal line 12.**

☐ **You were a semiweekly schedule depositor for any part of this quarter.** Complete Schedule B (Form 941), Report of Tax Liability for Semiweekly Schedule Depositors, and attach it to Form 941. Go to Part 3.

▶ **You MUST complete all three pages of Form 941 and SIGN it.** Next ▪▶

Page **2** Form **941** (Rev. 3-2022)

Source: Internal Revenue Service.

continued ▶

Quarterly Reporting, *continued*

Illustration 5.1: Form 941, continued

```
                                                                    950922
```

Name *(not your trade name)*	Employer identification number (EIN)

Part 3: Tell us about your business. If a question does NOT apply to your business, leave it blank.

17 If your business has closed or you stopped paying wages . . . . ☐ Check here, and

enter the final date you paid wages [/ /] ; also attach a statement to your return. See instructions.

18 If you're a seasonal employer and you don't have to file a return for every quarter of the year . . . ☐ Check here.

19 Qualified health plan expenses allocable to qualified sick leave wages for leave taken before April 1, 2021   19 [_____].

20 Qualified health plan expenses allocable to qualified family leave wages for leave taken before April 1, 2021   20 [_____].

21 Reserved for future use . . . .   21 [_____].

22 Reserved for future use . . . .   22 [_____].

23 Qualified sick leave wages for leave taken after March 31, 2021, and before October 1, 2021   23 [_____].

24 Qualified health plan expenses allocable to qualified sick leave wages reported on line 23   24 [_____].

25 Amounts under certain collectively bargained agreements allocable to qualified sick leave wages reported on line 23 . . . . .   25 [_____].

26 Qualified family leave wages for leave taken after March 31, 2021, and before October 1, 2021   26 [_____].

27 Qualified health plan expenses allocable to qualified family leave wages reported on line 26   27 [_____].

28 Amounts under certain collectively bargained agreements allocable to qualified family leave wages reported on line 26 . . . . .   28 [_____].

Part 4: May we speak with your third-party designee?

Do you want to allow an employee, a paid tax preparer, or another person to discuss this return with the IRS? See the instructions for details.

☐ Yes. Designee's name and phone number [_____] [_____]

Select a 5-digit personal identification number (PIN) to use when talking to the IRS. ☐ ☐ ☐ ☐ ☐

☐ No.

Part 5: Sign here. You MUST complete all three pages of Form 941 and SIGN it.

Under penalties of perjury, I declare that I have examined this return, including accompanying schedules and statements, and to the best of my knowledge and belief, it is true, correct, and complete. Declaration of preparer (other than taxpayer) is based on all information of which preparer has any knowledge.

X Sign your name here [_____]

Print your name here [_____]

Print your title here [_____]

Date [/ /]

Best daytime phone [_____]

Paid Preparer Use Only Check if you're self-employed . . . ☐

Preparer's name	[_____]	PTIN	[_____]
Preparer's signature	[_____]	Date	[/ /]
Firm's name (or yours if self-employed)	[_____]	EIN	[_____]
Address	[_____]	Phone	[_____]
City	[_____]	State [____]	ZIP code	[_____]

Page **3**   Form **941** (Rev. 3-2022)

Source: Internal Revenue Service.

Annual Reporting

Overview   Preparing and filing payroll forms are integral parts of the payroll process. The submission of required payroll forms is a means of tracking
compliance in various areas. These include reporting employer deposits,
employee income, independent contractor payments, tax withholding,
fringe benefits, and employer and worker identification. This section dis-
cusses frequently used federal payroll forms. In many cases state forms
are used for similar purposed, so a search for a state form by topic name
can often locate a necessary state form. In limited cases, such as with
federal form W-2, only a single form is necessary to comply with all reporting requirements.

Finding Forms   As with many payroll issues, a good source of information is the IRS
website at irs.gov. As well, an Internet search by topic or issue followed
by the term "forms" can also be useful. Finally, payroll software will normally generate the more frequently used forms as part of processing.

Form W-2 (Annual)

W-2 Basic Filing   An employer must prepare and submit a Form W-2 to the Social Security
Requirements   Administration for an employee if any of the following conditions exist:

- Any wages (cash or noncash) of at least $600/calendar year were paid
  to an employee for services in a trade or business regardless of whether
  any amounts were withheld or not. "Paid" means actual or constructive receipt by employee.
- Any income tax, social security, or Medicare tax is withheld
- Income tax would have been withheld if the employee had not claimed
  more than one allowance or had not claimed to be exempt from withholding on Form W-4
- There is a Form W-2G for types of gambling winnings.

Refer to instructions for Form W-2 for additional information.

A social security number verification service (SSNVS) is available
online for authorized employers and other authorized users. Go to
socialsecurity.gov/ employer/ssnv.htm for further information.

If a filing date falls on a Sunday or holiday, then the next business
day becomes the due date. For example if a filing date is normally
the last day of February, but this year February 28th is a Sunday, the
due date then becomes March 1.

continued ▶

Form W-2 (Annual), *continued*

Due Dates	Following December 31 of the current year:

- Provide to employees: no later than January 31 of the next year.
- Provide to taxing authorities: no later than January 31 (Exception: deadline for W-2G for gambling winnings is allowed a 30-day extension to federal taxing authorities.)
- A single 30-day extension of time may be requested on Form 8809. IRS will grant extensions only under extraordinary circumstances.

Source of W-2 Information

The employee earnings records (See page 201 example.) are primary sources of W-2 information. Supplementary records and reporting will provide tips and benefits information if not incorporated into individual earnings records. An employer should especially note the importance of maintaining consistency between internal records and reporting.

For example, employee earnings records, W-2s, and quarterly 941 or 943 forms must all show consistent amounts. The Social Security Administration checks W-2s and the annual total of quarterly reports for consistency.

Specific W-2 Circumstances

Table 5 2 on the next page addresses specific circumstances that may be occur in connection with the preparation and/or filing of Form W-2.

TIP

Identify yourself! – Do you know the differences between the forms: SS-4, SS-5, W-4 and W-9?

- A Form SS-4 application is mailed or faxed to the Internal Revenue Service or obtained online at IRS.gov/EIN in order to obtain an employer identification number (called EIN or "Tax ID").
- A Form SS-5 is filed with the Social Security Administration by an individual to obtain a social security number. A social security number is used by individuals and sole proprietors without employees as identification.
- A Form W-4 is used by employers to obtain employee information primarily to determine correct income tax withholding.
- A Form W-9 is used by business (also non-profits, pension plans, and government agencies) payers of income to obtain information from the recipient of the payments in order to determine reporting information and possible withholding. This request usually applies to independent contractors and recipients of dividends and interest. The party making the payments uses the information on Form 1099.

continued ▶

Form W-2 (Annual), *continued*

Table 5.1 Form W-2 Potential Issues

IF...	THEN...
a box on the form does not apply	leave that box blank.
a W-2 has been lost or destroyed,	send substitute copy as "reissued".
there are errors on W-2s that have been sent out,	immediately prepare and send out Form W-2c, "Corrected Wage and Tax Statement". (Illustration 5.4)
an employer refuses to issue a corrected W-2	employee may initiate a W-2 complaint with the IRS. 800-829-1040 or online taxpayer assistance.
an employee does not provide a social security number (SSN) at time W-2s are filed.	the employee must submit an application Form SS-5 within 7 days of beginning work. If the employee has applied but the number is not available write "Applied For" in box 'a' or all zeros in number box for electronic filing. A W-2c is later issued with correct number. An employer is required to obtain an employee's social security number.
employer cannot locate employee or current address,	retain the employee copy for four years.
an employee leaves the employer,	provide W-2 at any time after the employee leaves, but no later than the normal due dates.
an employee asks for a W-2 after leaving,	provide within 30 days of request or final wage payment.
an employee who previously left is rehired during the current calendar year,	provide W-2 according to normal due dates
100 or more issued (2022); 10 or more (after 2022).	filing must be done electronically.
an employer is going out business,	provide W-2s to employees and file no later than due date of final Form 941 or 944.
employee is deceased,	include in box 1 payments made in year of death, and paid amounts plus all accrued compensation in boxes 3 and 5. Use 1099 for accruals in year of death; after that year use 1099 for amounts paid.

Internet Delivery to Employees

An employer can provide W-2s to those employees who have affirmatively consented to Internet delivery of their W-2s. An employee's consent must be via the Internet and state that the employee has access. The website delivering the W-2s must be secure and use individual passwords. An employee must be notified of the W-2 availability and provided instructions on how to access it. Normal due dates apply, and the employer is required to keep W-2s available online until October 15 of the following calendar year.

continued ▶

Form W-2 (Annual), *continued*

Illustration 5.2: Form W-2

22222	VOID ☐	a Employee's social security number	For Official Use Only ▶ OMB No. 1545-0008	

b Employer identification number (EIN)	1 Wages, tips, other compensation	2 Federal income tax withheld
c Employer's name, address, and ZIP code	3 Social security wages	4 Social security tax withheld
	5 Medicare wages and tips	6 Medicare tax withheld
	7 Social security tips	8 Allocated tips
d Control number	9	10 Dependent care benefits
e Employee's first name and initial	Last name	Suff.	11 Nonqualified plans	12a See instructions for box 12
	13 Statutory employee ☐ Retirement plan ☐ Third-party sick pay ☐	12b
	14 Other	12c
		12d
f Employee's address and ZIP code		

15 State	Employer's state ID number	16 State wages, tips, etc.	17 State income tax	18 Local wages, tips, etc.	19 Local income tax	20 Locality name

Form **W-2** Wage and Tax Statement   2022   Department of the Treasury—Internal Revenue Service

Copy A—For Social Security Administration. Send this entire page with Form W-3 to the Social Security Administration; photocopies are **not** acceptable.

For Privacy Act and Paperwork Reduction Act Notice, see the separate instructions.

Cat. No. 10134D

Do Not Cut, Fold, or Staple Forms on This Page

Table 5.2 Summary of Instructions for completing Form W-2

Box	Description
a	**Employee social security number:** This should be available on Form W-4. (Note: After 2018, current regulations permit "truncated" numbers on employee copies (only) as follows: each of the first five digits of a social security number is replaced with "X".)
Void	This box is used when there is an error on a single form that is corrected on a following single form on one entire sheet of forms that is being prepared for taxing authorities.
b	**Employer identification number:** An employer identification number (EIN) is assigned by the IRS. An EIN can be applied for by completing and mailing or faxing Form SS-4 to the IRS or at IRS.gov/EIN. If no number is available and it has been applied for, enter "Applied For" in this space.
c	**Employer name, address and zip code:** Use the same information as used on Form 941 or 943.
d	**Control number:** This is optional - use only by employers with an internal system that is designed to identify employees or individual W-2s by an ID number.
e	**Employee name:** Use the exact same name as shown on employee social security card. If that is not available, use exact same name as on Form W-4.
f	**Employee address and zip code:** This information should be available on Form W-4.

continued ▶

Form W-2 (Annual), *continued*

Table 5.2: Summary of Instructions for completing Form W-2, continued

Box	Description
1	**Wages, tips, other compensation:** Show the employee taxable compensation that is actually or constructively (page 216) received during the calendar year: 1) wages, tips reported to employer, commissions, bonuses, prizes, and awards 2) taxable fringe benefits 3) certain employee expense reimbursements (under a non-accountable plan) 4) the cost of accident and health insurance for 2% or more shareholder-employees of a subchapter-S corporation 5) taxable benefits from a cafeteria plan 6) employer contributions to a qualified long-term care plan to extent such coverage is already available through a flexible spending plan 7) cost of group-term life insurance coverage in excess of $50,000 8) payments for non-job-related education expenses or payments under a non-accountable plan 9) payments of employee social security, Medicare, or income tax withholding 10) all other compensation including taxable compensation for which federal income tax was not withheld
2	**Federal income tax withheld:** Show the total federal income tax withheld from the employee's wages for the year.
3	**Social security wages:** Show the total wages paid (before payroll deductions) subject to employee social security tax (OASDI) but not including social security tips and allocated tips. If reporting these amounts in a subsequent year (due to lapse of risk of forfeiture), the amount must be adjusted by any gain or loss. See *Box 7—Social security tips* and *Box 8—Allocated tips.* Generally, noncash payments are considered to be wages. Include employee business expense reimbursements reported in box 1. If you paid the employee's share of social security and Medicare taxes rather than deducting them from wages, see *"employee's social security and Medicare taxes (or railroad retirement taxes, if applicable) paid by employer"* in W-2 instructions and pages 232–234. The total of boxes 3 and 7 cannot exceed the maximum social security wage base.)

Report in box 3 elective deferrals to certain qualified cash or deferred compensation arrangements and to retirement plans described in box 12 (codes D, E, F, G, and S) even though the deferrals are not includible in box 1. Also report in box 3 designated Roth contributions made under a section 401(k) plan, under a section 403(b) salary reduction agreement, or under a governmental section 457(b) plan described in box 12 (codes AA, BB, and EE).

Amounts deferred (plus earnings or less losses) under a section 457(f) or nonqualified plan or nongovernmental section 457(b) plan must be included in boxes 3 and/or 5 as social security and/or Medicare wages as of the later of when the services giving rise to the deferral are performed or when there is no substantial forfeiture risk of the rights to the deferred amount. Include both elective and non-elective deferrals for purposes of nongovernmental section 457(b) plans. |

continued ▶

Form W-2 (Annual), *continued*

Table 5.2: Summary of Instructions for completing Form W-2, continued

Box	Description
	Wages reported in box 3 also include: Signing bonuses an employer pays for signing or ratifying an employment contract. Taxable cost of group-term life insurance over $50,000 included in box 1. Cost of accident and health insurance premiums for 2%-or-more shareholder-employees paid by an S corporation, but only if not excludable under section 3121(a)(2)(B). Employee and non-excludable employer contributions to an MSA or HSA. However, do not include employee contributions to an HSA that were made through a cafeteria plan. Employee contributions to a SIMPLE retirement account.
4	**Social security tax withheld:** Show the total employee social security tax (OASDI) withheld (not employer share), including social security tax on tips. The amount should not exceed 6.2% × social security wage base. Include only taxes withheld (or paid by employer for the employee) for current year wages and tips. It is possible this amount may be greater than box 1 due to compensation not taxable for income tax purposes, but taxable for box 4 and 5 purposes.
5	**Medicare wages and tips:** The wages and tips subject to Medicare tax are the same as those subject to social security tax (boxes 3 and 7) except that there is no wage base limit for Medicare tax. Enter the total Medicare wages and tips in box 5. It is possible this amount may be greater than box 4.
6	**Medicare tax withheld:** Enter the total employee Medicare tax (including any Additional Medicare Tax) withheld. Include only tax withheld for current year wages and tips.
7	**Social security tips:** Show the tips that the employee reported to employer even if employer did not have enough employee funds to collect the social security tax for the tips. (The total of boxes 3 and 7 should not be more than the maximum amount for the social security wage base for current year). Report all tips in box 1 along with wages and other compensation. Include any tips reported in box 7 in box 5 also.
8	**Allocated tips:** If employer operates a large food or beverage establishment, employer should show the tips allocated to the employee. Do not include this amount in boxes 1, 3, 5, or 7. See Part III of Section 2 for a discussion of allocated tips. Employee uses Form 4137 to report box 8 amount.
9	Blank

continued ▶

Form W-2 (Annual), *continued*

Table 5.2: Summary of Instructions for completing Form W-2, continued

Box	Description
10	**Dependent care benefits:** Show the total dependent care benefits under a dependent care assistance program paid or incurred by you for your employee. Include the fair market value (FMV) of care in a daycare facility provided or sponsored by you for your employee and amounts paid or incurred for dependent care assistance in a cafeteria plan. Report all amounts paid or incurred (regardless of any employee forfeitures), including those in excess of the $5,000 exclusion. This may include (a) the FMV of benefits provided in kind by the employer, (b) an amount paid directly to a daycare facility by the employer or reimbursed to the employee to subsidize the benefit, or (c) benefits from the pre-tax contributions made by the employee under a dependent care flexible spending account. Include any amounts over $5,000 in boxes 1, 3, and 5.
11	**Nonqualified plans:** The purpose of box 11 is for the Social Security Administration (SSA) to determine if any part of the amount reported in box 1 or boxes 3 and/or 5 was earned in a prior year. The SSA uses this information to verify that they have properly applied the social security earnings test and paid the correct amount of benefits. Report distributions to an employee from a nonqualified plan or nongovernmental section 457(b) plan in box 11. Also report these distributions in box 1. Make only one entry in this box. Distributions from governmental section 457(b) plans must be reported on Form 1099-R, not in box 1 of Form W-2. Under nonqualified plans or nongovernmental 457(b) plans, deferred amounts that are no longer subject to a substantial risk of forfeiture are taxable even if not distributed. Report these amounts in boxes 3 (up to the social security wage base) and 5. Do not report in box 11 deferrals included in boxes 3 and/or 5 and deferrals for current year services (such as those with no risk of forfeiture).
12	Complete and code this box for all code items described in IRS instructions for Form W-2. Do not enter more than four codes; if more than four codes are needed use an additional W-2. Taxable amounts should also be included in box 1. For health coverage see codes J, R,W, and DD
13	Check all boxes that apply. Check statutory employee box for statutory employees whose earnings are subject to social security and Medicare taxes but not subject to federal income tax withholding. Do not check this box for common-law employees.
14	**Other:** Use this box for any other information that you want to give to your employee. Identify each item.
15–20	**Boxes 15–20:** Use these boxes to report state and local income tax information. Enter the two-letter abbreviation for the name of the state.

continued ▶

Form W-2 (Annual), *continued*

Who Receives a W-2?	An employer provides W-2 copies to the following parties: Forms to Social Security Administration: Paper forms are available in retail business stores as well as copies online; however, if there are 250 or more forms to file, the forms must be submitted electronically (on or after midnight January 31, 2022 100 or more and 10 or more same day in 2023). See Internet filing discussion below. Copy 1: To state and local taxing authorities Copy B: To employees for filing federal income tax returns Copy C: To employees for keeping in their records Copy 2: To employees for filing state and local income tax returns Copy D: Retained by the employer
Form W-3 Transmittal Form	Form W-3 is a transmittal form that must accompany Form W-2 when filed with taxing authorities. A single Form W-3 accompanies all copies of Form W-2. A W-3c accompanies W-2c forms.
Internet Filing	"W 2/W-3 forms are filed with the Social Security system, not the IRS, including electronic filing. The Social Security Administration strongly encourages all filers to use electronic filing; however, filers that file 250 or more forms must file electronically unless granted a waiver from the IRS. The following resources may prove useful: ■ Online filing: The Social Security Administration site for "business services" at https://www.ssa.gov/employer/ explains W-2 filing, how to register and links to resources including filing assistance. Also useful is www.SSA.gov/bso. See also the Social Security Administration Publication No. 42-007. Note that 3rd party software is available that allows an employer to import W-2/W-3 data to create a file that can be sent to Social Security. ■ W-2/W-3 forms available online: Online fill-in forms to fill in, save, print, and submit (except copy A), to a maximum of 50 items at a time. See https://www.irs.gov/pub/irs-pdf/fw2.pdf.

TIP

For the employee: what if no W-2 provided or employer does not change an incorrect W-2? If an employer refuses to provide a correct Form W-2, an employee can file Form 4852 with the annual income tax return Form 1040 using his/her own calculations (such as amounts from pay stubs), and with an explanation. This form will also work for independent contractors who have not received a correct Form 1099. The IRS also provides a number for assistance: 1-800-829-1040.

continued ▶

Form W-2 (Annual), *continued*

Illustration 5.3: Form W-3 Transmittal

DO NOT STAPLE

33333	a Control number	For Official Use Only ▶ OMB No. 1545-0008		

| b Kind of Payer (Check one) | 941 ☐ Military ☐ 943 ☐ 944 ☐ CT-1 ☐ Hshld. emp. ☐ Medicare govt. emp. ☐ | Kind of Employer (Check one) | None apply ☐ 501c non-govt. ☐ State/local non-501c ☐ State/local 501c ☐ Federal govt. ☐ | Third-party sick pay (Check if applicable) ☐ |

c Total number of Forms W-2	d Establishment number	1 Wages, tips, other compensation	2 Federal income tax withheld
e Employer identification number (EIN)		3 Social security wages	4 Social security tax withheld
f Employer's name		5 Medicare wages and tips	6 Medicare tax withheld
		7 Social security tips	8 Allocated tips
		9	10 Dependent care benefits
		11 Nonqualified plans	12a Deferred compensation
g Employer's address and ZIP code			
h Other EIN used this year		13 For third-party sick pay use only	12b
15 State Employer's state ID number		14 Income tax withheld by payer of third-party sick pay	
16 State wages, tips, etc.	17 State income tax	18 Local wages, tips, etc.	19 Local income tax
Employer's contact person		Employer's telephone number	For Official Use Only
Employer's fax number		Employer's email address	

Under penalties of perjury, I declare that I have examined this return and accompanying documents, and, to the best of my knowledge and belief, they are true, correct, and complete.

Signature ▶   Title ▶   Date ▶

Form **W-3** **Transmittal of Wage and Tax Statements**   **2022**   Department of the Treasury Internal Revenue Service

Send this entire page with the entire Copy A page of Form(s) W-2 to the Social Security Administration (SSA). Photocopies are not acceptable. Do not send Form W-3 if you filed electronically with the SSA. **Do not** send any payment (cash, checks, money orders, etc.) with Forms W-2 and W-3.

Source: Internal Revenue Service

TIP

A "TIN" (Taxpayer Identification Number) is a general term meaning a number that either an employee or employer is required to have. The term includes five number types: a social security number issued by the Social Security Administration and four types of numbers issued by the IRS as follows: 1) EIN (Employer Identification Number, sometimes called a Federal Employer Identification Number, or FEIN) required for businesses with employees, and for corporations, partnerships, and LLCs, as well as trusts, estates, non-profits and farmers' cooperatives; 2) ITIN (below) 3) ATIN (Adoption Taxpayer Identification Number), and 4) PTIN (Preparer Taxpayer Identification Number).

ITIN: An ITIN (Individual Taxpayer Identification Number) has only one function: to allow taxpayers without a social security number and ineligible for U.S. employment to file tax returns and or other tax information. Only resident aliens and non-resident aliens can apply for an ITIN (Form W-7 from IRS). An employer cannot use an ITIN for identification in place of a social security number. An ITIN begins with a "9" and has a different number format than a social security number. An employer is required to obtain an employee's social security number.

continued ▶

Form W-2 (Annual), *continued*

Illustration 5.4: Form W-2c

DO NOT CUT, FOLD, OR STAPLE THIS FORM

44444	For Official Use Only ▶ OMB No. 1545-0008

a Employer's name, address, and ZIP code

c Tax year/Form corrected　　/ **W-2**

d Employee's correct SSN

e Corrected SSN and/or name (Check this box and complete boxes f and/or g if incorrect on form previously filed.) ☐

Complete boxes f and/or g only if incorrect on form **previously filed** ▶

f Employee's **previously reported** SSN

b Employer's Federal EIN

g Employee's **previously reported** name

h Employee's first name and initial　Last name　Suff.

Note. Only complete money fields that are being corrected (exception: for corrections involving MQGE, see the General Instructions for Forms W-2 and W-3, under Specific Instructions for Form W-2c, boxes 5 and 6).

i Employee's address and ZIP code

Previously reported	Correct information	Previously reported	Correct information
1 Wages, tips, other compensation	1 Wages, tips, other compensation	2 Federal income tax withheld	2 Federal income tax withheld
3 Social security wages	3 Social security wages	4 Social security tax withheld	4 Social security tax withheld
5 Medicare wages and tips	5 Medicare wages and tips	6 Medicare tax withheld	6 Medicare tax withheld
7 Social security tips	7 Social security tips	8 Allocated tips	8 Allocated tips
9	9	10 Dependent care benefits	10 Dependent care benefits
11 Nonqualified plans	11 Nonqualified plans	12a See instructions for box 12	12a See instructions for box 12
13 Statutory employee ☐　Retirement plan ☐　Third-party sick pay ☐	13 Statutory employee ☐　Retirement plan ☐　Third-party sick pay ☐	12b	12b
14 Other (see instructions)	14 Other (see instructions)	12c	12c
		12d	12d

State Correction Information

Previously reported	Correct information	Previously reported	Correct information
15 State Employer's state ID number	15 State Employer's state ID number	15 State Employer's state ID number	15 State Employer's state ID number
16 State wages, tips, etc.	16 State wages, tips, etc.	16 State wages, tips, etc.	16 State wages, tips, etc.
17 State income tax	17 State income tax	17 State income tax	17 State income tax

Locality Correction Information

Previously reported	Correct information	Previously reported	Correct information
18 Local wages, tips, etc.	18 Local wages, tips, etc.	18 Local wages, tips, etc.	18 Local wages, tips, etc.
19 Local income tax	19 Local income tax	19 Local income tax	19 Local income tax
20 Locality name	20 Locality name	20 Locality name	20 Locality name

For Privacy Act and Paperwork Reduction Act Notice, see separate instructions.

Copy A—For Social Security Administration

Form **W-2c** (Rev. 8-2014)　**Corrected Wage and Tax Statement**　Cat. No. 61437D　Department of the Treasury　Internal Revenue Service

Forms 1099 (Annual): Non-Employee Payments and Miscellaneous Income

Form 1099–MISC   When payments made by a trade or business to non-employees and others are at least certain amounts, the trade or business (as well as other specified entities: nonprofits, qualified pension/profit-sharing plans, government agencies), must complete an information Form 1099 as indicated below by February 28 following December 31 of the prior calendar year. Electronic filers (100 items or more after January 31 2022; 10 or more 2023) have until March 31. (See 1099-NEC on Page 254 for non-employee compensation.) A copy is sent to each taxing authority and to the payment recipient. The minimum reportable amounts and payment types that require reporting are as indicated below, otherwise $10:

- **$600:**

For: Rents (box 1), other income payments types (box 3), medical and health care payments (box 6), any fishing boat proceeds (box 5), crop insurance proceeds (box 9), gross proceeds paid to attorneys (such as a settlement agreement) that are not fees for services ((box 10) that are not reportable on 1099-NEC.

- **$5,000**:

For: Direct sales of consumer products to a buyer other than a permanent retail establishment for resale (box 7)

- Any amount of backup withholding (boxes 4 and 15)

Not required: Payments to corporations (with limited exceptions, e.g. for health care or attorney fees), payments for merchandise, rent payments to real estate agents/managers, and payments to tax-exempt organizations are exempt from 1099 filing. Certain other payments are not required.

Further details, exceptions, and examples are available on the instructions for Form 1099-MISC. Also see the individual state 1099 requirements that may apply.

Other Common 1099 Forms   In addition to Form 1099-MISC, other types of 1099 forms report specific types of income. They are:

- **1099-INT**: For interest income of $10 or more from banks, credit unions, credit unions, and similar investments. It also reports $600 or more of other types of interest.
- **1099-C**: For debt cancellation of $600 or more.
- **1099-DIV**: For dividends of $10 or more and other corporate stock-related distributions
- **1099-G**: For government payments of $10 or more, most often tax refunds and unemployment compensation.
- **1099-K**: For distributions of any amount from 3rd party network debit and credit cards transactions; 3rd party network transactions exceeding $600. Also see www.irs.gov/GigEconomy.

continued   ▶

Forms 1099 (Annual): Non-Employee Payments and Miscellaneous Income, *continued*

Other Common
1099 Forms,
Continued

- **1099-NEC**: For non-employee compensation of $600 or more.
- **1099-PATR**: To report distributions of $10 or more from cooperatives. Also called "patronage dividends".
- **1099-R**: For distributions of $10 or more from pensions, annuities, retirement plans, IRA's, insurance contracts, etc.
- **1099-S**: Payments for real estate transactions.

Note: 1099 withholding information is also reported on Form 945.

Illustration 5.5: Form 1099-MISC

Source: Internal Revenue Service.

Form 1096
Transmittal
Form

Just as W-2 form requires an accompanying transmittal document, so does Form 1099. This is Form 1096. One 1096 must accompany each specific group of 1099 forms sent to the IRS. For example, there would be one 1096 for all 1099-MISC copies, one 1096 for all 1099-INT copies, and so on. Information returns may also be filed electronically using the FIRE (Filing Information Electronically) system, located at www.IRS.gov/FIRE. See page 238 "Tip"

continued ▶

Forms 1099 (Annual): Non-Employee Payments and Miscellaneous Income, *continued*

1099-NEC Overview	For any person who in the course of business was paid at least $600 for 1) Services performed as a non-employee, sole proprietor, partner, including parts and materials or use of entertainment facilities treated as compensation, (Also see independent contractor discussion in Section 1 regarding non-employee identification.), 2) Cash payments for fish or other aquatic life purchased from anyone engaged in a trade or business of catching fish, 3) Payments to attorneys for legal services, whether or not they work in a corporation. Report backup withholding related to these payments in boxes 4 and 5. File Form 1099-NEC with transmittal page by January 31.

Illustration 5.6: Form 1099-NEC

7171	☐ VOID	☐ CORRECTED		

PAYER'S name, street address, city or town, state or province, country, ZIP or foreign postal code, and telephone no.

OMB No. 1545-0116

Form **1099-NEC**

(Rev. January 2022)

For calendar year
20 ____

Nonemployee Compensation

PAYER'S TIN	RECIPIENT'S TIN	1 Nonemployee compensation $	**Copy A** **For Internal Revenue Service Center**
RECIPIENT'S name		2 Payer made direct sales totaling $5,000 or more of consumer products to recipient for resale ☐	**File with Form 1096.**
		3	For Privacy Act and Paperwork Reduction Act Notice, see the **current General Instructions for Certain Information Returns.**
Street address (including apt. no.)		4 Federal income tax withheld $	
City or town, state or province, country, and ZIP or foreign postal code		5 State tax withheld $	6 State/Payer's state no.	7 State income $
Account number (see instructions)	2nd TIN not. ☐	$		$

Form **1099-NEC** (Rev. 1-2022)   Cat. No. 72590N   www.irs.gov/Form1099NEC   Department of the Treasury - Internal Revenue Service

Do Not Cut or Separate Forms on This Page — Do Not Cut or Separate Forms on This Page

Source: Internal Revenue Service

TIP

Amounts reported in box 1 are often subject to self-employment tax. See Section 2, Part II discussion of self-employment tax.

Form 940 Employer Unemployment Tax (Annual)

Illustration 5.7: Form 940

Form **940 for 2021:** **Employer's Annual Federal Unemployment (FUTA) Tax Return**   850113
Department of the Treasury — Internal Revenue Service   OMB No. 1545-0028

Employer identification number (EIN)   ☐☐ – ☐☐☐☐☐☐☐

Name (not your trade name)

Trade name (if any)

Address
Number   Street   Suite or room number

City   State   ZIP code

Foreign country name   Foreign province/county   Foreign postal code

Type of Return
(Check all that apply.)

☐ **a.** Amended
☐ **b.** Successor employer
☐ **c.** No payments to employees in 2021
☐ **d.** Final: Business closed or stopped paying wages

Go to *www.irs.gov/Form940* for instructions and the latest information.

Read the separate instructions before you complete this form. Please type or print within the boxes.

Part 1:   Tell us about your return. If any line does NOT apply, leave it blank. See instructions before completing Part 1.

1a   If you had to pay state unemployment tax in one state only, enter the state abbreviation .   **1a** ☐ ☐

1b   If you had to pay state unemployment tax in more than one state, you are a multi-state employer . . . .   **1b** ☐ Check here. Complete Schedule A (Form 940).

2   If you paid wages in a state that is subject to CREDIT REDUCTION . . . .   **2** ☐ Check here. Complete Schedule A (Form 940).

Part 2:   Determine your FUTA tax before adjustments. If any line does NOT apply, leave it blank.

3   Total payments to all employees . . . .   **3** ☐

4   Payments exempt from FUTA tax . . . .   **4** ☐

Check all that apply: **4a** ☐ Fringe benefits   **4c** ☐ Retirement/Pension   **4e** ☐ Other
4b ☐ Group-term life insurance   **4d** ☐ Dependent care

5   Total of payments made to each employee in excess of $7,000 . . . .   **5** ☐

6   Subtotal (line 4 + line 5 = line 6) . . . .   **6** ☐

7   Total taxable FUTA wages (line 3 – line 6 = line 7). See instructions . . . .   **7** ☐

8   FUTA tax before adjustments (line 7 x 0.006 = line 8) . . . .   **8** ☐

Part 3:   Determine your adjustments. If any line does NOT apply, leave it blank.

9   If ALL of the taxable FUTA wages you paid were excluded from state unemployment tax, multiply line 7 by 0.054 (line 7 × 0.054 = line 9). Go to line 12 . . . . .   **9** ☐

10   If SOME of the taxable FUTA wages you paid were excluded from state unemployment tax, OR you paid ANY state unemployment tax late (after the due date for filing Form 940), complete the worksheet in the instructions. Enter the amount from line 7 of the worksheet . .   **10** ☐

11   If credit reduction applies, enter the total from Schedule A (Form 940) . . . .   **11** ☐

Part 4:   Determine your FUTA tax and balance due or overpayment. If any line does NOT apply, leave it blank.

12   Total FUTA tax after adjustments (lines 8 + 9 + 10 + 11 = line 12) . . . .   **12** ☐

13   FUTA tax deposited for the year, including any overpayment applied from a prior year .   **13** ☐

14   Balance due. If line 12 is more than line 13, enter the excess on line 14.
   • If line 14 is more than $500, you must deposit your tax.
   • If line 14 is $500 or less, you may pay with this return. See instructions . . . .   **14** ☐

15   Overpayment. If line 13 is more than line 12, enter the excess on line 15 and check a box below   **15** ☐

▶ You **MUST** complete both pages of this form and **SIGN** it.   Check one: ☐ Apply to next return.   ☐ Send a refund.

Next ▶

For Privacy Act and Paperwork Reduction Act Notice, see the back of the Payment Voucher.   Cat. No. 11234O   Form **940** (2021)

Source: Internal Revenue Service.

continued ▶

Form 940 Employer Unemployment Tax, *continued*

Illustration 5.8: Form 940, continued

850212

Name *(not your trade name)*	Employer identification number (EIN)

Part 5:   Report your FUTA tax liability by quarter only if line 12 is more than $500. If not, go to Part 6.

16 Report the amount of your FUTA tax liability for each quarter; do NOT enter the amount you deposited. If you had no liability for a quarter, leave the line blank.

16a **1st quarter** (January 1 – March 31) . . . . **16a** [.   ]

16b **2nd quarter** (April 1 – June 30) . . . . **16b** [.   ]

16c **3rd quarter** (July 1 – September 30) . . . . **16c** [.   ]

16d **4th quarter** (October 1 – December 31) . . . . . . **16d** [.   ]

17 **Total tax liability for the year** (lines 16a + 16b + 16c + 16d = line 17) **17** [.   ] **Total must equal line 12.**

Part 6:   May we speak with your third-party designee?

Do you want to allow an employee, a paid tax preparer, or another person to discuss this return with the IRS? See the instructions for details.

☐ **Yes.**   Designee's name and phone number [   ] [   ]

Select a 5-digit personal identification number (PIN) to use when talking to the IRS. [ ][ ][ ][ ][ ]

☐ **No.**

Part 7:   Sign here. You MUST complete both pages of this form and SIGN it.

Under penalties of perjury, I declare that I have examined this return, including accompanying schedules and statements, and to the best of my knowledge and belief, it is true, correct, and complete, and that no part of any payment made to a state unemployment fund claimed as a credit was, or is to be, deducted from the payments made to employees. Declaration of preparer (other than taxpayer) is based on all information of which preparer has any knowledge.

X Sign your name here [   ]   Print your name here [   ]

Print your title here [   ]

Date [/ /]   Best daytime phone [   ]

Paid Preparer Use Only   Check if you are self-employed ☐

Preparer's name [   ]   PTIN [   ]

Preparer's signature [   ]   Date [/ /]

Firm's name (or yours if self-employed) [   ]   EIN [   ]

Address [   ]   Phone [   ]

City [   ] State [   ]   ZIP code [   ]

Page **2**   Form **940** (2021)

Source: Internal Revenue Service.

Information Forms Summary

Common Information Forms Related to Payroll (Federal)

There are numerous types of information forms that must be submitted for many different circumstances. Common federal payroll-related information forms are:

- **Schedule H:** Attach to personal or estate/trust tax return (1040, 1040NR or 1041) to report household employee payments, income tax withheld and payroll taxes, unless you have IRS-approval for a third-party to do pay and report for you. If no return filed, Schedule H must still be filed. If a sole proprietor, these amounts instead may be included on Form 941. Deposit requirement: Pay amounts due with personal tax filing unless included on Form 941. See Publication 926.
- **W-2:** Annual reporting of employee wages, withholding, and related items, unless a notice is received from IRS. (**W-3**: Transmittal form for W-2.)
- **1099:** Various types for annual reporting of different kinds of payments to independent contractors and other recipients, not for wages/salaries.
- **940:** Annual federal unemployment tax (FUTA) report for obligation and amounts paid. Only employers pay FUTA. Deposit requirement: If tax liability exceeds $500 at any point during a calendar quarter, a payment must be made by the last day of the month following the end of the quarter. Liability below $500 carries forward as part of the next quarter. For an annual total less than $500, pay the amount due with the annual filing of Form 940.
- **941:** Quarterly reports of federal income tax withholding and deposits, FICA employer and employee deposits required, and FICA deposits made. (See page 237) Deposit requirement: See discussion for Form 941 under "Quarterly Deposits".
- **943:** Annual reports of agricultural employee income tax withholding and deposits, FICA employer and agricultural employee deposits required, and FICA deposits made. See Publication 51. (Illustration on page 258). Deposit requirement: 1) If $50,000 or less of tax liability for the second preceding year (lookback period) from the current year, deposits are monthly, made by the 15th day of a following month. 2) If tax liability exceeded $50,000 deposits are semi-weekly.
- **944:** File only with notified approval in writing by the IRS. This is for annual filing by small employers; eligibility is employment tax liability of $1,000 or less. Deposit requirements: 1) If less than $2,500 for the year, pay with filing of return. 2) Greater than $2,500 for the year but less than $2,500 for a quarter, deposit by the last day of the month following the end of the quarter. 3) If greater than $2,500 for a quarter, deposit monthly or semi-weekly as discussed for Form 941 (See page 219.). For approval, call 800-829-4933 by April 1; if new, before the first month a 941 is due.
- **945: Annual Return of Withheld Federal Income Tax:** Annual reporting for nonpayroll (Form 1099) withholding such as backup withholding (See page 130/131) for independent contractors. Covers back up withholding, pensions, military retirement, gambling winnings and Indian Gaming Profits. Deposit requirement: Same as form 943, above.

continued ▶

Information Forms Summary, *continued*

Common Information Forms Related to Payroll (Federal), Continued

- **1095-C**: Annual Medical insurance coverage disclosure from certain employers as required by the Affordable Care Act. Due to employees January 31 (extended to March 2 in 2020 and to IRS Feb. 28 (paper)/ Mar. 31 (electronic).
- **3921**: Notice of incentive stock option (ISO) exercise.
- **8027**: For annual reporting of total tips received and total receipts from business operations for large (averaging more than 10 employees working 80 hours daily for the prior year) food and beverage businesses. Tips are also reported as part of Form 941 and on Form W-2.

Illustration 5.9 Form 943

Source: Internal Revenue Service.

continued ▶

Information Forms Summary, *continued*

Illustration 5.10: Form 944

Form **944 for 2021:** **Employer's ANNUAL Federal Tax Return**

Department of the Treasury — Internal Revenue Service

OMB No. 1545-2007

Employer identification number (EIN)

Name *(not your trade name)*

Trade name *(if any)*

Address

Number	Street	Suite or room number
City	State	ZIP code
Foreign country name	Foreign province/county	Foreign postal code

Who Must File Form 944

You must file annual Form 944 instead of filing quarterly Forms 941 **only if the IRS notified you in writing.**

Go to *www.irs.gov/Form944* for instructions and the latest information.

Read the separate instructions before you complete Form 944. Type or print within the boxes.

Part 1: Answer these questions for this year. Employers in American Samoa, Guam, the Commonwealth of the Northern Mariana Islands, the U.S. Virgin Islands, and Puerto Rico can skip lines 1 and 2, unless you have employees who are subject to U.S. income tax withholding.

1 Wages, tips, and other compensation **1**

2 Federal income tax withheld from wages, tips, and other compensation **2**

3 If no wages, tips, and other compensation are subject to social security or Medicare tax **3** ☐ Check and go to line 5.

4 Taxable social security and Medicare wages and tips:

	Column 1		Column 2	
4a Taxable social security wages*		× 0.124 =		
4a (i) Qualified sick leave wages*		× 0.062 =		
4a (ii) Qualified family leave wages*		× 0.062 =		
4b Taxable social security tips		× 0.124 =		
4c Taxable Medicare wages & tips		× 0.029 =		
4d Taxable wages & tips subject to Additional Medicare Tax withholding		× 0.009 =		

*Include taxable qualified sick and family leave wages for leave taken after March 31, 2021, on line 4a. Use lines 4a(i) and 4a(ii) **only** to report wages paid for leave taken before April 1, 2021.*

4e Total social security and Medicare taxes. Add Column 2 from lines 4a, 4a(i), 4a(ii), 4b, 4c, and 4d **4e**

5 Total taxes before adjustments. Add lines 2 and 4e **5**

6 Current year's adjustments (see instructions) **6**

7 Total taxes after adjustments. Combine lines 5 and 6 . . . . **7**

8a Qualified small business payroll tax credit for increasing research activities. Attach Form 8974 **8a**

8b Nonrefundable portion of credit for qualified sick and family leave wages for leave taken before April 1, 2021 . . . . **8b**

8c Nonrefundable portion of employee retention credit **8c**

8d Nonrefundable portion of credit for qualified sick and family leave wages for leave taken after March 31, 2021 . . . . **8d**

▶ You MUST complete all three pages of Form 944 and SIGN it.

Next ▶

For Privacy Act and Paperwork Reduction Act Notice, see the back of the Payment Voucher.

Cat. No. 39316N

Form **944** (2021)

Source: Internal Revenue Service.

continued ▶

Information Forms Summary, *continued*

Illustration 5.10: Form 944, continued

Name *(not your trade name)*	Employer identification number (EIN)

Part 3:   Tell us about your business. If any question does NOT apply to your business, leave it blank.

14   If your business has closed or you stopped paying wages . . . . □ Check here, and

enter the final date you paid wages [/   /   ] ; also attach a statement to your return. See instructions.

15   Qualified health plan expenses allocable to qualified sick leave wages for leave taken before April 1, 2021   **15** [▪   ]

16   Qualified health plan expenses allocable to qualified family leave wages for leave taken before April 1, 2021   **16** [▪   ]

17   Qualified wages for the employee retention credit . . . .   **17** [▪   ]

18   Qualified health plan expenses for the employee retention credit . . . .   **18** [▪   ]

19   Qualified sick leave wages for leave taken after March 31, 2021 . . . .   **19** [▪   ]

20   Qualified health plan expenses allocable to qualified sick leave wages reported on line 19   **20** [▪   ]

21   Amounts under certain collectively bargained agreements allocable to qualified sick leave wages reported on line 19 . . . .   **21** [▪   ]

22   Qualified family leave wages for leave taken after March 31, 2021 . . . .   **22** [▪   ]

23   Qualified health plan expenses allocable to qualified family leave wages reported on line 22   **23** [▪   ]

24   Amounts under certain collectively bargained agreements allocable to qualified family leave wages reported on line 22 . . . .   **24** [▪   ]

25   If you're eligible for the employee retention credit in the third quarter solely because your business is a recovery startup business, enter the total of any amounts included on lines 8c and 10e for the third quarter . . . .   **25** [▪   ]

26   If you're eligible for the employee retention credit in the fourth quarter solely because your business is a recovery startup business, enter the total of any amounts included on lines 8c and 10e for the fourth quarter . . . .   **26** [▪   ]

Part 4:   May we speak with your third-party designee?

Do you want to allow an employee, a paid tax preparer, or another person to discuss this return with the IRS? See the instructions for details.

□ Yes.   Designee's name and phone number [   ] [   ]

Select a 5-digit personal identification number (PIN) to use when talking to the IRS. □ □ □ □ □

□ No.

Part 5:   Sign here. You MUST complete all three pages of Form 944 and SIGN it.

Under penalties of perjury, I declare that I have examined this return, including accompanying schedules and statements, and to the best of my knowledge and belief, it is true, correct, and complete. Declaration of preparer (other than taxpayer) is based on all information of which preparer has any knowledge.

X Sign your name here	[ ]	Print your name here	[ ]
		Print your title here	[ ]
Date	[ ]	Best daytime phone	[ ]

Paid Preparer Use Only

Check if you're self-employed □

Preparer's name	[ ]	PTIN	[ ]
Preparer's signature	[ ]	Date	[ ]
Firm's name (or yours if self-employed)	[ ]	EIN	[ ]
Address	[ ]	Phone	[ ]
City	[ ]	State [ ]	ZIP code	[ ]

Form **944** (2021)

Source: Internal Revenue Service.

continued ▶

Information Forms Summary, *continued*

Illustration 5.11: Form 945

| Form **945**
Department of the Treasury
Internal Revenue Service | **Annual Return of Withheld Federal Income Tax**
▶ For withholding reported on Forms 1099 and W-2G.
▶ For more information on income tax withholding, see Pub. 15 and Pub. 15-A.
▶ Go to *www.irs.gov/Form945* for instructions and the latest information. | OMB No. 1545-1430
2021 |

Type or Print	Name (as distinguished from trade name)	Employer identification number (EIN)	If address is different from prior return, check here. ▶
	Trade name, if any		
	Address (number and street)		
	City or town, state or province, country, and ZIP or foreign postal code		

A If you don't have to file returns in the future, check here ▶ ☐ and enter date final payments made. ▶ _____

1	Federal income tax withheld from pensions, annuities, IRAs, gambling winnings, etc.	**1**	
2	Backup withholding	**2**	
3	**Total taxes.** If $2,500 or more, this must equal line 7M below or Form 945-A, line M	**3**	
4	Total deposits for 2021, including overpayment applied from a prior year and overpayment applied from Form 945-X	**4**	
5	**Balance due.** If line 3 is more than line 4, enter the difference and see the separate instructions .	**5**	
6	**Overpayment.** If line 4 is more than line 3, enter the difference ▶ $ _____		

Check one: ☐ Apply to next return. ☐ Send a refund.

- **All filers:** If line 3 is less than $2,500, **don't** complete line 7 or Form 945-A.
- **Semiweekly schedule depositors:** Complete Form 945-A and check here . . . . ▶ ☐
- **Monthly schedule depositors:** Complete line 7, entries A through M, and check here . . . . ▶ ☐

7 Monthly Summary of Federal Tax Liability. (Don't complete if you were a semiweekly schedule depositor.)

	Tax liability for month		Tax liability for month		Tax liability for month
A January . . .		**F** June		**K** November . . .	
B February . . .		**G** July		**L** December . . .	
C March . . .		**H** August		**M** Total liability for year (add lines **A** through **L**)	
D April		**I** September . . .			
E May		**J** October			

Third-Party Designee Do you want to allow another person to discuss this return with the IRS? See separate instructions. ☐ Yes. Complete the following. ☐ No.

Designee's name ▶ _____ Phone no. ▶ _____ Personal identification number (PIN) ▶ ☐☐☐☐☐

Sign Here Under penalties of perjury, I declare that I have examined this return, including accompanying schedules and statements, and to the best of my knowledge and belief, it is true, correct, and complete. Declaration of preparer (other than taxpayer) is based on all information of which preparer has any knowledge.

Signature ▶ _____ Print Your Name and Title ▶ _____ Date ▶ _____

Paid Preparer Use Only	Print/Type preparer's name	Preparer's signature	Date	Check ☐ if self-employed	PTIN
	Firm's name ▶			Firm's EIN ▶	
	Firm's address ▶			Phone no.	

For Privacy Act and Paperwork Reduction Act Notice, see the separate instructions.   Cat. No. 14584B   Form **945** (2021)

Source: Internal Revenue Service.

State and Local Taxes

Overview

Most states tax income and have income tax withholding requirements. (Exceptions are: Alaska, New Hampshire (taxes investment income), Nevada, Florida, South Dakota, Tennessee (taxes investment income), Texas, Washington, and Wyoming. Note: However, these states have high sales and property taxes.) For those states that do tax income, the use of the state withholding tables and the withholding process is generally similar to what has so far been discussed.

W-2 Reporting

State income tax is reported in box 17 and related withholding is reported in box 19. Generally, box 16 and box 1 would be the same amounts; however, there can be exceptions: 1) If the amount of pre-tax income recognized is different for state purposes than for federal, the amounts will be different (for example, a state does not recognize 401(k) contributions as deferred income). 2) For work in multiple states box 16 can reference multiple amounts depending on the states in which the employee worked.

State Reporting Requirements

- States generally require quarterly payroll tax reports that show the total wages paid and the calculation of state payroll taxes due. In most cases the filing dates are the last day of the month following the end of the quarter being reported.
- Some states require employee wage reports, typically filed quarterly. These reports list individual employees, their wages for the period, and other required state information.
- Some states require a notice identifying individual employee information upon their termination of employment.
- Some states require a notice of reduction in employment identifying individual employee information upon their reduced employment due to lack of work.

Local Taxes

In some states, localities also impose local fair wage laws and local income taxes, which must be withheld and remitted to local authorities based on local rules. "Local" can mean by county or city. States with various local labor law jurisdictions include Alabama, California, Colorado, Delaware, Indiana, Iowa, Kansas, Kentucky, Maryland, Michigan, Missouri, New Jersey, New York, Ohio, Oregon, Pennsylvania, West Virginia, as well as District of Columbia, as of this writing. For multi-state taxation also see page 142.

State Deposit Requirements

Deposit requirements vary by state. Employers must check individual state regulations.

Where to File Forms

Overview

Directions for filing forms are available on the instructions for the forms. Do an Internet search by form number followed by "instructions".

Making Corrections

Overview

Forms 941-X, 943-X, 944-X, and 945-X are used to correct the forms listed. Form 940 is corrected on a paper form for the year filed.

- 941
- 941-SS (American Samoa, Guam, Northern Mariana, and U.S. Virgin, Islands)
- 943
- 944
- 945

IRS Audit

See Publication 5146 "Employment Tax Returns Examination and Appeal Rights" for a good summary of the employment tax returns examination process.

Earned Income Credit Required Notice

Overview of Earned Income Tax Credit

The earned income credit (EITC) is a refundable tax credit designed to help lower-income employees. It provides additional cash for living expenses and to help offset other employee taxes such as FICA. The amount of credit can range from $538 to $6,660 depending on income level and number of children. The credit is applied for with the filing of an individual's annual income tax return. At any time an employee can use the IRS "EITC Assistant" online to determine eligibility and amount of the credit.

Employer Notice Requirement

An employer is required to notify an employee of the availability of the EITC if: 1) The person was an employee at any time during the calendar year, and 2) The employer did not withhold income tax for that person during the year. Employees who claim an exemption from withholding on Form W-4 are not required to receive notice.

An employer must provide an employee with one of the following notices:

1) Copy B of Form W-2, which has required information on the back of copy B;
2) A substitute Form W-2 which has the same information on the back of the employee's copy;
3) Notice 797, "Possible Federal Tax Refund Due to Earned Income Tax Credit (EIC)";
4) A written statement that contains the same information as Notice 797.

Federal Penalties

Overview   All filing and payment requirements include penalties for failure to comply. The tables below show potential federal employer penalties for failure to conform to federal requirements for forms, return filing, and payment for some of the major items that we have discussed. States also impose penalties.

*Forms W-2
and 1099:*

Table 5.3: Frequently Imposed Federal Payroll Tax Penalties

Without Reasonable Cause, Failure to...	Penalty
Provide the IRS with form or correct form 2022	▪ $50 per item, to a maximum of $199,500 or $571,000 depending on business size if corrected within 30 days ▪ $110 per item, to a maximum of $571,000 or $1,713,000 depending on business size if corrected by August 1 ▪ Filed later than August 1: $280 per item to a maximum of $1,142,000 or $3,426,000 depending on business size ▪ Intentional disregard: $570 per W-2, no limit
Provide employees with form or correct form	The same as above, as an additional penalty

*Forms 940, 941,
944 and 945:*

Without Reasonable Cause, Failure to...	Penalty
Make timely deposits	▪ 1 to 5 days late: 2% of amount not timely deposited. ▪ 6 to 15 days late: 5% of amount not timely deposited. ▪ 16 or more days but at least 10 days before the date that first IRS was sent asking for payment: 10% of amount not timely deposited. ▪ Amounts that should have been deposited but instead were sent directly to the IRS or paid with the return, or otherwise incorrectly deposited: 10% of amount not correctly deposited. ▪ Averaged penalty of 2%-10% for monthly depositor if Form 941 line 12 equals or exceeds $2,500 and line 16 is incorrect. Same penalty for semiweekly depositor if Schedule B is not attached or is incorrect. ▪ Amounts that remain unpaid more than 10 days after the date of the first notice sent by the IRS or the date a demand is received from the IRS, whichever is earlier: 15% Deposits are generally applied to the most recent amounts due. If a penalty notice is received employer can designate the order of application to minimize penalty.
Pay the amount of tax due per correct tax return or to remit withholding	▪ .5% per month of the tax due to a maximum of 25%, plus interest at the current IRS rate. Payments reduce penalty if made on or before the first day of a month.

continued   ▶

Federal Penalties, *continued*

Without Reasonable Cause, Failure to...	Penalty
Pay the amount of tax due per correct tax return or to remit withholding	■ Re. withholding: willful (intentional or reckless disregard) failure: a penalty can be assessed against **any and all responsible individuals** in an amount equal to 100% of income tax and FICA tax to be withheld directly or indirectly (called "trust fund taxes" because withheld funds are considered to be held "in trust" by an employer, and the employer is trusted to: 1) collect, 2) account for, and 3) remit the funds). This is also called the "Trust Fund Recovery Penalty" or "TFRP" (not the same as FUTA trust fund). The IRS may also assess criminal penalties up to $10,000, imprisonment up to 5 years, or both. Even higher penalties can apply for willful failure to file a return or pay tax. ■ Tax lien: A lien is a legal claim against current and future property; a Federal tax lien is created by law if taxes are not paid. A public notice is filed with local agencies, such as county recorder. ■ Levy/seizure: A levy means seizure of property. The IRS can seize most property within 10 days of demand for payment, in order to obtain the value of unpaid tax.
File tax return	■ 5% of the tax due for any month to a maximum of 25% plus interest. If both a failure to file and a failure to pay (above) are assessed, the failure to file penalty is reduced by the amount of the failure to pay penalty. The maximum combined penalty for the first 5 months is 25%. Thereafter, the failure to file penalty continues at .5% per month for 45 months to a maximum of 22.5% with a total combined penalty of 47.5%. If a return is over 60 days late the minimum penalty is the lesser of $435 or 100% of tax due. (All the above should make it clear that filing a timely extension is essential to abate late filing penalties.)

Other Penalties
- Accuracy-related: 20% of underpayment (This means negligence or disregarding rules and regulations and/or substantial underpayment, unless a reasonable basis for position is provided. This penalty can be avoided if certain standards are satisfied called "substantial authority" and "more likely than not." This requires professional assistance.) Intentional disregard is $570/information return/no limit.
- Frivolous Tax Returns: $5,000 (For tax returns with completely unsupported data or using frivolous methods)
- Civil fraud: 75% of the underpayment
- Criminal fraud: Civil fraud penalty plus heavy fines and imprisonment

TIP

Unable to pay the full tax bill at once? The IRS makes installment agreements available. See Form 9465 or call the number on the tax bill (The IRS now answers only about 20% of the calls.) Also try: https://irs.gov/payments/online-payment-agreement.

IRS Abatement of Penalties and Tax

Overview of IRS Abatement

The term "abatement" means a reduction, decrease, or removal. In the context of our payroll topic, abatement refers to a reduction or removal of penalties and/or taxes imposed on an employer. Here, the most common circumstances to which abatement applies are reductions or removal of penalties imposed for failure to pay, failure to file, or failure to deposit. As well, in some cases the tax itself may also be abated. In this discussion, we focus on IRS penalty relief.

Rationale for Abatement of Penalty

Four categories of abatement rationale can apply. The first and probably most straightforward is statutory relief, which means that a law or regulation applies to specific circumstances such that a penalty should not be assessed. The second abatement category is administrative waiver (relief). This means that IRS administrative personnel address a policy by issuing a statement or news release clarifying or interpreting an IRS position on penalty assessment that provides relief from a penalty that might otherwise have been assessed. Third, a penalty may be abated by a taxpayer demonstrating reasonable cause for one of the failures stated above. The final category is correction of an IRS tax or penalty error.

Statutory Abatement

In order to obtain penalty abatement for this category, a taxpayer should identify the provision granting relief and carefully identify how each element of the relief provision applies to the taxpayer's specific situation. Some examples of statutory penalty relief provisions are: first employment tax deposit relief, accuracy-related deposit rule, and disaster relief. Section 530 (see Publication 1976) provides "safe harbor" relief for employers with a reasonable basis to treat workers as independent contractors and is available for employers who do not or cannot use VCSP (below).

First Time Penalty Abatement Waiver (FTA)

The most frequently-used administrative abatement is probably the First Time Penalty Abatement Waiver, a policy established in 2001. The waiver allows taxpayers who are compliant in the two years prior to late filing or payment to remove or reduce the assessment. As applied to payroll taxes, this abatement allows a taxpayer that is first time or frequency change non-compliant to abate the failure to pay, failure to file, and failure to deposit penalties for a single quarter. (Note: An FTA doesn't apply to Form W-2.) Business net worth must be $7million or less with no more than 500 employees.

- **Filing compliance:** The taxpayer must have filed all currently required forms and returns or a valid extension, and there cannot be an outstanding IRS request for an unfiled return. Apply 6 months before tax balance will be paid, or it may continue to accrue even after payment.
- **Payment compliance:** The taxpayer has paid, has received an extension to pay, or has arranged to pay via an installment agreement that is current, all taxes due. A taxpayer who is not in compliance with the above two requirements may be given the opportunity to comply in order to obtain an FTA before penalties are applied.

continued ▶

IRS Abatement of Penalties and Tax, *continued*

First Time Penalty Abatement Waiver (FTA), Continued

- **Penalty history:** The taxpayer cannot have had "significant" penalties assessed in the prior three years. If in doubt, when applying for relief, discuss this with the IRS contact person. An amount under $100 is probably not disqualifying. An estimated tax penalty or a prior reasonable cause abatement is not disqualifying. Receiving an FTA more than years prior is also not disqualifying. If there is a series of penalties, an FTA should be requested for the first year.

An FTA can be requested by telephone or mail. For telephone, a taxpayer can use the toll-free number that is on the penalty notice; at times, the IRS may want a written request. If by mail, the taxpayer must write all relevant facts and circumstances is a clear, direct manner to the IRS service center where the taxpayer files paper returns. (If the penalty results from an audit, the request should go to the source of the audit.) A failure to pay penalty will continue to accrue until the tax is fully paid, so a taxpayer should verify that the IRS will apply the FTA after the tax is paid, or that an FTA should be applied for at that point. As with all tax-authority physical mail correspondence, a taxpayer should be sure to retain tracking and delivery information with a copy of the correspondence; a post office return-receipt letter is best.

As sometimes happens, an intial FTA may be denied; however, the IRS can make incorrect determinations, sometimes as the result of automated systems output. If a request is denied, particulary if a letter does not seem to properly address the facts, a taxpayer should ask to discuss the issue with the IRS representative's manager-level administrator. If this fails, a taxpayer has the right to an appeals-level review, which may then grant relief.

Reasonable Cause

Penalties (but not interest, except for interest accruing on abated penalties or certain IRS delays) may be abated as the result of what the IRS determines as "reasonable cause". Reasonable cause by its nature is subjective; therefore, taxpayer rationale must be demonstrable and compelling. Generally, lack of funds does not constitute reasonable cause in most cases. When contacted by a taxpayer requesting a reasonable cause abatement, the IRS considers the following guidelines:

- Fire, earthquake, flooding, and other natural disasters.
- Loss of access to records beyond the taxpayer's control
- Death, serious illness, and incapacity of taxpayer or immediate family member, or key employee.
- Other circumstances beyond taxpayer control despite taxpayer ordinary business care and prudence (e.g. theft, embezzlement, fraud).

In presenting the facts, a taxpayer should clearly address the following questions with adequate documentation:

- What happened, parties involved, and when did it happen?
- What caused the taxpayer to be late in filing, or depositing payroll tax?

continued ▶

IRS Abatement of Penalties and Tax, *continued*

Reasonable Cause, Continued	■ Did taxpayer act with normal business care and prudence? ■ Did circumstances affect normal business activities? ■ When circumstances changed, what actions did the taxpayer take and when (i.e. did taxpayer attempt to resolve issues and to meet obligations as soon as possible –"timely manner" decided by IRS? The IRS also considers: ■ Taxpayer compliance history and payment patterns ■ Other tax filing (state and local)
Error Correction	A penalty can be imposed as the result of IRS error. This can be due to a range of common issues such as calculation, coding, identification, document loss, file maintenance, or incorrect IRS advice. Detailed calculation and documentation must be provided by the taxpayer. In practice, IRS errors are rarely a source of penalties.
Timing and Methods for Seeking Penalty Relief	Depending on circumstances, abatement potentially can be requested at any of the following points with the following methods: ■ Before the IRS assesses a penalty: At the time a paper return is submitted, include a penalty nonassertion request with the return addressing criteria. ■ After a penalty has been assessed, but before it is paid: Taxpayer requests a penalty abatement by calling or writing the IRS. ■ After a penalty has been paid: Taxpayer requests a refund using form 843 *Claim for Refund and Request for Abatement.* The form must be filed within three years of the filing or the original return, or within two years of the date the tax was paid, whichever is later. The form should be filed at the IRS service center where paper forms are currently filed.
Statutory Employment Tax Deposits Penalty Relief	Two statutory relief provisions apply specifically to employment tax deposit requirements: ■ Accuracy of deposit rule ■ First quarterly deposit waiver If penalties have been assessed due to late deposits, check to determine which periods the deposts have been applied to. The IRS may be applying subsequent deposits to earlier periods, thereby creating additional penalties in later periods. If so, a taxpayer may be able to reduce penalties by designating voluntary payments to later specific periods.
Voluntary Classification Settlement Program (VCSP) Relief Program	The IRS offers a program called the Voluntary Classification Settlement Program, or **VCSP**. It is intended for employers who are concerned that they have misclassified employees as independent contractors, and wish to correct the situation. Key features of the program are as follows: ■ The program allows employers to voluntarily apply for reclassification of workers by completing and submitting Form 8952.

continued ▶

IRS Abatement of Penalties and Tax, *continued*

Voluntary Classification Settlement Program (VCSP) Relief Program, Continued	▪ If approved, the employer will pay only 10% of reduced rate employment taxes that would have been due on compensation paid to workers being reclassified for the most recent tax year. ▪ The employer will not be liable for interest and penalties. ▪ The employer will not be audited for prior years for employment tax in regard to worker classification. ▪ Not all workers need to be reclassified. ▪ Application does not trigger an audit. ▪ The IRS does not share VCSP application information with the DOL or states. ▪ The applicant cannot currently be under employment tax audit.
Appeals	In addition to the above discussion, it is also important to keep in mind that there is an appeals process following an initial determination. This is required to be disclosed in taxpayer correspondence.
Offer in Compromise	An Offer in Compromise is an agreement to settle tax debt for less than the full amount and possibly be paid over a desginated period, based on hardship. Form 656 booklet explains the steps and eligibility. Collection is suspended for the duration of the offer or one year, whichever is greater.

DOL Abatement of Penalties and Tax

Overview of DOL Abatement	If, in the case of an employement law violation as determined by a Department of Labor audit, any possibility of abatement or minimization of penalties can be summarized by the following terms: 1) Good faith effort 2) Reasonable authority. While there is never formal assurance of penalty minimization, it is unlikely to occur if an employer, at its own risk, ignores the importance of proactive compliance efforts, especially if violations are willful or repeated. The same applies to other enforcement agencies as well (IRS, OSHA, EEOC, PBGC, NLRB, state employment authorities). ▪ An employer may receive a DOL notice of complaint filed by an employee. These notices require timely responses. FLSA statute of limitations for an employee to file a complaint for unpaid minimum wage or overtime is 2 years, and for willful employer violations, 3 years. (See https://www.dol.gov/whd/faq_workers.htm) ▪ An employer may receive a notice of investigation, which advises the employer that activities will be audited. These notices are optional; investigations may begin without notice. An investigator will require proof of consistent, good faith efforts to correctly apply labor law requirements, as well as correct interpretation of rules. Investigators have wide latitude in obtaining information, including requiring employer documentation and interviews with employees. Examples of proactive compliance are summarized below.

continued ▶

DOL Abatement of Penalties and Tax, *continued*

Good Faith Effort   A "good faith effort" demonstrates that an employer is making a genuine effort at compliance. "Demonstrates" primarily means documentation. If compliance efforts are not fully documented, they will provide little or no verification value when needed. At a minimum:

- Make a genuine effort to understand requirements and obtain guidance. This includes regular training, maintaining and using current reference material, and obtaining written legal advice. Documentation includes keeping training records, taking notes, developing action plans with references, and making follow-up notes.
- Check compliance regularly using a written self-audit plan and follow up with documented corrections for shortcomings, which should be reviewed by employment legal counsel. For example:

  1) Is there a regularly updated employee policy and procedures handbook? Is it used? Is it reviewed by employment legal counsel?
  2) Is there regular employment training and current reference materials?
  3) Are there compliance-based formal hiring/serverance procedures?
  4) Is there a compliant safety and health program in place?
  5) Have exempt and non-exempt classifications been checked?
  6) Have minimum wage and overtime calculations been checked?
  7) Is there a procedure for employee complaints and follow-ups?
  8) Is record-keeping complete and available? Are reports timely filed?
  9) Is retirement/health plan(s) compliance reviewed regularly?

- Maintain regular and open communication. Payroll compliance is a team effort, and all team members must coordinate their activities at various levels. Open communication also has the effect of reducing employee uncertainty and anxiety.

Reasonable Authority   "Reasonable authority" means sources such as authoritative published guidance, legal counsel, and professionally provided training. To ensure that the basis for a position is reliable, several concuring authoritative sources should be identified and retained. Stated another way, reasonable authority should at least ensure that it is more likely than not that an action or position taken is the correct one.

Deliquent Filer Voluntary Correction Program   The timely filing of Form 5500/5500-SF by companies with retirement plans is enforced by the DOL. This filing is regularly checked and involves potentially significant penalties for late filing. The Deliquent Filer Voluntary Correction Program (DFVCP) offers reduced civil penalties if the employer/administrator files the report prior to receiving a writen notice from the DOL of failure to file a timely report. The form should be electronically filed at efast.dol.gov and the box labled "DFVC" checked. The online calculator will calculate a penalty. After calculating the correct amount, submission and payment by mail is also accepted at: DFVCP, P.O. Box 6200-35, Portland, OR, 97228-6200. The IRS will also waive related penalties. If there are employees with deferred vested benefits, file IRS Form 8955-SSA.

continued ▶

DOL Abatement of Penalties and Tax, *continued*

*An Auditor's
Useful Advice*

The following page contains part of an article written by a former DOL Wage and Hour Division auditor. It is useful advice.

■ Much time and money can be saved by conducting a self-audit. This should be accomplished long before you become the subject of a DOL investigation.

• Ensure that your employment relationship and exemption determinations are correct and that your pay plans meet FLSA requirements.
• If nonexempt employees are paid commissions, make certain that overtime wages are being correctly computed. This DOL opinion letter http://www.dol.gov/whd/opinion/FLSANA/2008/2008 _09_22_12NA_FLSA.htm includes a clear explanation of the correct method to be used in computing overtime compensation. The same approach is usually applicable to job rate or piece rate arrangements.

■ If your FLSA practices are questioned by a DOL investigator–

• Listen to the explanations provided and ask relevant questions.
• Keep in mind that it is possible to disagree with the investigator without being arrogant.
• If you are not convinced that the investigator is correct in his/her assertions, request a "second level" conference with a District Office management official.
• If you have representation, make certain that your attorney will not be a "loose cannon" and that he/she is knowledgeable of the FLSA (or is willing to learn).
• Do not refuse to make needed corrections until you are certain that "fighting the battle" will be worth the investment.

Concluding Remarks

If the Wage and Hour Division conducts an investigation of your business or organization, be open-minded as to the possibility that there are violations. The investigator is probably more knowledgeable of technical FLSA rules than you or your attorney. However, that does *not* mean that you should not raise questions. DOL investigators do make mistakes. In some cases, the investigator reaches conclusions without considering key facts. Exemptions are occasionally overlooked. An intelligent and open-minded dialogue can encourage the investigator to reconsider the initial conclusions. Even if the assertions are essentially correct, there might at least be room for negotiation. The investigator should agree to allow you or your attorney a reasonable period of time (at least a week) to review the matter. Further, as I previously indicated, it is often productive to request a meeting with a District Office management official to discuss unresolved issues.

During the "final conference" or other discussions with the investigator, make extensive notes. A written report will *not* be provided to you.

continued ▶

DOL Abatement of Penalties and Tax, *continued*

An Auditor's Useful Advice, Continued

If the investigator presents a "summary of unpaid wages" and asks you to sign it, *do not do so* until you are convinced that you owe the back wages and that computations have been done accurately. You have the right to secure a copy of computations.

You should always consider obtaining representation when under DOL scrutiny. DOL does not have the authority to prevent an employer from securing professional guidance. In more than three decades of DOL enforcement experience, I dealt with hundreds of attorneys and consultants. They generally "brought to the table" knowledge, expertise, and negotiating ability that the employer did not possess. The attorney in this case study was clearly an exception.

Reprinted with permission, BizKeys

3rd Party Reporting

Typical Reports

In addition to required reporting to tax authorities, other reporting to outside parties is often needed. Typical reports that should be included in a checklist include:

- Workers' compensation reporting to insurance companies
- ERISA reporting information, as required, for employer-sponsored retirement plans and some health plans to plan administrators or Department of Labor and IRS, using EFAST2 or IFILE electronic submission systems; 5500 EZ filers may use paper filing.
- Reports to other agencies as applicable, such as OSHA for work-related injuries.
- Reports required at hiring and termination (See Section 1).

Payroll Management Forms and Reports: Overview

Overview

Payroll management reports provide payroll information that is used to analyze payroll-related costs and to improve payroll operating efficiency. The reports are created after each payroll is processed and are sent to designated management personnel. A wide variety of report types are possible; in practice, each report should be produced with a specific purpose in mind. Interesting but minimally useful reports or reports that are not or cannot be utilized as a source of actionable oversight should be avoided. With this in mind, the basic management reports followed by other possibly useful reports are discusssed below.

Basic Management Reports

Payroll Register	The most fundamental report is the payroll register. This is a detailed report of each employee's compensation, wages, and net pay as well as total amounts for each type of item. (See illustration 3.1 on page 196/197.) In practice a payroll register is not frequently provided to management. It is primarily used within the payroll and accounting departments for output review, internal control, journal entries, and as a permanent detailed reference for each payroll.
Payroll Summary Report	A payroll summary is the fundamental report that is submitted to management. This report reorganizes and summarizes much of the same data in a payroll register and breaks down totals into specified detail categories. Payroll software can generate a payroll summary report for a single payroll, a specific period, and year-to-date.
	One format example is illustrated below with a variety of compensation types. (Are they all needed or useful?) Potentially, sub-reports could provide additional details on specific categories, such as: hourly full-time, hourly tipped, and hourly part-time.
Labor Distribution Report	A labor distribution report allocates total labor cost to designated activity categories. For example, labor cost is allocated to advertising, sales, accounting, production jobs, or departments such as production departments, payroll, human resources, and so on. In order for this to happen, activity or department codes must be designated and applied to hours worked and any other compensation type. Defined "labor cost" can include not only gross compensation, but also employer payroll taxes, employer paid benefits, workers' compensation payments, and payroll penalties. Labor cost is usually allocated based on time worked in an activity.
Tracking "Excess Compensation"	A 21% excise tax is levied on "covered employees" receiving compensation exceeding $1,000,000 for many tax-exempt organizations called "applicable tax- exempt organizations", such as many charities, hospitals, universities ("501(c)(3)"), as well as political organizations, farmers' cooperatives, and public utilities. A covered employee is any employee who is one of the top five compensated employees for the tax year. Regulations are available online. Employers may wish to direct payroll or human resources to track compensation and advise the potentially covered employees.

Basic Management Reports, *continued*

Illustration 5.12: Payroll Summary Report

	Compensation Type	Current Payroll $	Year-to-Date $
Payroll Summary Report			*October 17, 2022*
Gross pay			
	Salary	13,000	130,000
	Salary – vacation pay	1,500	4,100
	Salary – sick leave	700	1,900
	Salary – other	-0-	-0-
	Hourly	14,080	144,200
	Hourly overtime	4,220	9,140
	Hourly – vacation pay	1,760	2,920
	Hourly – sick leave	1,900	4,550
	Hourly – other	-0-	-0-
	Commission	5,000	14,330
	Bonus	-0-	-0-
	In-kind – company car	-0-	-0-
	In-kind – meals, lodging	-0-	-0-
	Total gross pay	**42,160**	**311,140**
Gross pay reductions			
	401K	3,600	38,500
	Health insurance plan	450	4,500
	Adjusted gross pay	**38,110**	**268,140**
Withholding	Federal income tax	7,432	73,987
	State income tax	1,144	10,951
	Social security	2,614	19,291
	Medicare	611	4,512
	State disability	422	3,111
	Garnishment	280	2,854
	Total withholding	**12,503**	**114,706**
	Net pay	**25,607**	**153,434**
Employer payroll tax			
	Social security	2,614	19,291
	Medicare	611	4,512
	FUTA	-0-	420
	SUTA	-0-	3,780
	Total employer tax	**3,225**	**28,003**

Basic Management Reports, *continued*

Absenteeism Report

An absenteeism report is an efficiency measure for potential production and work time lost. A ratio is calculated as follows for a selected time period:

(Total hours missed)/(Total FTE work hours in the period)

"FTE" means "full time equivalent" employee; that is, someone working a 5-day, 8-hour per day, 40-hour workweek. For example, in a workweek, if 12 employees work ½ days, 40 × (12 × 1/2 = 6 FTE employees) work a total 240 FTE employee-hours. If 10 employees work 4 full days per week, 40 × (10 × 4/5 = 8 FTE employees) work a total of 320 FTE employee-hours. Or, reversing the procedure using total hours, 320 weekly hours/40 per week = 8 FTE for the week.

(Note: To calculate FTE using annual hours divide hours by 40 × 52 = 2,080. To calculate monthly FTE divide hours by 173.33. These amounts can be adjusted for vacation time and holidays and other reductions.)

This ratio becomes more effective when calculated separately for salaried employees and hourly employees. As well, a line item report can be produced showing individual employee names and days or hours absent.) For reference, maintain a record of average absence rate and if possible, compare it to similar companies. The Bureau of Labor Statistics has absence rate data online by occuption.

Example

During the quarter, 3 workers missed 1 day, 2 workers missed 2 ½ days, 3 missed 4 days, and 5 missed 5 days, all from absence (not vacation, holiday, PTO, etc.). There were 62 work days in the quarter and 30 full-time equivalent employees.

Employees		Days Absent		Total Hours
3	×	1	=	24
2	×	2.5	=	40
3	×	4	=	96
5	×	5	=	200
Total				360

360 / (62 × 8 × 30) = 2.4% operational time loss from absenteeism

The greater the percentage, the more negative the result. There may be additional costs associated with a high ratio, such as loss of customers, lower output by other employees who fill in, decrease in morale, and overtime work cost by other employees. In analyzing results it is also useful to keep in mind that most employees have unavoidable personal responsibilities that periodically require time away from work, and that job pressures are not equivalent for all employees. For example, constant understaffing and long hours may increase both absent days and employee turnover (below). In addition to adequate staffing, one useful method to help reduce total absentee time is implementing a flexible work week. (See page 85).

Basic Management Reports, *continued*

Employee Turnover Report	"Employee turnover" means an employee leaves and then has to be replaced. Turnover is expensive. In addition to productivity loss and an effect on morale, the cost to search, hire, and train is substantial. The employee turnover ratio calculates what percent of total employees leave and must be replaced, and is calculated as follows for a selected time period:

Total separated employees/Average* FTE employees

*The simplest average is: (beginning period total plus ending period total/2).

Example	During the last year, the assembly department of ABC Company has had difficulty meeting deadlines. In addition to checking absenteeism, ABC management also wants to check employee turnover in the department. During the year 4 employees left the department. At the beginning of the year there were 11 FTE employees in the department and at the end of the year there were 8.

$4/9.5 = 42\%$ annual turnover.

As with absenteeism, there can be numerous reasons for turnover, so a high ratio requires further investigation. Causes can be employee personal life changes or a company failure to provide sufficient compensation, benefits, or a desirable work environment. Second, the numerator of the ratio shows separations with the assumption that these require replacements; if there are any permanent position reductions or layoffs in this number, these should be excluded. As a point of reference, maintain a record of average turnover rate and if possible, compare it to similar companies. The Bureau of Labor Statistics has turnover rate information online by industry type.

Employee Cost Report	It can be useful to measure employee cost as a total amount in relation to some other measure, such as total employees, units or services revenue or product revenue. However, employee cost related to revenue can be difficult to use effectively because revenue is a function of various factors, particularly when based on product sales, such as pricing and volume decisions or seasonality.

Total employee cost for designated time period:
(salaries + wages including OT + bonuses, etc.) + employer-paid benefits + employer stock + employer payroll tax + workers' compensation + training + compliance costs (legal, penalties)

Cost per employee for designated time period:
Total employee cost per above/Average FTE employees

Example	Maple Company calculates total quarterly employee cost per above as $889,350. During the quarter there were 37 average FTE employees. Cost per employee for the quarter is $889,350/37 = $24,036. Annualized this is $24,036 × 4 = $96,144.

Basic Management Reports, *continued*

Payroll Department Cost Report	A payroll processing cost report can be created that indicates the payroll cost per employee. The calculation for a specified period is:

Total payroll processing costs/Average FTE employees

The following items are significant in determining total payroll processing cost:

For payroll department employees:

- Salaries, wages, bonuses, and other compensation
- Benefits
- Employer payroll tax
- Workers' compensation
- Training

Other employees:

- Supervisor timecard/time reporting checking cost
- Check signing, distribution

Other costs:

- Payroll software (updated annually)
- Annual depreciation on hardware/other assets required
- Supplies
- System maintenance
- Internet cost for mobile timekeeping
- Any overhead allocations specifically required for payroll
- If outsourced, payroll outsourcing cost
- IRS penalties and interest (DOL penalties generally relate to Human Resources department) directly connected to payroll department responsibilities.

As evident from the above list, numerous costs are connected to payroll department operations. How would management reduce these costs while at the same time not sacrificing internal control?

The greatest payroll department costs are employee costs, so it makes sense to focus on the use of automation to reduce manual hours and improve productivity. Timekeeping is an aspect of payroll that often involves significant manual time. For a discussion of various timekeeping methods and how to improve efficiency and reduce manual processing time, see Appendix II. Also, employee training both improves productivity and helps prevent compliance failures that result in penalty and interest costs.

Employee Payment Error Rate	The employee payment error rate ratio measures the total number of paycheck corrections as a percentage of total paychecks issued.

Total identified errors/All payroll-related entries

Section 6 Employment of Non-U.S. Persons

Overview

Introduction

There is essentially a separate method of taxation for non-U.S. persons. This section provides an introduction to procedures related to wage compensation of non-U.S. persons. The reader should keep in mind that this topic is broad in scope, and there can be further complexities that potentially affect both employers and employees. Also, wage payments to non-U.S. persons are affected by tax withholding and tax reporting requirements. Tax treaties can also apply. However, the Fair Labor Standards Act (FLSA) and fair employment laws generally apply to all employment in the U.S. and District of Columbia regardless of immigration status or lack of documentation.

What are Non-U.S. (Foreign) Persons?

For tax purposes, a non-U.S. person is defined within the context of *tax residency*. For tax residency purposes, there are three categories of non-U.S. persons.

- **Resident alien:** A resident alien is generally taxed in the same manner as a U.S. citizen.
- **Non-resident alien:** A non-resident alien is a "Foreign Person". There are special tax rules for foreign person income earned in the United States.
- **Dual-status alien:** A dual-status alien is a person who has been both a non-resident alien and a resident alien within the same tax year.

An "alien" is defined as any individual who is not a U.S. citizen or U.S. national (a person born in American Somoa or a certain part of the Northern Mariana islands, and electing U.S. national status instead of citizenship.) Note that if someone is treated as a resident of a foreign country resulting from the terms of a tax treaty, they are automatically treated as U.S. non-resident aliens for tax purposes.

For federal income tax purposes, a resident alien is determined by either of two tests:

- Green card test
- Substantial presence test

Resident Aliens

Definition

A resident alien is a person who for *tax purposes* (not always the same as for immigration and employment authorization purposes) has passed either the green card test or the substantial presence test for a full calendar year.

continued ▶

Resident Aliens, *continued*

Definition, Continued	The earlier of meeting either test begins the residency period. Note: it is also possible to be a resident alien for part of a year for a person who is a dual status alien. (Page 287)

Green Card Test	"Green card" refers to an alien registration card (Form I-551) from the U.S. Citizenship and Immigration Service granting a person approval to reside permanently in the United States as an "immigrant". A person who lawfully possesses a valid green card and has not had residency status taken away or has not abandoned residency status is considered to have passed the green card test, is considered to be a lawful permanent resident of the United States, and is therefore for tax purposes clasified as a resident alien.

Substantial Presence Test	The following is required to satisfy the substantial presence test:

- Be physically present in the United States for at least 31 days in the current calendar year, and
- Be physically present in the Unites States (excluding U.S. possessions and airspace) for 183 days or part of a day during a three-year period that includes the current calendar year, the prior calendar year, and the second prior calendar year, counting:

  - all days present in the current year,
  - 1/3 of the days present in the prior year
  - 1/6 of the days present in the second prior year

The following are not counted as "days":

- Days communting to the U.S. from a residence in Canada or Mexico
- Days in the U.S. for less than 24 hours when in transit between two places outside of the U.S.
- Days as a crew member of a foreign vessel.
- Days unable to leave the U.S. because of a medical condition arising in the U.S.
- Days for which a person is classified as an "exempt" person according to certain visa status or as a visiting athlete to compete in a charitable sports event.
- Initial days do not count as days for which there was a closer connection to the home country than the United States.

Note: Some visa classifications (such as F-1 or J-1 student visas, Teacher/Researcher/Trainee J-1 or Q visas) are generally considered "exempt" persons. These exempt status classifications are temporarily exempt from the substantial presence test requirement, typically for five or two years, subject to additional guidelines. Time spent in this status does not count toward the 183 day requirement.

Resident Aliens, *continued*

Employer Requirements

- **Status verification:** Employers must comply with the Immigration Reform and Control Act (IRCA). To demonstrate full compliance, employers must check authorization to work status of all new hires equally. This means asking for proof of citizenship or verification of lawful permanent residency (green card) or an employment authorization to work document (sometimes called a "work permit") or a visa that allows work for a particular employer. Employers must complete an Employment Eligibility Verification Form (Form I-9) for all new employees regardless of citizenship status. Employers also bear the resposibility of making a good-faith effort to examine documents of identity and eligibility to work and to determine if they appear to be genuine. Note: Under the law, a hiring policy of "U.S. citizens only" is illegal except where required under federal, state, or local law.
- **Withholding and payroll taxes:** Resident aliens are taxed in the same manner as U.S. citizens. Employers are subject to the same withholding and tax requirements as described earlier in this book for U.S. citizens. Resident aliens follow the same rules for completion of Form W-4 as U.S. citizens.
- **Identification numbers:** For a non-citizen who is eligible and desires to work in the United States, an unrestricted social security card or social security card authorizing work must be obtained and shown to the employer.

This means that some non-citizens will require both a social security number and a work permit. Generally, for a non-citizen to obtain a social security number, proof of permission to work from the U.S. Citizenship and Immigration Services (USCIS), a division of the Department of Homeland Security (DHS), is required unless a government agency requires a social security number. Both items can be applied for simultaneously from DHS using Form I-765.)

For tax withholding purposes, an employer requires a social security number and should not accept an Individual Taxpayer Identification Number (ITIN) in lieu of a social security number. An ITIN is only available to persons who are not eligible for U.S. employment and require tax identification for filing a return or other purposes. Note: An employer cannot withhold payment due to the absence of a social security number. The FLSA requires payment for all hours worked.

Non-Resident Aliens (NRA)

Overview

Non-resident aliens are generally subject to tax only on U.S. source income. Foreign source income may be taxable in limited circumstances. Table 6.1 below shows various determination of income sources for non-resident aliens.

continued ▶

Non-Resident Aliens (NRA), *continued*

Table 6.1: Determination of Income Source for Non-Resident Alien

Income Type	Determination of Source
Salaries and wages	Where services were performed
Other personal services	Where services were performed
Pension distribution	Where services were performed
Interest	Location of taxpayer residence
Dividends	Based on whether U.S. or foreign corporation, with some exceptions.
Rent	Location of property
Natural resources	Location of property
Sale of real estate	Location of property
Sale of purchased inventory	Location of sale
Sale of produced inventory	Technical allocation rules
Sale of depreciable personal property	Technical allocation rules
Sales of stocks, securities	Gains generally not taxable when trading for own account and not in trade or business in U.S. as a broker or securities dealer or connected with a U.S. trade or business, and individual is physically present less than 183 days or parts of days in the United States in a calendar year.

Overview, Continued

Note: Many of the above items (and others not listed) will require completion of forms 1042-S and 1042 by the entity making payments. Employers do not use these forms for employee wage compensation (Form W-2) or amounts reported on Form 1099 unless there is exempt income.

Employer Requirements for Non-Resident Aliens (NRA)

Employer

In respect to non-resident aliens, an "employer" includes:

- Any person paying wages to an NRA individual, or a foreign partnership or corporation not engaged in trade or business in the United States,
- Any person who has *control* of the payments of wages for services performed for another person who does not have control of payments,
- IRS guidelines for determining employer-employee relationship remain applicable.

Employer Requirements for Non-Resident Aliens (NRA), *continued*

Status
Verification
Review:
Employers must comply with the Immigration Reform and Control Act (IRCA). To demonstrate full compliance employers must check citizenship status of all new hires equally. This means asking for proof of citizenship or authorization to work from the Department of Homeland Security for non-citizens. Under the law a policy of "U.S. citizens only" is illegal except where required under federal, state, or local law. Employers must complete and retain an Employment Eligibility Verification Form (Form I-9) for all new employees regardless of citizenship status. Employers also bear the resposibility of making a good-faith effort to examine documents proving identity and eligibility to work to determine if they appear to be genuine.

Withholding
Generally an NRA is taxed only on U.S. source income, not worldwide income as is the case with U.S. citizens and resident aliens. NRA income is categorizied as either "effectively connected income" (ECI) or as "fixed, determinable, annual or periodical income" (FDAP).

- FDAP income is a very broad category that includes salaries, wages, commissions, and most passive income and requires payor withholding. Mandatory withholding is required at the time of payment unless exceptions (below) apply. The tax rate is 30% on gross income unless tax treaties or special categorical provisions apply.
- ECI income is generally income from a trade or business and is taxed at regular graduated tax rates. (The beneficial owner must file form W-8ECI and provide a taxpayer identification number.)

Form W-4
NRA employees must complete federal and state withholding withholding forms. For federal Form W-4 purposes, the following special rules apply:

- In Step 5, below line 4c write "NRA" in capital letters.
- An NRA cannot claim "exempt".

Identification: For a non-citizen who is eligible and desires to work as an employee in the United States, an unrestricted social security card or social security card authorizing work must be obtained and shown to the employer.

This means that non-resident aliens will require both a social security number and a work permit. Form SS-5 is used to apply for a social security number. Generally, for a non-citizen to obtain a social security number proof of permission to work from the U.S. Citizenship and Immigration Services (USCIS), a division of the Department of Homeland Security (DHS), is required unless a government agency requires a social security number. Both items can be applied for simultaneously from the USCIS using Form I-765 (Application for Employment Authorization).

continued ▶

Employer Requirements for Non-Resident Aliens (NRA), *continued*

Form W-4, Continued	For withholding tax purposes, an employer requires a social security number and should not accept an Individual Taxpayer Identification Number (ITIN) in lieu of a social security number. An ITIN is only available to persons who are not eligible for U.S. employment and require tax identification for filing a tax return or other purposes. Note: An employer cannot withhold payment due to the absence of a social security number. The FLSA requires payment for all hours worked.

Special Withholding Procedures

- An NRA cannot claim the standard deduction; this rule requires an additional withholding amount adjustment by an employer (See below). Generally the federal income tax rate for NRA with FDAP is 30%.
- Some NRAs are exempt or will have reduced withholding if tax treaties apply. See: *https://www.irs.gov/individuals/international-taxpayers/tax-treaties*. In this regard, an NRA must submit Form 8233 to the employer or other withholding agent, who in turn must review for completeness and documentation, and sign and forward the form to the IRS within 5 days of receipt. Employers unable to reasonably determine completeness and documentation or specific elements of a treaty not determinable until the end of a tax year will withhold at otherwise required rates and the employee will be able to claim a refund for any overwithholding at year-end by filing their personal tax return.
- Note that state and local withholding requirements may be different and result in different amounts than federal on Form W-2.

Exceptions to Mandatory Withholding

Wages and non-employee compensation are exempt from mandatory federal income tax withholding if all three of the following apply:

- The NRA who performed the services is present in the United States for a total not exceeding 90 days in a calendar year.
- The compensation for the services does not exceed $3,000
- The NRA performed the services as an employee of or under contract for an NRA individual or foreign corporation or partnership not engaged in a trade or business in the United States or the foreign office of U.S. citizen, corporation or partnership, or resident alien.

Also:
Wages and non-employee compensation are exempt from mandatory federal income tax withholding if both of the following apply:

- The NRA is in the U.S. based on F, J, or Q visa status
- The compensation for services is paid by an NRA individual or foreign corporation or partnership or the foreign office of U.S. citizen, corporation or partnership, or resident alien.

Also exempt from manadatory withholding:

1) Regular crew members of a foreign vessel, 2) Residents of Canada and Mexico engaged in transportation that frequently enter and exit the U.S. 3) Foreign agricultural workers on H-2A visas.

Employer Requirements for Non-Resident Aliens (NRA), *continued*

Withholding Adjustment

As indicated, an NRA does not receive a standard deduction; however, the standard deduction is built into tax tables used for withholding. Therefore, to adjust for this, employers must adjust (increase) withholding for NRAs. This is done by use of either table 6.2 or 6.3 below, following this procedure:

Step	IF...	THEN...
1	employee submitted a pre-2022 W-4 that has not been revised in 2022 or later,	use Table 6.2.
2	employee submitted a 2022 or later W-4,	use Table 6.3.

For the employee's payroll period shown in the table, add the indicated amount to the employee's compensation. Enter this total on the first line for total taxable wages for the payroll period of whichever employer worksheet is being used.

Note: The above calculations are for income tax withholding only. They do not affect total income tax, FICA, or FUTA taxes.

Note: NRA students and business apprentices from India are exempt from this procedure by treaty.

Table 6.2: NRA Wage Adjustment: Pre-2022 W-4

Payroll Period	Add $ Amount
Weekly	$ 166.30
Biweekly	322.70
Semi-monthly	360.40
Monthly	720.80
Quarterly	2,162.50
Semi-annual	4,325.00
Annual	8,650.00
Daily or miscellaneous	33.30

Table 6.3: NRA Wage Adjustment: 2022 & Later W-4

Payroll Period	Add $ Amount
Weekly	$249.00
Biweekly	498.10
Semi-monthly	539.60
Monthly	1,079.20
Quarterly	3,237.50
Semi-annual	6,475.00
Annual	12,950.00
Daily or miscellaneous	49.80

Employer Requirements for Non-Resident Aliens (NRA), *continued*

Example

Jon Schmidt is a single NRA and submitted a revised W-4 in 2022. Jon earns $7,100 monthly and has no other income additions, deductions or credits, so he completes only Steps 1 and 5 on his W-4. Jon's employer uses an automated payroll system and therefore Worksheet 1A. The employer should enter $7,100 + $1,079.20 = $8,179.20 on line 1a of Worksheet 1A (Percentage Method Tables for Automated Payroll Systems). Jon's monthly withholding, based on his annual compensation, will be: $15,213.50 + [($98,150.40 − $93,425) × .24] = $16,347.60/12 = $1,362.30. **Note:** this withholding method does not apply to supplemental payments if mandatory top tax rate or 22% flat rate is used.

Illustration 6.1: Withholding table for automated systems and Worksheet 1

2022 Percentage Method Tables for Automated Payroll Systems and Withholding on Periodic Payments of Pensions and Annuities

STANDARD Withholding Rate Schedules
(Use these if the Form W-4 is from 2019 or earlier, or if the Form W-4 is from 2020 or later and the box in Step 2 of Form W-4 is **NOT** checked. Also use these for Form W-4P from any year.)

If the Adjusted Annual Wage Amount on Worksheet 1A or the Adjusted Annual Payment Amount on Worksheet 1B is:

At least— (A)	But less than— (B)	The tentative amount to withhold is: (C)	Plus this percentage— (D)	of the amount that the Adjusted Annual Wage or Payment exceeds— (E)
Married Filing Jointly				
$0	$13,000	$0.00	0%	$0
$13,000	$33,550	$0.00	10%	$13,000
$33,550	$96,550	$2,055.00	12%	$33,550
$96,550	$191,150	$9,615.00	22%	$96,550
$191,150	$353,100	$30,427.00	24%	$191,150
$353,100	$444,900	$69,295.00	32%	$353,100
$444,900	$660,850	$98,671.00	35%	$444,900
$660,850		$174,253.50	37%	$660,850
Single or Married Filing Separately				
$0	$4,350	$0.00	0%	$0
$4,350	$14,625	$0.00	10%	$4,350
$14,625	$46,125	$1,027.50	12%	$14,625
$46,125	$93,425	$4,807.50	22%	$46,125
$93,425	$174,400	$15,213.50	24%	$93,425
$174,400	$220,300	$34,647.50	32%	$174,400
$220,300	$544,250	$49,335.50	35%	$220,300
$544,250		$162,718.00	37%	$544,250
Head of Household				
$0	$10,800	$0.00	0%	$0
$10,800	$25,450	$0.00	10%	$10,800
$25,450	$66,700	$1,465.00	12%	$25,450
$66,700	$99,850	$6,415.00	22%	$66,700
$99,850	$180,850	$13,708.00	24%	$99,850
$180,850	$226,750	$33,148.00	32%	$180,850
$226,750	$550,700	$47,836.00	35%	$226,750
$550,700		$161,218.50	37%	$550,700

Form W-4, Step 2, Checkbox, Withholding Rate Schedules
(Use these if the Form W-4 is from 2020 or later and the box in Step 2 of Form W-4 **IS** checked)

If the Adjusted Annual Wage Amount on Worksheet 1A is:

At least— (A)	But less than— (B)	The tentative amount to withhold is: (C)	Plus this percentage— (D)	of the amount that the Adjusted Annual Wage exceeds— (E)
Married Filing Jointly				
$0	$12,950	$0.00	0%	$0
$12,950	$23,225	$0.00	10%	$12,950
$23,225	$54,725	$1,027.50	12%	$23,225
$54,725	$102,025	$4,807.50	22%	$54,725
$102,025	$183,000	$15,213.50	24%	$102,025
$183,000	$228,900	$34,647.50	32%	$183,000
$228,900	$336,875	$49,335.50	35%	$228,900
$336,875		$87,126.75	37%	$336,875
Single or Married Filing Separately				
$0	$6,475	$0.00	0%	$0
$6,475	$11,613	$0.00	10%	$6,475
$11,613	$27,363	$513.75	12%	$11,613
$27,363	$51,013	$2,403.75	22%	$27,363
$51,013	$91,500	$7,606.75	24%	$51,013
$91,500	$114,450	$17,323.75	32%	$91,500
$114,450	$276,425	$24,667.75	35%	$114,450
$276,425		$81,359.00	37%	$276,425
Head of Household				
$0	$9,700	$0.00	0%	$0
$9,700	$17,025	$0.00	10%	$9,700
$17,025	$37,650	$732.50	12%	$17,025
$37,650	$54,225	$3,207.50	22%	$37,650
$54,225	$94,725	$6,854.00	24%	$54,225
$94,725	$117,675	$16,574.00	32%	$94,725
$117,675	$279,650	$23,918.00	35%	$117,675
$279,650		$80,609.25	37%	$279,650

Source: Internal Revenue Service

Employer Requirements for Non-Resident Aliens (NRA), *continued*

FICA Tax	In general, NRAs are subject to FICA, with the following exceptions, which are exempt status:

- A-visas: Employees, family members, servants of foreign governments if acting in official capacity as foreign government employees.
- D-visas: Crew members of a ship or aircraft if the the vesselis is foreign and the employer is foreign if services are performed outside of the United States.
- F, J, M, and Q-visas: NRA students, academics, trainees, researchers, and others in F-1, J-1, M-1, or Q-1/Q-2 immigrant status provided employment is compliant with status. There are certain detailed limitations on these exemptions.
- G-visas: Employees of international organizations
- H-visas: Non-immigrants in H-2 and H-2A status if either: 1) An H-2 resident of the Philippines who performs services in Guam 2) An H-2A admitted temporarily admitted to the United States to perform agricultural labor.

Note: because resident aliens do not have these exemptions, an employer must be aware if the residency status changes to avoid exempting employees who are ineligible.

FICA Totalization Agreements	The United States maintains bilateral agreements with countries who impose taxes that are similar in nature to FICA. These are called "totalization" agreements, and eliminate dual coverage and dual taxation. These agreements create exemptions for resident aliens, non-resident aliens, and even U.S. citizens in the circumstance when they relocate to the U.S. but still qualify as a resident of a signatory country, and U.S. citizens working in another country. Totalization applies only to FICA and not FUTA.
FUTA Tax	In general, NRAs are subject to FUTA, with the following exceptions, which are exempt status:

- Compensation to agricultural workers
- Compensation to household employees
- Compensation religious, charitable, educational, and certain tax-exempt organizaitons
- Compensation to NRAs temporarily in the U.S. in F-1, J-1, Q-1/Q-2 nonimmigrant status

Foreign Source Income	Foreign source income (income from outside the U.S.) is generally not taxed to a non-resident alien. There are limited circumstances in which the income can become taxable because either the income is generated from a U.S. place of trade or business or relates to conduct of business within the U.S.

Dual-Status Aliens

General Guidlines   A dual-status alien is a person who has been both a non-resident alien and a resident alien within the same tax year. A dual-status alien is taxed on income from all sources for the part of the year the person is resident alien, and is taxed as an NRA on U.S. – source income for the part of the year the person is an NRA. An employer will follow the guidelines previously discussed in this section.

Form Filing Requirements

Summary   In general, all the filing requirements discussed in previous sections still apply, with the addition of filing requirements that may apply for employers of non-resident aliens.

Employers and other payers to NRAs are typically required to file the following additional forms:

- Form 8233 received from an employee to claim exemption from wage withholding due to tax treaty. Filed within 5 days of receipt from employee.
- Form 1042-S to report NRA U.S. personal service income that is tax-exempt (by tax treaty), as well as resident alien treaty-exempt personal service income, and withholding repaid to a foreign person; however, not for income that is otherwise reportable on Form W-2 or on Form 1099 (e.g. the amount of wages or independent contractor income not exempt by treaty). Form 1042-S income also includes specified non-personal service NRA FDAP income types: interest and rents, dividends, royalties, annuities, pensions and amounts paid to students, trainees, teachers and researchers and non-excludable scholarship and fellowship income, and grants in excess of tuition. Use a separate form for each type. The form is due March 15 for the preceding year. An extension is available by filing form 8809 no later than March 5. Copy A is sent to the IRS with Form 1042-T, a transmittal form. Copies B, C, and D are sent to the employee (or recipient of other income) to be used in reporting their income (Form 1040 for resident alien, Form 1040NR for NRA). Note that an employee may receive both forms 1042-S and W-2 if some wages are exempt and some are not or certain kinds of income (such as certain scholarship income) has been earned.
- Annual Form 1042 is filed (separately) to report tax withheld whenever a Form 1042-S is filed. The due dates are the same.

Undocumented Workers

Overview

As we discussed earlier in Section 1, employers have a legal responsibility to verify the identity, citizenship, and residency status of potential employees, including Form I-9 requirements. Employment authorization from the Department of Homeland Security must be verified. As well, employers must immediately notify an employee of a tentative nonconfirmation and the Department of Homeland Security of a final nonconfirmation of eligibility (from E-Verify). Employers who violate these requirements are subject to fines and even criminal penalties (if there is a pattern of behavior). Also, the FLSA minimum wage and overtime requirements apply to undocumented workers.

Employer Tax Issues for Undocumented Workers

Undocumented workers are subject to income tax, and employers must withhold tax on wages, using backup withholding rates if necessary (or unknowingly using a false social security numbers supplied by an undocumented person on Form W-4). Other reporting requirements as previously discussed in earlier sections also apply. Undocumented worker income is also subject to FICA and FUTA requirements. See pages 10–13 for I–9 documentation requirements.

It should also be be noted that many undocumented workers choose to pay tax by using an ITIN number and filing a Form 1040 and state forms as needed when there has been no wage withholding.

Section 7 Internal Control

Internal Control Summary

Overview

As indicated in earlier sections, internal control means the policies, procedures, and organizational structure that safeguard assets from fraud and from loss due to mismanagement. Internal control applies to all the steps in the payroll process.

Payroll Risk Potential

1. Theft: Payroll is a multi-step process that leads to frequent, significant, cash payments, making the process inherently attractive to someone who would commit theft. Further, there are a variety of procedures within the process where a payroll fraud can occur.
2. Negligence/Error: Even when a fraud does not occur, significant losses can still happen. Virtually every aspect of the payroll process requires successfully navigating numerous federal, state, and sometimes local compliance requirements. Failure to properly satisfy these requirements can result in a high cost that potentially includes penalties, interest, additional pay, and a variety of lawsuits.

Using Checklists and Workflow Lists

The level of detail for tasks or workflow will vary by organizational level or department. Suggested detailed checklists for each step in the payroll process diagram are available at the end of this section. The first step, "Identify Employees" usually performed by a Human Resources department, requires only a periodic (at least annual) internal control review. The other checklists require regular and frequent use because cash payments are involved. Secondly, when possible there should be periodic rotation of either preparer or reviewer.

Not every internal control item in these checklists may apply, time may not be available to apply every item, and in different situations other procedures may be necessary. The application of internal control is a trade-off between likely risk and associated loss and the recurring cost. Use these checklists as a guide or reference. However, time spent on maintaining at least basic internal control is probably time well spent. Even a few key controls will add important protection.

Key controls: As you review the checklists you may notice similarity or repetition in some question types. These reflect the more fundamental internal control principles. Important examples are:

- Physical and computer data access is highly secure, controlled, and limited.
- Authorization/approval is required by someone with designated authority.
- Separation of duties and authority: no one person or department is allowed to perform most or all payroll functions. Authority is limited.
- Documentation is essential.

continued ▶

Internal Control Summary, *continued*

Using Checklists and Workflow Lists, Continued	Can internal control be applied in a small business with few employees and limited resources? Yes, but it requires regular owner oversight, which is crucial. If an owner cannot or will not become materially involved in internal control, then outside help is the only other solution. Historically, small businesses are always most at risk.
Professional Help & Audit	A certified public accountant is trained in audit and internal control procedures. Periodic and unannounced payroll audits will significantly help maintain internal control integrity for payroll. Internal audit is a viable alternative.

Internal Control: Special Considerations

Overview	As stated earlier, internal control should be considered in light of costs (including potential losses via data breach) and benefits. Some controls are essential while some might be too time-consuming or expensive for the potential security that is provided. However, some internal control issues require special mention, either because of potential losses involved, or because of employee interest. Key items are the following:
Rolling Payroll Calendar	A payroll calendar is essential for both internal control and the efficient operation of the payroll process. The calendar suggested here is a "rolling calendar" in which at the end of a period the current period is no longer used and a new period is added. At least a six-month calendar period should be used.

How to prepare: 1) If preparing for the first time, make an initial list of type of items probably involving deadlines, such as payroll tax deposits, reporting and filing, worker's compensation, and retirement plan information, 2) Refer to the following:

- IRS Publication 509 for current year
- Individual state labor office/state publications for current year
- U.S. Department of Labor (tel. 1-866-487-2365; www.dol.gov)
- Prior year's calendar
- Revise with updates as necessary (Be sure to include revision date.)

Below is an example of a master calendar for an entire payroll department (Individual calendars are also prepared for divisions or operations within payroll and for other departments.) Here it is assumed that the accounting department prepares and files federal and state tax forms; however, that could also be a payroll department task. Journal and ledger recording and oversight are a separate accounting department responsibility.

continued ▶

Internal Control: Special Considerations, *continued*

Illustration 7.1: Payroll Calendar

1	2	3	4	5
Receive timecards Initial payroll run	Final payroll run Funds to payroll acct.	Issue checks Summary to A/P	Check A/P: garn. pmt.	
8	**9**	**10**	**11**	**12**
Dept. Meeting 9:00		Mgmnt. reports review	Submit reports	Check A/P: Federal tax deposit State tax deposit
15	**16**	**17**	**18**	**19**
Receive timecards Initial payroll run	Final payroll run Funds to payroll acct.	Issue checks Summary to A/P	Mgmnt. reports Check A/P: garn. pmt.	
22	**23**	**24**	**25**	**26**
	Smith, Watson Training Seminar	Mgmnt. reports review	Check HR: Form 5500 Submit reports	
29	**30**	**31**		
Mgmnt. Meeting 9:00		Next month calendar		

Penalty Prevention

Potential payroll-related penalties are numerous and can be costly. The penalties originate with compliance failure from three primary sources: 1) fair labor laws, particularly the FLSA and ERISA enforced by the DOL (there are also state labor laws), 2) federal payroll tax as enforced by the IRS (and in some cases state tax laws), and 3) workers' compensation requirements. (Remember that even when payroll procedures are outsourced the employer remains fully responsible.) Pay particular attention to the following internal control checklist items:

- Process Step 1, items 10, 11, 18, 19, 28, and 29.
- Process Step 2, items 1e, 1f, and 3o, 6, and 12.
- Process Step 4, items 12 and 13.
- Process Step 5, items 1–5.

Online Data Breaches ("Hacking")

If an in-house payroll system is used, the best security is to keep it completely offline. This prevents online breaches either directly into payroll or through other departments in the company that ultimately allow access into payroll activities. When payroll is processed in-house online ("cloud" processing) the highest-level security should be in place including multi-level passwords, limited access, threat detection, firewalls, and regular employee training against "phishing" scams. Online data breaches, ransomware payments, and hacks can result in severe losses and business interruption.

Internal Control: Special Considerations, *continued*

Garnishment	Refer to pages 222–226 for more discussion on this topic. Because an employer is liable for timely and accurate garnishment payments, the following is recommended:

- Use a spreadsheet and sub-accounts that record the garnishment liability and payments made for each garnished employee. Spreadsheet should include beginning and ending dates, if relevant.
- Check exceptions report (see Process 2, Step 3, letter 1 checklist), regarding withholding, if garnishment amount is accurate.
- Verify that the garnishment amounts withheld have been timely paid.
- Many states require that a garnishment amount be identified on employee pay remittance advice (check stub). Verify that this is done if required.

PTO	Many employees want to monitor their PTO benefits, such as vacation pay and sick leave. With each payroll, review PTO as follows:

- Maintain a PTO spreadsheet for each employee, for each PTO type.
- Check balance against current accrual rate (A compensation rate change usually affects value of total PTO accrued time).
- Check PTO time accruals and uses, both in time and dollars.
- Reconcile spreadsheet to general ledger account liability balances (see Step 3 items 6 and 13).
- Consider: A payroll system that automatically tracks PTO and shows accruals on payroll remittance stub, and that employees can monitor online.

Employee Receivables	Although this should infrequently occur, a company may loan money to an employee or make a paycheck advance. Review the following:

- Check: is this in the policies and procedures manual?
- Conform to approval process in policies and procedures manual.
- Document all loan details and repayment schedule. Include in employee file.
- Maintain general ledger and sub-ledger accounts as with any receivable. Reconcile these accounts each payroll period.

A Payroll Budget to Analyze Cost	Creating and maintaining a budget is a very useful cost-saving device, provided that budgeted amounts are carefully thought out. A good system is to prepare about a 6-12 week rolling budget, in which the past week is dropped and a new budget week is added. The best use is to identify variances between actual and budgeted costs and use this as feedback to make necessary changes.

Internal Control: Special Considerations, *continued*

TIP

The following security tools should be seriously considered:
Software:

- Multi-level passwords, with regular changes
- File and ledger lockouts (limited access)
- User-defined transactions report (suspicious transaction types)

Additional for online use:

- Threat detection
- Firewalls
- Antivirus software automatically updated
- Two-factor authentication
- Password manager system for changing passwords
- A virtual private network (VPN) that is secure
- Never use a "save password" function
- Never automate username and/or password.
- Data encryption system

Internal Control Checklist

Identify Employees: (Human Resources Department)

The checklist below can be used as an internal control guide for functions comprising the first step in the payroll process: "Identify Employees". These functions occur primarily as human resource department duties, although other departments can be secondarily involved. As indicated at the end Section 1, a key issue is assuring compliance with a variety of legal requirements. Note: this checklist may require additions and/ or modifications based on the individual organization. See Section 1 concerning discussion of checklist items.

Prepared by:			Date:			
Reviewed by:			Date:			
Process Step 1: Internal Control Check Item			**Y**	**N**	**N/A**	**Comment**
1) Is there an up-to-date employee policies and procedures manual?						
2) If yes to #1, has the manual been reviewed by legal counsel?						
3) Is there documentation that policies and procedures are communicated and followed?						
4) Do all positions have job descriptions?						
5) Are job descriptions checked by counsel for non-discrimination compliance?						
6) Is there a secure file with all documents for each employee?						

continued ▶

Internal Control Checklist, *continued*

Prepared by:			Date:		
Reviewed by:			Date:		
Process Step 1: Internal Control Check Item	**Y**	**N**	**N/A**	**Comment**	
7) Is change to any status or data documented and signed by employee and approved by human resource department?					
8) Is file confidentiality well protected?					
9) New employee:					
a. Is there a standard application form reviewed by counsel?					
b. Do applicants sign application forms?					
c. Is a file opened for each interviewed employee?					
d. Are job openings offered to current employees?					
e. Is independent contractor vs. employee status documented?					
f. Is exempt vs. non-exempt employee status documented?					
g. Are there written guidelines for positions interview process?					
h. Do interview questions relate to the position and are they non-discriminatory? Are questions checked by counsel for non-discriminatory compliance?					
i. Is testing performed? Has it been checked for non-discrimination?					
j. Do background checks and reference checks conform to federal and state laws?					
k. Have EEOC guidelines been checked for adverse impact test?					
l. Is there a written offer of employment on company letterhead?					
m. Does offer accurately refer to job a description and duties?					
n. Has offer been signed by candidate and employer?					
o. Does medical exam meet legal requirements?					
p. Has employment contract been reviewed by counsel?					
q. Has form I-9 been completed?					
r. Is there tracking for non-resident alien I-9 expiration?					
s. Have other final tasks (see page 8) been completed?					
t. Has all documentation been completed (see page 10) ?					
u. Has the documentation been sent to all required recipients?					
v. Has employee orientation taken place?					

continued ▶

Internal Control Checklist, *continued*

Prepared by:		Date:			
Reviewed by:		Date:			
Process Step 1: Internal Control Check Item	**Y**	**N**	**N/A**	**Comment**	
10) Compliance: How is fair employment law monitored? Is training provided?					
11) Is there documentation that demonstrates that the organization complies with fair employment laws?					
12) Are job descriptions vs. actual duties still correct?					
13) Is employee compensation and benefits status reviewed and checked with payroll department before a payroll run?					
14) Is a leave reporting system in place and is each employee PTO balance current?					
15) Is an employee complaint process in place?					
16) Is there documentation of complaints and resolution details?					
17) Performance review: a. Is the review process regular and systematic? b. Is review process clear in policies and procedures manual? c. Is compensation tied to performance? d. Is there a standardized procedure that is duties-related? e. Are performance goals regularly established? f. What review input is used in the above procedure? g. Is the review discussed with the employee? h. Is review documented? i. Are performance improvement plans used? j. Are items 9e and 9f still correct?					
18) Is there training for non-discrimination behavior?					
19) Is there training for non-harassment behavior?					
20) Is there manager training for performance reviews?					
21) Is compensation regularly reviewed? Who approves a change in compensation and benefits and what is the process? Is this documented and followed?					
22) Is there an affirmative action plan to comply with federal and/or state contracts?					
23) Is there a master file for benefits with policy copies, cost, and allocation between employee and employer?					
24) Are employees informed of benefits available through a written summary?					

continued ▶

Internal Control Checklist, *continued*

Prepared by:			Date:		
Reviewed by:			Date:		
Process Step 1: Internal Control Check Item	**Y**	**N**	**N/A**	**Comment**	
25) Has COBRA compliance been checked with plan administrator at least annually?					
26) Are DOL/State/Local required posters being displayed?					
27) If retirement and medical plans are in place, are ERISA employee notice and reporting requirements current?					
28) Is workers' compensation reporting current?					
29) Have employee benefit plans been reviewed at least annually to ensure compliance and prevent loss of exclusion from tax?					
30) Were incidents investigated? Did changes result?					
31) Are insurance quotes competitive and documented?					
32) Are all necessary employee separation procedures completed? (See pages 29–32)					
33) Is there documentation of the procedures followed?					
34) Is the list and number of active employees accurate – always updated for hiring and separation?					
35) Is workers' compensation file up to date with employee remuneration, classification, and policy copy?					
36) If a computerized or online human resource system is in use, has an access login report been regularly checked?					
37) If a computerized or online human resource system is in use, are passwords regularly changed (A system can create reminders)?					
38) If a computerized or online human resource system is in use, has an employee data change report been regularly checked?					
39) Segregation of Duties: Are all Step 1 duties fully separated from Steps 2 -4 duties (see payroll process illustration), with no authority or oversight of one over the other? (Except for small business where owner performs these duties)					

Internal Control Checklist, *continued*

Calculate the Payroll: (Timekeeping Procedures and Payroll Department)

The checklist below can be used as an internal control guide for functions in the second step of the payroll process: "Calculate the Payroll". Note: This checklist may require additions and/or modifications based on the individual organization. Also note that most of these controls apply to both manual and computerized systems processing. (Step 2, items 3i, 3n, 3p, 3q, 9 and 10 are not required if processing is outsourced.) See Section 2 concerning relevant details for the checklist items.

Prepared by:		Date:			
Reviewed by:		Date:			
Process Step 2: Internal Control Check Item	**Y**	**N**	**N/A**	**Comment**	

1) <u>Timekeeping:</u>

   a. Have supervisors checked for employee signatures on time reporting documentation and that timecards contain no blank spaces above signature (non exempt employees)?

   b. Have supervisors checked and approved accuracy of time reporting documentation amounts and totals (non-exempt employees)?

   c. Exceptions: does payroll department compare time-cards received against list of timecard employees provided by Human Resources department and account for any differences? Does automated system flag exception items (e.g. max. hours)?

   d. Has PTO time been verified with Human Resources department and been checked by supervisor?

   e. Have department supervisors responded to requests for late or missing time reporting documents?

   f. For manual time reporting, has the payroll department checked all reporting for mathematical accuracy and reported exceptions?

   g. Is a consistent, DOL/state-approved, fractional-hour method being applied (non-exempt employees)?

   h. Is physical presence at work verified?

   i. Has work away from the primary work location been approved?

   j. Has approval for overtime hours been verified?

   k. Does a payroll department manager review and sign off on accuracy of time reporting documents before processing?

   l. Is access password protected?

   m. If time is allocated among tasks, has allocated time been checked and approved by supervisor?

   n. Are timekeeping records archived and safeguarded?

   o. Is confidentiality maintained for all timekeeping data?

continued ▶

Internal Control Checklist, *continued*

Prepared by:		Date:			
Reviewed by:		Date:			
Process Step 2: Internal Control Check Item	**Y**	**N**	**N/A**	**Comment**	
2) Other compensation:					
a. Is a checklist maintained for other compensation?					
b. Commissions: Do payroll and sales departments check each other's calculations?					
c. Tips: Forms 4070A or similar received from tipped employees?					
d. Piece rate: Do payroll and production departments check each other's calculations?					
e. PTO (sick leave, vacation pay, etc.). Refer to PTO reports.					
f. Bonuses and other compensation: Are they verified by Human Resources or manager with authority to approve?					
3) Payroll processing:					
a. Is system access password controlled and limited?					
b. Are there multi-level passwords?					
c. Is this the correct payroll period?					
d. Has an access login report been checked and archived?					
e. Are the following duties separated (not same employee) to the degree possible: 1) Timekeeping 2) Hours worked approval 3) Adding or removing employee names for check processing 4) Data entry vs. any verification or approval function:					
f. Has an active employee list been obtained from Human Resources prior to processing?					
g. Has employee current status (pay rate, exempt vs. non-exempt, withholding items and rates, employee vs. independent contractor, benefits) update report been obtained from Human Resources prior to processing? Are expense reimbursements verified to documents?					
h. Is an employee master file data change report automatic and sent by the payroll department to Human Resources department or a manager prior to trial run processing so it can be reviewed and approved?					
i. Is a trial run (no checks) payroll register processed? Is the payroll register used to: 1) verify gross and adjusted gross (after qualified plan reduction) pay 2) verify withholding 3) calculate net pay, and 4) make corrections?					
j. Are manual checks data included in the trial run (but no check will be printed for these)?					

continued ▶

Internal Control Checklist, *continued*

Prepared by:		Date:			
Reviewed by:		Date:			
Process Step 2: Internal Control Check Item	**Y**	**N**	**N/A**	**Comment**	
k. Is partial-period pay included and verified?					
l. **Exception reports**-examples: Are the following exception reports generated from trial run prior to final processing and changes (if any) have documented approval by Human Resources or other appropriate manager: 1) Pay rate difference 2) Salary difference 3) Individual (name) and total gross and/or net pay exceeds predetermined limits 4) Number of employees being paid not equal to active employee number 5) Terminated employee status is being paid 6) Negative withholding (this increases net pay) 7) Leave of absence/PTO pay not correct 8) Tipped employees: • Tips not enough to reach minimum wage required • Tax arrears due to deduction amounts exceeding cash wages 9) Gross pay equal to net pay? 9) Employee hours corrections average > 2 standard deviations above mean.					
m. Are benefit cost allocations between employer and employee withholding checked to a master file? Have costs changed?					
n. Whether or not the payroll is automated, does a second person (usually in accounting or finance) examine payroll register calculations and document their review?					
o. Are "regular rate", overtime, and minimum wage checked, at least on a sample basis, to verify compliance with FLSA, state, and local wage and hour rules (non-exempt employees)? No OT for exempt.					
p. Does a payroll supervisor approve the reviewed /corrected trial run payroll register before final processing?					
q. Has payroll (or accounting/finance) manager checked the final payroll register against: 1) the corrected and approved trial run register 2) the checks, for: compensation, withholding (include qualified plans gross pay reduction) and net pay 3) duplicate checks and missing checks?					
r. Is access to output (checks and final payroll register) carefully secured - physically locked and password protected?					
s. Are all payroll records secure –physically locked and password protected? Is data backed up?					

continued ▶

Internal Control Checklist, *continued*

Prepared by:		Date:			
Reviewed by:		Date:			
Process Step 2: Internal Control Check Item	**Y**	**N**	**N/A**	**Comment**	
4) Process trial runs until no further changes. Has the senior payroll manager approved the final run payroll register and completed payroll run? This person should not have any access to check signing or disbursements.					
5) Is there documentation that the payroll manager approved the final payroll run and final payroll register?					
6) Compliance: How is payroll tax law monitored? (Is training provided? Publication 15 reviewed? State publications? Is legal counsel consulted?)					
7) Segregation of Duties: Are all Step 2 duties fully separated from Steps 1 and 3 - 4 (see process illustration), with no authority or oversight of one over the other? (Except for small business where owner performs these duties)					
8) Has data been backed up and archived securely?					
9) Are vacations mandated for payroll employees?					
10) Are payroll employees cross-trained and rotated?					
11) If payroll processing is outsourced, does the processor provide an SOC report (Service Organization Compliance Report) of at least level 2 or 3 as an indicator of internal control adequacy and systems integrity?					
12) If tax-exempt and deferred tax benefits programs are in place, are they checked for compliance at least annually to avoid penalties and to ensure programs remain qualified?					

TIP

Positive pay service is a payroll internal control service offered by many banks to prevent check fraud. The bank matches items such as account number, check number, date, dollar amount, and other check information provided by the company against the checks presented for payment. The bank notifies the company electronically, sometimes with an image, of irregularities and exceptions and usually holds payment. This works most efficiently for checks that are drawn on a separate checking account used only for payroll. The bank generally charges a fee for the service, but this might be viewed as really an insurance premium.

Internal Control Checklist, *continued*

Record the Payroll: (Accounting Department)

The checklist below can be used as an internal control guide for functions comprising the third step in the payroll process: "Record the Payroll". These functions occur primarily as accounting department duties. Note: this checklist may require additions and/or modifications based on the individual organization. See Section 3 concerning relevant details for checklist items.

Prepared by:		Date:			
Reviewed by:		Date:			
Process Step 3: Internal Control Check Item	**Y**	**N**	**N/A**	**Comment**	
1) Was approved payroll register received per Step 2, item 3i?					
2) Are employee compensation expense classifications and allocations are correct?					
3) Check if any compensation expense has been or should be capitalized (recorded as an asset).					
4) Payroll register as source.					
a Are employee compensation, withholding, and net pay amounts journalized using totals per 1 above?					
b. In a computerized system, have manual checks been journalized and posted? Are they in payroll register?					
c. Payroll register totals reconciled to ledger account balances?					
5) Are employer payroll tax expenses journalized?					
6) Are employee PTO / benefits calculated and journalized?					
7) Is owed but unpaid compensation (salary, wages, commissions, etc.) accrued at end of accounting period?					
8) Are owed but unpaid employer payroll taxes accrued at end of period cutoff?					
9) Has workers' compensation been calculated and journalized?					
10) Is there any taxable employee compensation paid in another department that has not been recorded in payroll processing? (Especially look for stock and deferred compensation.) Has this been journalized?					
11) Are entries for items 5 – 10 posted in related ledger accounts and the account balances reconciled to calculations?					
12) Are general ledger reconciled payroll tax liability accounts also reconciled to payroll tax reports?					
13) Are general ledger controlling account balances reconciled to their related sub-account balance totals?					
14) Are general ledger wage and withholding account totals reconciled to employee earnings records totals?					

continued ▶

Internal Control Checklist, *continued*

Prepared by:				Date:	
Reviewed by:				Date:	
Process Step 3: Internal Control Check Item	**Y**	**N**	**N/A**	**Comment**	
15) Arepaymentstoindependentcontractorstracked(forform1099 purposes and backup withholding if no W-9)?					
16) Tax deposits being tracked by payee, date, and amount?					
17) Have PTO accruals and use been updated and checked?					
18) Are employee advances recorded and reconciled?					
19) Is a separate payroll checking account in use and reconciled with every payroll?					
20) Segregation of Duties: Are all Step 3 duties fully separated from Steps 1, 2, and 4 duties (see process illustration), with no authority or oversight of one over the other? (Except for small business where owner performs these duties)					

Make Payments (Accounts Payable)   The checklist below can be used as an internal control guide for functions comprising the fourth step in the payroll process: "Make Payments". Note: this checklist may require additions and/or modifications based on the individual organization. (Item 1 is not necessary if payroll is outsourced.) See Section 4 concerning relevant details for checklist items.

Prepared by:				Date:	
Reviewed by:				Date:	
Process Step 4: Internal Control Check Item	**Y**	**N**	**N/A**	**Comment**	
1) Automated check signing:					
a. If checks are mechanically signed as part of check printing when they are processed in payroll, is the signature plate easily separated from the printer that prints the checks?					
b. If a signature plate can be separated is a (are) specific individual(s) authorized to remove the plate and place it a locked and secure location?					
c. If plate cannot be removed from the printer or computer, is a (are) specific individual(s) authorized to place the printer or computer is a locked and secure location?					
d. Some systems have a meter that records the number of checks processed. Is this checked and logged regularly?					
e. When checks for other payroll-related items such as benefits, workers' compensation, or penalties are printed, is there accompanying documentation that verifies authenticity of the transaction, that has been approved by Human Resources or other non-payroll manager ?					

continued ▶

Internal Control Checklist, *continued*

Prepared by:		Date:			
Reviewed by:		Date:			
Process Step 4: Internal Control Check Item	**Y**	**N**	**N/A**	**Comment**	
2) <u>Manual check signing:</u>					
a. Does a high authority such as board of directors or owner designate who has authority to sign checks?					
b. If there is a list of authorized check signers, is this kept secure under control of only need-to-know managers?					
c. Are two signatures required for high dollar amounts?					
d. Are check signers away from the payroll department and away from the accounting department, for example in Human Resources, or some other management position?					
e. Are check signers prohibited access to stored checks, bank account data, and any deposit/payment transactions?					
f. Are check signers prohibited from doing bank reconciliations?					
g. When checks are made available for signature is there a written payroll department manager confirmation that checks were reviewed, that accompanies the checks?					
h. When checks for other payroll-related items such as benefits, workers' compensation, or penalties are signed, is there accompanying documentation that verifies authenticity of each transaction, which has been approved by Human Resources or other manager ?					
i. Does check signer confirm that checks are drawn on the correct account? A check appears regular on its face?					
j. Are rubber stamp signatures prohibited?					
k. Is signing blank checks prohibited?					
3) Is list of authorized check signers current? Are signature authorizations regularly verified (including signature plate used for automatic printing)?					
4) Has an approval report from payroll manager for amount of net pay (before transferring funds to the payroll checking account) been received?					
5) Has an approval report from payroll manager (or accounting department) for amount of payroll tax expense and additional benefit expense (before making payment) been received?					
6) Does the organization use a bank with a "positive pay service"?					
7) Are all checks sequentially pre-numbered?					
8) Are the reasons for uncashed checks investigated?					
9) Are voided checks marked "void" and retained in file?					

continued ▶

Internal Control Checklist, *continued*

Prepared by:		Date:			
Reviewed by:		Date:			
Process Step 4: Internal Control Check Item	**Y**	**N**	**N/A**	**Comment**	
10) Check distribution: 　a. Is employee ID required? 　b. Distribution on site: Does someone other than: 1) a payroll employee or 2) an employee's immediate supervisor distribute checks? 　c. Mailed checks: Does address match employee address in master file? 　d. Is any employee receiving more than one check?					
11) Direct deposits of employee pay: 　a. Are employees encouraged to use direct deposit service? 　b. Is all employee-approved direct deposit information (such as sample personal checks, bank name, account number, authorization signature, etc.) in employee file in human resource department? 　c. Is there only one direct deposit per employee? 　d. Is company alert for phishing scams in which other parties claim to be "official" and request information from "a" above? 　e. Does any change require both employee and Human Resources signed approval, which is documented in employee file?					
12) Payroll tax deposits: 　a. Is a payroll tax calendar being used (For IRS: Pub. 509. Refer to state employment department)? 　b. Has EFTPS (federal) and equivalent state service been set up? 　c. Have payroll deposits deadlines been reviewed? 　d. Have deposits been timely made?					
13) If payments are outsourced: 　a. Have correct payments to tax authorities been verified? 　b. Were payments timely? 　c. Were funds frozen prematurely?					
14) Segregation of Duties: Are all Step 4 duties fully separated from Steps 1–3 duties (see process illustration), with no authority or oversight of one over the other? (Except for small business where owner performs these duties)					

Internal Control Checklist, *continued*

TIP

Pay cards are an alternative to payroll checks. Pay cards are essentially debit cards with net pay loaded into the card. Advantages are: reduced payroll processing cost for employer, elimination of check fraud, cards are useful for lower-income employees who do not have bank accounts and want to avoid check-cashing fees-although the cards often have fees that should be compared, cards have security codes, and lost cards can usually be replaced at remaining balance, although this may be an extended process. Disadvantages: state and local law possible limitations, time to replace a lost card, level of fees, and not all service providers accept debit cards. The DOL requires: 1) Pay cards cannot be mandatory but rather offered as an alternative, 2) Employer must disclose fees (which cannot reduce pay below minimum wage) and program details, 3) Provider must offer at least 60-day account history information.

Submit Forms and Reports

The checklist below can be used as an internal control guide for functions comprising the fifth step in the payroll process: "Submit Forms and Reports". This step will primarily involve accounting and payroll departments; Human Resources department will submit other compliance reports. Note: this checklist may require additions and/or modifications based on the individual organization. See Section 4 concerning relevant details for checklist items.

Prepared by:			Date:		
Reviewed by:			Date:		
Process Step 5: Internal Control Check Item	**Y**	**N**	**N/A**	**Comment**	
1) Is a checklist used with a tax calendar to identify required federal, state, and local tax forms and other reports due to taxing and regulatory authorities and to employees?					
2) Is a checklist used for other required/3rd party reports as required by employment laws at hiring and termination (such as EEO-1 report, PRWORA report) and benefit providers (Human Resources department)?					
3) Is a checklist used for regular 3rd reporting such as for workers' compensation and ERISA?					
4) Are tax forms reconciled to general ledger accounts and deposit records prior to submission?					
5) Year-end: Always reconcile the totals of individual Forms W-2 to Form W-3. Then reconcile the W-3 totals to the totals on Form 941 and/or other applicable forms submitted to the IRS such as 940, 943 or 944. Retain all reconciliations.					

continued ▶

Internal Control Checklist, *continued*

Prepared by:		Date:			
Reviewed by:		Date:			
Process Step 5: Internal Control Check Item	**Y**	**N**	**N/A**	**Comment**	
6) Is certified mail return receipt or delivery tracking system used for forms that are mailed?					
7) Is a record or ledger account maintained for penalties, interest, and other charges incurred due to payroll error?					
8) Is there a checklist and deadlines for management reports?					
9) Is a payroll summary report prepared and sent to each department supervisor and budget supervisor?					
10) Are all management reports reconciled to payroll register and general ledger prior to submission?					

11) Useful human resource department reports:
    a. Vacation accrual and use summary
    b. Other PTO accrual and use summary
    c. Retirement account summary
    d. New hires and separations listing					

Appendix I

States and Territories With Daily Overtime Laws

States With Overtime Requirements and Related Laws Exceeding the FLSA

Overview

The following states and U.S. territories have daily and other overtime requirements that can materially exceed FLSA overtime: Alaska, California, Colorado, Nevada, Puerto Rico, and U.S. Virgin Islands.

General Rule: Pay the Highest Amount

The general rule in each location is that the total wage calculation must be compared to the FLSA wage calculation, and the highest amount is always what must be paid.

Common examples of differences are overtime dollar rates, hourly requirements, and exempt worker categories.

For example, California has a double-time dollar overtime rate in some circumstances, and the FLSA does not. All of these states have daily overtime hourly requirements and the FLSA does not.

Overtime can be greater under the FLSA when it does not exempt certain worker categories from overtime, even though a state might exempt that category. As well, the reverse can be true; some states may not exempt workers from overtime in some situations while the FLSA does (resulting in higher worker pay because of the state law).

Check State and Local Law

It is important to verify requirements (such as rates and exempt worker categories) by contacting the relevant state, territory, and local employment authority. In general, one should contact a "wage and hour division". Professional assistance may be another wise option to confirm understanding or clarify uncertainty.

Alaska Overtime and Related Rules

Overtime Rules for Non-exempt Employees	**1.5 times the regular rate of pay:** ■ Hours per weekly workday in excess of 8 ■ Weekly hours exceeding 40 (Same as Fair Labor Standards Act) Overtime is calculated by comparing the total weekly overtime hours to the total daily overtime hours and using the greater total of hours. Overtime is not required for employers with fewer than four employees in the regular course of business or twelve in designated circumstances, when FLSA overtime does not apply. Consult the Department of Labor and Workforce Development for details. (Alternative workweek is allowed if employees voluntarily agree and that by law does not circumvent overtime.)
Exempt Employee	In general, exempt employee classification is similar to the FLSA with exemption for administrative, executive, professional, and certain other job categories. However, it is important that classifications, definitions, and other compliance details for Alaska- specific exempt job types be verified with the Alaska Department of Labor and Workforce Development, Division of Labor Standards and Safety. (901-465-4855; statewide. wagehour@alaska.gov). Consider professional employment counsel in this area. As a starting point, three basic general requirements can be applied in many cases. To be classified as exempt: ■ **Salary requirement**: "White collar" employees must be paid two times the minimum wage (see below) for the first weekly 40 hours worked. Actual hours worked of greater or less than 40 are not considered; in other words, only the full 40-hour salary agreement is required. (Note: this requirement applies only to "executive" classification, not to administrative or supervisory duties.) ■ **A "white collar" job**: Employee actual activity must consist primarily of executive, administrative, professional, or other designated job types, as defined by the FLSA and Alaska law. ■ **Independent Judgment**: The term "discretion and independent judgment" is used to describe the nature of decision-making. This means that decisions can be made independently of direct and immediate supervision, even though decisions can be reviewed at a higher level later.
State Hourly Minimum Wage	Effective January 1, 2022 the state minimum wage in Alaska remains at $10.34 per hour. School bus drivers receive a minimum wage of two times this rate.

continued ▶

Alaska Overtime and Related Rules, *continued*

Employee Wage Claims	Employee wage claims are filed with the Alaska Dept. of Labor and Workforce Development, Division of Labor Standards and Safety. The statute of limitations for overtime and minimum wage claims requires filing within two years from date work was performed. Regular wage and benefit claims must be filed within three years from date work was performed. Employee must first have requested payment from employer (Request should be verifiable). Employee may alternatively pursue independent legal action.
Regular Rate	In Alaska the regular rate is the total weekly compensation received (after any statutory exclusions) divided by the total weekly hours actually worked. If a salary contract contains a fixed hour amount and employer and employee follow terms of the contract, the fixed hour amount is used; otherwise, the regular rate is based on the salary divided by an 8-hour day, 40-hour week, different than the FLSA.
Overtime Example #1	Joyce is a non-exempt employee who worked 44 hours Monday through Friday, working 8-hour days Monday–Wednesday, 11 hours on Thursday and 9 hours on Friday. Her pay rate is $25 per hour; she also received a non-discretionary bonus of $800 during the week. The regular rate and compensation are:

- Regular compensation: $800 + ($25 × 44) = $1,900
- Regular rate: $1,900/44 hours = $43.18
- Overtime rate: ($43.18 × 1.5) = $64.77
- Total compensation: ($25 × 40) + $800 + ($64.77 × 4) = $2,059.08

Overtime Example #2

Vonetta is a non-exempt employee who earns $20 per hour in a workweek beginning on Monday and worked the following hours in the two workweeks below:

	Monday	Tuesday	Wednesday	Thursday	Friday	Saturday	Sunday	Total
Total Hrs.	0	8	9	12	0	0	0	29
Reg. Hrs.		8	8	8				24
Total OT			1	4				5

	Monday	Tuesday	Wednesday	Thursday	Friday	Saturday	Sunday	Total
Total Hrs.	6	9	8	10	8	13	10	64
Reg. Hrs.	6	8	8	8	8	8	8	40 max.
Total OT		1		2		5	2	64–40

continued ▶

Alaska Overtime and Related Rules, *continued*

Overtime Example #2, Continued	**Calculate Overtime**

Week #1: (29 total hours)

Step	Action	Example
1	Overtime hours: Subtract the total of regular hours worked per day (to a maximum of 40) from total hours worked.	29 – 24 = 5 hours overtime (8 + 8 + 8 =24)
2	Time and one-half: Multiply by regular $ rate × 1.5.	5 × $20 × 1.5 = $150

Total compensation: (24 regular hours × $20) + $150 = $630
Check: total hours accounted for: (24 + 5) = 29

Week #2: (64 total hours)

Step	Action	Example
1	Overtime hours: Subtract the total of regular hours worked per day (to a maximum of 40) from total hours worked.	64 – 40 = 24 hours overtime
2	Time and one-half: Multiply by regular $ rate × 1.5.	24 × $20 × 1.5 = $720

Total compensation: (40 regular hours × $20) + $720 = $1,520
Check: total hours accounted for: (40 + 24) = 64

California Overtime and Related Rules

Overtime Rules for Non-exempt Employees

1.5 times the regular rate of pay:

- Hours per weekly workday in excess of 8 up to and including 12
- First 8 hours worked on seventh consecutive day of workweek
- Weekly hours exceeding 40 (same as Fair Labor Standards Act)

Double the regular rate of pay:

- Hours per day in excess of 12
- All hours exceeding 8 on seventh consecutive day of workweek

Compare the total weekly overtime hours to the total daily and 7th consecutive day hours and use the higher result. See examples below.

Consult the Division of Labor Standards for further details. A workweek is the same as the FLSA. (Alternative workweeks are permitted that do not circumvent overtime by law; as well, overtime may be required in certain situations.)

Exempt Employee

In general, exempt employee classification is similar to the FLSA with exemption for administrative, executive, professional, and certain other job categories. However, it is important that classifications, definitions, and other compliance details for California-specific exempt job types be verified with the office of the Commissioner of Labor Standards, also known as the Division of Labor Standards Enforcement (DLSE2@dir.ca.gov). Consider professional help in this area.

As a starting point, three basic general requirements can be applied in many cases. To be classified as exempt:

- **Salary requirement**: An employee must earn a minimum monthly salary of at least twice the state full-time hourly minimum wage based on a 40-hour week. Example: If an employee earns a $5,000 per month salary, then the equivalent hourly rate is [($5,000 × 12)/52]/40 = $28.85, which satisfies the current requirement-see below. (The FLSA requirement is $684 per week.) Note: commission employees requirement is 1.5 times minimum wage.
- **A "white collar" job**: Employee actual duties must consist customarily and regularly of primarily (more than half) executive, administrative, professional, or other designated job types, as defined by the FLSA and California law.
- **Independent Judgment**: The term "discretion and independent judgment" is used to describe the nature of decision-making. This means that decisions can be made independently of direct and immediate supervision, even though decisions can be reviewed at a higher level later.

continued ▶

California Overtime and Related Rules, *continued*

State Hourly Minimum Wage

Effective Date	Employers With 25 or Less Employees	Employers With More Than 25 Employees
1/1/2020	$12	$13
1/1/2021	$13	$14
1/1/2022	$14	$15
1/1/2023	$15	$15

No tip credit.

Employee Wage Claims

Employee wage claims for unpaid or under-paid wages are filed with the Division of Labor Standards Enforcement. The statute of limitations for filing a claim is 3 years from date of the most recent violation, and in some cases, up to 4 years. An alternative is a separate legal action.

Regular Rate

The "regular rate" of pay in California is defined differently than under the FLSA when there is a non-discretionary flat-sum bonus or salary. Absent this bonus, the weekly regular rate of all other non-salary compensation received (after any statutory exclusions) is divided by weekly total hours actually worked, as generally required under the FLSA. However, the regular rate in California related to this type of bonus is determined by dividing by hours worked *not exceeding 40 hours*; that is, non-overtime hours. (See *Alvarado vs. Dart Container Corp.*) For salaried non-exempt employees, the divisor for regular rate is the weekly hours per the salary agreement, *not exceeding 40 hours*.

Overtime Example #1

Joyce is a non-exempt employee who worked 44 hours Monday through Friday, working 8-hour days Monday–Wednesday, 11 hours on Thursday and 9 hours on Friday. Her pay rate is $25 per hour; she also received a non-discretionary, flat-sum bonus of $800 during the week. The regular rate, overtime, and compensation are:

- Regular pay ($25 × 44) = $1,100
- Regular rate on regular pay: $25 (or $1,100/44 hours = $25)
- Regular rate on bonus: $800/40 = $20
- Overtime rate at 1.5: [($25 + $20) regular rate × 1.5] = $67.50

Total compensation: ($25 × 40) + $800 + ($67.50 × 4) = $2,070

Overtime Example #2

Vonetta is a non-exempt employee who earns $20 per hour in a workweek beginning on Monday and worked the following hours in the three workweeks below:

	Monday	Tuesday	Wednesday	Thursday	Friday	Saturday	Sunday	Total
Total Hrs.	0	0	8	0	0	8	16	32
Reg. Hrs.			8			8	8	24
Total OT							8	8

continued ▶

California Overtime and Related Rules, *continued*

Total Hrs.	8	8	10	8	8	10	15	67
Reg. Hrs.	8	8	8	8	8	8	0	40 max.
Total OT			2			2	15	67–40

Total Hrs.	15	15	3	15	15	4	4	71
Reg. Hrs.	8	8	3	8	8	4		39
Total OT	7	7		7	7		4	32

Overtime Example #2, Continued

Calculate Overtime

Week #1: (32 total hours)

Step	Action	Example
1	Overtime hours: Subtract the total of regular hours worked per day (to a maximum of 40) from total hours worked	32 – 24 = 8 hours overtime (8 + 8 + 8 = 24)
2	Double-time: Multiply double-time hours times regular $ rate × 2.	16 –12 = 4 double-time hours (Sunday > 12 hrs. but not a 7th consecutive day): 4 × $20 × 2 = $160
3	Time and one-half: Subtract double-time hours from total overtime hours and multiply by regular $ rate × 1.5.	8 – 4 = 4 time/half hours 4 × $20 × 1.5 = $120

Total compensation: (24 regular hours × $20) + $280 = $760
Check: total hours accounted for: (24 + 4 + 4) = 32

Week #2: (67 total hours)

Step	Action	Example
1	Overtime hours: Subtract the total of regular hours worked per day (to a maximum of 40) from total hours worked.	67 – 40 = 27 hours overtime
2	Double-time: Multiply double-time hours times regular $ rate × 2.	15 – 8 = 7 double-time hours (Sunday > 8 hrs. on a 7th consecutive day): 7 × $20 × 2 = $280
3	Time and one-half: Subtract double-time hours from total overtime hours and multiply by regular $ rate × 1.5.	27 – 7 = 20 time/half hours 20 × $20 × 1.5 = $600

continued ▶

California Overtime and Related Rules, *continued*

Overtime Example #2, Continued

Total compensation: (40 regular hours × $20) + $880 = $1,680
Check: total hours accounted for: (40 + 7 + 20) = 67

Week #3: (71 total hours)

Step	Action	Example
1	Overtime hours: Subtract the total of regular hours worked per day (to a maximum of 40) from total hours worked.	71 – 39 = 32 hours overtime (8 + 8 + 3 + 8 + 8 + 4 = 39)
2	Double-time: Multiply double-time hours times regular $ rate × 2.	15 – 12 = 3 on 4 days 12 × $20 × 2 = $480 (3 + 3 + 3 + 3 = 12)
3	Time and one-half: Subtract double-time hours from total overtime hours and multiply by regular $ rate × 1.5.	32 – 12 = 20 time/half hours 20 × $20 × 1.5 = $600

Total compensation: (39 regular hours × $20) + $1,080 = $1,860
Check: total hours accounted for: (39 + 12 + 20) = 71

Local Laws

There are numerous cities in California with their own minimum wage/other work rules. If local law requires more, employers must comply.

Colorado Overtime and Related Rules

Overtime Rules for Non-Exempt Employees	**1.5 times the regular rate of pay:** - Hours per weekly workday in excess of 12 - Hours in excess of 12 continuous hours (excluding duty-free meal periods) without regard to starting and ending times - Weekly hours exceeding 40 (Same as Fair Labor Standards Act) Compare the total weekly overtime hours to the total daily hours and use the higher result. See examples below. Consult the Division of Labor Standards and Statistics for further details. A workweek is the same as the FLSA (Alternative workweek is allowed if employees voluntarily agree and that by law does not circumvent overtime.)
Exempt Employee	In general, exempt employee classification is similar to the FLSA with exemption for administrative, executive, professional, and certain other job categories. However, it is important that classifications, definitions, and other compliance details for Colorado- specific exempt job types be verified with the Colorado Division of Labor Standards and Statistics (888-390-7936; cdle_labor_standards@state.co.us). Consider professional help in this area. As a starting point, three basic general requirements can be applied in many cases. To be classified as exempt: - **Salary requirement**: An executive employee must receive more than Colorado total minimum wage for all weekly hours worked (see minimum wage below) to be exempt; therefore, below-minimum rate salaried employees will never be exempt. Administrative and professional employees have no Colorado minimum salary requirement, so FLSA $679 minimum requirement always applies for these categories. - **A "white collar" job**: Employee actual duties are primarily executive, administrative, professional, or other designated job types, as defined the FLSA and Colorado law. - **Independent Judgment**: The term "discretion and independent judgment" is used to describe the nature of decision-making. This means that decisions can be made independently of direct and immediate supervision, even though decisions can be reviewed at a higher level later.
State Hourly Minimum Wage	Effective January 1, 2022 state minimum wage in Colorado is $12.56 per hour. Tipped employee rate is $9.54 net of tip credit up to $3.02. Government workers minimum is $15.00
Employee Wage Claims	Employee wage claims are filed with the Colorado Division of Labor Standards and Statistics, with a maximum $7,500 claim. The statute of limitations for overtime and minimum wage claims requires filing within two years from the date the wages became due and payable (3 years for willful violations). Employee should first file a written demand with employer, preferably within 60 days. Employee may alternatively pursue independent legal action.

continued ▶

Colorado Overtime and Related Rules, *continued*

Regular Rate	In Colorado the regular rate is the total weekly compensation received (after any statutory exclusions) divided by the total weekly hours actually worked. For salaried non-exempt employees, the regular rate is the salary divided by the number of hours the salary has been agreed to compensate, with a .5 premium above 40 hours; hours worked above agreed hours are at a 1.5 rate. If there are no fixed hours, the regular rate is based on hours worked up to 40 hours, unless there is a flexible hour agreement in which actual hours worked would be used.
Overtime Example #1	Joyce is a non-exempt employee who worked 52 hours Monday through Friday, working 8-hour days Monday–Wednesday, 15 hours on Thursday and 13 hours on Friday. Her pay rate is $25 per hour; she also received a non-discretionary bonus of $800 during the week. The regular rate and compensation are:

- Regular compensation: $800 + ($25 × 52) = $2,100
- Regular rate: $2,100/52 hours = $40.39
- Overtime rate: ($40.39 × 1.5) = $60.59
- Total compensation: ($25 × 40) + $800 + ($60.59 × 12) = $2,527.08

Overtime Example #2	Vonetta is a non-exempt employee who earns $20 per hour in a workweek beginning at 9 am beginning on Monday (except in week 1, beginning at 6 pm and ending Tuesday at 8 am, 1 hour non-duty-free meal break) and worked the following hours in the three workweeks below:

	Monday	Tuesday	Wednesday	Thursday	Friday	Saturday	Sunday	Total
Total Hrs.	6	7	9	14	0	0	0	36
Reg. Hrs.	6	6	9	12				33
Total OT	<---1--->			2				3

	Monday	Tuesday	Wednesday	Thursday	Friday	Saturday	Sunday	Total
Total Hrs.	8	8	14	8	4	10	15	67
Reg. Hrs.	8	8	12	8	4	10	12	40 max.
Total OT			2				3	67–40

	Monday	Tuesday	Wednesday	Thursday	Friday	Saturday	Sunday	Total
Total Hrs.	12	12	12	12	12	0	0	60
Reg. Hrs.								40 max.
Total OT								60–40

continued ▶

Colorado Overtime and Related Rules, *continued*

Overtime Example #2, Continued

Calculate Overtime

Week #1: (36 total hours)

Step	Action	Example
1	Overtime hours: Subtract the total of regular hours worked per day (to a maximum of 40) from total hours worked.	36 – 33 = 3 hours overtime (6 + 6 + 9 + 12 = 33)
2	Time and one-half: Multiply by regular $ rate × 1.5.	3 × $20 × 1.5 = $90

Total compensation: (33 regular hours × $20) + $90 = $750
Check: total hours accounted for: (33 + 3) = 36

Week #2: (67 total hours)

Step	Action	Example
1	Overtime hours: Subtract the total of regular hours worked per day (to a maximum of 40) from total hours worked.	67 – 40 = 27 hours overtime
2	Time and one-half: Multiply by regular $ rate × 1.5.	27 × $20 × 1.5 = $810

Total compensation: (40 regular hours × $20) + $810 = $1,610
Check: total hours accounted for: (40 + 27) = 67

Week #3: (60 total hours)

Step	Action	Example
1	Overtime hours: Subtract the total of regular hours worked per day (to a maximum of 40) from total hours worked.	60 – 40 = 20 hours overtime
2	Time and one-half: Multiply by regular $ rate × 1.5.	20 × $20 × 1.5 = $600

Total compensation: (40 regular hours × $20) + $600 = $1,400
Check: total hours accounted for: (40 + 20) = 60

Nevada Overtime and Related Rules

Overtime Rules for Non-Exempt Employees

1.5 times the regular rate of pay:

For an employee who earns less than 1.5 times the applicable minimum wage (see below):

- Hours per 24-hour period (starting when employee begins work) in excess of 8
- Weekly hours exceeding 40 (Same as Fair Labor Standards Act)

Others: Weekly hours exceeding 40 (Same as Fair Labor Standards Act)

Overtime is calculated by comparing the total weekly overtime hours to the total daily overtime hours and using the greater total of hours. Overtime is not required for employees of businesses with gross sales of less than $250,000, when FLSA overtime does not apply. Consult the Office of the Labor Commissioner for details. A workweek is the same as the FLSA. (Alternative workweek is allowed if employees voluntarily agree and that by law does not circumvent overtime.)

Exempt Employee

In general, exempt employee classification is similar to the FLSA with exemption for administrative, executive, professional, and certain other job categories. However, it is important that classifications, definitions, and other compliance details for Nevada-specific exempt job types be verified with the Nevada Office of the Labor Commissioner (702-486-265; mail1@Labor.nv.gov). Consider professional help in this area.

As a starting point, three basic general requirements can be applied in many cases. To be classified as exempt:

- **Salary requirement**: "White collar" employees are exempt in Nevada and the FLSA minimum weekly requirement of $679 applies.
- **A "white collar" job**: Employee actual duties must consist primarily of executive, administrative, professional, or other designated job types, as defined by the FLSA and Nevada law.
- **Independent Judgment**: The term "discretion and independent judgment" is used to describe the nature of decision-making. This means that decisions can be made independently of direct and immediate supervision, even though decisions can be reviewed at a higher level later.

State Hourly Minimum Wage

Effective July 1, 2022 state minimum wage in Nevada changes from $9.75 per hour to $10.50 per hour. The minimum wage for employees that have qualifying health benefits made available by their employers changes from $8.75 per hour to $9.50 per hour. No tip credit.

continued ▶

Nevada Overtime and Related Rules, *continued*

Employee Wage Claims	Employee wage and benefit claims are filed with the Nevada Office of the Labor Commissioner. Claims must be filed within 2 years from date work was performed. Employee must first have requested payment from employer (Request should be verifiable). Employee may alternatively pursue independent legal action.

Regular Rate	In Nevada the regular rate is the total weekly compensation received (after any statutory exclusions) divided by the total weekly hours actually worked. For salaried non-exempt employees, the regular rate is the salary divided by the number of hours the salary has been agreed to compensate, with a .5 premium above 40 hours; hours worked above agreed hours are at a 1.5 rate. If there are no fixed hours, the regular rate is based on hours worked.

Overtime Example #1	Joyce is a non-exempt employee who worked 44 hours Monday through Friday, working 8-hour days Monday–Wednesday, 11 hours on Thursday and 9 hours on Friday. Her pay rate is $25 per hour; she also received a non-discretionary bonus of $800 during the week. The regular rate and compensation are:

- Regular compensation: $800 + ($25 × 44) = $1,900
- Regular rate: $1,900/44 hours = $43.18
- Overtime rate: ($43.18 × 1.5) = $64.77

Total compensation: ($25 × 40) + $800 + ($64.77 × 4) = $2,059.08

Overtime Example #2	Vonetta is a non-exempt employee who works a fixed workday beginning at 9:00 am and earns $20 per hour (greater than 1.5 times Nevada minimum wage) in a workweek beginning on Monday and worked the following hours in the two workweeks below:

	Monday	Tuesday	Wednesday	Thursday	Friday	Saturday	Sunday	Total
Total Hrs.	0	8	9	12	0	0	0	29
Reg. Hrs.		8	8	8				24
Total OT			1	4				N/A

	Monday	Tuesday	Wednesday	Thursday	Friday	Saturday	Sunday	Total
Total Hrs.	6	9	8	10	8	13	10	64
Reg. Hrs.	6	8	8	8	8	8	8	40 max.
Total OT		1		2		5	2	64–40

continued ▶

Nevada Overtime and Related Rules, *continued*

To Calculate Overtime

Week #1: (29 total hours)

Step	Action	Example
1	Overtime hours: Subtract the total of regular hours worked per day (to a maximum of 40) from total hours worked.	29 – 24 = 5 hours overtime (8 + 8 + 8 = 24)
2	Time and one-half: Not applicable. Vonetta earns more than 1.5 times Nevada minimum wage. She did not exceed FLSA 40 hours per week.	-0-

Total compensation: (24 regular hours × $20) + (5 hours × $20) = $580
Check: total hours accounted for: (24 + 5) = 29

Week #2: (64 total hours)

Step	Action	Example
1	Overtime hours: Subtract the total of regular hours worked per day (to a maximum of 40) from total hours worked.	64 – 40 = 24 hours overtime
2	Time and one-half: Multiply by regular $ rate × 1.5.	24 × $20 × 1.5 = $720

Total compensation: (40 regular hours × $20) + $720 = $1,520
Check: total hours accounted for: (40 + 24) = 64

Overtime Example #3

Assume that Vonetta earns $11 per hour and has no health plan and worked the following hours:

	Monday	Tuesday	Wednesday	Thursday	Friday	Saturday	Sunday	Total
Total Hrs.	0	8	9	12	0	0	0	29
Reg. Hrs.		8	8	8				24
Total OT			1	4				5

	Monday	Tuesday	Wednesday	Thursday	Friday	Saturday	Sunday	Total
Total Hrs.	6	9	8	10	8	13	10	64
Reg. Hrs.	6	8	8	8	8	8	8	40 max.
Total OT			1	2		5	2	64–40

continued ▶

Nevada Overtime and Related Rules, *continued*

*Overtime
Example #3,
Continued*

Week #1: (29 total hours)

Step	Action	Example
1	Overtime hours: Subtract the total of regular hours worked per day (to a maximum of 40) from total hours worked.	29 – 24 = 5 hours overtime (8 + 8 + 8 = 24)
2	Time and one-half: Multiply by regular $ rate × 1.5.	5 × $11 × 1.5 = $82.50

Total compensation: (24 regular hours × $11) + $82.50 = $346.50
Check: total hours accounted for: (24 + 5) = 29

Week #2: (64 total hours)

Step	Action	Example
1	Overtime hours: Subtract the total of regular hours worked per day (to a maximum of 40) from total hours worked.	64 – 40 = 24 hours overtime
2	Time and one-half: Multiply by regular $ rate × 1.5.	24 × $11 × 1.5 = $396

Total compensation: (40 regular hours × $11) + $396 = $836
Check: total hours accounted for: (40 + 24) = 64

Puerto Rico Overtime and Related Rules

Overtime Rules for Non-exempt Employees

1.5 times the regular rate of pay for employees hired on or after January 26, 2017:

- Hours per weekly workday in excess of 8
- Weekly hours exceeding 40 (same as Fair Labor Standards Act)

2 times the regular rate of pay for employees hired before January 26, 2017:

- Hours per weekly workday in excess of 8
- All hours worked on seventh consecutive day of workweek
- Weekly hours exceeding 40

Additional:
A Christmas bonus generally ranging from $300 to $600 is required. Various detailed provisions apply that require careful review.

Overtime is calculated by comparing the total weekly overtime hours to the total daily and 7th consecutive day hours and using the greater total of hours. Consult with the Department of Labor and Human Resources for details. A workweek is the same as the FLSA. (Alternative workweek is allowed if employees voluntarily agree and that by law does not circumvent overtime.)

Exempt Employee

In general, exempt employee classification follows the FLSA with exemption for administrative, executive, professional, and certain other job categories. It is important that classifications, definitions, and other compliance details for Puerto Rico-specific exempt job types be verified with the Puerto Rico Department of Labor and Human Resources (trabajo.pr.gov; 787-754-2120). Consider professional help in this area.

As a starting point, three basic general requirements can be applied in many cases. To be classified as exempt:

- **Salary requirement**: The FLSA minimum level of $455 weekly still applies to Puerto Rico.
- **A "white collar" job**: Employee actual duties must consist customarily and regularly of primarily executive, administrative, professional, or other designated job types, as defined by the FLSA and Puerto Rico law.
- **Independent Judgment**: The term "discretion and independent judgment" is used to describe the nature of decision-making. This means that decisions can be made independently of direct and immediate supervision, even though decisions can be reviewed at a higher level later.

Hourly Minimum Wage

The hourly minimum wage is $8.50. Government construction contracts may require a higher minimum. Tip credit same as FLSA. Employees not covered by the FLSA: Rate is 70% of the FLSA rate ($5.08) or the state rate, whichever is higher.

continued ▶

Puerto Rico Overtime and Related Rules, *continued*

Employee Wage Claims	Employee wage claims for unpaid or under-paid wages are filed with the Department of Labor and Human Resources. There are initial employment probationary periods ranging fro 9–12 months. The statute of limitations for filing a claim is 1 year from the date the employee ceased work with the employer. Employee may alternatively pursue independent legal action. Note: Employment in Puerto Rico is not "At-Will", meaning that employees cannot be fired at any time for any legal reason.
Regular Rate	The regular rate is the total compensation received (after any statutory exclusions) during a period divided by the total hours actually worked during the same period. For salaried non-exempt employees, the regular rate is the salary divided by the number of hours the salary has been agreed to compensate, with a .5 premium above 40 hours; hours worked above agreed hours are at 1.5 rate. If there are no fixed hours, the regular rate is based on hours worked up to 40 hours, unless there is a flexible hour agreement in which actual hours worked would be used.
Overtime Example #1	Joyce is a non-exempt employee hired after January 26, 2017 who worked 44 hours Monday through Friday, working 8-hour days Monday–Wednesday, 11 hours on Thursday and 9 hours on Friday. Her pay rate is $25 per hour; she also received a non-discretionary fixed bonus of $800 during the week. The regular rate, overtime, and compensation are:

- Regular compensation: $800 + ($25 × 44) = $1,900
- Regular rate: $1,900/44 hours = $43.18
- Overtime rate: ($43.18 × 1.5) = $64.77
- Total compensation: ($25 × 40) + $800 + ($64.77 × 4) = $2,059.08

Overtime Example #2

Vonetta is a non-exempt employee hired after January 26, 2017 who earns $20 per hour in a workweek beginning on Monday and worked the following hours in the two workweeks below:

	Monday	Tuesday	Wednesday	Thursday	Friday	Saturday	Sunday	Total
Total Hrs.	0	8	9	12	0	0	0	29
Reg. Hrs.		8	8	8				24
Total OT			1	4				5

	Monday	Tuesday	Wednesday	Thursday	Friday	Saturday	Sunday	Total
Total Hrs.	6	9	8	10	8	13	10	64
Reg. Hrs.	6	8	8	8	8	8		40 max.
Total OT		1		2		5	10	64–40

continued ▶

Puerto Rico Overtime and Related Rules, *continued*

Overtime Example #2 Continued	Calculate Overtime

Week #1: (29 total hours)

Step	Action	Example
1	Overtime hours: Subtract the total of regular hours worked per day (to a maximum of 40) from total hours worked.	29 – 24 = 5 hours overtime (8 + 8 + 8 = 24)
2	Double-time: Multiply double-time hours by regular $ rate × 2.	Does not apply. Employee hired after January 26, 2017.
3	Time and one-half: Multiply by regular $ rate × 1.5.	5 × $20 × 1.5 = $150

Total compensation: (24 regular hours × $20) + $150 = $630
Check: total hours accounted for: (24 + 5) = 29

Week #2: (64 total hours)

Step	Action	Example
1	Overtime hours: Subtract the total of regular hours worked per day (to a maximum of 40) from total hours worked.	64 – 40 = 24 hours overtime
2	Double-time: Multiply double-time hours by regular $ rate × 2.	Does not apply. Employee hired after January 26, 2017.
3	Time and one-half: Multiply by regular $ rate × 1.5.	24 × $20 × 1.5 = $720

Total compensation: (40 regular hours × $20) + $720 = $1,520
Check: total hours accounted for: (40 + 24) = 64

Overtime Example #3	Vonetta is a non-exempt employee hired before January 26, 2017 who earns $20 per hour in a workweek beginning on Monday and worked the following hours in the two workweeks below:

	Monday	Tuesday	Wednesday	Thursday	Friday	Saturday	Sunday	Total
Total Hrs.	0	8	9	12	0	0	0	29
Reg. Hrs.		8	8	8				24
Total OT			1	4				5

	Monday	Tuesday	Wednesday	Thursday	Friday	Saturday	Sunday	Total
Total Hrs.	6	9	8	10	8	13	10	64
Reg. Hrs.	6	8	8	8	8	8		40 Max.
Total OT		1		2		5	10	64–40

continued ▶

Puerto Rico Overtime and Related Rules, *continued*

Overtime Example #3 Continued	**Calculate Overtime**

Week #1: (29 total hours)

Step	Action	Example
1	Overtime hours: Subtract the total of regular hours worked per day (to a maximum of 40) from total hours worked.	29 – 24 = 5 hours overtime (8 + 8 + 8 = 24)
2	Double-time: Multiply double-time hours by regular $ rate × 2.	5 × $40 = $80
3	Time and one-half: Multiply by regular $ rate × 1.5.	Does not apply. Employee hired before January 26, 2017.

Total compensation: (24 regular hours × $20) + $80 = $560
Check: total hours accounted for: (24 + 5) = 29

Week #2: (64 total hours)

Step	Action	Example
1	Overtime hours: Subtract the total of regular hours worked per day (to a maximum of 40) from total hours worked.	64 – 40 = 24 hours overtime
2	Double-time: Multiply double-time hours by regular $ rate × 2.	24 × $40 = $960
3	Time and one-half: Multiply by regular $ rate × 1.5.	Does not apply. Employee hired before January 26, 2017.

Total compensation: (40 regular hours × $20) + $960 = $1,760
Check: total hours accounted for: (40 + 24) = 64

U.S. Virgin Islands (USVI) Overtime and Related Rules

Overtime Rules for Non-exempt Employees

1.5 times the regular rate of pay:

- Hours per weekly workday in excess of 8
- Weekly hours exceeding 40 (Same as Fair Labor Standards Act)
- Any hours on the 6th and 7th consecutive work day

Overtime is calculated by comparing the total weekly overtime hours to the total daily overtime hours and using the greater total of hours. Consult the USVI Department of Labor for details.

Exempt Employee

In general, exempt employee classification is similar to the FLSA with exemption for administrative, executive, professional, and certain other job categories. However, it is important that classifications, definitions, and other compliance details for USVI- specific exempt job types be verified with the USVI Department of Labor. (340-773-1994 or 340776-3700); vidol.gov). Consider professional help in this area.

As a starting point, three basic general requirements can be applied in many cases. To be classified as exempt:

- **Salary requirement**: The FLSA minimum level of $455 weekly still applies to the USVI.
- **A "white collar" job**: Employee actual activity must consist primarily of executive, administrative, professional, or other designated job types, as defined by the FLSA and USVI law.
- **Independent Judgment**: The term "discretion and independent judgment" is used to describe the nature of decision-making. This means that decisions can be made independently of direct and immediate supervision, even though decisions can be reviewed at a higher level later.

State Hourly Minimum Wage

Effective June 1, 2018 minimum wage in the USVI is $10.50 per hour. Statute requires a minimum 10-minute break every four hours apart from meal breaks and not at the beginning or end of work. Tipped rate is $4.20 direct wage minimum and $10.50 minimum that includes tips.

Employee Wage Claims

Employee wage claims are filed with the USVI Dept. of Labor. There is a six-month probationary period upon initial employment. The statute of limitations for employee wage claims requires filing within six years from date of the violation. (See *Rennie vs. Hess Oil Virgin Islands*). Note: Employment in the USVI is not "At-Will", meaning that employees cannot be fired at any time for any legal reason.

continued ▶

U.S. Virgin Islands (USVI) Overtime and Related Rules, *continued*

Regular Rate	In the USVI the regular rate is the total weekly compensation received (after any statutory exclusions) divided by the total weekly hours actually worked. For salaried non-exempt employees, the regular rate is the salary divided by the number of hours the salary has been agreed to compensate, with a .5 premium above 40 hours; hours worked above agreed hours are at a 1.5 rate. If there are no fixed hours, the regular rate is based on hours worked up to 40 hours, unless there is a flexible hour agreement in which actual hours worked would be used.

Overtime Example #1

Joyce is a non-exempt employee who worked 44 hours Monday through Friday, working 8-hour days Monday–Wednesday, 11 hours on Thursday and 9 hours on Friday. Her pay rate is $25 per hour; she also received a non-discretionary bonus of $800 during the week. The regular rate and compensation are:

- Regular compensation: $800 + ($25 × 44) = $1,900
- Regular rate: $1,900/44 hours = $43.18
- Overtime rate: ($43.18 × 1.5) = $64.77
- Total compensation: ($25 × 40) + $800 + ($64.77 × 4) = $2,059.08

Overtime Example #2

Vonetta is a non-exempt employee who earns $20 per hour in a workweek beginning on Monday and worked the following hours in the three workweeks below:

	Monday	Tuesday	Wednesday	Thursday	Friday	Saturday	Sunday	Total
Total Hrs.	0	8	9	12	0	0	0	29
Reg. Hrs.		8	8	8				24
Total OT			1	4				5

	Monday	Tuesday	Wednesday	Thursday	Friday	Saturday	Sunday	Total
Total Hrs.	6	9	8	10	8	13	10	64
Reg. Hrs.	6	8	8	8	8			38
Total OT		1		2		13	10	26

	Monday	Tuesday	Wednesday	Thursday	Friday	Saturday	Sunday	Total
Total Hrs.	12	9	8	14	8	0	9	60
Reg. Hrs.	8	8	8	8	8		8	40 max.
Total OT	4	1		6			1	60–40

continued ▶

U.S. Virgin Islands (USVI) Overtime and Related Rules, *continued*

*Overtime
Example #2,
Continued*

Calculate Overtime

Week #1: (29 total hours)

Step	Action	Example
1	Overtime hours: Subtract the total of regular hours worked per day (to a maximum of 40) from total hours worked.	29 – 24 = 5 hours overtime (8 + 8 + 8 =24)
2	Time and one-half: Multiply by regular $ rate × 1.5.	5 × $20 × 1.5 = $150

Total compensation: (24 regular hours × $20) + $150 = $630
Check: total hours accounted for: (24 + 5) = 29

Week #2: (64 total hours)

Step	Action	Example
1	Overtime hours: Subtract the total of regular hours worked per day (to a maximum of 40) from total hours worked.	64 – 38 = 26 hours overtime (6 + 8 + 8 + 8 + 8 = 38)
2	Time and one-half: Multiply by regular $ rate × 1.5.	26 × $20 × 1.5 = $780

Total compensation: (38 regular hours × $20) + $780 = $1,540
Check: total hours accounted for: (38 + 26) = 64

Week #3: (60 total hours)

Step	Action	Example
1	Overtime hours: Subtract the total of regular hours worked per day (to a maximum of 40) from total hours worked.	60 – 40 = 20 hours overtime (8 + 8 + 8 + 8 + 8 = 40)
2	Time and one-half: Multiply by regular $ rate × 1.5.	20 × $20 × 1.5 = $600

Total compensation: (40 regular hours × $20) + $600 = $1,400
Check: total hours accounted for: (40 + 20) = 60

States That Moderately Exceed FLSA Overtime Requirements

Overview	The following states provide some moderately more favorable overtime multiples and additional hours than the FLSA and less than states previously discussed. Minimum wage rates vary widely among the states. As always, the highest total wage is what must be paid. "Week" refers to a 7-consecutive day work week.
Kansas	For non-exempt workers that do not otherwise qualify for overtime under the FLSA, Kansas requires 1½ times the regular rate for hours in excess of 46 per week. Certain minors and public employees receive 1½ times the regular rate after working 28 consecutive days if at least 258 hours have been accumulated. (Kansas Department of Labor: 785-296-5000)
Kentucky	Kentucky requires that a seventh consecutive day of work by non-exempt employees be paid at 1½ times the regular rate. (Kentucky Labor Cabinet: 502-564-3534)
Oregon	For certain occupations, Oregon requires 1½ times the regular rate for hours in excess of 10 per day and has weekly total hour limits. (Oregon Bureau of Labor and Industries: 971-673-0762)
Rhode Island	Rhode Island requires that non-exempt employees working Sundays and holidays be paid at 1½ times the regular rate and guaranteed at least 4 hours of work. (Rhode Island Department of Labor and Training: 401-462-8000)
Washington	Washington requires that most non-exempt employees, including possibly most agricultural workers, receive overtime at 1½ times the regular rate for hours in excess of 40 per week. (Washington State Department of Labor and Industries 360-902-5799)
Wisconsin	Wisconsin requires that workers under 18 earn 1½ times the regular rate for hours in excess of 10 per day and may not work more than 50 hours per week. (Wisconsin Department of Workforce Development: 608-266-3131)

Appendix II

Timekeeping Methods

The Critical Function of Timekeeping

Overview

The timekeeping function is a key part of the second step in the payroll process: "Calculate the Payroll". Its effects are extensive. Timekeeping is most directly connected to hourly employee wage calculations but also potentially affects employees receiving commissions, bonuses, tips, piecework, and non-exempt salaried employees, for legal compliance requirements primarily related to minimum wage and overtime. In general, timekeeping activities primarily impact three activities: 1) calculating gross pay amounts, 2) allocating hours to other payroll expense types (PTO, vacation, etc.) typically by use of pay codes, and 3) allocating hours to jobs and deparments, also by use of codes. Here, our discussion focuses primarily on the first activity, in order to: 1) reduce payroll-related costs by reducing payroll processing time and reducing errors. 2) comply with FLSA, state, and local wage and hour laws as discussed in earlier parts of this book.

In this regard, the reader may wonder if there are situations where timekeeping does not apply; i.e. create cost savings by simply not needing the procedures. These situations are few, because: 1) a business must demonstrate that it complies with all non-exempt exempt employee minimum wage and overtime hourly requirements, 2) even salaried exempt employees may require time-related PTO tracking or may later be classified as non-exempt following DOL or state audits, 3) time allocations may be needed for other purposes such as job costing, 4) time tracking is required for regular management reports (which often use FTEs as discussed earlier) and oversight, and 5) customers that require time verification for work performed.

Instead of eliminating the process, in some cases hours could be recorded only by exception, but these situations must be very reliable and relatively simple. Examples are: 1) Do not record salaried employee hours if their exempt status is certain, there is no PTO time, and no other time recording requirements. 2) Always record hourly employees at 40 hours unless they report overtime, the overtime is infrequent, and weekly hours for each employee are otherwise reliably provable under audit.

Strictly speaking, the timekeeping function is separate from other payroll activities such as computing and/or changing withholding, printing paychecks, and performing minimum wage and overtime dollar calculations.

continued ▶

The Critical Function of Timekeeping, *continued*

Overview, Continued	However, in smaller businesses, all these activities may be combined into a single department or performed by one individual. The more consolidated the activities, the greater the need for active internal control (Section 7). Following is a brief summary of internal control for timekeeping activities.

Key Timekeeping Internal Control Procedures

Overview	Essential timekeeping practices should include the timekeeping internal control procedures that are described below. These are part of every time-keeping activity; however, the list is not exhaustive. The procedures apply in most situations, but specific circumstances may dictate additional or changed procedures. Note: internal control procedures related to hours worked applies primarily to non-exempt employees. Following is a brief summary of key procedures.
Employee Recording and Supervisor Approval	However time is recorded, each employee must confirm his or her to-tal time (recording on a daily basis is DOL-required, identifying in-and-out times) with a signature, initial, or other recordable method. The time should also be reviewed by supervisor(s) for approval. A supervisor should not approve a report that contains blank spaces above signature or allows any further data input after approval. The purpose of supervisor approval is to check for reasonableness and appropriateness for required work duties; other internal control methods (below) are also available as a check on time reporting fraud. Time submission and supervisor review must be timely; payroll should never be processed without supervisor-reviewed verification.
Password Use	Electronic time sheet systems should require passwords and require password changes at regular intervals. Supervisor approvals should require separate passwords. Passwords should not be shared for spreadsheets or be accessible for any other reason. Password requirements and input control applies at all levels of the payroll process.
Separation of Duties	For a small business, the timekeeping and the payroll calculation and recording duties are often performed by a single person. In this case "separation of duties" means that payroll preparation is separated from all other activities, and no other person is authorized to enter any data, calculate the payroll, or perform any other payroll activity, except authorized management for supervisory purposes. This key internal control procedure helps prevent collusion between employees and influence or data entry by non-payroll employees. In a larger business with more employees and a higher volume of work, the timekeeping duties are further separated from other duties within the payroll department. In all cases, output of any kind should be reviewed and approved by someone not part of the activity creating the output.

Key Timekeeping Internal Control Procedures, *continued*

Small Business Duties Concentration Risk	In a small business it is often the case that one person performs not only timekeeping, but all payroll duties. Frequently this is done through a computerized payroll system. This creates a significant internal control issue, when a single person has access to timekeeping, employee database information, paycheck creation, deposit and filing duties, performs payroll checking account reconciliation and payroll expense reports and probably has access to general ledger accounts. In this circumstance it is essential for the owner(s) to carefully review each payroll element with every payroll, and regularly review employee database information.
Retention and Delivery to Timekeeping	If a paper-based system is in use, no employee should have access to other employee timesheets after supervisor approval. A supervisor should collect and retain timesheets and deliver them to timekeeping.
Exceptions Reports	Exceptions reports should be created to identify variations from policy relating to such items as total hours, overtime, leave, and absences. For many items exceptions flagging features are available as part of automated timekeeping and payroll systems.
Changes Approval	Changes to any timekeeping output must be reviewed by an independent party. All changes should be included on an exceptions report.
Document Security	All timekeeping source data must be retained and protected. In the case of paper data, physical security and controlled access is required. In the case of electronic information proper off-site file storage should be required. Orginal data become very important, for example, in the case of Department of Labor audits to evaluate labor law compliance. Suggested retention time is four years, unless state and local law requires more.
Federal and State Data Requiremnts	Timekeeping must provide data that can determine compliance with federal and state employment law requirements. This is particularly essential for minimum wage calculations and overtime calculations. This can include not only designated duties, but time for rest periods, training time, orientation time, on-call time, and away from office time.
Payroll Bank Account	A separate payroll bank account faciltitates tracking payroll-related deposits and expenditures. It also limits access to the general bank account(s).
Timekeeping Audit	Payroll, including the timekeeping function, should be periodically audited and internal controls reviewed by competent internal or external independent parties.

Timekeeping Best Practices

Overview

Best practices relate to policies and procedures. Payroll policies, which are indicator of management objectives in this context, should be comprehensive, clear, and available to all employees. Following such a standard will prove to be useful should the need at some point arise to demonstrate compliance with applicable laws. Procedures typically result from policies. Procedures usually involve a checklist of actions that must be taken.

Timekeeping Policies

Policies are created with objectives in mind. In the matters of payroll and timekeeping, policies revolve around compliance and internal control. The most basic requirement of a payroll policy is awareness–management should be able to demonstrate that all policies are documented and that employees have been made aware of policies and changes in policies. Key policies that should be included (that affect the timekeeping function) are:

- Integrity: Honesty in all aspects of recording work hours and job time is expected and required.
- Accuracy: Precision in the timekeeping process is required to ensure correct compensation to employees and correct expense to employer. "Precision" is defined in all applicable contexts, (e.g. hours rounded to a tenth of an hour).
- Documentation: All data that are part of or used in timekeeping must be recorded.
- Security: All recorded data is kept secure with procedures in place for limited access by specified employee classifications (e.g. in a small business, only the owner has access).
- Verification: Verification means obtaining proof of accuracy or evidence of an event. In the context of timekeeping this generally means periodic physical checking or electronic verification, such as for presence at work.
- Approvals: Approvals by a designated authority are required for specificed events.
- Limitations: Limitations may placed on activities, such as a limitation on overtime.
- Errors/Corrections: All timekeeping errors must be corrected upon discovery with approval.
- Meals and rest periods: Periods are set for specified employees.
- Work away from the office: Notice and approval are required.
- Leaves (paid and unpaid): Times are identified and reported to payroll.
- Employee privacy: Privacy matters are identified and procedures are implemented (e.g. paycheck amounts).
- Procedure enforcement: Procedures must be followed and enforcement standards are set in coordination with potential disciplinary actions.
- Disciplinary actions: Events requiring disciplinary actions are clearly identified and the action(s) that may be taken are identified.

Rounding Rules

If all hours worked are paid, the DOL permits a consistent and regular method, but prefers rounding to the nearest 5 minutes, tenth of an hour, or quarter of an hour.

Timekeeping Methods: Offline

Overview

There is a wide variety of timekeeping methods. This is a consequence of the wide variety of business conditions and activities. As a result, there is no "one size fits all" method; a timekeeping method (or methods) must be carefully selected to address the requirement(s) of each business. The following discussion reviews timekeeping methods that do not use the Internet. The important advantage of offline payroll and human resources processing is the minimization of the theft of employee personal and bank information. Damaging Internet viruses and intrusive code are also prevented. Various methods are discussed below.

Timesheets

A manual timesheet is a formatted and preprinted paper document on which an employee writes hours worked. Timesheets are for specific periods, such as weekly, and hours are recorded daily. Usually hours worked are recorded by client or by job. Separate timesheets also can be used for separate jobs to simplify tracking. Timesheets are easy to use and any number of employees can use timesheets under most conditions. The disadvantages of timesheets are: 1) It is easy to make errors in recording and checking 2) It is easy to falsify hours 3) A large number of timesheets create a heavy load on the payroll department and a slow process, requiring extensive manual checking. 4) Also, with a large number of employees the necessity for repeated reminders to turn in timesheets will slow processing.

Electronic timesheets are also available; an employee logs in at his/her workstation, records time worked, and the information is stored in the company database for processing. Standardized code numbers are often used to identify client and/or type of work performed. Electronic timesheets have applications that can generate scheduling, management reports, and automated invoicing and billing. Falsified hours are still possible when log-in information is shared, although probably is less than with paper timesheets, particularly if any personal information is accessible. Fraud is also possible if a change in the computer's timeclock would change in/out times.

Timecards

Timecards have been a standard method for recording employee hours. A timecard is an oblong form preprinted on heavyweight paper called card stock. A card is preprinted with spaces for beginning and ending work times in daily blocks, and an employee name is entered on the card. A timecard can be filled out by hand; however, in many businesses employees insert their cards into a timeclock device that timestamps date and hour on the card to record in and out times in the daily blocks. Overtime can also be recorded. After a standard period such as a week, the an employee checks amounts and signs the card, which is then collected by a supervisor who reviews the times and amounts, also signs the card, and sends all collected timecards to the payroll department.

continued ▶

Timekeeping Methods: Offline, *continued*

Timecards, Continued

Use of paper timecards is a very manual process. Except for timestamp devices, which are not expensive, timecards require no other out-of-pocket investment except for cards. This means that cards can be used in multiple business locations at a reasonable cost. Cards generally have enough space to record up to two weeks of daily time. Disadvantages are: 1) Because the process is highly manual, it is slow, and significant recording, checking, correcting, and manual input time is required. 2) Manual time recording and payroll data entry is subject to a significant error rate; (about 1-8% of data input according to the American Payroll Association). 3) Timecards are subject to a common employee fraud called "buddy punching" in which a friend or associate of an employee will record time in and out for an employee who is not at work. 4) When timestamp devices are used, lines can form when many employees arrive simultaneously. 5) Timecards function best in locations where employees are not spread out.

Computer System Linked Timeclocks

In this system, a "card" is a plastic badge or card with a magnetic data stip, bar code, or chip that an employee passes in front of a card-reading scanner. The scanner is really an extension of the in-house payroll software; the scanner identifies an employee and records time in and out; as well, it can peform other functions. The payroll software identifies the scanned data and downloads it for use by the software, where it is used in processing the payroll. There is no manual data entry.

The essential advantage of this system is the major time savings provided over manual recording, checking, locating and correcting errors, and manual key entry. These manual hours are significant and continuous; this system essentially eliminates such hours. A second signifcant advantage is the reduction in error rate over a manual system. Also, as indicated above, additional functions are available. Examples are: 1) shift and overtime controls in which employee time can only be recorded during certain periods (although this has potential for FLSA violations if the employee still performs work) or requires manager authorization 2) tracking paid and unpaid break time 3) restricting work by location 4) Real-time reporting of early/late punch-ins 5) codes that identify work performed by type and by job or department allocation. 6) Multiple wage and hour calculations that help prevent Federal, state, and local labor law violations.

The main disadvantage over timesheets and manual timecards is higher cost, although this is not excessive for two reasons: 1) There is a range of prices and features available for off-line installed cost per scanner below $750 and easily below $1,000; however, there have been negative reliability issues with the cheaper installations. Some suppliers will lease devices

continued ▶

Timekeeping Methods: Offline, *continued*

Computer System Linked Timeclocks, Continued	at a monthly rate. 2) The value of the processing time savings will exceed the initial cost of a device, especially when usage is high or significant hiring can be anticipated within the next several years which would result in additional processing work. For example, an employee performing manual timekeeping duties described above 8 hours per month at $20 per hour is $1,920 per year. Disadvantages are installation time, that cards can be lost and that "buddy punching" is still possible.
Biometric: Facial and Eye Recognition	"Biometric" means the use of physical characteristics, such as facial, fingerprint, handprint, eye, and voice. Biometric systems operate in the same manner as computer system-linked timecards; the only difference is that the input is through a physical recognition device used as the means of identification. The input device for facial recognition is a specialized camera.
	In addition to being faster than manual processing, biometric systems eliminate buddy punching fraud. Another advantage with facial and eye (and voice) recognition is that it does not require touching any devices, which is important for employers such as hospitals, medical offices, and food service that need to minimize infection. Disadvantages of facial/eye recognition devices are: 1) They can be more expensive than card scanning systems, and training time may be required 2) Processing time is slightly slower than card scanning devices.
Biometric: Fingerprint Recognition	This system operates in the same manner as computer system-linked timecards; the only difference is that the input is through a fingerprint recognition device. In addition to being faster than manual processing, this system eliminates buddy punching fraud. Disadvantages of fingerprint recognition devices are: 1) They can be somewhat more expensive than card scanning systems and training time may be required, 2) Processing time is slightly slower than card scanning devices. 3) There can be reliability issues where fingers are not clean 4) The devices must be touched and can transfer bacteria/viruses.
Biometric: Handprint Recognition	This system operates in the same manner as computer system-linked timecards; the only difference is that the input is through a handprint recognition device. In addition to being faster than manual processing, this system eliminates buddy punching fraud. Handprint scanners provide more reliable and precise data than fingerprint scanners. Disadvantages of handprint recognition devices are: 1) They can be somewhat more expensive than card scanning systems and training time may be required, 2) Processing time is slightly slower than card scanning devices. 3) There can be reliability issues where hands are not clean 4) The devices must be touched and can transfer bacteria/viruses.

Timekeeping Methods: Online

Overview

Online (Internet) time tracking carries both significant benefits and risks. In addition to time savings in many circumstances, the main benefits are access flexibility and possible lower initial costs than in-house systems. Data is maintained in an Internet database; employees simply log in to the Internet from any location and use an appliction that records the work time. The cost of multiple fixed device installations for geographically dispersed employees is not required. Any of the previously-discussed methods can be developed for use in an Internet format.

The most significant risks of online use are data theft and destructive software intrusion. Other constraints are: 1) loss or unavailability of Internet access. 2) need for a company-specific application to transfer online data into a company's payroll software system, when the processing is performed in-house. 3) limited or no control over falsified hours when log-in information is shared (except biometric) or when log-in is not performed when actually at work. (However, geolocation applications are avaible that idenify location and/or allow log-in only within a certain location). Three costs: installation, operating, and replacement should be compared for each potential use, both between methods and between offline and online systems.

Summary of Methods

- **Timesheets**: These have the same features and limitations and are used in a similar manner as electronic timesheets previously described.
- **Computer system linked timeclocks**: Because the key advantage of Internet use is access from any location, fixed timeclocks are not used. Instead, a "timeclock" is really an application on a mobile device such as a tablet or smart phone. An employee logs in and uses the application to record time and possibly other data, such as standarized time allocation codes. Although geographically flexible, the process is slower than a paper timecard punch in or card swipe. Therefore, if workers are concentrated in one or a few locations, fixed timeclocks may be faster overall.
- **Biometrics**: Online biometric identification services are available. The identification can be processed by use of a fixed device or on mobile devices. The process is slower with mobile devices, so as above, if workers are concentrated in one or a few locations, fixed devices may be faster overall.
- **Smart phones, laptops, tablets**: The ultimate in access flexibility is the use of mobile devices. These devices are most useful for employees who travel frequently, need to record time at various work locations, and may need to access resoues while on the job away from the employer's location. Also, employees find it useful to be able to access their own payroll and PTO information and make allowed changes, such as to benefits (which saves time in the HR department). Mobile devices are not likely to be a net cost benefit when employee work is concentrated in one or two employer locations. As with methods described above, the data entry process is somewhat slower than with fixed location devices.

continued ▶

Timekeeping Methods: Online, *continued*

Summary of Methods, Continued

It should be noted that prior to the development of these various methods and devices, work time and location were simply entered, usually contemporaneously, in a paper notebook or log when traveling. In simple situations or with few employees traveling, this may still be an overall net lower cost, even with the necessity of later reviewing and keying-in the information.

Use the table below as an initial filtering device to prioritize timekeeping needs and identify applicable methods. For each constraint item, enter a value of 0 to 10 to represent your feelings for the relative importance of a constraint item. Then, in each column multiply the value by the parenthetical amount to determine a score for the particular method. Enter the score and total the scores in each column. The process can be repeated with different constraint values. Columns with the highest totals represent methods that might be better choices for fulfilling timekeeping needs. Follow up with more detailed research on these methods.

Method / Constraint	Value 0–10	Paper Time sheet	Standard time clock	Integrated with in-house computer system			
				Time clock	Facial/eye recognition biometric time clock	Fingerprint biometric time clock	Handprint biometric time clock
1. Minimize time required to record, check and transcribe time data		(0)	(1)	(10)	(10)	(8)	(9)
2. Minimize employee wait time to record in/out		(10)	(9)	(10)	(8)	(8)	(8)
Select one: 3 – 6							
3. Cost < $100 per installation		(10)	(1)	(0)	(0)	(0)	(0)
4. Cost $100–$750 per installation		(0)	(10)	(5*)	(5*)	(5*)	(5*)
5. Cost $751–$1,000 per installation		(0)	(5)	(7*)	(7*)	(7*)	(7*)
6. Cost >$1,000 per installation		(0)	(1)	(10*)	(10*)	(10*)	(10*)
7. Basic reliability/functionality		(10)	(9)	(6,7,9*)	(6,7,9*)	(5,7,9*)	(6,7,9*)
8. Expanded features		(0)	(0)	(2,7,9*)	(2,7,9*)	(2,7,9*)	(2,7,9*)
9. Error rate minimized		(1)	(5)	(10)	(10)	(10)	(10)
10. Minimize employee fraud loss		(0)	(5)	(9)	(10)	(10)	(10)
11. Minimize personal data theft		(10)	(10)	(10)	(10)	(10)	(10)
12. Many work locations separated		(10)	(3)	(3)	(3)	(3)	(3)
13. Minimize disease transmission		(8)	(6)	(9)	(9)	(1)	(1)
14. Federal/state/local compliance	10	30 (3)	50 (5)	90 (9)	100 (10)	100 (10)	100 (10)
Total							

continued ▶

Timekeeping Methods: Online, *continued*

Parenthetical amounts: estimates of the likelihood or availability of a constraint fulfillment relative to other methods.

1 – 2: Higher amounts indicate greater efficiency at minimizing time required.

3 – 6: Higher amounts indicate greater likelihood of finding the method/ system within the cost range. Cost is initial total cost that includes installation and testing, for each separate installation. Cost per installation can decrease with more installations due to some fixed costs. Note that operating costs and replacement costs are not considered.

7. Indicates ability to reliably perform basic functionality. Items with * indicate generally better reliability and more functionality with higher cost methods; use higher amounts as selected costs increase.

8. These are features such as PTO tracking, time allocations by job, and overtime settings for rate and time.

9. Higher amounts indicate minimizing timekeeping errors.

10 – 11: Higher amounts indicate minimizing employee fraud and personal data theft relative to other methods.

12. Higher amounts indicate efficient use when work locations are spread out.

13. Higher amounts indicate lower likelihood of disease spread relative to other methods.

14. Higher amounts indicate greater likelihood of FLSA and state and local compliance because of ability to accurately record and monitor data. It is assumed compliance is a high priority and value of 10 has been inserted.

TIP

One advantage of online systems is that archived data is stored off-site, away from the company location, which provides protection against physical disasters such as fire, flood, earthquake, etc. However, even if payroll is processed offline, in-house, copies of payroll data should nevertheless be periodically stored in a secure offsite location. This should not be difficult if the company has non-payroll online access to archiving sites, or simply uses backup memory devices that can store significant amounts of data.

continued

Timekeeping Methods: Online, *continued*

	Internet-based (integrated with in-house computer system)				
	Time clock	Facial/eye recognition biometric time clock	Fingerprint biometric time clock	Handprint biometric time clock	Mobile device
1.	(9)	(9)	(9)	(9)	(9)
2.	(10)	(8)	(8)	(8)	(10)
3.	(0)	(0)	(0)	(0)	(0)
4.	(6*)	(6*)	(6*)	(6*)	(9)
5.	(9*)	(8*)	(8*)	(8*)	(9)
6.	(10*)	(10*)	(10*)	(10*)	(10)
7.	(6,7,9*)	(6,7,9*)	(5,7,9*)	(6,7,9*)	(10)
8.	(2,7,9*)	(2,7,9*)	(2,7,9*)	(2,7,9*)	(10)
9.	(10)	(10)	(10)	(10)	(10)
10.	(9)	(10)	(10)	(10)	(10)
11.	(7)	(7)	(7)	(7)	(6)
12.	(3)	(3)	(3)	(3)	(10)
13.	(10)	(9)	(1)	(1)	(10)
14.	100 (10)	100 (10)	100 (10)	100 (10)	100 (10)

What About Exempt Employees?

Exempt employees–for the most part, salaried employees (see Section 2) - are not subject to timekeeping needs for minimum wage and overtime requirements… generally. Why "generally"? Because if errors are made and an exempt employee turns into a nonexempt employee upon audit or a classification change by management, then years of hourly data for that employee can become important. Unpaid overtime and possibly benefits can become issues. Also, payroll cost allocations between jobs requires timekeeping. For salaried employees who may not be currently or in the future exempt, it may be worthwhile to record all hours –above and below 40, depending on the hourly calculation method used to determine overtime hours.

Appendix III

Document Retention Guidelines

Overview

The list of items below summarizes requirements that affect many employers, but is not comprehensive. Virtually all employers will be subject to a combination, if not all, of the requirements below. **These are summaries and minimum amounts**; prudence would dictate adding a margin of error. As well, records may be useful for other events that can arise later than the minimums. A time-saving policy might be to select the two or three longest guidelines that encompass all items. However, if an employee has filed a charge or complaint or an enforcement action has begun, all related records must be maintained until the issue is fully resolved. Finally, check state and local law.

Department of Labor (DOL)

The Department of Labor administers and enforces the Fair Labor Standards Act as well as several other important laws, all of which affect compensation and key working conditions. The DOL requires that an employer create and retain certain documents for a minimum of 3 years from the date of last document entry for each covered, worker. These include:

- Payroll records
- Sales and purchase records
- FMLA disputes
- Medical certifications and histories relating to FMLA (kept in separate files)
- Collective bargaining agreements
- Dates FMLA leaves are taken
- FMLA written notices
- Employee benefits records
- Paid and unpaid leave policy

The DOL requires that an employer create and retain records on which wage computations are based for a minimum of 2 years from date of last document entry for each covered, nonexempt worker. These include:

- Time cards/daily hours worked
- Wage rate tables
- Increase and decrease wage adjustments
- Justification for pay differences, particularly to different sexes.
- Piece rate tickets

continued ▶

Document Retention Guidelines, *continued*

Department of Labor (DOL), Continued

- Work and time schedules
- Exceptions to fixed schedule hours

The DOL also requires the following employee documented information but does not state specific minimum retention guidelines, which suggests the records should be kept indefinitely:

- Full name and social security number
- Birth date if younger than 19
- Address including zip code
- Sex and occupation

Equal Employment Opportunity Commission (EEOC)

The Equal Employment Opportunity Commission (EEOC) administers and enforces laws that prohibit discrimination in the workplace. The EEOC has a number of different document retention guidelines depending on the type of issue such as demographic records, personnel action records, hiring, payroll, seniority, benefits, and others. In general, policy that would address these various items should use the later of 3 years from the last/revised effective date of a document or a related plan, except records concerning race and ethnicity that require permanent retention.

Internal Revenue Service (IRS)

The IRS document retention rule related to employment includes the following required documentation:

- Employer ID number
- Basic employee information and dates
- Payroll data used for calculation
- Refunds
- Cash payments and deposits
- Regular time
- Withholding
- All payroll-related forms filed
- All salary/wage and compensation information and calculations
- Employment contracts
- Reconciliation of taxable to gross pay
- Overtime
- Fringe benefits

The employment records retention requirement is a minimum of 4 years from the latest of the dates that that a tax becomes due or is paid. However, records must be maintained while under examination, and the IRS is able to extend the statute of limitations for examination deadlines. Finally, there is no statute of limitations for fraudulent reporting or a failure to file.

FORM I-9

Form I-9 is a required form that is used to verify identity and employment authorization of a person hired for employment in the United States. A division of the U.S. Citizenship and Immigration Service administers

continued ▶

Document Retention Guidelines, *continued*

FORM I-9, *Continued*	and enforces compliance. Form I-9 must be completed by employee and employer with an employment before a final. An employer must keep a completed I-9 form (and any supporting documentation) on file for each person on the payroll who is required to complete the form. The form is retained until the later of 3 years after an employee begins to work for pay or 1 year following the date of employment termination.
Employee Retirement Income Security Act (ERISA)	ERISA is designed to safeguard employee retirement funds. It is administered and enforced by the DOL, the IRS, and the Pension Benefit Guaranty Corporation (PBGC). Most private sector employers with retirement plans are affected by ERISA. The document retention requirement is a minimum of 6 years from the time a document is filed. Therefore, this rule affects documents such annual Form 5500, required notices including to employees, audited financial statements, and other plan-level and plan-related documents. ERISA does not specify retention time for individual employee information so this should be retained indefinitely.

Other Records

Item	Suggested Minimum Years Retention
Pre-employment documents, such as job applications, resumes, references, interview records, help wanted, etc.	1 year after termination
Drug and alcohol testing results	5 years
Lily Ledbetter Fair Pay Act: Individual personnel files of each employee	2 years after termination
Affirmative action programs	5 years
OSHA injury and illness report	5 years
OSHA employee medical and exposure records	Employment + 30

Appendix IV

New Business/First-Time Payroll Checklist

Checklist Summary

Employer Identification Number

If there are one or more employees, a Keogh plan, or the business is a corporation or partnership, obtain an Employer Identification Number (EIN) online by searching for the form online or at https://tax-irs-ein .com. Certain other businesses also require an EIN. A sole proprietor with no employees is also allowed to obtain an EIN.

OR: simply search "obtain EIN". The form is filed as follows:

- Business location is in one of the 50 states or District of Columbia: Use the following address: Internal Revenue Service, Attn: EIN Operation, Cincinnati, OH, 45999. Fax number: 855-641-6935.
- No legal residence, principal place of business or office in any state: Use the following address: Internal Revenue Service, Attn: EIN International Operation, Cincinnati, OH, 45999. Fax number: 855-215-1627 (in the U.S) or 304-707-9471 (outside the U.S.)

States also require employer identification numbers. Be sure to check identification requirements for your own state.

Electronic Payment System

Federal payroll tax deposits of $2,500 or more generally must be made electronically; an Electronic Federal Tax Payment System (EFTPS) account should be created if this is the case, or to streamline the process. Some financial institutions and accounting firms provide similar service. For enrollment instructions and procedures go to https://www.eftps.gov. If you obtain an employer identification number (above) you will automatically be enrolled in eftps. However, it is still necessary to access the site to have information validated, receive a personal identification numbe (PIN), and access instructions. Instructions are also available in Publications 966 and 4990. Be sure to check state requirements and resources, which may be different.

Tax Calendar

This is easy, but essential. Go online to locate Publication 509 for federal deadlines. Also determine state and local deadlines from your own state. Refer to the calendar(s) often. Some of the most common reasons for payroll tax penalties are late filing and payment.

Checklist Summary, *continued*

Legal Business Type Selection	Each type has pros and cons. Most common: sole proprietorship, LLC, (Limited Liability Company) S Corp. and C Corp. In all cases, distributions of business assets are not subject to payroll tax. A sole proprietor calculates self-employment (SE) tax on profits on the individual tax return. When no election is made a single-person LLC pays SE tax, as does a general partner. Salaries in corporations are subject to payroll tax, and to IRS rules on salary size vs. profit distributions.
Payroll Bank Account	A separate payroll bank account used only for payroll transactions makes it easier to trace payroll cash transactions such as deposits and cleared checks. As well, it reduces the time needed for cash reconciliation procedures. It also improves internal control.
Tax Year	Select a tax year. Typically these are either years ending on December 31 (calendar year) or another month-end (fiscal year). Ideally a year should end at a quiet time. A tax year and financial accounting year should generally be the same.
Pay Period	Every business with employees must have a regular pay period(s)–different pay periods are also permitted for different employee classifications. There is no one single best period; deciding on a pay period is a question of optimizing alternatives. See page 84 for a summary of the alternatives and pros and cons.
Deposit Schedule	For federal purposes a new business generally has a monthly payroll tax deposit schedule until a lookback period (see page 218) can be established. Be sure to double-check your own case, and check state and local requirements.
Employee Handbook	A payroll policy handbook should be developed, discussed with employees and regularly updated. This is a task for which it may be wise to consider legal assistance from experienced employment law counsel. Communicating and following a legally supportable policy for employees is really a form of insurance against lawsuits and audit penalties.
Your Location and Overtime and Fair Labor Laws	Will the company likely be paying overtime? Check city and locality overtime wage rates in your area. Local overtime rates vary from no requirements to requirements that exceed state and federal rates. As well, other payroll-related costs may be imposed such as local fair labor laws. (See Section 1 discussion.) Although legislation can change, if acceptable location alternatives exist, lower rates and costs should be considered, which are especially important for a startup. The same considerations apply between state locations.
Insurance Requirements	Most states require some form of workers' compensation insurance. Check state requirements and select from whatever options are available for businesses in your state.
Direct Deposit for Employees	Setting up a direct deposit link for each employee will save substantial time over the long run, and provide some internal control safeguards. Try to communicate all the advantages of this to employees so they will enroll.

Checklist Summary, *continued*

Software Systems	Payroll functions are excellent applications for computerized systems, and there are numerous software systems available that can eliminate a great deal of manual time related to processing and calculation functions, especially as the number of employees increases. However, purchase of these systems requires research, and there are both upfront investments and software updating costs, and training time costs.

Employment Laws

There are numerous payroll laws that create a complex web of potential compliance requirements, which are often unexpected. Pages 10, 23–28 provide a summary. If after review you are in doubt about compliance requirements, you can do your own inexpensive research by contacting the Department of Labor, the IRS, the Social Security Administration, and other administrative agencies; however, also consider obtaining professional legal assistance. Regular employee training by professional firms to ensure compliance should be considered.

Professional Help

Professional assistance includes numerous alternatives at varying costs. These are some options:

- **Outsourcing to payroll services**: Some banks as well as specialized payroll companies provide payroll processing services. However, this approach does not eliminate employer compliance liability such as under various labor laws and wage and hour compliance under the Fair Labor Standards Act, as well as other duties that may not be provided under the outsourcing agreement, such as timekeeping or reporting.
- **Outsourcing to accounting firms**: Small to moderate-size accounting firms frequently provide payroll processing services. An advantage of using these services is that accounting firms, particularly CPAs, is the building of a relationship with a resource that also provides other necessary services such as accounting systems setup, financial statement preparation, and tax advice. Payroll processing costs might be higher than payroll processing companies; services might be combined.
- **Legal advice**: Although this can be expensive, an intial consultation may be advisable for a new business in order to ensure that all compliance issues, especially DOL, will be properly addressed.
- **Business startup literature**: Both the IRS and individual states offer start-up advice. Check IRS Publication 583.
- **Contact IRS for help**: Online contact is available at www.irs.gov/help. For telephone contact, individuals: 800-829-1040; for business: 800-828-4933; for non-profits: 877-829-5500. For hearing impaired: 800-829-4059.
- **Reduced filing - Form 944:** A new business with under $1,000 annual liability can request IRS approval for this form (must be written). Call 800-829-4933 before the first day of month the first current year Form 941 is due.
- **Small and disadvantaged businesses**: For federal labor law compliance help, contact the Office of Small and Disadvantaged Businesses at 1-888-972-7332, or search for the website by the same name. Online address is https://www.dol.gov/agencies/oasam/business-operations-center/osdbu/compliance-assistance
- **SCORE - Service Corps of Retired Executives**: Provides mentoring and a variety of training for small businesses. Visit website at score.org.

Checklist Summary, *continued*

Cash or Accrual Accounting Method?	Affecting payroll, an important decision for a new business is the selection of an accounting method for keeping the books. There are two basic choices: cash method or accrual method. (In some situations there are hybrids.) The cash accounting method records revenues only when cash is received (also see "constructive receipt") and records expenses only when cash is paid; receivables and payables are not used. It is a simple but relatively inaccurate method. For the purpose of recording revenues and expenses, the accrual method ignores when cash is received or paid. The accrual method records revenues when earned and records expenses into the periods that they relate to revenue-earning activity, even if none is earned. The result is more accurate net income each period, but is more complex to apply. Accrual accounting requires the use of receivables, payables, and other accounts that are not used in cash basis (except in informal records). Cash basis is typically used by small service and small merchandising businesses. For related tax rules, see IRS Publication 538.

Revenue Examples	ABC Company provided November advertising services and billed the client $4,000 in December.

CASH BASIS	
IF Client Paid...	**THEN Record Revenue In...**
In advance on October 1	October
On December 18	December
On January 27	January
ACCRUAL BASIS	
In advance on October 1	
On December 18	November
On January 27	

Expense Examples	On May 9, ABC received an $800 bill for April utility expenses, and paid it June 2.

CASH BASIS	
IF Company Paid...	**THEN Record Expense in...**
In advance on March 2	March
On April 12	April
On June 2	June
ACCRUAL BASIS	
In advance on March 2	
On April 12	April
On June 2	

99) B 100) B 101) C 102) D 103) B 104) A 105) D

106) A 107) B 108) D 109) C 110) C 111) B 112) A

113) C 114) A 115) C 116) B 117) C 118) B 119) C

120) C 121) D 122) A 123) A 124) C 125) A 126) B

127) A 128) B 129) D 130) C 131) A 132) D 133) D

134) D 135) A 136) B 137) C 138) C 139) A 140) B

141) A 142) C 143) B 144) B 145) B 146) C 147) C

148) A 149) C 150) C 151) C

1) D   2) D   3) D   4) B   5) C   6) D   7) D
8) B   9) B   10) C   11) D   12) A   13) B   14) A
15) B   16) C   17) B   18) C   19) D   20) C   21) C
22) D   23) A   24) C   25) D   26) C   27) B   28) B
29) B   30) C   31) C   32) A   33) C   34) C   35) B
36) A   37) B   38) B   39) B   40) D   41) D   42) A
43) A   44) X   45) B   46) B   47) D   48) D   49) B
50) A   51) A   52) C   53) B   54) A   55) A   56) D
57) D   58) D   59) D   60) A   61) A   62) A   63) C
64) A   65) D   66) A   67) B   68) B   69) A   70) A
71) C   72) A   73) C   74) C   75) C   76) C   77) D
78) B   79) D   80) B   81) B   82) D   83) B   84) B
85)   86)   87)

Index

351